HUNGARIAN CUISINE

HUNGARIAN CUISINE

A COMPLETE COOKERY BOOK

BY JÓZSEF VENESZ

CORVINA PRESS

Collaborators:

ISTVÁN MÓZER, JÁNOS RÁKÓCZY, EMIL TURÓS,
GÉZA SCHULHOF and MRS. L. SZINDER

Cover and jacket by Mária Hódossy

Photos:

KÁROLY GINK, KÁROLY SZELÉNYI

Third, revised edition

ISBN 963 13 0219 9

CONTENTS

INTRODUCTION

This book, prepared for the English public, is not like other cookery books previously published in foreign languages about Hungarian cuisine and its specialities. It gives more, being the first Hungarian cookery book in English which covers all aspects of Hungarian culinary art, including the products of olden times and traditions, together with those borrowed from the cooking of other peoples and adapted to suit the taste and cooking practice of Hungary.

We hope that this book—a very popular one in Hungary, already reprinted seven times up till now—will give pleasure to all English specialists and housewives who are looking for variety.

Hungarian culinary art has adapted many recipes from other peoples' cooking, in the first place from the French. It has long since been the aim of our qualified specialists, restaurant keepers and trained cooks to learn, and to give their customers, all the products of French culinary art. Such an adaptation could not be undertaken, of course, without sometimes changing the ingredients or cooking methods of the meals, according to Hungarian taste, and following the requirements of the raw foodstuffs available in Hungary. Thus it is quite possible that the English reader may find in the book variations of dishes, well known to him, differing somewhat from similar French recipes. The variations will surely evoke great interest.

Next to French cooking Hungarian culinary art was influenced by the cooking of neighbouring countries, and of the peoples living in close proximity. Among these, Viennese cooking should be mentioned first of all, which played a great role in the development of Hungarian culinary art not only by its recipes, but by acting as intermediary for the specialities of other nations (Italian cookery especially) as well.

Hungarian cooking, in the course of time, has adapted many specialities from the cuisine of the Slav peoples who live in and around the country, and also from the Rumanians, accepting specialities which correspond with Hungarian taste.

Hungarian cooking has been composed from all these elements in the course of time and because of its originality and great variety it enjoys great popularity by all who have the opportunity of becoming well acquainted with it.

We do not deem it necessary to give general introductory explanations in the case of recipes which are also well known in West-European cooking, or of recipes included in this book which are similar. They will be understood by all people who are familiar with the rudiments of cooking and baking. It is important, however, in view of the Hungarian specialities described in the book, to enlighten the reader briefly about Hungarian cooking, by means of a few general remarks.

The really special characteristics of Hungarian cooking are to be found mostly in cooking methods, in the composition of meals and in the raw food-stuffs used.

As regards the preparation of dishes, one of the most characteristic and well known specialities of Hungarian cooking consists of the braising of certain meat dishes on a foundation of onions, seasoned with paprika. These meat dishes, such as the various goulashes, stews and meals prepared with paprika and black pepper, are adequately dealt with in our cookery book.

Soups and in particular many kinds of vegetables are characteristically prepared in the Hungarian cuisine with a roux, as in French cooking. But there are two special ways of thickening in Hungarian cooking: one by adding a mixture of flour and sour cream to the dish (thickening), and the other by simply sprinkling with flour (dusting).

The preparation of pastries and sweets also offers special Hungarian traits, such as pulling out the pastry for *rétes* (Genoese pastry) into thin, film-like sheets, and its different uses. (See p. 247.)

Another Hungarian farinaceous product should also be mentioned; it is called *tarhonya* (granulated dried pasta made of flour and eggs), the use of which, according to some authors, had been introduced by our nomad forbears in the distant past. Tarhonya consists of pasta kneaded from eggs and flour, granulated in a special way into small pellets and dried. (See p. 232.) Tarhonya may be kept in dried condition for a long time. It can be used, just like rice, fried lightly in lard, then cooked in water until tender and served chiefly as an accompaniment to meat dishes, served with plenty of gravy.

As regards the composition of meals, the introduction in the menu of pastas by way of sweets, especially when sweet substances (sugared nuts, poppy seeds, fruit jellies or jams) are added, may be unknown to Western cooking.

As far as raw foodstuffs are concerned, we should point out the significant role of pork, as compared with Western cooking, and a certain loss of importance of mutton, to be explained on the one hand by the excellent tasty quality of Hungarian pork, and on the other, by the fact that the breeding of sheep for meat does not come up to the standard of sheep brought up on the West-European salty, seaside pastures.

Of all fats used for cooking, lard is preferred in the Hungarian cuisine to other animal or vegetable fats.

Among the many milk products used for cooking, sour cream, derived from sour milk, may be regarded as a special Hungarian cooking ingredient, frequently to be met in our recipes, just as the cheese-curd, prepared from sour milk, is known in France as a basic substance of cheese-making, but is practically never used in its original form for cooking purposes.

Because of the country's geographical situation, Hungarian cooking must be content with the use of freshwater fish. There are, however, two kinds of freshwater fish available for Hungarian cuisine; their excellent quality renders all sorts of preparation possible, including the methods, used in French cooking, in preparing sea fish. These fish are the sturgeon (sterlet), living both in the Danube and the Tisza, and one kind of pike-perch, called *fogas*, which inhabits Lake Balaton. (For further details, see p. 98.) The silurus (sheat-fish), a fish rarely to be found in West-European waters, but an inhabitant of our rivers, also plays an important role in Hungarian cooking.

Two vegetables, kohlrabi and vegetable marrow, used less in French cooking, are frequently and readily employed in Hungarian cooking. Celery is grown in Hungary but rarely; Hungarian cooking uses celeriac (celery root) instead.

Speaking of cooking ingredients, we should also discuss seasoning in detail. Among special seasonings in Hungarian cooking, first place undoubtedly belongs to *paprika*. This fine choice spice is made from the cleaned, dried and finely ground ripe red fruit of the paprika plant (Capsicum annuum). (The same fruit, while still green, may be used in vegetable dishes and salads.)

Fine quality paprika ("sweet choice" or "rose paprika" of Szeged), has a specific, slightly sweetish flavour: not stronger, however, than that of the pepper, for instance, generally used in Western countries. In addition to its special flavour, very suitable for the seasoning of meals, the paprika lends dishes a beautiful colour as well. Occasional complaints may be due to the incorrect use of poor quality paprika, but that is the sort of thing that should not happen either in a well-managed restaurant kitchen or in your own home.

Dill and marjoram, though not exclusively Hungarian specialities, are more frequently and readily used in Hungarian cooking than in the Western cuisine.

Poppy-seeds *(grains de pavot)* are also unknown in French cooking, but are very popular not only in Hungarian cooking, but also in other East-European cuisines as well. They are used here in a ground form, sweetened with sugar, cooked or raw, for the filling of pastries.

We hope, this book will enable its readers to prepare Hungarian dishes they have tasted either in Hungary or somewhere else abroad and of which they still have pleasant recollections; and then, encouraged by success, perhaps they will also try to prepare dishes unknown to them before.

Unless otherwise stated, quantities in our recipes are generally sufficient for five people.

FUNDAMENTAL CONCEPTIONS OF COOKING AND BAKING

Hungarian cooking, in common with French cooking, knows five fundamental methods of cooking: boiling, braising, frying, roasting and frying in bread-crumbs.

We call the process boiling by which certain foodstuffs, meat or any kind of vegetables, are heated and brought to the boil in plenty of water, meat stock or some other liquid, in order to prepare them for human consumption and to make them easily digestible by tenderizing the fibres. We may start boiling in two ways: in cold or hot water, depending on the aim we wish to achieve. If we want to make a good, strong meat stock, for instance, we must always start to cook the meat and bones in cold water, but if we wish to prepare tasty and juicy boiled meat, we must bring the water to the boil and then put in the meat and bones, because this way the precipitating enzymes seal in the juices of meat effectively, rendering it juicy, palatable and more nourishing. The same methods may be applied in the case of fish, poultry or other cooked foods as well.

Stewing or braising may be easily distinguished from boiling, because the foodstuff to be stewed is placed on a certain foundation, then covered with a very little fluid and stewed. Meats and vegetables are stewed, so to speak, almost in their own juice, until tender. For this reason, it is very important, in the case of braising, that meat, for instance, should first be browned in a very small amount of fat, because the hot fat seals the meat and this prevents loss of flavour in the course of braising. Water, meat stock or any other liquid should subsequently be added only in very small quantities, sufficient to produce steam, in which meat may be braised until really tender.

Frying should always be done in *hot* fat, oil or butter. If we attempt to fry onions in *warm* fat, they only wither, but do not brown; not to mention that potatoes put into lukewarm fat will absorb twice as much of it as those put into hot fat, and will not brown so nicely and gradually. The same rule may be applied in the case of mushrooms and all other foodstuffs. Roast meat should also be roasted in hot fat, because fat, when hot, seals the surface of the meat or other foodstuffs and thus prevents the evaporation of juices in the course of roasting, and helps to preserve flavour and the aroma of the meat, acquiring a fine colour in the meantime, and becoming crisp and tasty.

Roasting should be done on a grill, on a spit, or in a closed oven; meat may be grilled over a wood, coal or gas flame, and meat can be roasted on turn-spit turned frequently in the course of roasting. If roasting is done in a closed space, in an oven, it is a rule to start the roasting or baking process when the oven is hot, with the exception of a few light pastries, sponge-cakes and soufflés. When the meat or any other foodstuff acquires a nice brown colour, we should finish the roasting at a moderate, steady heat.

Coated or crumbed meats, fish and croquettes must be fried in plenty of hot fat.

The various kinds of thickening belong to the very important culinary processes. According to Hungarian cooking, soups, vegetables, sauces may be thickened in four different ways: thickening with a roux, thickening with sour cream and flour, sprinkling or dusting with flour and thickening with a mixture of flour and butter. As mentioned previously in the foreword, adding sour cream with flour and sprinkling and dusting with flour are special Hungarian methods of thickening.

It is very important that the roux should be made with hot fat, oil or butter, browned, lightly or to a darker colour—as needed. When thickening dishes with a roux, take care to prevent lumpiness. To avoid this, dilute roux when ready and browned with a small quantity of cold water, and mix well until smooth and add to the dish only afterwards—mixing constantly. (See also p. 219.)

Thickening with sour cream and flour is actually done by adding flour to sour cream, diluting with a small quantity of water and straining; this mixture should be added to the dish gradually, stirring constantly. (The mixture should be strained to avoid curdling.) This method of thickening is mostly used in the case of fruit sauces or cold fruit soups.

Sprinkling or dusting with flour can be applied when we want to thicken dishes only to a small extent. For instance, when preparing fresh and tender peas, we should stew peas in a small quantity of butter or lard until soft, and when their juice is reduced, sprinkle with a little flour, mix well, and finally dilute with stock or water.

The mixture of flour and butter should be used for the quick thickening of a thin sauce or cream soup. Mix a small quantity of butter well with flour and stirring soup or cream constantly with a whisk, break this mixture into it, gradually, and stir constantly to prevent curdling; leave over the fire until sufficiently thick.

Meats should be sliced with great care. Uncooked fillets or cutlets as well as already roasted or boiled meat should be sliced so as always to cut fibres crosswise and not lengthwise; in this way the meat will not be tough, but tender, and more easily digestible. Meat intended for *pörkölt* (stewed meat with seasoning and potatoes) should be cut into bigger pieces, meat for goulash into smaller cubes, while for stews (meat stewed with black pepper) into strips of about an inch and half in length.

When roasting poultry, the legs should be fastened to the sides of the bird and the bird trussed in order to retain its shape during roasting; the trussing string must be removed before serving. Boneless ham should also be properly trussed before boiling, as well as fillets of pike-perch or sheat-fish, meant for a cold dish, to facilitate carving.

Blanching is one of the cooking methods frequently used too. Early kohlrabi, cauliflower, or mutton, for instance, may be blanched to remove strong flavour, by dipping into boiling water for a minute. It should subsequently be strained and rinsed with cold water and cooking continued in fresh water.

Aerating is one of the frequently recurring culinary processes, by which expression we understand the leavening and kneading of dough, the mixing and dressing of various pastes, butter creams and the beating of cream until stiff and foamy. The aim is to force as much air into a mixture as possible, thereby increasing its bulk and making it lighter. We must take care therefore, when beating is prescribed in recipes to beat properly, in order to ensure the success of our pastas, pastries or butter creams.

To prevent cloudiness in meat stock or aspic, clarify by mixing slightly beaten egg white with a little water and pouring it into the soup or aspic, stirring all the while; then bring to boil. When boiling, take off the fire, leave to settle down and then strain slowly through a fine cloth.

There are other important culinary processes which are also frequently met with in the course of cooking, such as larding, marinading, coating, etc., the description of which may be found in various recipes.

Cooking and baking should be undertaken with pleasure and real joy and excellent results will follow. But the real pleasure and real joy should be developed in spirit; it cannot be found in any recipes. One thing is certain: all recipes are but mute letters, unless we undertake cooking with great care and interest and start our responsible work of cooking with due devotion and skill. Housewives and cooks, who do their work with pleasure and enthusiasm, can develop the craft of cooking and baking into a real art.

SOUPS AND GARNISHES

Soups in Hungarian cooking are grouped generally into white and brown soups. The expression "brown" and "white" does not indicate the colour of the soup. Soups prepared without thickening, such as bouillon, clear soup, bone stock, are called white soups, and thickened soups are called brown.

Bouillon is one of our most popular soups. The first rule to be observed in making a fine bouillon is always to put the meat and bones, having first washed them thoroughly, into cold water and bring to boil not too quickly. In the course of a slow and gradual heating and in consequence of the long cooking the nutritive juices of the meat are completely extracted. The meat cooked this way will lose much of its flavour, but the soup will contain all the nutritious juices of the meat, and it will possess a fine flavour and have high nutritive value.

If we want to obtain tasty meat, we should start its cooking in hot water. The second essential rule for making bouillon is to keep soup boiling steadily and slowly after having brought it to boil; put vegetables into it and skim well in order to obtain a good crystal-clear and transparent liquid. Bouillon cooked over an open fire, by quick boiling, is bound to become cloudy, broken and tasteless. Finally, it is also important to put the soup aside for about 10—15 mins. after having taken it off the fire, to allow complete settling, and only then strain through a clear cloth or a fine hair sieve. Strain soup gradually by ladling it with a spoon (do not pour), with due care, to avoid its becoming cloudy, and to keep it fine and clear. Garnishings for bouillon (for instance fine noodles, squares of pasta, etc.) should be boiled separately and added to the soup just before serving.

Consommé is one of the almost indispensable soups for festive occasions. The method for making bouillon may also be applied for consommé, with the difference that meat must not be cooked in one piece in this soup, but lean beef should be minced and mixed well in a basin together with appropriate quantities of white of egg and tomato purée with a wooden spoon. Then dilute it with cold water stirring constantly, put on a steady fire, and bring to boil (stirring at times to prevent the minced meat and white of egg from burning). Salt and season soup, put in vegetables and boil over a slow and steady fire to avoid its becoming cloudy. Do not stir after having brought to boil. Strain as for bouillon. If consommé is cloudy for some reason, clarify with white of egg; first beat white of egg with a little cold water for a short time, then mix it well, adding some of the cloudy liquid and putting it on fire, boil slowly for a few mins. until the liquid is completely clarified. Take off the fire, leave it to settle and ladling carefully with a spoon, strain through a clean cloth. Skim consommé before serving.

Consommé may also be prepared from poultry or wildfowl. Cook the chicken, pheasant or partridge in the soup and then, removing the flesh from the bones, cut it into neat, thin slices and serve in the strained soup. Consommé should be served with special garnishings, and its name will change according to the garnishes used.

Brown soups may also be divided into several groups, according to the method of preparation or the ingredients used.

1. Simple brown soups: e. g. mushroom soup, French bean-soup.
2. Purées: e. g. lentil purée, liver purée.
3. Cream soups: e. g. asparagus or cauliflower cream.
4. Fruit soups: e. g. apple soup, cherry soup.
5. Mixed or special soups: *gulyás*, Újházi's chicken soup.

The basic ingredients (such as vegetables, etc.) of simple brown soups in Hungarian cooking should be cut into fine noodles, small slices or cubes, seasoned and cooked adequately and thickened with a roux. The basic ingredients are served in the soup. Purées should be passed through a fine sieve when cooked, mixed until smooth, and then served. Cream soups are really purées, thickened before serving with a mixture of egg-yolks and cream or butter. Fruit soups differ from simple brown soups inasmuch as they are thickened not with a roux, but with a mixture of flour and sour cream, and are usually put on ice during the summer season and served cold. Finally, we list in the group of mixed and special soups all those which are served together with meat, in addition to the various kinds of vegetables and other garnishes. Such soups are: gulyás, Újházi's chicken soup, some of the more popular foreign soups, which are also well-known in our country, e. g. the Russian borshch and Russian shchi; the Italian minestrone.

The first condition for preparing a good soup is to choose the ingredients carefully. Really good soups can be made only from fine, fresh and suitable basic raw foodstuffs.

Bone stock prepared from calf's or pig's bones is used for the making of brown soups, because it lends the soup strength and flavour. (Soups can also be prepared without bones, but they are not as full-bodied and tasty if bone stock is omitted.)

It is advisable in the case of certain brown soups, such as vegetable soup and mushroom soup, to brown mixed vegetables and mushrooms in fat before cooking, because there are many aromatic substances produced by frying in hot fat. It is quite important to boil soups thoroughly, to ensure their proper smoothness, and also, because boiling brings out the flavour of the soup much better.

Great care should be taken always to suit the individual taste and wishes of guests as regards spices, but strong spices must be avoided at all costs, because they may spoil the characteristics of the soup, and even render it quite unpalatable.

The thickness of soup is a question of taste. There are people who prefer thinner, and others who like thicker soups. As a rule, people dislike any soup if served too thin or too thick, and we should keep this in mind when preparing soup in bigger quantities.

SOUPS

Clear Meat Soup

Ingredients: 1¾ lb. beef, 5¼ oz. carrots, 2 oz. parsnips, 2 oz. celery, 2 oz. kohlrabi, 2 oz. savoy, 1 oz. onions, 1 oz. mushrooms, 1 clove of garlic, 1 oz. tomato purée, 5 whole black peppers, 1 oz. salt (1 green paprika when in season), 2 oz. fine noodles (vermicelli).

Wash beef and put into 4 pt. of water, bring slowly to boil and skim well all the time. Clean and wash all vegetables. Add carrots, parsnips, mushrooms, onions, tomato purée and salt and cook until meat is tender. Strain. Serve clear soup with fine noodles (vermicelli), cooked separately, and with sliced vegetables and mushrooms.

Bouillon

Ingredients: 14 oz. beef bones, ½ lb. lean beef, 3½ oz. carrots, 2 oz. parsnips, 2 oz. celery, 2 oz. kohlrabi, 2 oz. savoy, 1 oz. onions, 1 oz. mushrooms, 1 clove of garlic, 1 oz. tomato purée, 5 whole black peppers, 1 oz. salt, 1 white of egg (1 green paprika when in season).

Mince meat and mix well with the white of egg and tomato purée; add 4 pt. of cold water, stirring well all the time. Then add vegetables, onions, mushrooms, salt, pepper and garlic, bring to boil, simmer gently for 4 hrs., then strain.

Bouillon à la Jardinière

Ingredients: 5 oz. carrots, 3½ oz. parsnips, 3½ oz. celery, 2 oz. asparagus-tips, 2 oz. tender green peas, 3½ oz. cleaned cauliflower.

Wash carrots, parsnips and celery, cut with small vegetable scoop into pellets and wash well; then cook in slightly salted water until tender. At the same time cook separately green peas, asparagus-tips and also small sprigs of cauliflower. When tender (but not too tender), strain, then mix together with soup ladle, and dividing evenly, place into soup bowls. Serve with hot bouillon.

Bouillon with Goose-liver and Egg-jelly

Ingredients: 3½ oz. goose-liver, 2 oz. béchamel sauce (see: Sauces), pinch of ground black pepper, salt, 1 whole egg, 2 egg-yolks, ½ oz. butter.

Rub goose-liver through a fine wire sieve, add cooled and not too thick béchamel sauce, salt and pepper. Mix whole egg smoothly together with yolks. Butter basin or mould of appropriate size and pour mixture into it. Cover basin with small lid and put into a saucepan or casserole with cold water, reaching up to the middle of the mould. Cover saucepan and steam in a medium-hot oven until the egg-jelly is set. Do not boil water, lest condensing steam should make jelly watery. Steam for about 10—15 mins., then remove from oven, place basin in cold water to cool, then turn jelly out of its mould. Cut into neat, even slices, and serve, evenly divided, with hot bouillon.

Bouillon with Profiteroles

Ingredients: 2½ oz. flour, 1 oz. butter, pinch of salt, pinch of ground black pepper, 2 eggs.

Boil about a pt. of water in a small saucepan, together with 1 oz. butter, salt and pepper. Pour flour into the boiling water, the whole quantity at the same time, and stir over flame until it is quite smooth and does not stick to the saucepan. Then remove from heat, cool a little (do not cool completely) and break one whole egg into the mixture mixing well; then add second egg again mixing very well. In the meantime butter clean baking tin with ⅓ oz. of butter. Put mixed dough into forcing-bag, fitted previously with small round nozzle. Press dough on to the buttered baking tin, in small round buns, not too near to each other. Bake in a hot oven. When baked, the small buns swell into a kind of light roll with hollow inside. Serve separately on paper serviettes, together with bouillon. The rolls may be filled before serving, with warm goose-liver (purée), warm cream-cheese or brains and eggs.

Bouillon with Brains on Fried Croutons

Ingredients: 2 rolls, 3 oz. butter, 5 oz. dressed calves brains, 1 tsp. salt, pinch of ground black pepper, 1 egg, 1 tsp. finely chopped parsley, 2 oz. grated cheese.

Cut crust off rolls and divide into 15 pieces of neat and even heart-shapes or other forms. Fry in butter until slightly browned and place on clean baking tin. Fry in the meantime finely chopped brains in some butter, sprinkle with salt, pepper and finely chopped parsley and fry it together with egg. Stir on fire until it turns into a thick, pliable paste. Divide this paste evenly on pieces of toast, spread them daintily, sprinkle each one with grated cheese, put some melted butter on them and toast in the oven until slightly browned and crisp. Serve—as soon as taken from oven—separately on paper serviettes, together with hot bouillon in bowls.

Ujházi's Chicken Broth Served ▷

Consommé (Bone Soup)

Ingredients: 1½ lb. bones of beef, 5 oz. carrots, 2 oz. parsnips, 2 oz. celery, 1 oz. kohlrabi, 2 oz. savoy, 1 oz. onions, 1 oz. mushrooms, 1 clove of garlic, 1 oz. tomato purée, 5 whole black peppers, 1 tsp. salt, 1 green paprika (in season), 2 oz. pasta squares.

Put bones, washed and cleaned, to cook in 4 pt. of water. Bring to boiling point and simmer it gently, skimming thoroughly. Clean and wash vegetables, mushrooms, onions, garlic, then add to soup, together with tomato purée and salt, and cook for 3 hrs., then strain. Cook pasta separately, chop cooked vegetables, mushrooms, and serve in consommé.

Gulyás Soup

Ingredients: ½ lb. beef (preferably shin of beef), 3 oz. onions, 1 tsp. salt, 1 clove of garlic, pinch of caraway seed, 2 lb. potatoes, 3½ oz. ready stewed onions, tomatoes and green paprika (tinned *lecsó*), half a tsp. red paprika, 1½ oz. lard.

Fry onions in lard, add red paprika, beef cut in squares, finely chopped garlic, caraway seed, fresh or tinned *lecsó*, salt it, pour on cold water and steam until almost tender. Add potatoes cut into cubes, cover potatoes and meat with water and cook well.

Mock Gulyás Soup

Ingredients: 2 lb. potatoes, 1½ oz. lard, 3½ oz. onions, 1 tsp. salt, 1 clove of garlic, 3½ ready stewed onions, tomatoes and green paprika (tinned lecsó), half a tsp. red paprika, pinch of caraway seed.

Fry finely chopped onions in lard, add garlic and red paprika, then pour 2 pt. of water on it. Clean and wash potatoes, and cut into cubes, put them in the soup, add caraway seed, *lecsó* and boil until potatoes are cooked.

Giblet Soup

Ingredients: 11 oz. giblets, 5 oz. carrots, 2 oz. parsnips, 3½ oz. fresh green peas or 1½ oz. tinned green peas, 1 oz. mushrooms, 1 oz. salt, pinch of ground black pepper, 1 small bunch of parsley, 2 oz. lard, 2 portions of brain dumplings, 2 oz. flour.

Before cooking, giblets must be thoroughly cleaned and washed in plenty of water and cut into pieces. Clean and chop vegetables and mushrooms into small squares and cook in salted water, seasoned with shelled green peas and ground pepper, until vegetables are tender. Make a light sauce (roux) from flour and lard, add finely chopped parsley to it, then pour a little cold water over it, mix it in the soup, bring to boil, boiling the brain dumplings in the soup as well.

Cream of Chicken Soup

Ingredients: 1 lb. chicken, 5¼ oz. carrots, 1¾ oz. parsnips, 2 oz. celery, 1 oz. onions, 1 tsp. salt, pinch of ground black pepper, 1 small bunch of parsley, 2 oz. butter, 2 oz. flour, 1 gill cream, 1 egg-yolk, ¼ lemon.

Cleanse and wash chicken and prepare a good strong chicken soup with onions, vegetables, salt and pepper. Strain, when chicken tender. Then remove breast of chicken, skin and cut into fine, thin slices and put it aside for the time being. Remove rest of meat from bones, mince and rub through a fine sieve. In the meantime thicken strained soup with a light roux—made from butter and flour, but not browned—bring to boil, then add chicken purée, stirring constantly. Salt and season soup afterwards, adding some lemon-juice; before serving, pour egg-yolk mixed with cream into soup, stirring all the time. Finally divide the finely sliced cooked breast. Serve hot in bowls.

Minced Lights Soup

Ingredients: 11 oz. bones (veal or pork), 3½ carrots, 2 oz. parsnips, ½ lb. lights (veal or pork), 2 oz. flour, 1 tsp. salt, 1 oz. onions, ½ clove of garlic, 1 tbsp. mustard, a good pinch of red paprika, pinch of ground black pepper, ½ lemon, 1 bay leaf, 1 oz. butter, 1 roll, 2 oz. lard.

Make stock from bones and vegetables with 3 pt. of salted water, boiling it for 2 hrs. Cook the lights separately and mince. Fry finely chopped onions in 1 oz. of lard, add minced lights, ground pepper, bay leaf and fry. Pour strained soup over it and season with mustard and lemon. Make a light roux from 1½ oz. of flour with lard sprinkle with red paprika, add a little cold water to it, mix it into the soup and boil, stirring well for 10 mins. Fry neat dices of roll in 1 oz. of butter and when serving, sprinkle into soup. May be cooked without stock; the gravy from the lights may be used instead.

Újházi's Chicken Broth

Ingredients: 3 lb. fowl, 7½ oz. carrots, 1¾ oz. parsnips, 2 oz. celery, 1 oz. onions, 1 clove of garlic, 1 oz. tomato (purée), 2 oz. mushrooms, 1 green paprika (in season), ¾ oz. salt, 5 whole black peppers, 3 oz. flour, ½ egg.

Clean, draw and wash fowl, then put on to boil in 4 pt. of salted water, together with cleaned and chopped vegetables, celery, onions, garlic, mushrooms and pepper, until fowl is tender. Strain. Make paste from flour and ½ egg, knead it, cut into thin slices and boil it in the strained soup. Slice cooked vegetables and mushrooms as well, add to soup and serve hot.

Vegetable Soup

Ingredients: 11 oz. bones (veal or pork), 7½ oz. carrots, 3 oz. parsnips, 2 small bunch of parsley, 1 oz. mushrooms, 2 oz. celery, 2 oz. flour, 1½ oz. lard, 1 tsp. salt, 5 oz. fresh green peas or 2 oz. tinned green peas, 2 portions of buttered dumplings.

Make stock from the bones with 1¾ oz. of carrots, 1 oz. of parsnips, simmering them in 3 pt. of salted water for 2 hrs. Strain. Slice remaining carrots and parsnips, celery and mushrooms, add shelled peas, and cook in the stock. Prepare roux from lard and flour, add finely chopped parsley, mix with a little cold water, then add to soup, boil for 10 mins. cooking small buttered dumplings in soup. (For buttered dumplings see Garnishes for Soups.)

Italian Vegetable Soup (Minestrone)

Ingredients: 11 oz. bones (veal or pork), 7½ oz. carrots, 5 oz. parsnips, 4 oz. savoy, 3½ oz. potatoes, 3½ oz. kohlrabi, 3½ oz. celery, 1½ oz. lard, 1 tsp. salt, 1 oz. tomato (purée), 1 small bunch of parsley, 2 oz. spaghetti, 2 oz. grated cheese, 2 oz. bacon.

Make stock from bones with 2 oz. of carrots, 2 oz. of parsnips, boiling it in 3 pt. of salted water for 2 hrs. Braise in lard cleaned and sliced vegetables, savoy cabbage, potatoes, celery, kohlrabi. Dice bacon and fry together with tomato purée. Strain stock, add stewed vegetables, fried bacon, spaghetti, and boil for 20 mins. Serve hot with grated chesee, in individual plates.

Fish Soup

Ingredients: 1 lb. fish (carp or sheat-fish), 1 tsp. salt, half a tsp. red paprika, 1 oz. sugar, 1 tbsp. vinegar, 1 bay leaf, 1½ oz. lard, 2 oz. flour, 1 gill sour cream, 1 roll, pinch of ground black pepper, 5 oz. carrots, 5 oz. parsnips, 1 oz. onions, 1 small bunch of parsley, 1 tsp. butter.

Clean and dress fish, and cook it in 3 pt. of salted water, together with vinegar, bay leaf, black pepper and onions. Cook cleaned and sliced vegetables in strained liquid until tender. Prepare white roux from lard and flour, add finely chopped parsley and red paprika, mixing with cold water. Mix it in the soup, together with sour cream, and boil for 10 mins. Dice roll, fry it in butter until crisp, and add some of it to each plate when serving soup. Remove fish from bones and serve in the soup.

Cream of Fish Soup

Ingredients: 2 lb. fish bones (or 1 lb. cleaned and gutted small fish), 3½ oz. carrots, 3½ oz. parsnips, 1 oz. onions, 1 tsp. salt, 5 whole black peppers, 1 bay leaf, ¼ lemon, 2 oz. butter, 2 oz. flour, 1 gill cream, 1 egg-yolk.

Put fish bones, washed clean (or small fish, cleaned and gutted) to simmer, seasoned with onions, various vegetables, salt, pepper, bay leaf and lemon. Cook until fish is tender, then strain. Remove flesh from fish bones, and rub through a fine sieve. Thicken soup with a light roux, prepared from butter and flour, not browned. Add fish, mix it until smooth and boil it well. Season and, before serving, add cream mixed well with egg-yolk, stirring it all the time with a whisk. Serve garnished with croutons of toast (rolls cut in squares and fried crisp in butter).

Lebbencs Soup

(Clear soup with boiled potatoes and pasta cut into irregular squares)

Ingredients: 1 lb. peeled potatoes, 1 tsp. salt, 1½ oz. lard, 3½ oz. bacon, 1 oz. onions, 3½ oz. flour, ½ egg, 3½ oz. tinned lecsó (stewed onions, tomatoes, and green paprika prepared with red paprika, salt and lard), ¼ tsp. red paprika.

Dice peeled and washed potatoes and boil in 3 pt. of salted water, until half cooked. Knead pasta made from flour and half an egg, cut into squares and fry it in a little fat; then fry bacon together with finely chopped onions, sprinkle with red paprika and put into soup, together with lecsó and paste. Boil for 10 mins.

Lentil Soup

Ingredients: 11 oz. bones (pork or veal), 3½ oz. carrots, 2 oz. parsnips, 7½ oz. lentils, 1 tsp. salt, 1½ oz. lard, 2 oz. flour, 1 oz. onions, 1 oz. sugar, 1 bay leaf, 1 tbsp. vinegar, ¾ oz. mustard, 1 gill sour cream.

Cook cleaned and washed lentils until tender. Make stock from bones and vegetables, boiling them in 3 pt. of salted water for 2 hrs., strain liquid and pour over cooked lentils, then add bay leaf. Prepare roux from flour and lard, with finely chopped onions, pour in some cold water and mix it into the soup, season with vinegar and sugar and boil for 10 mins. Mix mustard and cream together well with a whisk and add to soup before serving.

Cream of Lentil Soup

Ingredients: 11 oz. bones (pork or veal), 3½ oz. carrots, 2 oz. parsnips, 7½ oz. lentils, 2 oz. flour, 2 oz. butter, 1 tsp. salt, 1 oz. onions, 1 gill cream, 1 egg-yolk, 1 roll.

Cook cleaned and washed lentils until tender. Make a stock from bones and vegetables, boiling them in 3 pt. of salted water for 2 hrs. Strain liquid and pour over cooked lentils. Prepare roux from 1½ oz. butter and 2 oz. flour with finely chopped onions, mix it in the soup, boil for 10 mins. Rub lentils through a fine sieve. Cut roll into small squares and fry until crisp in 1 oz. of butter. Whisk egg-yolk with cream, pour it into the soup (slightly cooled to prevent curdling) and serve garnished with croutons of rolls.

Potato Soup with Sour Cream

Ingredients: 11 oz. bones (veal or pork), 3½ oz. carrots, 2 oz. parsnips, 1 tsp. salt, 1¼ lb. peeled potatoes, 1½ oz. lard, 2 oz. flour, 1 oz. onions, 1 small bunch of parsley, 1 sprig of green celery, 1 gill sour cream.

Make stock from bones and vegetables, cooking them in 3 pt. of salted water for 2 hrs. Strain liquid, add to it peeled potatoes cut into small cubes and boil. Prepare white roux from flour and lard, then brown it slightly, add finely chopped onions, celery and parsnips. Pour cold water over this and mix well into soup. Boil it well. Add sour cream before serving.

Cream of Potato Soup

Ingredients: 11 oz. bones (veal), 3½ oz. carrots, 2 oz. parsnips, 1 tsp. salt, 2 oz. celery, 2 oz. butter, 2 oz. flour, 1¼ lb. potatoes, 1 egg-yolk, 1 gill cream, 1 roll.

Make stock from bones, vegetables and celery, boiling them in 3 pt. of salted water for 2 hrs. Strain liquid. Simmer peeled onions cut into rounds in 1½ oz. of butter, then add flour, brown slightly and pour stock over it. Boil for ½ hr. and then rub through a fine sieve. Whisk egg-yolk with cream well before serving and pour it into the soup when slightly cooled. Cut roll into small squares, fry crisp in ½ oz. of butter and serve soup garnished with them.

Tarhonya Soup

Ingredients: 11 oz. bones (pork or veal), 3½ oz. carrots, 2 oz. parsnips, 1½ oz. lard, 1 oz. onions, 1 oz. red paprika, pinch of ground black pepper, 1½ oz. bacon, 2 sprig of parsley, 3½ oz. tinned lecsó (dish of ready stewed onions, green paprikas, tomatoes, and red paprika), 3½ oz. tarhonya.

Make stock from bones and vegetables, boiling them in 3 pt. of salted water for 2 hrs. Brown *tarhonya* in lard, together with finely chopped parsley, and diced bacon, and put, together with lecsó, into the strained liquid. Cook until tender.

Cauliflower Soup

Ingredients: 11 oz. bones (veal or pork), 3½ oz. carrots, 2 oz. parsnips, 1 tsp. salt, 1 lb. cauliflower (cleaned), 1½ oz. lard, 2 oz. flour, 1 small bunch of parsley, 1 gill sour cream.

Make stock from bones and vegetables, boiling them in 3 pt. of salted water for 2 hrs. Strain liquid. Break cauliflower into flowerets and cook it in stock until tender. Prepare light roux from lard and flour, add finely chopped parsley, mix with soup, and bring to boil. Add sour cream before serving.

Cauliflower Purée Soup (Cream Soup)

Ingredients: 11 oz. bones (veal or pork), 2½ oz. carrots, 2 oz. parsnips, 1 lb. cleaned cauliflower, 2 oz. butter, 2 oz. flour, 1 gill cream, 1 egg-yolk, 1 tbsp. salt.

Make stock from bones and vegetables, boiling them in 3 pt. of salted water for 2 hrs. Strain liquid. Cook cauliflower in stock until tender. Prepare light roux from butter and flour, thicken cauliflower soup with it, bring to boil, then rub through fine sieve. Whisk egg-yolk and cream well together, and pour into warm (not hot) soup before serving.

Mushroom Soup

Ingredients: 11 oz. bones (veal), 3½ oz. carrots, 2 oz. parsnips, 1 tsp. salt, 5 oz. mushrooms, 1½ oz. lard, 2 oz. flour, ¼ pt. sour cream, 1 sprig of parsley, 1 oz. onions, pinch of ground black pepper.

Make stock from bones and vegetables, boiling them in 3 pt. of salted water for 2 hrs. Strain liquid. Clean, wash and slice mushrooms. Fry finely chopped onions in ⅓ oz. of lard, add sliced mushrooms, stew, season with black pepper, and put into stock. Prepare roux from 1 oz. lard and 2¼ oz. flour adding finely chopped parsley. Mix into soup and boil for 10 mins. Mix sour cream into soup before serving.

Cream of Mushroom Soup

Ingredients: 11 oz. bones (veal or pork), 3½ oz. carrots, 2 oz. butter, 5 oz. mushrooms, 2 oz. flour, 1 tsp. salt, 1 gill cream, pinch of ground black pepper, 1 egg-yolk.

Make stock from bones and vegetables, boiling them for 2 hrs. in 3 pt. of salted water. Clean, wash and chop mushrooms well, let them simmer in butter, season with pepper; add flour and brown, then pour stock over it, bring to boil and rub through a fine sieve. Whisk egg-yolk with cream well and mix into warm (not hot) soup before serving.

Kohlrabi Soup

Ingredients: 11 oz. bones (veal or pork), 3½ oz. carrots, 2 oz. parsnips, 1 lb. kohlrabi, 1½ oz. lard, 2 oz. flour, 1 tsp. salt, pinch of ground black pepper, 1 tsp. sugar, 1 gill sour cream.

Make stock from bones and vegetables, boiling them in 3 pt. of salted water for 2 hrs. Strain liquid. Slice cleaned kohlrabi finely, braise in lard, mix with flour, brown and add chopped parsley. Add stock, season with pepper and boil until kohlrabi tender. Mix in sour cream before serving.

French Bean Soup

Ingredients: 11 oz. bones (veal or pork), 1 small bunch of parsley, 14 oz. fresh French beans or 1 lb. tinned French beans, 1½ oz. lard, 4 oz. flour, 1 tsp. salt, ¼ tsp. red paprika, 1 oz. onions, ½ egg, 1 gill sour cream, a little vinegar, 1 clove of garlic.

Make stock from bones and vegetables, boiling them in 3 pt. of salted water for 2 hrs. Strain liquid. Clean and wash beans, slice and cook in stock until tender. Prepare roux from lard, 2 oz. flour, with finely chopped onions, parsley, garlic and red paprika, add a little cold water to it, and mix into the soup. Boil for 5 mins. Prepare pasta from 2½ oz. flour and half an egg with a little water, make small pellets from pasta and cook them in soup. Mix in sour cream before serving.

Green Pea Soup

Ingredients: 11 oz. bones (veal or pork), 3½ oz. carrots, 2 oz. parsnips, 2 lb. fresh green peas or 1 lb. tinned green peas, 1½ oz. lard, 4½ oz. flour, 1 tsp. salt, 1 tsp. sugar, 1 small bunch of parsley, ½ egg.

Make stock from bones and vegetables, boiling them in 3 pt. of salted water for 2 hrs. Strain liquid. Shell and wash peas, cook them in stock and sweeten with sugar. Prepare light roux from lard and 2¼ oz. flour, add finely chopped parsley, dilute with a little cold water, mix into soup and boil for 10 mins. Prepare paste from 2¼ oz. flour and ½ egg with a little water, make small pellets from pasta and cook in the soup.

Cream of Green Pea Soup

Ingredients: 11 oz. bones (veal or pork), 3½ oz. carrots, 2 oz. parsnips, 2 lb. fresh green peas or 1 lb. tinned green peas, 2½ oz. butter, 2 oz. flour, 1 tsp. salt, 1 tsp. sugar, 1 gill cream, 1 egg-yolk, 1 roll.

Make stock from bones and vegetables, boiling them in 3 pt. of salted water for 2 hrs. Strain liquid. Shell and wash green peas, cook them in stock and sweeten with sugar. Make a light roux with 1½ oz. butter and 2 oz. flour, dilute with a little cold water, mix into soup and boil for 10 mins. Then rub through a fine sieve. Whisk egg-yolk and cream well and pour into warm (not hot) soup before serving. Serve soup garnished with croutons of rolls, fried crisp in 1 oz. of butter.

Asparagus Soup

Ingredients: 11 oz. bones (veal or pork), 3½ oz. carrots, 2 oz. parsnips, 1 lb. fresh asparagus or 11 oz. tinned asparagus, 1 tsp. sugar, 1½ oz. butter, 2½ flour, 1 tsp. salt, 1 sprig of parsley, 1 gill milk, 2 portions of buttered dumplings.

Make stock from bones and vegetables, boiling them in 3 pt. of salted water for 2 hrs. Strain liquid. Wash, prepare and dice asparagus, sweeten with sugar and cook in stock. Prepare a light roux with butter, flour and finely chopped parsley, dilute with a little cold water, mix it into the soup, together with milk, and boil for 5 mins. Cook and serve buttered dumplings in soup.

23

Cream of Asparagus Soup

Ingredients: 11 oz. bones (veal or pork), 3½ oz. carrots, 2 oz. parsnips, 1 lb. fresh asparagus or 11 oz. tinned asparagus, 1 tsp. sugar, 2 oz. butter, 2 oz. flour, 1 gill milk, 1 tsp. salt, 1 gill cream, 1 egg-yolk, 1 roll.

Make stock from bones and vegetables, boiling them in 3 pt. of salted water for 2 hrs. Strain liquid. Clean and cut asparagus, cook in stock until tender, sweeten with sugar. Make a light roux with 1½ oz. butter and 2 oz. flour, dilute with a little cold water, add milk, mix into soup and boil for 10 mins. Then rub through a fine sieve. Whisk cream with egg-yolk before serving and add to warm (not hot) soup. Fry and brown croutons of rolls in ¾ oz. butter until crisp, and serve soup garnished with them.

Sorrel Soup with Sour Cream

Ingredients: 11 oz. bones (veal or pork), 3½ oz. carrots, 2 oz. parsnips, 1 lb. sorrel, 2 oz. lard, 2½ oz. flour, 1 tsp. salt, 1 oz. sugar, 1 gill sour cream, 1 roll, 1 oz. butter, 1 oz. onions.

Make stock from bones and vegetables, boiling them together in 3 pt. of salted water for 2 hrs. Strain liquid. Fry sliced onion-rings in 1 oz. of lard, add cleaned and washed sorrel, let it simmer for 30 mins. and pour stock over it. Prepare a roux with 1 oz. lard and 2 oz. flour, dilute with a little cold water, mix into soup, boil for 10 mins., then rub it through a sieve. Add sour cream to soup before serving. Garnish with croutons fried crisp in butter.

Cabbage (Sauerkraut) Soup with Smoked Pork Sausages

Ingredients: 14 oz. sauerkraut, 1½ oz. lard, 2 oz. flour, 1 oz. onions, pinch of red paprika, half a tsp. salt, 3½ oz. smoked pork sausages, 2 oz. bacon. ¼ pt. sour cream.

Cook sauerkraut in 3 pt. of water until tender. Dice bacon and fry, slice sausages, put in the soup and salt it. Make a roux with flour and lard, add finely chopped onions and red paprika, dilute with a little cold water, mix into soup and boil for 10 mins. Mix in sour cream before serving.

Tomato Soup

Ingredients: 11 oz. bones (veal or pork), 3½ oz. carrots, 2 oz. parsnips, 1 lb. fresh tomatoes or 7½ oz. tomato (purée), 1¼ oz. lard, 2 oz. flour, 1 tsp. salt, 1 oz. onions, 1 oz. sugar, 1 sprig of green celery, 2 oz. rice.

Make a stock from bones, carrots, parsnips, onions, green celery, boiling them in 3 pt. of salted water for 2 hrs. Add fresh tomatoes, cooked separately, or purée, and sweeten with sugar. Make a light roux from lard and flour, dilute with a little cold water, mix into soup and boil for 10 mins. Then strain. Cook rice in water separately, and add to soup before serving.

Bean Soup

Ingredients: 11 oz. bones (pork), 3½ oz. carrots, 2 oz. parsnips, 1 tsp. salt, 5 oz. haricot beans, 1½ oz. lard, 1 oz. onions, 1 clove of garlic, 2 oz. flour, ¼ pt. sour cream, pinch of red paprika, 1 small bunch of parsley.

Make a stock from bones and vegetables, boiling them in 3 pt. of salted water for 2 hrs. Strain liquid. Clean and wash haricot beans, soak in water for a few hrs., then cook until tender and add stock. Make a roux from lard and flour, add finely chopped onions, garlic, parsley and red paprika, dilute with a little cold water, mix into soup and boil for 10 mins. Add sour cream before serving.

Cream of Pea Soup

Ingredients: 11 oz. bones (veal or pork), 3½ oz. carrots, 2 oz. parsnips, 1 tsp. salt, 7½ oz. peas, 1½ oz. lard, 2 oz. flour, 1 oz. onions, pinch of ground black pepper.

Make stock from bones and vegetables, boiling them in 3 pt. of salted water for 2 hrs. Strain liquid. Wash peas and cook separately until tender, then add stock. Make a roux with lard, flour and finely chopped onions, mix into soup, season with pepper, and boil for 10 mins., then rub through a fine sieve. Reheat before serving.

Cream of Barley Soup

Ingredients: 11 oz. bones (pork or veal), 3½ oz. carrots, 2 oz. parsnips, 1 tsp. salt, 1½ oz. butter, 1½ oz. flour, 3½ oz. pearl-barley, 1 gill milk, 1 gill cream, 1 egg-yolk.

Make stock from bones and vegetables, boiling them in 3 pt. of salted water for 2 hrs. Strain liquid. Clean and wash barley and cook in stock until tender. Make a light roux from butter and flour, dilute with a little water and milk, mix into soup, boil for 10 mins. and pass through a hair sieve. Whisk cream and egg-yolk well, and add into warm (not hot) soup before serving.

Cream of Rice Soup

Ingredients: 11 oz. bones (veal or pork), 3½ oz. carrots, 2 oz. parsnips, 5 oz. rice, 2 oz. butter, 1 tsp. salt, 1 gill milk, 1 egg-yolk, 1 gill cream, 1 roll.

Make stock from bones and vegetables, boiling them in 3 pt. of salted water for 2 hrs. Strain soup. Cook cleaned and washed rice in stock, pass through a sieve, add milk, and 1½ oz. of butter and boil for 10 mins. Mix egg-yolk mixed in cream into warm (not hot) soup, before serving. Garnish soup with fried croutons (rolls cut into squares and fried crisp in ½ oz. of butter).

Cream of Spinach Soup

Ingredients: 11 oz. bones (veal or pork), 3½ oz. carrots, 2 oz. parsnips, 1 lb. spinach, 2 oz. butter, 2 oz. flour, 1 tsp. salt, pinch of ground black pepper, 1 gill cream, 1 egg-yolk, pinch of bicarbonate of soda.

Make stock from bones and vegetables, boiling them in 3 pt. of water for 2 hrs. Clean and wash spinach, and cook separately with bicarbonate of soda, rinse with cold water when cooked, pass through a sieve and add to strained stock. Make a light roux with butter and flour, dilute with a little cold water, mix into soup and boil for 10 mins. Whisk egg-yolk and cream well together before serving and add to the warm (not hot) soup.

Cream of Celery Soup

Ingredients: 11 oz. bones (veal or pork), 3½ oz. carrots, 2 oz. parsnips, 1 tsp. salt, 11 oz. cleaned celery, 1 sprig of green celery top, 2 oz. butter, 2 oz. flour, 1 gill cream, 1 egg-yolk, 3 whole black peppers.

Make a good strong soup from the bones, carrots and parsnips, seasoned with salt and pepper. Cut cleaned celery roots in slices and together with the washed green celery head braise in a little butter, in a closed pot, until almost tender. Pour cooked and strained soup on celery and cook together until quite soft. When ready, remove green celery head. Make a roux with butter and flour and mix into soup. Boil well, pass through a fine sieve, and whisk until smooth. Season before serving and add, stirring all the time, egg-yolk mixed with cream. Serve hot in soup bowls. Garnish with crisp croutons on paper serviettes. Slice roll into neat even squares or thin strips, brown in a medium-hot oven on a buttered pan until golden.

Cream of Liver Soup

Ingredients: 11 oz. bones (veal), 3½ oz. carrots, 2 oz. parsnips, 1 tsp. salt, 7½ oz. calf's liver or pig's liver, 2 oz. lard, 2 oz. flour, 1½ oz. onions, 1 gill cream, 1 egg-yolk, pinch of ground black pepper.

Make stock from bones and vegetables, boiling them together in 3 pt. of salted water for 2 hrs. Fry onions in ¾ oz. of lard, add diced liver, salt and pepper, simmer until tender, then pass through a sieve and mix into strained soup. Make a light brown roux with 1 oz. lard and 2 oz. flour, mix into soup and boil for 10 mins. Mix egg-yolk into cream and pour into soup (not hot) before serving.

Cream of Brains Soup

Ingredients: 11 oz. bones (veal), 3½ oz. carrots, 2 oz. parsnips, 1 tsp. salt, 1 oz. onions, 7½ oz. dressed calf's or pig's brains, ¼ lemon, pinch of ground black pepper, 2 oz. butter, 2 oz. flour, 1 gill cream, 1 egg-yolk.

Cook a good strong soup from the bones, various vegetables, salt and pepper. Fry finely chopped onions in a little butter, add diced brains salt and pepper and let it simmer. Pour cooked and strained soup over brains. Make a roux with butter and flour, do not brown it, and mix into soup. Season with salt, ground pepper, lemon-juice, and a pinch of grated lemon peel, then boil well, and pass through a fine sieve. Whisk until smooth and add to it, before serving, egg-yolk and cream mixed well. Serve hot in soup bowls, garnished with crisp croutons, squares or slices of fried crisp rolls browned in butter until golden.

Frankfurter Cream Soup

Ingredients: 11 oz. bones (veal or pork), 3½ oz. carrots, 2 oz. parsnips, 1 oz. onions, 1 tsp. salt, pinch of ground black pepper, 14 oz. cleaned savoy cabbage, 1½ oz. butter, 2 oz. flour, 1 oz. bacon, 1 pair of frankfurter sausages, 1 gill cream, 1 egg-yolk.

Make a good strong soup from the bones, various root vegetables, onions and salt. Slice savoy, wash well, place in a pot, pour soup over it, salt and season with ground pepper and cook until tender. Make a light roux with butter and flour and mix into soup when cooked. Bring to boil, cook well and pass through a fine sieve. Whisk until smooth and mix into it egg-yolk and cream beaten well together, stirring it all the time. Dice bacon, fry it in a pan, add skinned sausages cut in slices, fry together, browning them quickly, while turning all the time. Divide into equal portions and add to soup served hot in bowls.

Cold Apple Soup

Ingredients: 1 lb. apples, 1½ oz. flour, ½ tsp. salt, 3 oz. sugar, 1 tbsp. white wine, 1 pt. milk, 1 gill cream or sour cream, 2 cloves, very little cinnamon, ½ lemon.

Clean apples, removing seeds and cores, then cut into small cubes. Cook apples well in water, together with sugar and seasoning, until tender. Add white wine, and finally pour on milk. Whisk cream with flour until smooth, add to soup thickening it, bring to boil, cook well and season it again. Serve chilled.

Cold Morello Soup

Ingredients: 1½ lb. morello cherries, 2 oz. flour, a little salt, ½ lemon, 3½ oz. sugar, 1 gill red wine, 2 cloves, a little cinnamon, 1 pt. milk, 1 gill cream.

Wash morello cherries well and take out stones. Cook, together with sugar, seasonings and red wine, in water, until tender. Add milk, mix cream and flour together, pour into soup, whisk until smooth, and boil well. Season again and serve when cold.

SPECIAL SOUPS

Lobster Bisque

Ingredients: 11 oz. bones (veal), 5½ oz. carrots, 3 oz. parsnips, 20 crayfish, 1 oz. onions, 5 whole black peppers, a little thyme, 1 bay leaf, ½ clove of garlic, 1 oz. tomato purée, 1 tsp. salt, 2 oz. flour, 4½ oz. butter, 1 tbsp. cognac, 1 gill white wine, ¼ pt. cream, 1 egg-yolk, 2 oz. rice, 1 oz. tinned green peas.

Make a stock from bones and vegetables (2 oz. carrots, 1 oz. parsnips) and salt, boiling them for 2 hrs. Dice cleaned vegetables and onions and fry, together with thyme, bay leaf, ground pepper and tomato purée in 1¾ oz. of butter until brown. Wash and gut crayfish. (Use live specimens only.) Put them in the saucepan, together with the vegetables, pour cognac over them, light it and stir all the time while it is alight. Pour white wine and a small quantity of soup over it afterwards and steam it, under cover, for 10 mins., then take out crayfish, clean shells and claws. Put aside 5 shells for garnish. Pound the rest in a mortar, until quite fine, then add paste into the liquid with vegetables and peas, add stock, boil it well, and pass it through a sieve.

Make a light roux with 1¼ oz. butter and flour, dilute with a little cold water, mix into the soup and boil for 10 mins. Rinse and clean rice, steam in ¾ oz. butter, and a little salt water, till tender, add green peas to rice and fill clean shells with it. Whisk egg-yolk and cream well and pour into warm (not hot) soup before serving. Place into each soup bowl or plate the flesh of four crayfish and 1 shell, filled with rice and green peas.

Palóc Soup *

(For ten people)
Ingredients: 3 lb. mutton, 1 oz. onions, 2 oz. lard, 1 pt. sour cream, ⅓ tsp. red paprika, 1 lb. tender French beans (or butter beans), 1½ lb. potatoes, pinch of caraway seed, pinch of ground black pepper, ½ bay leaf, 2 tsp. salt, 2 cloves of garlic, 1½ oz. flour, 3½ oz. bacon, 1 small bunch of parsley.

Cut the bacon into small cubes and fry in a saucepan. Add onions, chopped finely and fry them lightly, then sprinkle with red paprika and place mutton

---

* Palóc are inhabitants of a part of North-Eastern Hungary.

in the saucepan, washed well and cut into neat and even cubes. Mix together, salt, season with ground pepper and bay leaf, and add caraway seed and garlic as well, the latter chopped finely. Put roast mutton, under closely fitting lid, in a very little liquid, stirring it at times, add a little water from time to time so as to prevent burning, and partially cook. In the meantime cook cleaned and sliced green beans separately in slightly salted water until tender. Make a golden roux. Put tender meat, potatoes and strained French beans together, dilute with stock, adding the quantity needed for soup, mix in roux and boil well. Season again before serving, mix well sour cream into soup, bringing it to boil once more, and serve hot in a bigger bowl, garnished with finely chopped parsley.

Soup from the Scraps of Sucking Pigs with Sour Cream

(For ten people)
Ingredients: 3 lb. scraps (trotters, ears, tails, liver, etc.) of sucking pigs, 3½ oz. lard, 7½ oz. onions, ½ tsp. red paprika, 2 tsp. salt, 1½ oz. flour, 1 pt. sour cream, pinch of ground black pepper, ½ bay leaf, ¼ lemon.

Clean and wash scraps of sucking pigs well (as is done with giblets for giblet soup). Cut scraps into small pieces. Fry finely chopped onions in 1¾ oz. of lard, sprinkle with red paprika and add scraps to it. Salt, season with ground pepper and bay leaf, and let it simmer under close fitting lid, stirring at times, until almost tender. Dilute with as much water as necessary for soup and bring to boil. Make a roux in the meantime with flour and lard, brown it slightly, mix into soup and boil until scraps are quite tender. Season again before serving, add lemon-juice, mix sour cream with soup and serve hot in a soup-tureen.

Russian Cabbage Soup I

(For ten people)
Ingredients: 3 lb. bones (pork), 3½ oz. onions, 1 oz. flour, 2 oz. bacon, 2 oz. lard, 11 oz. mixed vegetables, 1 lb. fresh tomatoes, 1 bunch of parsley, small bunch of fresh dill (leaves of dill), 3½ oz. pickled gherkins, 1 tsp. salt, good pinch of ground black pepper, ⅓ tsp. red paprika, 11 oz. common white cabbage, 1 lb. potatoes, ½ pt. sour cream.

Wash bones well and make a good, strong stock from bones and from half the quantity of vegetables, boiling them together in 8 pt. of salted water for 2 hrs. Clean, wash and chop onions, parsley and dill in the meantime. Clean, wash and dice the rest of the various vegetables as well, including potatoes. Slice cabbages finely, or cut into thin pieces with a knife. Dice bacon and fry lightly, then add onions, and fry them gently. Put various vegetables with parsley and dill into the saucepan, and let them simmer under closely fitting lid, adding a little stock from time to time, until half cooked. Strain stock into saucepan and add cabbages, potatoes, and the diced fresh tomatoes (washed and cleaned well) or some tomato purée in the winter, salt it again, season with ground pepper and cook until quite tender. Make a golden roux in the meantime from lard and flour, colour it with red paprika and mix it into the soup. Peel and dice gherkins and add to soup. The taste may be improved with a little vinegar from the gherkins as well. Add half of sour cream now. Remove meat from bones and mix it into soup. Care must be taken to keep soup rather thin. The soup is rather sour in flavour, owing to the taste of gherkins and sour cream. It can be served with beef cooked in the soup. Serve beef cut in slices in soup, allowing 3 lb. of beef for 10 persons. Serve hot in a soup-tureen.

Ox-tail Soup

(For ten people)
Ingredients: 6 lb. ox-tails, 8 pt. stock, 2 lb. various vegetables, pinch of thyme, 5 whole black peppers, 2 oz. lard, 2 oz. butter, 2 eggs, 2½ oz. flour, ½ bay leaf, 3½ oz. onions, 1 tbsp. cognac.

Cut ox-tails into pieces, 1—2 inches long, wash thoroughly and fry in lard in the oven until golden together with sliced onions and 11 oz. of various vegetables, chopped finely. Remove fat and dilute with the strained and skimmed stock. Season carefully with pepper, bay leaf, thyme, and cook under cover slowly and steadily for a long time, until tender. When cooked, strain through a fine cloth. Skim off any fat, season it with cognac, and re-season if necessary with salt. Divide ox-tails into equal portions, when serving, adding to the soup 1 lb. of various vegetables, cooked separately in slightly salted water. Garnish soup with small buttered dumplings, prepared from butter, flour and eggs and boiled separately. Serve soup hot, together with garnishes. Sometimes this soup is prepared with a roux. The method is the same, but instead of cognac, add a thin, light roux.

Consommé à la Française

(Made from beef and chicken, for 10 people)
Ingredients: 2 lb. beef, 3 lb. chicken for soup, 2 lb. marrow-bones, 1 lb. mixed vegetables, 3½ oz. kohlrabi, 3½ oz. celery, 1 lb. cauliflower, 5 oz. onions, 2 cloves of garlic, 1 oz. salt, 8 whole black peppers, 1 oz. tomato purée, 5 oz. green peas, 3½ oz. mushrooms.

Clean and wash chicken and put to boil, together with beef, marrow-bones, as is done in the case of clear meat soup. Add vegetables, seasoning and simmer on steady fire, until almost tender. Clean and wash cauliflower in the meantime, break it into flowerets and parboil separately, until almost tender, in a little water. Cook green peas also in separate saucepan, as well as the well-washed mushrooms. Strain soup, slice beef and divide the chicken meat into ten equal parts. Chop various vegetables, cooked in the soup, into thin even slices. Divide beef and fowl into ten fire-proof bowls, or individual casseroles. Divide mixed vegetables also evenly, as well as cauliflowers, mushrooms, green peas and lastly the strained soup. Cover bowls, place on a baking tin and cook in the oven, slowly, evenly, until meat is tender. When ready, serve at once, in the same bowls. Divide marrow from the bones and put it on 10 toasted slices of rolls, salt and pepper them and serve hot, on paper serviettes, together with soup.

Borshch Soup

Ingredients: ½ lb. beef, 2 oz. lard, ½ lb. potatoes, 7 oz. beetroots, 7 oz. cabbages, 2 oz. tomatoes, 2 oz. onions, 5 oz. parsnips, 2 oz. tomato purée, 2 oz. flour, 1 tbsp. vinegar, 1 gill sour cream, half a bay leaf, pinch of ground black pepper, 1 tsp. salt.

Put on the meat to boil in 3 pt. of water. Slice the vegetables into thin strips, braise in a little lard, adding some stock to it. When vegetables are tender, mix in the shredded cabbage and the potatoes cut into cubes, pour the stock off the meat over it and adding the pepper and bay leaf, boil it for 25—30 mins. When soup is nearly ready mix in a little thin roux, add the cooked meat cut into little cubes, lastly add the quartered tomatoes 10 mins. before serving. Add a spoonful of sour cream to each plate of soup.

Raskolnik Soup with Kidney

Ingredients: ½ lb. ox-kidney, 2 oz. lard, 2 oz. sorrel, 3½ oz. celery root (celeriac), 2 oz. onions, 2 oz. leeks, ½ lb. potatoes, 5 oz. parsnips, 5 oz. pickled cucumbers, 1 gill sour cream, pinch of ground black pepper, half a bay leaf.

Trim kidney, cut into four, scald and wash it well. Cook the cleaned and sliced kidney in 3 pt. of water for one hour. Clean and chop onions, slice cleaned vegetables into strips and braise them in a little lard till golden-brown. Add sliced cucumbers, potatoes cut into strips, bay leaf and pepper. Dilute with stock off the meat and cook it for 25—30 mins. To improve the flavour, a little liquor off the cucumbers and some shredded sorrel may be added. Add sour cream just before serving and sprinkle with finely chopped parsley. Pork-kidney may be used, if preferred. Trim kidneys carefully before scalding.

Russian Cabbage Soup II

Ingredients: 3 lb. of pork-bones, ½ lb. pork-hearts, 2 oz. lard, 10 oz. cabbages, 3½ oz. potatoes, 3½ oz. carrots, 3½ oz. beetroot, 2 oz. celery root (celeriac), 1½ gill sour cream, half a bay leaf, 2 oz. onions, small bunch of parsley, 1 tsp. salt, pinch of ground black pepper, 2 oz. tomato purée.

Cut beetroot, carrots, celeriac and onions into strips, braise in lard, then add tomato purée and 3 pt. of stock made of pork-bones and hearts. When the vegetables are nearly tender, add potatoes and the cooked pork-hearts cut into neat cubes. Serve with sour cream.

Harcho (Soup Made in the Gruzian Way)

Ingredients: 1 lb. breast of mutton, 3½ oz. onions, 3½ oz. rice, 2 oz. of pickled plums, 1 bunch of fresh dill, 2 oz. butter, 1 oz. tomato purée, 1 clove of garlic, 1 small bunch of celery tops, 1 tsp. of salt.

Cut the breast of mutton into small cubes, then put to boil in 3 pt. of water. Skim off the froth, add salt and finely chopped onions, bring to boil again. Heat the butter, mix in the tomato purée and add it to the soup, then add rice, crushed garlic, finely chopped celery tops and pickled plums. Let it simmer for 20 mins. longer. Sprinkle with finely chopped fresh dill before serving.

Green Shchi

Ingredients: 1 lb. meat, 7 oz. sorrel, 2 oz. onions, 3 oz. flour, 10 oz. spinach, 2 oz. parsnips, 3 oz. lard, 2 tsp. of salt, 1 bay leaf, ⅓ tsp. ground black pepper, 1 hard-boiled egg, 1 gill sour cream.

Wash, then cook spinach in boiling water till tender; put through sieve. Clean and shred sorrel. Clean and chop onions and parsnips and fry in lard till golden, add the flour and brown it a little longer. Mix in the spinach purée, stir well, pour in the stock, and the water off the spinach. Cut the boiled meat into strips, add to the soup together with bay leaf, ground black pepper and salt, and cook it for 15—20 mins. Add the finely shredded sorrel just before serving. Serve with sliced hard-boiled egg and sour cream.

Vegetarian Borshch

Ingredients: 2 lb. cabbage, ½ lb. tomatoes, 10 oz. beetroots, 10 oz. carrots, 7 oz. potatoes, 2 oz. butter, small bunch of fresh dill, 1 bunch of parsley, half a lemon, 1 tsp. salt.

Clean and slice beetroots, sprinkle with salt and lemon-juice, braise it in butter and a little water for 20 mins. Add the sliced carrots, then the shredded cabbage, pour on sufficient water and cook it for 10 mins. Lastly add the cubed potatoes and continue cooking till vegetables are tender. Add quartered tomatoes and sour cream just before serving. Sprinkle with finely chopped parsley.

Lebbencs Soup ▷
Hortobágy Pancake

Cold Borshch

Ingredients: 1 lb. beetroot, 3½ oz. potatoes, 7 oz. fresh cucumbers, 2 oz. onions, 1 dessert-spoon sugar, 1 tsp. salt, 1 tsp. vinegar, 1 gill sour cream, 1½ hard-boiled eggs, 1 tsp. French mustard.

Peel and cube beetroots, cook them in 3 pt. of water into which vinegar is added. When tender drain and cool it. Add the already cooked and chopped potatoes, cucumbers, onions and egg, salt, add the mustard and pour on it the stock off the beetroots and the sour cream. Mix well. Sprinkle with finely chopped parsley or fresh dill just before serving.

GARNISHES FOR SOUPS

Fine Vermicelli or Diced Pasta

Ingredients: 3½ oz. flour, 1 egg, pinch of salt.

Knead egg with a little water together with the flour into a hard paste, then roll it out until quite thin. Cut into fine noodles or small squares and boil it in hot soup or separately in salted water and mix into soup when ready.

Trickled Pastry (Snippets)

Ingredients: 1 egg, 2 oz. flour, pinch of salt.

Mix well egg, flour and salt, and trickle it into hot soup, then boil for 5 mins.

Pancake Noodles

Ingredients: 1 gill milk, 2 oz. flour, 1 egg, 1½ oz. lard, pinch of salt.

Mix egg well with flour, add milk, salt it and fry pancakes from the batter. Cut them into thin strips when ready.

Semolina Dumplings

Ingredients: 3½ oz. semolina, 2 oz. lard, pinch of salt, 1 egg.

Mix egg well with lard, add semolina, salt it and form dumplings from batter with spoon and cook them in hot soup.

Butter Dumplings

Ingredients: 5 oz. flour, 2 oz. butter, 1 egg, pinch of salt.

Mix butter with the egg, salt it, then add flour. Form dumplings from the batter with a spoon and cook them in hot soup.

◁ Egg Dish
Liverpaste

Chicken Dumplings

Ingredients: 3½ oz. boneless chicken meat, 3½ oz. boneless white veal, 2 oz. butter, 1 oz. flour, 1½ tsp. salt, 2 eggs, pinch of ground black pepper and 1 gill whipped cream.

Skin chicken meat, and remove and cut away stringy parts from veal and pass both through a mincing-machine, with a fine disc, twice. Prepare a paste of flour (panada) in the meantime. Take as much water as is necessary to match ¾ oz. flour and boil with ⅓ oz. of butter and a little salt, then add all the flour into liquid and stir it quickly and constantly on the fire, until quite smooth and does not stick to saucepan any more. Then put aside to cool. When cooled, put into a mortar, adding minced meat, butter, 1 egg and 1 egg-yolk to it and pound it well into a paste so that it may be passed through a sieve more easily. Rub through a rough sieve first, and next through a fine one. Place into a porcelain dish, add salt and pepper (season it also with a little grated nutmeg) and put on ice for 10—15 mins. Remove from ice and, adding whipped cream to paste gradually, stir constantly. Dip spoon into hot water and cut with it small, even dumplings from the paste, and cook them in a flat saucepan. Butter saucepan first and place dumplings on it, then cover with hot soup and bring to boil on the cooker. Now cover saucepan with buttered grease-proof paper, put lid on top, place in a medium hot oven and cook for 7—8 mins. Take out dumplings with round skimming-ladle and serve in hot bouillon.

Dumplings Made from Rolls

Ingredients: 1½ rolls, 1 oz. lard, 3 oz. flour, ⅓ tsp. salt, 1 oz. onions, pinch of ground black pepper, 1 small bunch of parsley, 2 eggs.

Dice rolls and brown in ½ oz. lard, frying finely chopped onions and parsley at the same time in ½ oz. lard. Mix flour and eggs, together with a little water, salt and season with ground pepper. Mix well fried dices, onions and finely chopped parsley, form dumplings from dough and cook them in hot soup.

Liver Dumplings

Ingredients: 5 oz. pig's or calf's liver, 1½ oz. flour, 1½ oz. lard, 1 oz. fine breadcrumbs, ½ tsp. salt, pinch of ground black pepper, ¾ oz. onions, a little marjoram (sweet), 1 egg, 1 roll, 1 sprig of parsley.

Fry finely chopped onions in lard until slightly brown. Mince liver, add roll, soaked in water first, season with salt, pepper and marjoram, then add fried onions, egg, bredcrumbs, flour and finely chopped parsley, mix well, make dumplings from this dough and cook them in hot soup.

Fried Drops

Ingredients: 1 gill milk, 2 oz. flour, 1 egg, 3 oz. lard, pinch of salt.

Mix egg well with flour and milk, season with salt, pour into a colander with big holes and drip into hot lard. Mix in lard with fork, and when golden-brown, drain and put some of them into each plate, when serving soup.

Genoese Pastry (Rétes) Filled with Lights

Ingredients: 5 oz. flour, 1 oz. lard, a little marjoram, ½ lb. lights, ½ egg, 1 oz. onions, good pinch of salt, pinch of ground black pepper, 1 sprig of parsley.

Prepare dough for *rétes* (Genoese pastry) from flour and fill with the following stuffing: First cook lights, then mince them. Fry finely chopped onions in lard, and season with green parsley, salt, ground pepper and marjoram. Brush top of filled pastry with egg, bake it and cut into pieces and when serving soup, place one into each plate.

Boiled Ravioli Filled with Minced Lights

Ingredients: 5 oz. flour, 1 egg, ½ lb. lights, 1 oz. lard, 1 oz. onions, pinch of salt, pinch of ground black pepper, a little marjoram, 2 eggs, 1 oz. breadcrumbs, 1 sprig of parsley.

Knead flour and 1 egg into a hard paste with a little water, roll it, and make pockets from it. Use following stuffing: Cook and mince lights. Fry finely chopped onions in lard with parsley, add minced lights. Season with salt, ground pepper and marjoram, mix well with slightly browned bredcrumbs. When cooled fill pockets with this stuffing, seal edges with egg, and put them into hot soup to cook.

Brain Dumplings

Ingredients: 3½ oz. brains, 1 whole egg, 1 egg-yolk, 1 roll, 2 oz. breadcrumbs (from rolls), 1 gill milk, 1 tsp. salt, pinch of pepper, pinch of marjoram, 1 small bunch of parsley.

Rub uncooked brains through a sieve, mix in basin until smooth and add roll, soaked in milk, breadcrumbs, egg, salt and seasoning. Mix well, form small dumplings from this dough, boil in salted water and serve in clear meat soup.

Griddle Cake Filled with Mushrooms

(Mushroom patties or mushroom pies)
Ingredients: 3 oz. mushrooms, 2 eggs, 2 oz. flour, 1 tsp. lard, pinch of ground black pepper, 1 small bunch of parsley.

Clean, wash and chop finely mushrooms. Fry them in lard, together with parsley, season with salt and ground pepper. Beat two whole eggs, and warm them slowly on steady fire whisking constantly, whip when cold, until egg is stiff, add 1½ oz. flour and fried cold mushrooms into eggs, mix well. Cook in buttered and floured frying pan on slow fire; cut into cubes, and put some cubes into each plate when serving soup.

Jelly Made from Eggs

Ingredients: 3 gill milk, 3 eggs, 1 tsp. butter, pinch of salt.

Mix milk with eggs, add salt, pour into small, buttered saucepan or double saucepan. Pour water into bigger saucepan, or bottom of double saucepan, place saucepan with milk over this and steam in a slow oven. Rinse jelly when ready with cold water. May be used for garnish in bouillons.

Matzoh Dumplings

(Dumplings made from unleavened bread)
Ingredients: 3¾ oz. matzoh, 2 oz. lard, 1 whole egg, 1 egg-yolk, 1 oz. onions, a little salt, pepper, parsley and ground ginger.

Beat 1 oz. lard until creamy, add whole egg, a tbsp. of water, and finely chopped onions fried in lard, chopped parsley, seasoning, and last the matzoh finely ground and mix everything well together. Put aside for half an hour to settle. Form small dumplings from this dough with a knife dipped into water, cook them in salted water or in clear soup, partly covered, for 20—30 mins.

SAUCES

ON SAUCES IN GENERAL

Sauces play a significant part in the composition of our meals. Their purpose is double: as an accompaniment to various dishes, on the one hand, they improve the edibility of our food with their seasonings; and, on the other hand, the important nutritious raw foodstuffs (cream, egg, butter, etc.), used for their making, supplement the nutritive value of the main courses.

Sauces are divided into two groups: cold and hot sauces. Certain so-called basic sauces may be picked out among both categories, from which various other sauces can be made by adding seasonings or subsidiary ingredients to them. Mayonnaise sauce may be regarded as a basic sauce, serving as a basis for most of our cold sauces. The basic warm sauces are the following: 1. brown (Espagnole) sauce; 2. béchamel (milk) sauce; 3. white (velouté) sauce; 4. Hollandaise sauce; 5. tomato sauce.

Recipes in this chapter are thus grouped in order to acquaint the reader with each of the basic sauces in turn, together with the variations prepared from them. At the end of the chapter are sauces which cannot be included in any of the basic groups, and are made simply with a roux or with the mixture of sour cream and flour or by other thickening methods.

We should start our work by choosing the ingredients carefully. Good sauces can only be made from good ingredients. If the raw foodstuffs are without blemish, the preparation itself is no hard task, because exact information may be found in all the recipes. There are only a few exceptions, for instance, mayonnaise, or Hollandaise sauce, the making of which requires some skill. Great care should be taken when preparing mayonnaise to choose table oil of good quality and fresh eggs, the yolks of which are used. Stir yolks quickly with a whisk, while adding the oil to them drop by drop at first, or in a very thin trickle, then gradually pouring more freely, as quickly as yolks can absorb the oil. When preparing Hollandaise sauce, care should be taken to keep it at suitable temperature; beat over a not too strong flame, mixing in the butter at the right moment, because if added too early, the sauce may collapse, and if too late, the eggs may curdle.

It is important in the case of all sauces to ensure the right thickness, avoiding its becoming either too thick or too thin. If the sauce is too thick, it may be thinned with meat stock, milk, fresh cream or some other liquid, according to the sauce in question. If the sauce is too thin, it may be reduced: boil it on a low, steady fire, stirring at times, until it is thick enough. Sauces with egg-yolk in them should not be boiled, however, because the yolks may curdle when boiling, and the sauce can be spoilt. If there is no time to thicken sauce by reducing, a little butter may be well kneaded together with some flour, then mixed with a whisk into the boiling sauce, bit by bit; keep on boiling for 1—2 more mins. It is advisable, however, to strain a sauce thus thickened once more, to avoid lumpiness. Great attention should be paid to the process of straining, in order to ensure the velvety smoothness of sauces.

Flavouring is also an important factor. A sauce should be seasoned so as to emphasize its character, and to supplement the course we serve it with, by accentuating, bringing out the taste, the flavour of the fish—or meat—dish. Our recipes give the amounts of flavouring, seasonings and spices exactly. If it is not possible to weigh the quantities, we should rely on our taste in apportioning spices.

When making hot sauces, time the preparation well, so that they should be ready immediately before serving. This is especially important in the case of sauces prepared with butter, cream and beaten with eggs (e. g. Hollandaise, béarnaise, etc.), because they are inclined to collapse after a while. If we have to prepare the sauce in advance, for one reason or other, we must always keep it in a porcelain or enamelled dish, over hot water, until serving.

To avoid the formation of skin, break a lump of butter onto the surface of the sauce, instead of keeping hot over water. This butter should be mixed well into the sauce with a whisk before serving.

The boiling and reducing of spices and seasonings (pepper, thyme, tarragon leaf, etc.) figure in the recipes for some sauces. We boil and reduce them by cooking in water, wine or vinegar, under cover, until the liquid is almost entirely reduced. The distillate of spices should always be well drained through a fine cloth, and subsequently added to the sauce, to improve its taste and flavour. Draining is necessary, to keep the spices out of the sauce, because they would spoil its smoothness and flavour.

Sauces are mostly served separately, only occasionally poured over some fish- or meat-dish (e. g. carp in red wine sauce).

We should keep cold sauces in a cool place, in a cold sauce-boat, and warm sauces in a pre-heated, warm sauce-boat and serve while hot.

COLD SAUCES

Mayonnaise

Ingredients: ⁴/₅ pt. oil, 3 egg-yolks, 1 lemon, ½ tsp. salt. (1 lb. of ready sauce).

Mayonnaise should be beaten well with a whisk, so as to force as much air as possible into the mixture of oil and yolks, turning it into a light, cream-like, thick sauce. Place egg-yolks in a basin and salt them. Add the oil, drop by drop, stirring the whole time, to prevent curdling. If it gets too thick, stop and add the juice of half a lemon. Mix well, and when the mayonnaise has thinned from lemon-juice, continue to add oil, stirring constantly, until all the oil is added. Squeeze the other half of the lemon into this sauce and mix it well again. Mayonnaise, thus prepared, is a thick and stiff paste, serving as a foundation for many cold sauces (Tartare, Sauce Rémoulade, etc.). It may be used for several varieties of cold dishes: it is suitable for salad dressings, for decoration, as with beaten butter, and for the coating of cold egg dishes or fish. In this case mix with a little melted, tepid aspic the egg or fish. And last, it may be used, with the addition of a little cream and well seasoned with salt and lemon-juice, as a cold sauce, but note that it must not be too thick or too cold.

It is important that the oil used for the preparing of mayonnaise should be neither too cold nor too hot, because of tendency to run, i. e. the yolk does not mix well with the oil. If this should happen, pour two tsp. of hot water into the mixture, and beat it quickly, until it is thick. The same method may be applied if the mayonnaise is used at a later time.

Mayonnaise Sauce

Ingredients: 14 oz. mayonnaise, 1 gill sour cream or cream.

Mix the mayonnaise well with the cream, and re-season it with salt and lemon-juice.

Rémoulade Sauce

Ingredients: 13 oz. mayonnaise, 1 tsp. mustard, 1 oz. parsley, 1 oz. gherkins, 1 gill cream, 1 oz. chives, 1 tsp. tarragon leaves, juice of ¼ of lemon, pinch of Cayenne pepper, a little Worcester sauce.

Add cream, mustard and a little lemon-juice to mayonnaise. Clean and wash chives, parsley, tarragon leaves and peel gherkins; chop them finely on board and mix into the sauce. Season with a little Cayenne pepper, Worcester sauce and flavour with lemon-juice.

Tartare Sauce

Ingredients: 11 oz. mayonnaise, 1 gill white wine, 1 oz. castor sugar, half a tsp. salt, ½ lemon, 1 oz. mustard, 1 gill cream, dash of Worcester sauce, pinch of Cayenne pepper.

Mix mayonnaise well with lemon-juice, white wine, mustard, castor sugar, salt, cream and a pinch of Cayenne pepper, and season with Worcester sauce. Sour cream (but not too sour) can be used instead of cream. Cayenne pepper may be substituted by a dusting of ground black pepper.

Mustard Sauce

Ingredients: 7½ oz. mayonnaise, 2½ oz. mustard, ¼ tsp. salt, 1 gill cream (whipped), ½ tsp. castor sugar, 3½ oz. pickled horse-radish (horse-radish in vinegar).

Mix mayonnaise well with mustard and whipped cream, season with salt and castor sugar, then drain horse-radish through cloth and after squeezing well add to sauce also. Serve with cold meat.

Horse-radish Sauce with Apples

Ingredients: 5 oz. horse-radish, 1 tbsp. vinegar, ½ tsp. salt, 5 oz. apples, 1 tsp. oil, ½ tsp. castor sugar, 1 gill bouillon.

Clean horse-radish and apples, and grate on a fine grater (grate the apples on a glass grater if possible). Mix well together with vinegar, oil and cold Worcester sauce, flavour with salt and castor sugar. Generally served with cold, boiled beef.

Tarragon Sauce

Ingredients: 11 oz. mayonnaise, 1 gill sour cream, 1 tsp. tarragon vinegar, ½ tsp. mustard, 1 tsp. tarragon leaves, ¼ tsp. salt, ½ tsp. castor sugar.

Clean and wash tarragon leaves, place into a jar and pour enough vinegar on it to cover. Keep for a few days, and use liquid when tarragon vinegar is needed. Mix mayonnaise well with sour cream, season with salt, castor sugar, mustard and tarragon vinegar, and also add finely chopped green tarragon leaves to it. Served with brains, roast lamb, cold calf's tongue.

Ravigote Sauce

Ingredients: 6 oz. oil, 2 tbsp. vinegar, 1 oz. caper, 1 small bunch of parsley, ¼ tsp. salt, 1 hard-boiled egg, 2 oz. onions, 1 small bunch of chives, ½ tsp. tarragon leaves, pinch of ground black pepper.

Wash and clean chives, tarragon leaves, parsley, remove shell from hard-boiled egg, clean onions, and capers. Chop everything finely, place in a dish and add oil, vinegar, flavour with salt, and ground pepper.

Russian Sauce

Ingredients: 11 oz. mayonnaise, 1 gill cream, ½ lemon, 1 tsp. mustard, 1 tsp. caviare.

Mix mayonnaise well with mustard and cream and add caviare. Flavour with lemon-juice.

Tyrolean Sauce

Ingredients: ½ lb. mayonnaise, 1 gill cream, pinch of Cayenne pepper, 2 oz. ketchup or thick tomato purée, 2 pt. white wine, ½ tsp. salt, castor sugar.

Mix well ketchup or tomato purée with mayonnaise, adding cream, white wine, and seasoning with salt, Cayenne pepper and castor sugar. Whisk until smooth.

Vinaigrette Sauce

Ingredients: Same as for Ravigote sauce, but egg is not needed.

Prepare in the same way, but leave out hard-boiled egg.

Gribiche Sauce

Ingredients: 5 oz. mayonnaise, ½ tsp. salt, 1 oz. capers, 1 bunch of parsley, 1 oz. onions, 1 lemon, 2 hard-boiled eggs, 2 cucumbers, ½ tsp. tarragon leaves, 1 oz. chives, 1 oz. mustard, pinch of Cayenne pepper, 2 tbsp. cream.

Wash tarragon leaves, parsley and chives well, clean onions, remove shell of hard-boiled eggs, peel pickled cucumbers, and chop everything, together with caper, quite finely. Place mayonnaise into a porcelain dish, mix well with cream and lemon-juice, add to it chopped eggs, caper, etc., flavour with salt, mustard and Cayenne pepper.

Serve in sauce-boat with cold or hot boiled beef, with cold, underdone roasted leg of mutton, etc.

Mayonnaise Sauce with Caviare

Ingredients: 1 lb. mayonnaise, 1 oz. caviare.

Mix caviare into the mayonnaise sauce.

Cumberland Sauce

Ingredients: 7½ oz. red-currant jelly, 1 orange, 1 lemon, pinch of Cayenne pepper, 1 tbsp. Madeira wine, 1 gill red wine, ¼ tsp. English mustard, 1 tsp. cognac.

Peel orange and lemon very carefully, removing the inner white parts from skin. Cut peel into very fine slices, cook in red wine and a little water until tender, reducing liquid while cooking, then cool. In the meantime rub red-currant jelly through hair sieve, add whipped and strained juice from orange and lemon, English mustard, Madeira wine and cognac, and finally the cooked and cooled peel of the lemon and orange, and mix everything well together until smooth. Serve mostly with cold or hot game, in separate sauce-boat.

Horse-radish in Vinegar

Ingredients: ½ lb. horse-radish, 1 oz. sugar, 1 gill vinegar, ½ tsp. salt, 1 gill bouillon.

Clean, wash and grate horse-radish on a fine grater, then blanch to remove strong taste. Strain, mix with not-fatty bouillon or clear meat soup, season with salt, sugar, vinegar, according to taste. Mostly served with boiled beef, Újházi's chicken broth, cold wild-boar, always in separate sauce-boats. May also be prepared with water if there is no bouillon or clear meat soup.

Green Sauce

Ingredients: 11 oz. mayonnaise, ½ tsp. salt, ½ tsp. tarragon leaves, 1 tsp. castor sugar, 2 oz. fresh spinach, 1 bunch of parsley, 1 tbsp. white wine, 1 gill cream.

Clean and wash fresh spinach and cook in slightly salted water until quite tender. Strain, cool, squeeze well and rub through a fine sieve. Wash and chop finely parsley and tarragon leaves. Mix mayonnaise well with cream, white wine, castor sugar, add sieved and cooled spinach as well as chopped parsley and tarragon leaves and re-season with salt, according to taste.

Chive Sauce

Ingredients: 3½ oz. mayonnaise, 1 bunch of chives, 1 gill sour cream, 3 hard-boiled egg-yolks, ½ tsp. castor sugar, 2 rolls, ¼ lemon (juice).

Soak rolls in tepid water, squeeze them and pass through sieve, together with the yolks of hard-boiled eggs. Mix mayonnaise with sour cream, lemon-juice, castor sugar, and add finely chopped chives, then add sieved eggs and soaked rolls, salt again and if too thick, thin it with cold, skimmed bouillon or clear meat soup. Mostly served with cold or hot boiled beef, in separate sauce-boat.

Chaudfroid Sauce (Brown)

Ingredients: 2 gills ready-made brown Espagnole sauce, 1 tbsp. Madeira wine, 9 leaves of gelatine, 1 gill red wine, 2 oz. mushrooms, 2 tbs. aspic, ¼ tsp. salt.

Clean and wash mushrooms well and slice them. Cook mushrooms in red and Madeira wine, until liquid is reduced. Add brown Espagnole sauce to it, salt it and cook for 10 mins. Skim off fat frequently with a paper serviette, then add gelatine leaves, previously well soaked in water and well squeezed; mix it well with a whisk and bring to boil again. Skim once more, strain through fine cloth, beat with a whisk until smooth and cool, stirring it frequently. If too thick, dilute with tepid, melted aspic. This sauce is used for the coating of cold pheasant, venison, goose-liver and eggs and as a garnish.

Chaudfroid Sauce (White)

Ingredients: 2 gills white velouté sauce, 10 leaves of gelatine, 2 tbsp. aspic, 1 gill cream, ¼ tsp. salt, 2 oz. Champignon mushrooms.

Clean and wash well the fresh, white Champignon mushrooms and slice them finely. Cover with water and cook until liquid has almost boiled away. Strain into white velouté sauce, boiled well, and cook together for 10 more mins. Skim off fat carefully with a paper serviette, then add gelatine leaves, previously soaked in cold water and well squeezed. Whisk well and cook for 1–2 mins. Remove all grease, skimming frequently. Then strain through fine cloth, cool stirring frequently, and when cooled, whisk in cream. In case it is too stiff, melt aspic and mix into it while tepid. Chaudfroid sauce is mostly used for the coating of cold fowl, fish, egg-dishes, for garnishes and various decorations.

HOT SAUCES

When brown sauce is being used as foundation for a sauce, in the recipes containing white wine (for instance in hunter sauce, Provençale sauce, etc.) use white wine instead of red for the brown sauce as well.

Brown (Espagnole) Sauce

Ingredients: 1 lb. bones (veal), 2 oz. lard, 1 tsp. sugar, 1 gill red wine, 2 oz. tomato purée, 2 cloves of garlic, pinch of thyme, 5 oz. mixed vegetables, 2 oz. flour, ½ tsp. salt, 6 whole black peppers, 2 oz. onions, 1 bay leaf, 1 tbsp. Madeira wine.

Cut veal bones small, clean and slice mixed vegetables, onions, garlic, and fry together with bay leaf and whole peppers in a little lard until brown; dilute with 2 pt. of water, salt, and then bring to boil. Brown sugar in lard until golden-brown, add flour and fry until quite brown. Thicken stock with it, add tomato purée, red wine, thyme and Madeira wine, and let it simmer for a further 3 hrs. slowly and steadily. Stir from time to time, skim, and if too thick, dilute with stock or water; if thin, reduce until thick enough. Remove bones, when ready, and pass sauce through a fine hair sieve.

Italian Sauce

Ingredients: 2 gills ready-made brown sauce, 2 oz. lean ham, 1 tbsp. white wine, 2 oz. tomato purée, pinch of ground black pepper, 2 oz. mushrooms, 1 small bunch of parsley, 1 oz. onions, 2½ oz. butter and ¼ tsp. salt.

Clean onions and chop them finely. Clean, wash and chop mushrooms and parsley; chop ham, separately. Then heat 2 oz. butter, fry chopped onions in butter first until half ready, then add mushrooms and parsley, salt, and pepper and brown everything together. Add ready-made brown sauce to it, mix in white wine, tomato purée, chopped ham; mix them well together and cook for 10 mins. Remove from heat, add the rest of the butter gradually, mixing sauce all the time with a whisk. Serve without draining. Goes well with boiled brains and fillets of pork, etc.

Demi-glace Sauce

Ingredients: 2 gills brown sauce, 1 tsp. meat extract (home-made glaze), 1 tbsp. Madeira wine, pinch of ground black pepper, 2 oz. butter, 1 oz. tomato purée, 2 oz. mushrooms.

Clean, wash and slice mushrooms properly. Put on boil in enough water to cover them and cook well covered until liquid is almost boiled away. Then add ready-made brown sauce, tomato purée, meat extract, Madeira wine, and ground pepper, cook for 10 mins., and rub through a fine straining cloth. Add butter gradually, mixing well with a whisk, before serving. May be used with beefsteak, tenderloin steak, veal steak, etc.

Hunter Sauce

Ingredients: 2 gills demi-glace sauce, 2 gill tomato sauce, 1 small bunch of green parsley, 1 tbsp. white wine, ½ tsp. tarragon leaves, pinch of ground black pepper, 1 oz. onions, 3½ oz. mushrooms, 2½ oz. butter, 1 tsp. cognac, ¼ tsp. salt.

Clean and chop onions finely. Slice mushrooms. Wash and chop parsley and tarragon leaves separately. Heat 1 oz. of butter, fry finely shopped onions in it until half cooked, add sliced mushrooms, parsley, salt, pepper and continue frying until ready. Mix in ready-made demi-glace sauce and tomato sauce, white wine, cognac and boil for 10 mins. Take off the fire, add the rest of the butter gradually, sprinkle with finely chopped tarragon leaves and mix with a whisk until smooth. Serve hot with rumpsteak, cutlets, etc.

Brown Tarragon Sauce

Ingredients: 2 gills ready-made brown sauce, 1 tsp. tarragon leaves, 2 oz. butter, 1 tbsp. tarragon vinegar.

Wash and chop tarragon leaves finely, boil together with tarragon vinegar and a little water well covered until liquid is almost boiled away. Add brown sauce, boil for 10 mins. and rub through fine straining cloth. Mix in butter before serving, adding gradually, while whisking. Mostly used with mutton cutlets and lamb chops.

44

Brown Mushroom Sauce

Ingredients: 2 gills ready-made brown sauce, 1 small bunch of parsley, ¼ tsp. salt, 1 tbsp. Madeira wine, 5 oz. mushrooms, pinch of ground black pepper, 2½ oz. butter.

Clean, wash and slice mushrooms. Clean parsley, wash and chop finely. Heat 1 oz. of butter, and chopped mushrooms and parsley, salt, season with ground pepper, and cook on an open flame, mixing frequently, for 3—4 mins. Strain butter, add ready-made brown sauce and boil for 10 mins. Take off the fire, flavour with Madeira wine and add rest of the butter gradually, mixing with a whisk all the time. Mostly served with tenderloin steak, sirloin steak or veal chops.

Sherry Sauce

Ingredients: 2 gills ready-made brown sauce, 2 gills sherry.

Bring ready-made brown sauce to boil together with sherry.

Robert Sauce

Ingredients: 2 gills ready-made brown sauce, 2 oz. onions, 3½ oz. pickled cucumbers (gherkins), 2 tsp. sugar, ½ tsp. vinegar, pinch of ground black pepper, 1 oz. mustard.

Clean and chop onions finely, and cook well covered in a little water, mixed with vinegar, until liquid is almost boiled away. Strain into ready-made brown sauce, add peeled and diced pickled gherkins, season with mustard, sugar and ground pepper, boil for 4—5 mins. and serve hot. Mostly used with tenderloin steak, pork chops, fillets of pork, etc.

Provençal Sauce

Ingredients: 7½ oz. fresh tomatoes or 2 oz. tomato purée, 3½ oz. butter, 1 clove of garlic, pinch of ground black pepper, 2 gills white wine, 2 oz. onions, ½ tsp. salt, 3½ oz. mushrooms, 2 gills ready-made brown sauce.

Bring to boil ready-made brown sauce together with white wine. Chop onions finely, clean, wash and dice mushrooms well. Wash fresh tomatoes, then blanch them in hot water for a min. to remove skin; remove seeds as well and cut into even cubes. Clean garlic, crush with a knife on choppingboard and chop finely. Heat 2½ oz. of butter, mix in finely chopped onions, fry partly, add mushrooms, fresh tomatoes, garlic, flavour with salt, ground pepper and fry on open flame, stirring at times, for 2—3 mins. Pour over it brown sauce boiled well with white wine and cook for 4—5 mins. Take off the fire and add the rest of the butter to it gradually, before serving, mixing sauce all the time. Mostly served with tenderloin steak and tournedos (mutton chops).

Madeira Sauce

Ingredients: 2½ gills ready-made brown sauce, 1 tbsp. Madeira wine.

Flavour ready-made brown sauce with Madeira wine and bring to boil. Cognac may be used for flavouring instead of Madeira wine, if desired. This sauce may be used with various dishes, e. g. with stewed ox-tongue, boiled ham, tournedos, sirloin steak, etc.

Bordelaise Sauce

Ingredients: 2½ gills ready-made brown sauce, 1 oz. onions, pinch of whole black peppers, 1 gill red wine, 1 bay leaf, 3½ oz. bone marrows.

Chop onions finely and cook them, together with bay leaf and whole black pepper. Boil, well covered, until liquid is almost boiled away. Add ready-made brown sauce, boil for 10 mins., then rub through a straining cloth. Grate marrows into it on a fine grater, mix well with a whisk until smooth and boil for 1—2 mins. Mostly served with rumpsteak, entrecotes or tournedos.

Burgundy Sauce

Ingredients: 2 gills ready-made brown sauce, 1 gill Burgundy wine.

Boil ready-made brown sauce well with Burgundy wine, rub through straining cloth and serve. Mostly used with beef fillets or tenderloin steak or stewed rumpsteak.

Hot Brown Sauce (Fines-herbes Sauce)

Ingredients: 2 gills ready-made brown sauce, 3½ oz. mushrooms, 1 clove of garlic, 1½ oz. butter, ¼ tsp. salt, 1 oz. onions, pinch of ground black pepper, 2 tbsp. white wine, 1 small bunch of parsley.

Mix ready-made brown sauce well with white wine and put to cook. Clean mushrooms well, wash them carefully, drain water and chop them finely, together with parsley, previously washed and cleaned. Clean onions, chop them small. Clean garlic as well, and crush with the blade of a knife and chop finely. Heat butter in the meantime, place chopped onions in it, fry lightly, then add garlic mushrooms with parsley, chopped finely. Fry them together for a while and add them afterwards into the boiling sauce, then flavour with salt and ground pepper. Boil for 10 more mins. and mix well with a whisk until smooth, then serve. Mostly used with veal or mutton chops.

Béchamel Sauce

Ingredients: 3 oz. butter, ½ tsp. salt, 3 oz. flour, pinch of Cayenne pepper, 1 pt. milk.

Make a light roux (not browned) with 2¼ oz. of butter and the whole quantity of flour; dilute with hot milk and mix quickly and well with a whisk until smooth, flavour with salt and Cayenne pepper and boil for 30 mins. on steady fire, then rub through muslin and add gradually 1 oz. of butter, mixing all the time. This sauce may be used as a basis for various other sauces, but will do also as a binding agent, for various croquettes, puddings, etc., in which case more butter and flour and less milk should be used, according to need, in order to ensure the necessary thickness.

Mornay Sauce or Sauce au Gratin

Ingredients: 3 gills ready-made béchamel sauce, 3 egg-yolks, 2 oz. grated cheese, 2 oz. butter, 2 tbsp. cream, ¼ tsp. salt.

This sauce must be somewhat thicker than usual, because it should be served with dishes prepared au gratin. For this reason béchamel sauce, serving as foundation, should also be cooked somewhat thicker. When béchamel is thick enough and cooked, take off the fire, and stirring all the time, blend, gradually with cream and egg-yolks, mixed well previously with a whisk. Add grated cheese afterwards, salt and, stirring all the time, add butter gradually. This sauce must not be boiled after cream and yolks are added, because eggs may curdle. The thickness of the sauce must be such as to serve for coating (fillets of fish or cauliflower for instance) without running.

Crayfish Coral Butter

Ingredients: 7½ oz. butter, 7½ oz. crayfish shells, pinch of red paprika.

Pound well in a mortar the bones of 20 crayfish (without the flesh and soft parts) together with butter. Place in a saucepan and fry on the fire, then add red paprika and dilute with 1 pt. of water, bring to boil, cook well, remove and put to cool. Crayfish butter will come up to the surface, remove it and cook it again then drain and put on ice, until needed. Crayfish coral (butter) may be used not only for crayfish sauce, but for crayfish stews, and crayfish meridons (sauces) or other hot crayfish dishes as well. Crayfish butter may be kept in a glass or porcelain container for a long time in an ice-box or refrigerator.

Crayfish Sauce

Ingredients: 2½ oz. butter, ¼ tsp. salt, 1 tbsp. cognac, 1 gill cream, 2 gills milk, 1½ oz. flour, pinch of Cayenne pepper, 2 egg-yolks, 3 oz. crayfish butter.

Make a light roux with 1½ oz. of butter and the flour, but do not brown. Dilute with the milk and mix until smooth. Salt, and flavour with Cayenne pepper and cook slowly and steadily for 30 mins. Then take off the fire, and add cream well mixed previously with egg-yolks beating all the time. Flavour with cognac and rub through fine muslin, then add, gradually and stirring constantly, the rest of the butter and crayfish butter as well. This sauce should be fine and smooth, adequately thick and rosy in colour, from crayfish butter. Mostly served with crayfish dishes, white fish and mutton chops.

Soubise Sauce

Ingredients: 3½ oz. butter, 2 oz. flour, ¼ tsp. salt, 1 gill cream, 4 oz. onions, 2 gills milk, pinch of Cayenne pepper.

Clean and slice onions well. Make a light roux with 1½ oz. butter and flour (do not brown), add chopped onions and fry together for some time, then dilute with milk and mix well. Flavour with salt and Cayenne pepper and cook on slow, steady flame for 1 hr. Mix in cream, then rub through a fine hair sieve. Add butter gradually, mixing all the time with a whisk. Served mostly with white fish and mutton chops.

Cheese Sauce

Ingredients: 2½ oz. butter, 1½ oz. flour, ¼ tsp. salt, 2 tbsp. cream, 2 egg-yolks, 2 gills milk, pinch of nutmeg, 2½ oz. of grated cheese.

Make a light roux with 1½ oz. of butter and the flour, dilute with milk, mix until smooth, flavour with salt and grated nutmeg and cook for 10 mins. Add grated cheese, boil for 5 more mins. and take off the fire, beat yolks and mix them well with cream and add to sauce. Drain through fine muslin and add butter to it gradually, mixing it well all the time.

Cheese sauce may be used with hot entrées, for instance with cheese puddings, cheese doughnuts, cheese pancakes, etc.

HOLLANDAISE SAUCE
AND VARIOUS SAUCES MADE FROM IT

Hollandaise Sauce

Ingredients: 5 egg-yolks, 1 gill cream, ½ lemon, 11 oz. butter, pinch of salt, pinch of Cayenne pepper.

48

Melt butter and put aside on the fire, to keep warm. Break yolks into a fireproof basin, adding cream, salt it and keeping basin on the edge of the cooker, beat constantly until thickened into a light, foamy paste. Then remove from fire and add gradually, mixing slowly and steadily, melted and warm butter. Flavour with lemon juice and Cayenne pepper. Keep over steam until served (in a porcelain dish if possible), but the water must not boil. Hollandaise sauce must be velvet smooth and transparently light. If too thick, thin it before serving with a little cream. Take care it does not boil, while egg-yolks and cream are beaten up, because it may curdle and spoil. Therefore it is important that the sauce should be constantly kept on the edge of the cooker, and stirred continually on a steady, slow heat. If this is not possible (for instance on gas fire), then place basin over steaming hot water and beat sauce thus.

Hollandaise sauce may be used with many dishes. For instance with white fish, especially with pike perches and jack salmons, with boiled asparagus, cauliflower, hot egg dishes (e. g. poached eggs), bouchés, pastes, etc.

Florentine Sauce

Ingredients: 2 gills ready-made Hollandaise sauce, 3 oz. fresh spinach.

Clean fresh spinach, wash well and cook in slightly salted water until tender, then drain, rinse, squeeze off liquid and rub through a fine hair sieve. Colour sauce with this spinach purée to give it green colour, before serving. Serve with fillets of perches or poached eggs.

Béarnaise Sauce

Ingredients: 5 egg-yolks, 1 oz. onions, ½ tsp. tarragon leaves, 1 bay leaf, good pinch of ground black pepper, 1 oz. Worcester sauce, 1 gill (2 tbsp.) white wine, 11 oz. butter, ½ tsp. salt, pinch of Cayenne pepper, ½ lemon, 1 tsp. tarragon vinegar, 1 gill cream.

Chop onions finely and put to cook, together with bay leaf, $\frac{1}{6}$ oz. of tarragon leaves—washed and chopped finely previously—, ground pepper and some lemon peel, tarragon vinegar and white wine; cover well and simmer till liquid is almost boiled dry. Then drain through a muslin into a thick-sided basin, add egg-yolks, cream and salt and beat it with a whisk evenly and continuously on the edge of the cooker on slow, steady heat, until thickened into a foamy sauce. Take off the fire and rub through a sieve with butter, melted previously and kept warm on the fire. Lastly flavour with lemon-juice, Cayenne pepper and Worcester sauce and mix the rest of the well washed and finely chopped tarragon leaves into it. Take care—as with Hollandaise sauce—it does not boil while beating, or while adding butter or afterwards. If too thick, thin with a little cream, but be careful; it must be thicker than usual, because it is often used for the coating of egg dishes or slightly underdone meat courses (prepared in the English way), and it must not run. Keep hot until ready to serve, in a porcelain bowl, over steam, but take care that the water does not boil.

Moscow Sauce

Ingredients: 2½ gills ready-made Hollandaise sauce, 1 oz. caviare.

Mix caviare lightly and carefully, so as not to crush it, into the ready-made sauce a few minutes before serving. This sauce may be served mostly with white fish, e. g. with pike perches and jack salmons.

Choron Sauce

Ingredients: The same ingredients are used as for béarnaise sauce with 2 oz. thick tomato purée in addition.

Prepare it the same way as béarnaise sauce, but mix in 2 oz. thick tomato purée with a whisk before serving. May be prepared with fresh tomatoes instead of tomato purée. Tomatoes should be skinned and seeds removed; then cut into small even cubes. Fry them in a small quantity of butter on open fire, mixing quickly and well, until slightly brown and then add them to the already prepared béarnaise sauce. Choron sauce may be served with white fish primarily, but also with slightly underdone meat, tenderloin and sirloin steaks, and mutton chops.

Tomato Sauce

Ingredients: 2 lb. fresh tomatoes or 5 oz. tomato purée, 1 oz. lard, ½ tsp. salt, 1 sprig of green celery, 1 oz. onions, 2 oz. flour, 2 oz. sugar, 2 gills stock.

Clean and wash fresh tomatoes and cut them into slices. Clean and wash onions and green celery, and put them to boil, together with tomatoes. Cook —stirring frequently—until it turns into a thick tomato purée. Remove onions and green celery from purée and rub through a hair sieve. Make a not too brown roux in the meantime with lard and flour, mix tomato purée into this, dilute with stock, flavour with sugar and salt, beat with a whisk until smooth, and reduce, boiling slowly and on steady fire, stirring at times, until of desired consistency. Strain again through fine sieve and serve hot. May be prepared with tinned tomato purée the same way.

Portuguese Sauce

Ingredients: 3½ oz. butter, 1 bunch of parsley, pinch of Cayenne pepper, 1 oz. onions, ½ tsp. salt, 11 oz. fresh tomatoes, 1 gill ready prepared tomato sauce.

Wash fresh tomatoes, then put them in hot water for a min. to ease skinning. Skin and slice them, and remove seeds, then dice finely. Chop well cleaned onions and washed parsley, heat 1¾ oz. butter on the open fire in a frying pan, add chopped onions, brown slightly, then mix in finely diced fresh tomatoes and chopped parsley as well. Salt, season with Cayenne pepper and fry on quick, open fire for 4—5 mins., then add already prepared tomato sauce, bring to boil again and take off the fire. Break 1¾ oz. butter into sauce gradually, stirring all the time. Serve mostly with egg dishes and mutton chops.

WHITE (VELOUTÉ) SAUCE
AND VARIOUS SAUCES MADE FROM IT

White (Velouté) Sauce

Ingredients: 2 oz. butter, 1 pt. white clear meat or fish stock, 2 oz. flour, ½ tsp. salt, pinch of Cayenne pepper.

Make a light, slightly browned roux with the butter and flour, dilute with white meat stock, and beat with the whisk until smooth; salt, flavour with Cayenne pepper and boil well for ½ hr. (If sauce is to be served with fish, use fish instead of meat stock.) Skim off fat from time to time. When well cooked, pass it through a muslin, and use as a foundation for various other sauces (Normandy, supreme).

Asparagus Cream Sauce

Ingredients: 2 gills white (velouté) sauce, ½ lb. cleaned and dressed asparagus, ½ tsp. salt, 1 tbsp. cream, 1 tsp. sugar, 1 small bunch of parsley, 2 oz. butter.

Clean and wash asparagus, and cook in slightly salted and sweetened water until tender, then drain. Cut heads and tender parts into small, fine slices, put these aside, pass the rest through a sieve and put into the already prepared white sauce. Flavour with salt and sugar, add washed and finely chopped parsley and cook for 10 mins. Strain, and add—mixing all the time—cream and butter, and beat with whisk until smooth. Now place asparagus heads into sauce, bring to boil once more and serve hot.

The stock of asparagus may also be used for the making of asparagus cream sauce. Dilute white (velouté) sauce, serving as a foundation, with it, bring to boil and strain. Mostly served with veal cutlets, chops, roast chicken, etc.

Tarragon Sauce

Ingredients: 2 gills ready prepared white (velouté) sauce, 2 egg-yolks, 1 tbsp. tarragon leaves, 1 tbsp. cream, ¼ tsp. salt, 2 oz. butter.

Clean, wash and chop tarragon leaves finely, mix into ready prepared white sauce and boil for 10 mins. Take off the fire. Mix egg-yolks well with cream and beat them into sauce with a whisk; salt and break all the butter into it gradually and slowly, stirring all the time, and beat until smooth. Served mostly with mutton.

Lemon Sauce

Ingredients: 2 gills ready prepared white (velouté) sauce, 1 tbsp. cream, ¼ tsp. salt, 1½ lemons, 2 oz. butter, 2 egg-yolks.

Squeeze the juice of a lemon and pour into the already prepared white (velouté) sauce. Slice lemon peel, wash well and mix also into sauce; salt and boil for 10 mins. Take off the fire, grate a little lemon peel into it, and squeeze the juice of the half lemon left into it: lastly add egg-yolks mixed well previously with cream. Beat until smooth and pass through fine muslin. Break butter into the sauce, before serving, mixing it constantly with a whisk. Do not boil or cook sauce after the addition of cream and yolks. Served mostly with cooked veal brains, with sweetbread stewed in butter or with white fish.

Normandy Sauce

Ingredients: ²/₅ pt. white (velouté) sauce, 3½ oz. Champignon mushrooms, 2 egg-yolks, 1 gill white wine, ¼ tsp. salt, 1 tbsp. cream, 2 oz. butter, ¼ lemon.

Clean and wash well fine white Champignon mushrooms and slice them thinly. Put to boil in white wine and enough water to cover them; cover with lid, and reduce liquid until only about $^1/_{10}$ pt. remains. Add already prepared white (velouté) sauce, salt and cook for 10 more mins. Take off from the fire and add cream and egg-yolks, mixed well together previously, beat with a whisk until smooth, flavour with lemon-juice and pass through fine muslin. Before serving, break butter into sauce, gradually, mixing it all the time and whisk until smooth. Do not boil sauce after the addition of cream and egg-yolks. This sauce may be served primarily with white fish, hot egg dishes, etc.

Supreme Sauce

Ingredients: ½ lb. bones (veal), 5 oz. mixed vegetables, 2 oz. mushrooms, 2 oz. flour, 2 tbsp. cream, 6 whole black peppers, 5 oz. chicken giblets, 1 oz. onions, 3½ oz. butter, 1 egg-yolk, ¼ tsp. salt.

Clean and dress chicken giblets and feet, neck, etc., chop them and wash together with bones cut neatly, then put to cook in 2 pt. of water. When boiling, skim well and frequently, then add mixed vegetables, cleaned and washed well previously, onions and mushrooms. Salt and flavour with whole peppers.

Bring to boil again, and place on slow heat, on the edge of the cooker to keep simmering reducing steadily, until only 2 gills of liquid remain. Make a light, not browned roux with $1\frac{3}{4}$ oz. butter and flour. Dilute with about $^3/_5$ pt. of drained meat stock, and beat quickly with a whisk until smooth. Stir from time to time and cook for 20 more mins. Mix cream and yolks together thoroughly and taking the sauce off the fire—mixing it constantly with the whisk—pour mixture slowly and gradually into the sauce. Pass through a fine muslin and break into it $1\frac{3}{4}$ oz. butter stirring constantly. Supreme sauce may be served with hot egg dishes, pastries in butter (bouchés) or chicken breast fillets.

Poulette Sauce

Ingredients: 2 gills already prepared supreme sauce, ½ lemon, 5 oz. Champignon mushrooms, pinch of Cayenne pepper, 1 sprig of parsley.

Clean Champignon mushrooms and wash them well. Slice them neatly, squeeze lemon-juice on mushrooms, then dilute with enough water to cover and cook, well covered, with a pinch of salt, until tender. When liquid is already almost reduced, and only some thick mushroom gravy is left, mix it into the already prepared supreme sauce. Season with finely chopped parsley and Cayenne pepper.

Poulette sauce may be served with cooked brains, sweetbread stewed in butter, boiled calf's feet or head.

White Wine Sauce

Ingredients: 3 tbsp. fish or white meat stock, 2 gills white wine, 2 egg-yolks, 3 tbsp. cream, $3\frac{1}{2}$ oz. butter, ¼ tsp. salt, ½ lemon, 2 oz. flour.

Make white wine sauce as needed, with fish stock if served with fish, with meat stock if served with meat. Make a light roux with $1\frac{3}{4}$ oz. butter and flour, dilute with fish or meat stock, add white wine and salt and cook on steady, slow fire for 20—25 mins. Take off the fire and add gradually, stirring all the time, cream and egg-yolks previously mixed together. Flavour with lemon-juice and pass through a muslin. Sauce must not boil after the addition of yolks and cream. Keep sauce on steam, perhaps in a porcelain dish and serve hot. Break into sauce the rest of the butter before serving, whisking constantly. This sauce should be very smooth, and neither too thick nor too thin. If too thick, thin it with a little white wine or cream.

Valenciennes Sauce

Ingredients: 2 gills already prepared white wine sauce, $3\frac{1}{2}$ oz. fresh spinach.

Clean spinach and wash well several times. Then put to boil in slightly salted water and cook until tender. Drain, rinse well with cold water, squeeze and pass through a fine hair sieve. Add spinach purée thus prepared to the ready-made white wine sauce to give it a slight green colour; beat well with a whisk until smooth and serve. Use with hot egg dishes or white fish.

OTHER SAUCES

Mushroom Sauce with Sour Cream

Ingredients: 1½ oz. lard, 5 oz. mushrooms, 1 gill sour cream, 1 oz. onions, ¼ tsp. salt, pinch of ground black pepper, 1 small bunch of parsley, ½ pt. meat stock.

Clean mushrooms well and wash in cold water, then place on a sieve and drain. Clean, wash and then chop onions and parsley finely. Heat lard and fry onions in it first, until half done; add sliced mushrooms afterwards, together with finely chopped parsley. Simmer well under cover for 4—5 mins. until mushrooms are tender, sprinkle with flour, dilute with stock, flavour with salt, and ground pepper and mix well until smooth. Cook for 10 mins., then add sour cream, bring to boil again and serve hot.

Mushroom sauce may be served with boiled beef, various hot entrées (croquettes, puddings, pancakes filled with brains, etc.), or else together with braised veal chops or fillets, roast beef, etc.

Mushroom Sauce with Cream

Ingredients: Prepare the same way as mushroom sauce with sour cream, but take the same quantity of cream instead of sour cream and 2 oz. butter in addition.

This sauce should be served with chicken breast fillets or pike perch fillets.

Cream Sauce

Ingredients: 3½ oz. mixed vegetables, 1 bay leaf, 1 tsp. sugar, ¼ tsp. salt, 2 oz. flour, 1 oz. mushrooms, scant ½ pt. meat stock, 2 oz. onions, whole black pepper, ½ lemon, 2 oz. lard, 1 gill sour cream, 1 tbsp. white wine, 1 tsp. mustard.

Clean, wash and slice mixed vegetables, and mushrooms as well. Clean and chop onions finely. Heat lard, brown sugar slightly in it, and add vegetables, chopped onions, mushrooms, bay leaf, whole black pepper, and simmer them together, well covered, adding meat stock from time to time. Then salt, sprinkle with flour and dilute with stock; squeeze lemon-juice into it, add a little bit of lemon peel too; pour white wine over mixture, stir well together and cook until vegetables are completely tender. Mix in sour cream, bring to boil once more, pass through a hair sieve, mix until smooth and serve hot. Often served with fillet of pork, pork chops, tenderloin minced and roasted whole, etc.

Paprika Sauce

Ingredients: 3 fleshy, ripe green paprikas, 1 oz. red paprika, ¼ tsp. salt, pinch of ground black pepper, 2 tbsp. red wine.

Remove seeds of 3 fleshy, ripe paprikas (the red, so-called tomato-paprikas can be used), and grind their flesh very finely into a pulp. Mix red paprika, salt and pepper together with red wine into a fine sauce. Add paprika purée to it, mix well together and serve with grilled meats.

SAUCES TO BE SERVED WITH BOILED BEEF

Fresh Dill Sauce

Ingredients: 1½ oz. lard, ¼ tsp. salt, 1 oz. sugar, 2 oz. flour, 1 small bunch of fresh dills, 1 oz. onions, 1 tsp. vinegar or ¼ lemon, 1 gill sour cream, ³/₅ pt. meat stock.

Clean and wash fresh dill, then chop finely. Make a light roux with lard and flour, add finely chopped onions, and half of the chopped dill; dilute with ³/₅ pt. of meat stock, flavour with sugar, salt, vinegar or lemon-juice and cook for 20 mins. Strain through a hair sieve, add rest of chopped dill and sour cream, bring to boil once more and beat with a whisk until smooth.

Onion Sauce

Ingredients: 1½ oz. lard, ¼ tsp. salt, 1 pinch of ground black pepper, 2 oz. flour, 3½ oz. onions, 1¹/₂ oz. sugar, 1 tsp. vinegar, ½ pt. meat stock.

Brown sugar in lard, add flour and thus make a brown roux. Clean onions in the meantime, slice thinly and add to brown roux. Mix well and brown together, until onions are also golden in colour. Dilute with meat stock, mix together, flavour with salt, ground pepper, vinegar and, stirring from time to time, cook for 20 mins. Pass through a sieve, beat with a whisk until smooth and serve hot (with sour cream mixed in if desired).

Garlic Sauce

Ingredients: 1½ oz. lard, 1 oz. garlic, 1 gill sour cream, 2 oz. flour, ¼ tsp. salt, ³/₅ pt. meat stock.

Clean garlic cloves, crush them with the blade of the knife, and chop finely. Make a not too brown roux with lard and flour, add finely chopped garlic, mix well, dilute with meat stock. Salt, add sour cream, beat well until smooth and bring to boil.

Caper Sauce

Ingredients: 1 oz. capers, 2 oz. flour, ½ tsp. sugar, ³/₁₀ pt. sour cream, 1½ oz. lard, ¼ tsp. salt, 1 tsp. vinegar, ³/₅ pt. meat stock.

Make a light roux with lard and flour, dilute with meat stock, beat well with whisk until smooth, add capers and sour cream, then flavour with salt, sugar and vinegar, mix again well until smooth, and cook for a few mins.

Anchovy Sauce

Ingredients: ½ tube of anchovy paste, 2 oz. flour, 2 tbsp. sour cream, 1½ oz. butter, ¼ tsp. salt, ⁴/₅ pt. meat stock.

Make a light roux from butter and flour, dilute with meat stock, and beat well with whisk until smooth. Salt and cook for 10 mins., then add anchovy paste and sour cream, mix well again until quite smooth and bring to boil once more.

Sorrel Sauce

Ingredients: 1 lb. sorrel, 1¾ oz. onions, ⅓ oz. salt, 1 gill sour cream, 1½ oz. lard, 2¼ oz. flour, 1¾ oz. sugar, ½ pt. meat stock.

Clean and wash sorrel thoroughly to get rid of sand completely. Chop onions finely and fry them lightly in lard. Add sorrel and cook them together, stirring frequently, for 8—10 mins. until quite thick and creamy. Sprinkle with flour, dilute with meat stock, add sour cream, flavour with salt and sugar, mix well and cook for 5 more mins. Pass through a fine hair sieve, beat with a whisk until smooth and serve hot.

Celery Sauce

Ingredients: 7½ oz. celery roots, 2 oz. flour, ½ tsp. salt, 1 tsp. sugar, ½ pt. meat stock, 1 oz. lard, 1 oz. onions, pinch of ground black pepper, 1 gill sour cream, ⅓ oz. green celery tops.

Clean, wash and dice celery roots finely. Wash and chop green celery tops as well. Clean and chop onions, put them in lard and brown them a little, then add chopped celery and celery tops, salt and let it simmer, together with a little meat stock, until liquid is reduced and celery is almost tender. Sprinkle with flour, dilute with meat stock, flavour with ground pepper and sugar and mix well, then cook until celery is completely tender. Add sour cream, bring to boil once more, stir until smooth and serve hot.

Beetroot Sauce

Ingredients: ½ lb. cooked beetroots, 2 oz. flour, 1 oz. sugar, 1½ oz. lard, ½ tsp. salt, ²/₅ pt. sour cream, ³/₅ pt. meat stock, 1 tbsp. vinegar.

Cook and peel the beetroots, dice them finely and put to boil in meat stock. Make a light roux in the meantime with lard and flour, thicken sauce with it, flavour with salt, sugar and vinegar, add sour cream, beat with the whisk until smooth, and bring to boil once more.

Horse-radish Sauce

Ingredients: 5 oz. horse-radish, 2 oz. flour, 2 tsp. sugar, 1 tsp. vinegar, 1½ oz. lard, ¼ tsp. salt, 1 gill sour cream, ½ pt. meat stock.

Scrub, peel and finely grate horse-radish, then blanch to remove strong taste. Make a light roux in the meantime with lard and flour, dilute with meat stock, mix well until smooth, salt it, and add grated and blanched horse-radish to it. Cook for a few mins., mix sour cream into it, flavour with sugar, vinegar, bring to boil once more and serve hot.

Apple Sauce

Ingredients: 12 oz. apples, 2 oz. flour, ½ lemon, 1½ gills sour cream, 2 oz. sugar, 1 oz. butter, ¼ tsp. salt, 1 clove, 1½ gill milk.

Peel apples, remove seeds and cores, cut fruit into small cubes. Put to boil, together with sugar, clove and milk, salt and add a little lemon peel, then boil for a few mins. Make a light roux in the meantime with butter and flour, thicken sauce with this, add sour cream and lastly flavour with lemon-juice. Stir thoroughly until smooth and bring once more to boil.

Morello Sauce

Ingredients: 12 oz. morello cherries, 2 oz. flour, ¼ tsp. salt, 1 tbsp. red wine, 1 clove, 1½ oz. butter, 2½ oz. sugar, ³/₁₀ pt. milk, ½ lemon, 1½ gills sour cream.

Wash morello cherries and stone them. Put to cook, together with sugar, salt, red wine, clove and a little grated lemon peel, in ³/₅ pt. of water, and boil for 10 mins. Make a light (not browned) roux in the meantime with butter and flour and thicken sauce with it, then add sour cream, stir until smooth and bring to boil once more.

Cherry Sauce

Prepare the same way as Morello sauce, but instead of morello cherries, take the same quantity of cherries, cleaned and stoned, and use cream instead of sour cream.

57

Gooseberry Sauce

Ingredients: 1 lb. gooseberries, 2 oz. flour, ¼ tsp. salt, 1½ oz. butter, 3 oz. sugar, ³/₁₀ pt. sour cream, ½ pt. meat stock.

Put cleaned and washed gooseberries to cook in meat stock, salt and flavour with sugar. Make a light roux in the meantime with butter and flour and when gooseberries are well cooked, thicken sauce with roux. Add sour cream, beat well until smooth, and bring once more to boil.

Red Currant Sauce

Ingredients: 1 lb. red currants, 2 oz. flour, ¼ tsp. salt, 1½ oz. butter, 3 oz. sugar, 1 gill sour cream.

Pick currants from stalks, wash well and put into boiling water. When boiling, drain and strain off on a sieve. Make a light roux with butter and flour, dilute with ²/₅ pt. of water, beat well with the whisk until smooth, salt and flavour with sugar. Add sour cream and cook for 5 mins. Mix in boiled red currants, boil again for 4—5 mins. and serve hot. If too thick, thin with meat stock.

Cucumber Sauce

Ingredients: ½ lb. pickled cucumbers (gherkins), 2 oz. flour, ⅓ tsp. salt, 1 oz. lard, 1 tsp. sugar, 2 tbsp. sour cream, ½ pt. meat stock.

Peel pickled gherkins and cut them into neat, even cubes. Make a light roux with lard and flour, dilute with meat stock and beat well until smooth.

Add chopped gherkins, sour cream, flavour with salt and sugar and boil for a few mins. May also be flavoured with a little vinegar from the gherkins.

COLD AND HOT ENTRÉES AND SANDWICHES

ON ENTRÉES IN GENERAL

Entrées are light dishes and combinations of various dishes, served generally before or after the soup, but always before the main course. Entrées may be either hot or cold. They can be prepared from eggs, fish, various kinds of meat, offal, all sorts of vegetables and greens, and different farinaceous products.

Entrées are meant to whet the appetite and to supply a good foundation for the courses to follow. They lend colour and variety to our meals.

When planning menus, entrées may play the role of adjuster inasmuch as we can serve a light, easily digestible entrée before a heavy meat course, and if the main course is not so richly garnished, the entrée, as a sort of balancer, can be more substantial and more nourishing.

Great attention should be paid therefore in planning well-balanced meals to choosing the most suitable entrées for them.

The consumption of entrées is also recommended by the fact that they contain foodstuffs of high nutritive value, which are only to be found in other courses of the menu to a lesser degree or not at all. Entrées, especially cold ones, save time too. We may prepare them long before the meal and keep in readiness in a suitable cool place until the time of serving, thus allowing plenty of time for the careful preparation and serving of the next, the main course, which possibly demands more attention and more labour.

Hot or cold hors-d'oeuvres are rather popular among the entrées. The variations of mixed hors-d'oeuvres are almost endless. Ingenuity and individual taste can play a big role in their preparation. In serving hors-d'oeuvres, attention should be paid to variation in colour, taste and character. For instance, do not place various cold fish side by side, on the dish, while cold stuffed tomatoes and smoked salmon, being of more or less the same colour, do not go well together. Hors-d'oeuvres may be flavoured and seasoned fairly freely, because they are meant to tempt the appetite. Mixed hors-d'oeuvres consist of various mayonnaise dishes, jellies, galantines, patés, salads, tinned fish (sardines, tunny-fish, anchovies), smoked meat of fish. We may, in addition, use fish milt and roe, crayfish or prawns, prepared in different ways, and also herring salad, small red radishes, baked paprikas in French dressing, asparagus, cauliflowers, mushrooms, artichokes, aubergines; we may serve meat salads or chaudfroids, prepared from poultry or game, calf's brains, etc.

Several entrées may be prepared from fish. They may be fried (or baked) either whole or in fillets. Boiled fish should be cooled well, and served either whole or in slices, removing the flesh from the backbone.

Croquettes can be prepared from poultry, eggs, fish, game, ham, mushrooms, or crayfish.

The meat of cooked crayfish should be removed from the shell, claws and tail, and used for stews or ragouts when warm, and for salads and crayfish mayonnaise when cold.

Tasteful serving is important in the case of entrées as well. This goes especially for cold entrées. They provide good opportunities for skill and imagination and their dishing and garnishing represent one of the most decorative parts of culinary art. It is an enjoyable task to choose the materials for the purpose of decoration. One needs at least as much ingenuity, taste and sense of beauty for this, as skill is necessary for the preparation of a cold dish itself. It is essential that we should always use edible materials for decorating and that they should always be in harmony with the flavour, colour and the whole character of the cold dish.

For decoration we may use caviare, smoked salmon, crayfish or prawns, eggs, truffles, carrots, French beans, lettuces, tarragon leaves, small red radishes, red or green paprika, fresh tomatoes and aspic.

COLD ENTRÉES

Aspic (Jelly)

Aspic may be prepared from meat, fowl, bone or fish soup. The simplest way of preparing aspic from calves' bones, is as follows.

Ingredients: 1 lb. bones (veal), 3½ oz. mixed vegetables, 1 oz. onions, 1 tbsp. vinegar, 1 tbsp. white wine, 1 oz. tomato purée, 1 bay leaf, some whole black peppers, 1 tsp. salt, 1 small bunch of tarragon leaves, 1 clove of garlic, 1½ oz. gelatine, 2 whites of eggs.

Cut bones neatly, bring to boil, pour away water and rinse bones well with cold water. Put to boil again in about 3 pt. of water, skim well, and add vegetables, salt liquid and let it simmer slowly and steadily for 3 hrs., making about 2 pt. of soup. Then strain and carefully remove all grease. When somewhat cooled, beat up two whites of eggs well in a basin until almost stiff, add tomatoes, tarragon leaves, vinegar and then add, stirring constantly, meat stock. Lastly place gelatine in the soup, after having soaked it in cold water for a while, and bring to boil, stirring all the time. Then place saucepan to the edge of the cooker and cook steadily and slowly for 10—15 mins. Wash clean muslin in cold water, squeeze well, then pass aspic through cloth into an enamelled dish. Remove grease from the surface, brown with caramel (when prepared from fish stock leave white colour) and put to cool, i. e. on ice. Aspic may also be prepared from calves' feet, in which case gelatine is not needed, because calves' feet posses a great deal of glutinous matter.

Mixed Savoury

Ingredients: 3½ oz. ham, 3½ oz. butter, 2 oz. sardines, 1 portion of fish mayonnaise, 1 portion of meat salad, 5 halfs of Casino mayonnaise eggs, 1 portion of goose-liver paté, 5 small stuffed tomatoes, 10 crayfish, 5 asparagus heads, 1 portion of mixed salad (Macedoine), ½ pt. tartare sauce.

Cover plate or platter with a folded serviette, place small round or oval dishes on it, and fill them tastefully with the cold dishes listed above. The combination may be quite simple, but several variations can be used. All sorts of tinned fish, various patés, galantines, chaudfroids prepared from various poultry, ham cornets, caviare, various dishes in jelly, radishes, salads, cheese, various vegetables, crayfish and sea lobsters, etc. Choose from the dishes mentioned, according to taste and quantity needed, and serve as hors-d'oeuvres.

Fish Roe Salad

Ingredients: 2 lb. carp roes, 2 oz. onions, ½ tsp. salt, 1 bay leaf, 1 tbsp. vinegar, 5 oz. vegetables, ½ pt. vinaigrette sauce, 1 small bunch of parsley.

Wash carp roes well and cook in slightly salted water, with a little vinegar, together with onions and bay leaf, then drain and when cooled, mix into vinaigrette sauce. When cold, remove carp roes from liquid, strain, skin and place, cut into pieces, on a glass dish. Pour vinaigrette sauce with vegetables over it and sprinkle with chopped parsley. Garnish with corn salad or lettuce leaves.

Fish Mayonnaise

Ingredients: 1½ lb. fish (the meat only without bones), carp, sheat-fish or pike perch, 3 hard-boiled eggs, 1 oz. salt, 1 lemon, 5 rings of anchovies, 5 oz. aspic, ²/₅ pt. oil, 3 egg-yolks, 1 tbsp. vinegar, ½ lb. mixed salad, ½ head of lettuce, pinch of ground black pepper.

Cook fish in salted water, together with vinegar, and put to cool. Mix 2 egg-yolks together in a porcelain basin (with a whisk) with a little salt, lemon-juice and, stirring it constantly, add gradually ²/₅ pt. of oil carefully to prevent curdling. Re-season with salt, pepper and lemon-juice. Cut fish—after having removed bones—into small cubes and mix well together with half the mayonnaise sauce. First place on glass tray mixed salad, to form a foundation, then add fish salad in a cone form; put on a coating of mayonnaise sauce. Decorate with rings of anchovies, lemons and hard-boiled eggs, garnish with diced aspic and lettuce leaves.

Crayfish Mayonnaise

Ingredients: 25 crayfish, ½ lb. boiled fish, 1 oz. salt, 4 hard-boiled eggs, 2 egg-yolks, ½ pt. oil, ½ lemon, pinch of ground black pepper, ½ tsp. caraway seed, small bunch of parsley, 2 and half portions of mixed salad, 5 oz. aspic.

Cook crayfish in salted water with caraway seeds and parsley and remove shells. Prepare mayonnaise sauce, as described for fish mayonnaise. Re-season with salt and pepper, cut the meat of claws of crayfish and boiled fish into neat pieces and mix well with mayonnaise sauce. (Put some mayonnaise sauce aside for the coating, before mixing in fish and crayfish.) Put mixed salad on glass platter as a foundation, place crayfish salad in a mound on top and cover with sauce-coating. Decorate mound with the meat from the tails. Place finely diced aspic round the cone and hard-boiled eggs cut in quarters. Garnish with lettuce leaves.

Herring Salad

Ingredients: 1½ lb. herrings, 7½ oz. apples, 11 oz. potatoes, 7½ oz. pickled gherkins, 5 eggs, ½ pt. tartare sauce, 1 oz. onions, ½ lemon, pinch of black pepper, 5 rings of anchovies, 7½ oz. fish aspic.

Clean herrings and remove flesh from backbones, cut into slices ½ inch wide. Boil and skin potatoes, put them to cool. Cut boiled potatoes and peeled apples into thin slices, and chop gherkins and 3 hard-boiled eggs into thin rings. Flavour with lemon-juice, salt, pepper, finely chopped onions (pickled onions may be used as well) and mix together with tartare sauce. Serve on glass dish in cone-shape and decorate with diced fish aspic. Garnish with slices of hard-boiled eggs, anchovies (rings) and lettuce leaves.

Chicken Salad

Ingredients: 2 lb. chicken, 11 oz. potatoes, 5 oz. apples, 1 head of lettuce, 1 tsp. salt, 3 eggs, ½ pt. mayonnaise sauce, ½ lemon, pinch of ground black pepper, 7½ oz. meat aspic.

Cook chicken, skin, put meat of breast aside, cut flesh from legs into thin slices. Slice boiled potatoes, peeled apples, lettuce leaves, and 1½ hard-boiled eggs as well, flavour with lemon-juice, salt, pepper and mix well together with mayonnaise sauce. Serve on glass dish in cone, put on a coating of mayonnaise from the rest of the sauce, and decorate the top with thin slices of chicken breast. Garnish with diced aspic, hard-boiled eggs cut in fours and lettuce leaves.

Russian Meat Salad

Ingredients (for 10 people): 1¼ lb. roast or boiled meat, 1 lb. potatoes, 7½ oz. apples, 11 oz. cucumbers, 1 tsp. mustard, 1 oz. salt, pinch of ground black pepper, 4 eggs, ³/₅ pt. tartare sauce, 1 oz. onions, ½ lemon, 1 small bunch of parsley, 7½ oz. meat aspic.

Cook and peel potatoes. Slice thinly meat, cold cooked potatoes, peeled apples, pickled cucumbers, and 2 hard-boiled eggs. Flavour with lemon-juice, mustard, salt, pepper and finely chopped onions, and mix together with $^2/_5$ pt. of tartare sauce. Sprinkle with chopped parsley and decorate dish with neatly diced aspic. Garnish with hard-boiled eggs cut in fours, lettuce leaves and beetroots.

Ox-cheek Salad

Ingredients (for 10 people): 1 lb. ox-cheek, $^1/_5$ pt. vinegar, 5 oz. onions, 1 tsp. salt, pinch of ground black pepper, $^1/_5$ pt. oil, ½ tsp. sugar, small bunch of parsley, 1 bay leaf, 1 small bunch of tarragon leaves.

Cook ox-cheek in salted water until tender and put to cool. Cut into thin slices, place in a deep bowl, add onions cut in rings, flavour with salt, pepper, chopped tarragon leaves, bay leaf and chopped parsley. Pour vinegar thinned with water and good quality table oil over the mixture and pickle in this liquid for a few hrs.

Tomatoes Stuffed with Fish

Ingredients: 10 tomatoes, 14 oz. boiled fish, 1 oz. salt, pinch of ground black pepper, 3½ oz. mayonnaise sauce, ½ lemon, 11 oz. mixed salad, ½ pt. tartare sauce, 7½ oz. aspic, 1 small bunch of parsley.

Dip tomatoes in hot water, skin them and remove cores and seeds. Break boiled fish into pieces, mix together with mayonnaise sauce and flavour with salt, pepper and lemon-juice. Salt and pepper tomatoes and fill them with fish mayonnaise, sprinkle with chopped parsley. Garnish with neatly diced aspic and lettuce leaves.

Tomatoes Stuffed with Meat Salad

Ingredients: 10 medium-sized tomatoes, 14 oz. meat salad, 14 oz. mixed salad, ½ tsp. salt, pinch of ground black pepper, ½ pt. tartare sauce, 7½ oz. aspic, 1 small bunch of parsley.

Prepare this salad as for tomatoes stuffed with fish, but use meat salad for filling instead of fish.

Tomatoes Stuffed with Crayfish

Ingredients: 10 medium-sized tomatoes, 25 crayfish, 14 oz. mixed salad, 1 oz. salt, ½ pt. mayonnaise sauce, pinch of ground black pepper, 7½ oz. aspic, ½ lemon, 2 tbsp. cream, ½ tsp. caraway seeds.

Dip tomatoes in hot water, skin them, remove seeds and cores. Crack claws of boiled crayfish, remove meat, pry the body meat loose with fork and remove as well, cut into small pieces and mix into the salad. Flavour with salt, pepper and lemon-juice. Salt and pepper tomatoes, fill them with salad and put on a coating of mayonnaise sauce mixed with cream. Decorate the top of each tomato with a crayfish tail, and garnish with diced aspic and lettuce leaves.

Forcemeat (Farce) for Dumplings, Stuffing, Puddings and Soufflés

Ingredients: 1 lb. veal, 1 pt. cream, 2 eggs, 1 tbsp. milk, 1 oz. butter, 2 oz. flour, 1 tsp. salt, pinch of nutmeg, pinch of ground black pepper.

Boil milk with butter, mix in the flour and when the sauce does not stick to the saucepan any more, put it on a plate and set to cool (panada). Pound meat in a mortar, add cooled panada, and continue pounding, adding eggs to the mixture, one at a time. When quite smooth, pass through a fine hair sieve, then mix the forcemeat well together in a mixing basin, put on ice and leave undisturbed two hrs. Beat cream until stiff and mix with the forcemeat, a spoonful at a time. Flavour with salt and grated nutmeg. Small dumplings for soup may be prepared from this forcemeat. Cut out small dumplings with a small teaspoon and place in a buttered frying pan, then pour enough slightly salted hot water over them to cover. Boil gently, then put aside and place into the soup after a few minutes with a flat ladle. To prepare a pudding or soufflé form forcemeat, the mixture must be lightened with a few spoonfuls of beaten cream. Prepare forcemeat by this method from poultry, game, lean ham or fish to be used for dumplings, stuffing, puddings and soufflés.

PATTIES AND GALANTINES

Chicken Galantine

Ingredients: 1½ lb. chicken, ½ lb. veal, 2 oz. bacon, 2 oz. smoked tongue, 3½ oz. gooseliver, 1 oz. truffles, 1 tsp. pistachio nuts, 3 tbsp. cream, 2 tbsp. milk, 1 oz. flour, 1 oz. butter, 1 tsp. cognac, 1 egg, 2 oz. vegetables, 1 oz. onions, 1 bay leaf, 2 tsp. salt.

Cut the skin of the chicken at the back with a sharp knife and remove the whole skin carefully. Afterwards draw chicken and remove all meat from the bones. Pound the breast of chicken with a meat beater and replace in the skin. Mince the meat from the legs, together with the veal. Boil ⅕ pt. of milk with the butter, add flour and when it is cooked and does not stick to the saucepan any more, put to cool. (This paste is called panada.) Pound the minced meat together with the panada and an egg in a mortar, pass through a sieve and place in a mixing bowl. Add cream gradually to the minced meat, a spoonful at a time, and mix until smooth, flavour with salt, pepper and cognac and mix carefully together with diced goose-liver, bacon, smoked tongue, truffles and pistachio nuts. Open the skin of the chicken, fill with the stuffing and folding the skin over it, sew it up with a needle and thread. Roll it tightly in a serviette and tie up both ends with a string; tie it in the middle too, once or twice. Fill saucepan with water, put in chicken bones, vegetables, onions, bay leaf, a few whole black peppers and salt it, then bring to boil. When boiled, put the stuffed chicken in the serviette (galantine) into it and boil for 50 mins. well covered, then put aside. When somewhat cooled, take out, tie up once more tightly, press and put on ice. Take out from serviette before serving, pull out thread, slice neatly and thinly, place on a bed of mixed salad and garnish with finely diced aspic.

Patty Cases Made of Puff Pastry

Ingredients: ½ lb. flour, ½ lb. butter, ½ tsp. salt, ¼ lemon, 1 egg, 1 oz. flour, for sprinkling.

Chill puff pastry well, then roll out into half a finger thickness, and cut out forms with a round, fancy cake cutter. Place on a baking tin, brush thinly with egg, and put another one on top, the middle of which has been cut out with a smaller pastry cutter. Brush top thinly with egg, and bake in a hot oven, together with the cut out parts. Be careful to prevent the egg running down the sides while brushing pastry, because this may stop pastry from rising.

Small cases made in the above way can be filled with various stuffings. When serving, give two bouchées for each person. When pastry is kept in one piece for 6—8 people (vol-au-vent), the stuffing must be cut less finely too.

Ham Patties

Ingredients: 1 lb. ham, 10 patty cases, 1 pinch of ground black pepper, ½ tsp. salt, 1 egg-yolk, 3 tbsp. béchamel sauce, 3 portions of Madeira sauce, ½ tsp. red paprika.

Chop boiled ham finely, mix together with béchamel sauce, heat it well, and add 1 yolk to bind. Fill patties with this stuffing, pour Madeira sauce over, place cut out tops on each one and serve hot.

Chicken Patties

Ingredients: 10 patty cases, 1 lb. 11 oz. chicken, pinch of ground black pepper, ½ tsp. salt, 1 egg-yolk, 1 oz. onions, 3½ oz. vegetables, 2 oz. butter, small bunch of parsley, 1 pt. supreme sauce.

Boil chicken together with vegetables and onions, skin when cooked, remove meat from bones and chop finely. Fry lightly ¾ oz. finely chopped onions in butter, add chicken meat, a little supreme sauce, 1 yolk; heat mixture, flavour with salt, pepper and chopped parsley. Fill patties with this stuffing, pour the rest of supreme sauce over them, place the small lids on each patty and serve hot. Sauce may be served separately, and patties may be served on paper doily or on a neatly folded serviette.

Game Patties

Ingredients: 10 patty cases, 1 lb. stewed venison or hare, 2 oz. butter, ½ tsp. salt, pinch of ground black pepper, 1 tbsp. cognac, 2 oz. onions, ⁴/₅ pt. Madeira sauce.

Chop venison or hare meat finely. Fry chopped onions in butter until golden brown in colour, add game, with a little Madeira sauce, flavour with salt, pepper and a little cognac. Pour the rest of the cognac into the sauce, fill patties with the stuffing, place the tops over them and serve hot.

Mushroom Patties

Ingredients: 10 patty cases, 22 oz. Champignon mushrooms, 2 oz. onions, 3½ oz. butter, 1 egg, 1 tsp. salt, pinch of ground black pepper, 1 small bunch of parsley, 1 pt. Madeira sauce.

Clean Champignon mushrooms, wash and chop them: Chop onions finely and fry in butter until golden-brown, add mushrooms, salt, pepper, and fry together with chopped parsley until brown, add 1 beaten egg to bind mixture. Fill patties with this stuffing, place small tops to cover and serve hot with the sauce.

Rich Patties (Lucullus Patties)

Ingredients: 10 patty cases, 3½ oz. goose-liver, 3½ oz. mushrooms, 2 oz. cockscomb, 2 oz. cocks' kidney, 3½ oz. smoked tongue, 2 oz. butter, ⅓ oz. salt, 1 pt. Madeira sauce.

Dice goose-liver and mushrooms finely, salt and pepper and brown in butter. Cut boiled cockscomb and cooked smoked tongue into small cubes, add cooked cocks' kidney and mix the whole stuffing well together with a little Madeira sauce. Fill patties with this stuffing. Serve like other patties.

Strasbourg Patties

Ingredients: 10 patty cases, 1 lb. goose-liver, 2 oz. onions, 1 bay leaf, pinch of ground black pepper, pinch of marjoram, 2 sprigs of thyme, 2 oz. butter, 1 oz. lard, 1 oz. flour, 1 tbsp. cognac, 1 tsp. salt, 1 pt. Madeira sauce.

Cut onions into rings and fry in lard until light brown in colour; add sliced goose-liver, season and brown together, then sprinkle with flour and continue frying for a short time; pour cognac over it, as well as ¹/₅ pt. of Madeira sauce, bring to boil and afterwards pass through a hair sieve. Heat in a saucepan and add fresh butter. Fill patties with this mixture, pour Madiera sauce over them, put small centres on top and serve hot.

Goose-liver Paste Prepared in the Strasbourg Way

Ingredients (for 10 people): 2 lb. first-class goose-liver, 1 oz. onions, 2 oz. truffles, ½ lb. bacon, 1 tsp. mixed herbs, 1 tbsp. cognac, 1 tbsp. Madeira wine, ½ bay leaf.

Take a fine, well fattened, first-class goose-liver for the making of goose-liver paste, remove heart and gall bladder carefully and soak in cold water for a few hrs. Dry on a cloth, remove filmy, skinny parts and sinews with a small knife. Score the pieces of liver with a knife, and push slices of truffles into each slit. Salt, season with mixed herbs, place in a porcelain bowl, sprinkle with cognac and Madeira wine and steam the liver for a few hrs. in this savoury liquid. Use half of the liver for this; then brown part of the other half with onions in lard; then pass through a sieve. Rub the raw liver through a sieve as well, mix both pastes together, flavour with salt, and mixed herbs; add savoury liquid left over from liver slices and mix well. Line the inside of a porcelain bowl with thinly sliced bacon. Arrange part of the paste on the bottom and on sides, place some of the steamed goose-liver in the bowl, put another layer of paste on top of it, then goose-liver again; repeat until the basin is full. When the basin is full, put the rest of the paste on top, cover with slices of bacon and put a porcelain lid over the basin. Put it in a saucepan, pour water in the saucepan to reach the middle of the basin, and bring to boil. When boiling, place into a hot oven and steam for about 3 hrs., then take out of the oven and put to cool. It is ready when the fat in the basin is quite clear; it turns completely clear only when the liver is well cooked. Take the basin out of the saucepan; when it has cooled a little, remove lid, and put a wooden platter on top of it, pressing it down with a 10 lb. weight. Take off weight after a day's pressing and remove wooden platter as well; wipe the edges and outside of the porcelain basin thoroughly, with a cloth dipped in lukewarm water, and pour melted goose fat or lard on top, to the thickness of about an inch. May be kept in a cool, dark place for months.

Goose-liver Galantine

Ingredients (for 10 people): 1 lb. goose-liver, 3½ oz. butter, 1½ oz. lard, ²/₅ pt. cream, ½ tsp. cognac, pinch of mixed herbs, pinch of ground black pepper, 2 oz. onions, 1 tsp. Madeira wine, ¹/₅ pt. béchamel sauce, 1 lb. aspic, lettuce or parsley to garnish.

Clean goose-liver carefully, remove gall bladder; cut liver into smaller slices. Chop onions into rings and fry in lard until golden-brown; add goose-liver, flavour with salt, pepper and bay leaf and let it simmer. When ready, pass through a hair sieve and put to cool. Beat butter well until creamy, add goose-liver purée, béchamel sauce and mix well on ice until smooth. Season with mixed herbs, cognac, Madeira wine, add 3½ oz. melted aspic gradually, a spoonful at a time, and lastly add whipped cream. Pour mixture into a mould lined with aspic, decorated with truffles, or smoked tongue, pour aspic on top and place on ice. Dip mould in hot water before serving, then turn galantine out on a glass dish, garnish with diced aspic and chopped parsley or lettuce leaves.

Ham Galantine

Ingredients (for 10 people): 1 lb. ham, 1 oz. butter, $^3/_{10}$ pt. milk, 1 oz. flour, pinch of ground black pepper, ¼ tsp. red paprika, 1 tsp. cognac, $^3/_{10}$ pt. cream, 1 oz. smoked tongue, 1 lb. aspic, ½ pt. tartare sauce, 1 head of lettuce.

Make a light roux with 1 oz. butter and 1 oz. flour, dilute with the milk, bring to boil, then cool. Pass cooked lean ham and the cooled milk sauce through a sieve. Put on ice in a dish, then add 3½ oz. melted aspic to it gradually, a spoonful at a time, and mix well until smooth. Flavour with salt, pepper, red paprika and cognac, and if light in colour, use a little red colouring to darken. Mix beaten cream into the mixture carefully and pour into a pudding mould, lined previously with aspic, and decorated with smoked tongue and truffles. Pour melted aspic on top and put on ice to chill. Dip mould into hot water before serving and turn out on a glass dish, garnish with diced aspic and lettuce leaves. Serve together with tartare sauce.

Fish Galantine

Ingredients (for 10 people): 2 lb. pike perch, 3½ oz. butter, 1 oz. flour, $^1/_5$ pt. milk, $^3/_{10}$ pt. cream, $^1/_5$ pt. white wine, 1 oz. onions, pinch of ground black pepper, pinch of nutmeg, 1 lb. aspic, 1 oz. smoked salmon, 3 portions of tartare sauce, 1 head of lettuce.

Clean and salt fillets of pike perch, steam in a buttered saucepan, together with onions and white wine, and when tender, put to cool. Make a thick roux with ¾ oz. butter, 1 oz. flour, $^1/_5$ pt. milk and dilute with the stock of the fish. Mince the fish together with this sauce and pound well with the rest of the butter in a mortar, then pass through a hair sieve. Place in a dish on ice and add 3½ oz. melted jelly to it gradually, a spoonful at a time, and mix well until smooth. Flavour with salt, pepper and grated nutmeg, and carefully mix in whipped cream; then pour into a pudding mould, previously lined with aspic and decorated with smoked salmon. Pour aspic on top and put on ice to freeze. Dip mould into hot water before serving, turn galantine out on a glass dish, garnish with finely diced aspic and lettuce leaves. Serve together with tartare sauce.

Hare Pie

Ingredients (for 10 people): 1 lb. 6 oz. hare meat, 7½ oz. pork, 1 saddle of hare, 14 oz. bacon, 5 oz. ham, 7½ oz. goose-liver, 11 oz. bacon, 2 oz. truffles, 1 tsp. mixed herbs, 1 oz. salt, 1 tbsp. cognac, 2 eggs, pinch of ground black pepper.

Pastry: ½ lb. flour, 4 oz. butter, 1 egg, pinch of salt, ¹/₅ tepid water.

If possible prepare pastry one day earlier and fold twice.

Cut fillets from the saddle of hare, salt and pepper, and partially fry them. When cooled, cover it with slices of bacon. Cut goose-liver, half of the bacon and ham into thick fingers, half an inch in thickness; salt and sprinkle them with mixed herbs and cognac. Cut hare meat, pork and bacon in small pieces, mince them, then put in a mortar and pound them together with 2 eggs; then pass through a sieve. Salt, flavour with seasonings and add the rest of the cognac, then mix well. Line pudding or pastry mould with thin pastry, and put thinly sliced bacon at the bottom as well; put in one layer of meat mixture first, place hare fillets in the middle, adding goose-liver, bacon and ham fingers together with truffle dices at the sides, covering everything again with the meat mixture, until mould is full. Finally cover with the meat mixture, put thin slices of bacon on top to prevent sticking, brush the edges with egg and cover with thinly rolled pastry. Make 3 holes in the middle for the steam to escape during cooking. Decorate top with pastry ring, according to taste. Brush with egg and bake in a hot oven for 35—40 mins. for each 2 lb. weight of the uncooked pie. (For instance if the pie weighs 4 lb. the time of baking should be 80 mins. in all.) The next day, when cooled, fill through the holes in the centre with Madeira jelly. Place on ice and when frozen, carve with a sharp knife and serve together with Cumberland sauce.

SANDWICHES

Sandwiches may be made from sliced French bread, rolls, or simply from thin slices of bread cut into oval or square shapes, as well as from toasted bread or rolls.

There is a difference between sandwiches and the so-called open sandwiches, or canapés. Both have a lot of variations, and can be made in many different ways, according to the ingredients and methods used.

This is the method for making simple sandwiches: spread the slices of bread or rolls thinly with creamed butter, place chopped ham, salami, cold meat or cheese on them, and cover with other slices of bread or rolls, also spread with butter.

Canapés are very popular, because a great variety of ingredients can be used. They are often preferable, because they can be made very quickly, in almost a few minutes. Canapés decorated tastefully and placed, when ready, on sandwich plates, according to their flavour and colour-scheme, make attractive dishes.

Canapés can be made with sliced or finely chopped ham, winter salami, smoked sausages, cold meat, cold fish, caviare, herring, hard-boiled eggs, Liptauer cheese, various kinds of cheese, cold roast goose-liver, etc.

Cut slices of bread or rolls into neat even pieces (not too big and not too small).

Sandwiches are generally spread with butter, beaten up previously until smooth, and slightly salted, but goose-liver sandwiches, for instance, may be spread with cold goose fat. Sandwiches made from various fish (sardines, herrings, etc.) should be spread with butter flavoured with anchovy rings or paste.

It is important that sandwiches should always be decorated according to their character, tastefully and with moderation. Thus sandwiches made from cold fish, for instance, may be decorated with caviare, hard-boiled eggs, slices of lemon, etc., while ham sandwiches, on the other hand, may be garnished with aspic, grated horse-radish; cheese sandwiches with radishes, butter, green paprika; meat sandwiches with cucumbers, lettuce leaves, and so on. Sandwiches may also be effectively decorated with aspic, glazed with finely chopped aspic, creamed butter or sprinkled with mayonnaise, etc.

Sandwich Bread

Ingredients: 2 lb. flour, 1 oz. yeast, 5 oz. mashed boiled potatoes, a little salt, 1½ oz. sugar, 2 oz. butter, 3/5 pt. milk.

Mix yeast together with 11 oz. flour, sugar and tepid water, and leave it to rise in a warm place. Then add this leaven to flour, together with 3/5 pt. tepid milk, and 2/5 pt. tepid water, and with the mashed potatoes, and knead well together; continue kneading, and lastly add melted butter, also mixing well, and put to prove in a lukewarm place. When the dough is ready, make different shapes on a floured pastry board, place in buttered baking tin, and leave to prove again for 25—30 mins. The bread is then brushed over with eggs, melted butter, or honey and baked in a medium-hot oven.

Sandwiches can also be made from a kind of light sweet bread dough (with less sugar) raised with yeast; from which small round and oval brioches (about 3/4—1 oz. in weight) can be baked. They may be used as sandwiches or as canapés.

Sandwiches Made from Brioches

Brioches are cut in two, spread with salted butter, filled with ham or goose-liver slices, various meats; ham, liver or fish paste and covered with the other half of the brioches, also spread with butter.

70

Canapés Made from Brioches

Cut off the top of the brioches, spread with salted butter, place caviare or ham, fresh or tinned fish, lobster, smoked meat, fillets or slices prepared from chicken glazed with white (velouté) sauce. Fillets or slices of game may also be used, glazed with brown sauce and put on sandwiches garnished neatly and previously glazed with jelly.

Sandwich Cake

Remove crust from a round brown or white loaf. Slice neatly and thinly, spread slices with salted butter, and put ham, goose-liver paste or minced meat on top in turn, place slices on top each other, press well and put on ice. When cooled, cut neatly to achieve cake form, spread butter on side and sprinkle with finely chopped ham or hard-boiled egg-yolks, or finely chopped white of eggs. The top of the cake may be decorated with salted butter or garnished with smoked salmon, ham or herrings, and cut in slices when served, like fancy cakes. Sandwich cakes may also be prepared from long loaves of bread; when chilled, cut into triangles and arrange them in the shape of a round cake.

Meat Paste for the Filling of Sandwiches

Mince 11 oz. any kind of roasted meat, of ham, boiled goose or calf's liver; mix with 2 oz. of béchamel sauce, pass through a sieve, then mix well with 2 oz. of creamed butter and $^1/_5$ pt. cream, salt and pepper, and flavour with cognac. Fish paste can be prepared the same way from boiled fresh or tinned fish, but cognac must not be used as a flavouring; use some lemon-juice instead.

Sandwiches with Smoked Ox-tongue

(For ten people)
Ingredients: 7½ oz. sandwich bread, 2½ oz. butter, 5 oz. ox-tongue, 3½ oz. aspic, 3 or 4 red radishes.

Cut sandwich bread into 10 thin slices, spread them with slightly salted butter, then put slices of ox-tongue on top, cut them round neatly, and put a thin slice of radish in the middle of each sandwich, lastly pipe butter on them through a paper tube, then glaze with aspic.

Sandwich Squares with Chopped Ham

(For ten people)
Ingredients: 7½ oz. white bread, 7½ oz. ham, 2 oz. butter, a little salt.

Cut squares from bread, spread both sides with slightly salted butter, and afterwards roll in finely chopped ham.

Sandwich with Eggs

(For ten people)
Ingredients: 7½ oz. sandwich bread, 2 oz. butter, 10 anchovy rings, 3 hard-boiled eggs, 3½ oz. aspic.

Cut sandwich bread in 10 thin slices and spread with slightly salted butter. Cut eggs into thin neat rings (with an egg-slicer if available) and place two rings on each slice of bread, then put one anchovy ring in the middle of every one and decorate with finely chopped aspic.

Sandwich with Herring

(For ten people)
Ingredients: 7½ oz. sandwich bread, 2 oz. butter, 1 big herring, 2 hard-boiled eggs, some tomato purée.

Cut sandwich bread in 10 thin slices and spread slices with slightly salted butter. Cut herring in half lengthwise, remove backbone, and cut fillets into 20 small slices, then place two pieces of herring on each slice of bread slantwise so as to leave some space free at both ends and in the middle. Chop separately whites and yolks of hard-boiled eggs, quite finely; place chopped whites of eggs at both ends of the slice and chopped yolks in the middle. Slices of herrings may be decorated with tomato purée piped through a paper tube in small rosettes.

Sandwiches with Sardines

(For ten people)
Ingredients: 7½ oz. sandwich bread, 3 oz. butter, 5 neat sardines, 3½ oz. aspic, spoonful of tomato purée.

Cut sandwich bread into thin slices, spread with slightly salted butter, and place half a sardine on each of them. Mix a little melted aspic into the tomato purée, and when cooled, draw bars on sardines by forcing through a paper tube. Finally decorate sandwich again with the help of a paper forcing bag, putting the rest of the butter on top.

Sandwiches with Caviare

(For ten people)
Ingredients: 7½ oz. sandwich bread, 2 oz. butter, 3 hard-boiled eggs, 1 oz. caviare.

Cut sandwich bread into thin slices and spread with slightly salted butter. Chop whites and yolks of hard-boiled eggs separately and finely, and put on one half of the bread some of the yolks, and on the other half some of the whites, pressing them down slightly. Arrange thin stripes of caviare in the middle.

Sandwiches with Goose-liver Paste

(For ten people)
Ingredients: 7½ oz. sandwich bread, 2 oz. butter, 7½ oz. goose-liver paste, 3½ oz. aspic.

Cut sandwich bread into thin slices and spread with slightly salted butter; place slices of goose-liver paste on top, cut with a spoon previously dipped in hot water. Glaze with melted and cooled aspic. If there is no goose-liver paste available, use paste made from chicken or calf's liver, piping it through a star-shaped nozzle.

Cheese Sandwiches

(For ten people)
Ingredients: 7½ oz. sandwich bread, 5 oz. cheese, 3 oz. butter, red radishes, 1 oz. cream cheese, ⅓ tsp. red paprika.

Cut sandwich bread into thin slices and spread with slightly salted butter. Cut cheese into 10 thin slices, cut them round to fit the size of the bread slices, and place them on top. Decorate with radishes cut in rings, and with small balls prepared from cream cheese and rolled in red paprika. Colour the rest of the butter with a little red paprika and force through a paper tube on top of the sandwiches.

Sandwiches may also be filled with Liptauer cheese mixed with butter.

Sandwiches with Tomatoes

Ingredients: 7½ sandwich bread, 2 oz. butter, 1 lb. tomatoes, chopped parsley, salt, pepper.

Cut sandwich bread into thin slices and spread with slightly salted butter. Cut skinned tomatoes in thin slices, salt them slightly, flavour with pepper and place on the slices of bread. Sprinkle with chopped parsley.

HOT ENTRÉES

Meat Pudding

Ingredients: 1 lb. boiled or roasted veal, 3½ oz. butter, 2 oz. flour, 1 pt. milk, 6 eggs, 1 tsp. salt, pinch of ground black pepper.

Pass the meat, together with 1¾ oz. butter twice through the mincer until quite fine. Make a light roux with 1¾ oz. butter and flour, dilute with hot milk, then beat until smooth and bring to boil. Add to meat purée and pass through a wire sieve. Then mix well the yolks, salt and pepper, and lastly add carefully the whites of the eggs, well beaten until quite stiff. Butter and flour pudding basin carefully, pour meat purée into it and steam slowly under cover until ready. Add supreme sauce to it.

Puddings may be prepared by the same method from fowl, game, ham, fish or left-over meat, but should of course be served together with the appropriate sauces. Puddings made from white meats, for instance, should be served with supreme or mushroom sauce, dishes prepared from ham or game may be served together with Madeira sauce, while fish dishes are usually served together with white wine sauce or lobster sauce.

CROQUETTES

Chicken Croquettes

Ingredients: 2 lb. chicken, 1½ oz. butter, 1½ oz. flour, 1 tsp. salt, ¹/₅ pt. milk, ¹/₅ pt. chicken soup, 2 egg-yolks, pinch of ground black pepper, 5 oz. lard.

Cook chicken, remove skin and then remove flesh from bones. Mince or cut chicken meat finely. Make a light roux with butter and flour, dilute with chicken soup and milk and bring to boil, stirring constantly. Into this thick sauce add minced chicken meat, together with 2 egg-yolks, salt and pepper, and mix well over the fire; then put to cool. When cooled, form croquettes, about 2½ inches long and ¾ inch thick from the mixture; roll in flour, egg and bread-crumbs and fry in hot fat. May be served with tomato, tartare or supreme sauce.

Fish Croquettes

Ingredients: 2 lb. fish, 1½ oz. flour, 1½ oz. butter, 1 tsp. salt, pinch of ground black pepper, pinch of nutmeg, 2 egg-yolks, ²/₅ pt. milk, 5 oz. lard.
For coating: 2 eggs, 5 oz. bread-crumbs, 2 oz. flour.

Clean fish well, then cook in salted water. Cut the meat into squares when cooled. Make a light roux with 1½ oz. butter and 1½ oz. flour, dilute with hot milk and boil until thick. Into this thick sauce add 2 egg-yolks, season with pepper and salt and with nutmeg, mix carefully with the fish and then put on ice. When cooled, form croquettes, about 2½ inches long and ¾ inch thick from the mixture; roll in flour, egg and bread-crumbs and fry in hot fat. Should be served with Hollandaise or tartare sauce.

Ham Croquettes

Ingredients: 1 lb. ham, ²/₅ pt. milk, 1½ oz. butter, 1½ oz. flour, 2 egg-yolks, pinch of nutmeg, pinch of ground black pepper, 5 oz. lard.
For coating: 2 eggs, 5 oz. bread-crumbs, 2 oz. flour.

Cut thin slices from boiled ham, and chop it finely. Make a light roux with 1½ oz. flour and 1½ oz. butter, dilute with ²/₅ pt. hot milk and cook until thick. Add chopped ham, together with 2 egg-yolks to this sauce, season with salt, pepper and grated nutmeg, mix well over the fire and put to cool. When cooled, make different shapes from the mixture, according to taste, cutlets, croquettes or rings; roll in flour, egg and bread-crumbs and fry in hot fat. Madeira sauce should be served separately with ham croquettes.

Calf's Brains Croquettes

Ingredients: 3 calf's brains, 1 oz. salt, 1 oz. onions, 1½ oz. butter, 1½ oz. flour, $^3/_{10}$ pt. milk, pinch of ground black pepper, pinch of marjoram, 3 eggs, 1 small bunch of parsley, 7½ oz. lard.

For coating: 3 oz. flour, 2 eggs, 5 oz. bread-crumbs.

Wash brains well in cold water, trim and skin, then drain and chop finely. Fry finely chopped onions in lard until golden-brown, add brains, and season with salt, pepper and marjoram, adding parsley, and brown lightly. Make a light roux with 1½ oz. flour and 1½ oz. butter, dilute with $^3/_{10}$ pt. milk, and cook until thick. When thickened, add brains, 1 egg and 2 yolks, stir it well, mix a small quantity of bread-crumbs into this sauce and put to cool. When cooled, form croquettes, about 2½ inches long and ¾ inch thick from this mixture, roll in flour, dip in the egg and bread-crumbs and fry in hot fat. May be served with mushroom or tomato sauce.

Venison Croquettes

Ingredients: 1 lb. boiled venison, 1½ oz. butter, 1½ oz. flour, $^2/_5$ pt. milk, 1 oz. onions, 1 tsp. salt, pinch of mixed herbs, 2 egg-yolks, 5 oz. lard.

For coating: 2 oz. flour, 2 eggs, 5 oz. bread-crumbs.

Fry finely chopped onions in 1½ oz. butter, until pale golden colour, add flour and stir for a minute or two, then dilute with hot milk and bring to boil; then add minced venison, 2 egg-yolks, and season with salt and mixed herbs. Mix well over the fire, then put to cool. When cooled, form croquettes, about 2½ inches long and ¾ inch thick from this mixture; roll in flour, egg and bread-crumbs and fry in hot fat. Serve with game sauce, prepared with sour cream or Madeira sauce.

Croquettes may be made in the above way from hare, pheasant or partridge garnished with potato purée.

Vegetable Croquettes

Ingredients: 11 oz. mixed vegetables, 7½ oz. kohlrabi, 3½ oz. green peas, 2 oz. mushrooms, 7½ oz. French beans, 3½ oz. flour, 5 oz. lard, 1 oz. salt, 1 egg, $^1/_5$ pt. milk.

For coating: 2 oz. flour, 2 eggs, 5 oz. bread-crumbs.

Dice all vegetables after cleaning, and cook in slightly salted water until tender. Cool and drain. Fry chopped mushrooms in butter, add boiled vegetables and heat it well, then add 3½ oz. flour as well, and stir this mixture a little. Dilute with milk, add 1 whole egg and boil until thick, then put to cool. Form small croquettes, about 2 inches long, from this mixture, roll in flour, egg and bread-crumbs and fry in hot fat. May be served with different sauces.

Rice Croquettes

Ingredients: ½ lb. rice, 1 oz. butter, 1 tsp. salt, 2 oz. cheese, 5 oz. lard, 2 egg-yolks.
For coating: 2 oz. flour, 2 eggs, 5 oz. bread-crumbs.

Salt ⁴/₅ pt. of water, add 1 oz. butter and bring to boil. Add washed rice and steam until tender. When ready, mix in grated cheese and 2 egg-yolks, mix well, then put to cool. Form small croquettes about 2½ inches long from cooled rice, roll in flour, egg and bread-crumbs and fry in hot fat.

Mushroom Croquettes

Ingredients: ½ lb. mushrooms, 1 oz. butter, 1 oz. onions, pinch of ground black pepper, pinch of marjoram, ½ pt. milk, 5 oz. lard, 2 oz. flour, 1 egg, small bunch of parsley.
For coating: 2 oz. flour, 2 eggs, 5 oz. bread-crumbs.

Clean mushroms and chop them finely. Fry finely chopped onions in butter, add mushrooms, parsley, season, and cook until tender. When mushrooms are ready, sprinkle with 1¾ oz. flour and dilute with milk, then add 1 egg to this mixture and boil until thick. Then place in a buttered basin and cover with buttered paper. When cooled, form croquettes, about 2½ inches long from the mixture, roll in flour, egg and bread-crumbs and fry in hot fat.

May be served with Madeira or tartare sauce.

MUSHROOMS

Stuffed Mushroom

Ingredients: 2 lb. mushrooms, 2 oz. lard, 2 oz. butter, 2 oz. onions, 1 small tsp. salt, 3 oz. bread-crumbs, 1 egg, 2 oz. grated cheese, pinch of ground black pepper, 1 small bunch of parsley, 1 pt. Madeira or tomato sauce.

Clean and wash mushrooms well. Put bigger heads aside, counting 4 heads for each person. Take off stalks. Chop these stalks, together with the rest of the mushrooms, finely. Fry finely chopped onions in lard until light brown, add chopped mushrooms, salt, pepper and parsley, and fry lightly. Thicken when cooked well with ¹/₅ pt. of Madeira sauce, 1 egg and 1½ oz. of bread-crumbs. Place heads of mushrooms into a buttered pan, sprinkle with salt and ground pepper, then stuff with minced mushrooms, sprinkle with grated cheese and bread-crumbs, besprinkle with melted butter and bake in a hot oven. Serve on a bed of rice, and pour Madeira or tomato sauce around mushrooms when serving.

76

Mushrooms with Sour Cream

Ingredients: 2 lb. mushrooms, 3 oz. lard, 1 oz. onions, ½ oz. salt, pinch of ground black pepper, 1 oz. flour, ³/₅ pt. sour cream, small bunch of parsley.

Clean mushrooms well and cut them into thin slices. Fry finely chopped onions in lard until light brown, add mushrooms, season with salt and pepper, let simmer for a while, then sprinkle with chopped parsley and dilute with sour cream mixed well with the flour; then cook thoroughly. May be served with garnish of rice or 1—2 fried eggs for each person.

Tomatoes Stuffed with Mushrooms

Ingredients: 10 medium-sized tomatoes, 1 lb. mushrooms, 3½ oz. bread-crumbs, 3½ oz. lard, 2 oz. butter, 1 oz. flour, 1 egg, 2 oz. onions, 1 oz. salt, pinch of ground black pepper, 2 oz. grated cheese, 1 small bunch of parsley, 3 portions of tomato sauce, 3 portions of boiled rice.

Wash tomatoes, remove core and seeds and squeeze juice. Place in a buttered pan or tin and put it aside. Fry finely chopped onions in lard until light brown, add finely chopped Champignon mushrooms, season with salt, pepper and finely chopped parsley and simmer. When the liquid is reduced, sprinkle with flour, dilute with a little meat soup or bone stock and bring to boil; thicken it by the addition of an egg. If not thick enough, add some bread-crumbs and mix together well. Sprinkle tomatoes with salt and ground pepper, and stuff with the mushroom filling; sprinkle with grated cheese and bread-crumbs, then besprinkle with melted butter and bake in a hot oven. Place tomatoes on a bed of rice, when serving, and pour tomato sauce around them.

Mushrooms Fried in Bread-crumbs

Ingredients: 1½ lb. mushrooms, 1 tsp. salt, 2 oz. flour, 2 eggs, 5 oz. bread-crumbs, 7½ oz. lard, 1 bunch of parsley, pinch of ground black pepper, 1 pt. tartare sauce.

Take medium-sized Champignon mushrooms, clean and wash them well, and remove stalks. Salt heads, pepper them, then dip in flour, egg and roll in bread-crumbs and fry in hot fat. Place on a bed of rice when serving; garnish with parsley fried in hot fat and serve tartare sauce separately.

Mushroom Heads the Orly Way

Ingredients: 1½ lb. mushrooms, 1 tsp. salt, 5 oz. flour, ²/₅ pt. beer, ³/₅ pt. oil, 2 eggs, 7½ oz. lard, 1 bunch of parsley, pinch of ground black pepper, 1 lb. tomato sauce.

Take neat, medium-sized Champignon mushrooms, clean and wash them well and remove stalks. Salt and pepper mushroom heads, dip in flour and coating batter and fry in hot fat. Serve on a bed of rice, garnish with parsley fried in hot fat and serve tomato sauce separately.

Method for making batter for coating: Prepare thick, pancake-like batter in a basin, from ¼ lb. of flour, ²/₅ pt. beer, ³/₅ pt. oil and 2 egg-yolks, salt and add the stiff beaten whites of two eggs.

Mushroom with Eggs

Ingredients: 14 oz. mushrooms, 3½ oz. lard, 1 oz. onions, pinch of ground black pepper, 15 eggs, 1 small bunch of parsley.

Clean and wash mushrooms and cut them into thin slices, then fry in lard together with finely chopped onions until light brown. Season with salt and pepper, sprinkle with chopped parsley, pour well beaten eggs on top and fry like scrambled eggs, until ready.

RISOTTOS

When preparing dishes from rice, it is important to know how to steam rice, and for how long it should be boiled, etc. Take 11 oz. of rice for five persons. Fry 1½ oz. of chopped onions in a saucepan in 3 oz. of lard, until tender, add rice and heat up well. Then dilute with 1 pt. of hot, white stock, mix well, season with salt and when brought to boil, steam under cover in the oven for 20 mins. Take out of the oven, mix in 2 oz. of butter.

If prepared this way, the grains of the rice do not stick together, but stay apart after cooking.

Risotto with Goose-liver

Ingredients: 11 oz. rice, 1 lb. goose-liver, 7½ oz. mushrooms, 5 oz. tinned green peas, 3½ oz. lard, 2 oz. butter, 2 oz. onions, small tsp. salt, pinch of ground black pepper, 3½ oz. grated cheese, pinch of marjoram, 1 small bunch of parsley.

Cut goose-liver into cubes, slice mushrooms, and fry, together with a small quantity of chopped onions, in lard or butter; then flavour with a little tomato sauce and meat gravy. Mix in rice, prepared as described above, add green peas, season and mix well together, adding grated cheese as well. Press into a buttered basin, then turn out from basin onto a dish, put grated cheese on top and pour tomato sauce or meat gravy around it. Risotto may also be prepared with chicken-liver.

Chicken Risotto

Ingredients: 22 oz. chicken, ½ lb. rice, 4½ oz. lard, 2 oz. butter, 5 oz. onions, pinch of ground black pepper, 2 oz. grated cheese, 1 small bunch of parsley, 7½ oz. mixed vegetables, 1 oz. salt.

Cook chicken in salted water, till tender, remove meat from bones and chop finely. The stock should be used for steaming the rice. Cut mushrooms into slices, and fry lightly with some onions. Prepare rice as described above, then add meat, mushrooms, green peas; season with salt and pepper, and mix in finely chopped parsley and half of the grated cheese.

Press into a buttered basin, then turn out onto a dish, sprinkle top with grated cheese and garnish with tomato or supreme sauce.

Stefania Risotto

Ingredients: 11 oz. rice, 3½ oz. lard, 2 oz. butter, pinch of ground black pepper, 5 eggs, 3½ oz. mushrooms, 3½ oz. tinned green peas, 3½ oz. carrots, 2 oz. celery, 3½ oz. grated cheese, 1 oz. salt, 1½ oz. onions.

Chop all vegetables finely and cook in slightly salted water until tender. Chop mushrooms finely and fry in a small quantity of lard. Cut hard-boiled eggs into rings and add, together with vegetables, mushrooms and green peas, to rice. Add half of the grated cheese as well, sprinkle with finely chopped parsley, season with salt and pepper and mix well. Press into a buttered basin, then turn out onto a dish, sprinkle top with grated cheese and pour tomato sauce around it.

Ham Risotto

Ingredients: 11 oz. ham, 11 oz. rice, 7½ oz. tinned green peas, 5 oz. mushrooms, 3½ oz. lard, 2 oz. butter, 1 tsp. salt, 1 small bunch of parsley, 3½ oz. grated cheese.

Cut mushrooms into slices and fry in lard, add diced ham and green peas and heat well. Mix everything together with the rice, prepared as described above, season with salt and pepper, add chopped parsley and half of the grated cheese, then mix well together. Press into a well buttered basin, then turn out onto a dish, sprinkle top with grated cheese and pour Madeira sauce or meat gravy around it.

Veronese Risotto

Ingredients: 11 oz. salami or Veronese sausage, 11 oz. rice, 7½ oz. mushrooms, 3½ oz. lard, 2 oz. butter, 1 tsp. salt, 3½ oz. grated cheese, pinch of ground black pepper, a little more than a pt. of tomato sauce.

Cut mushrooms into small squares and fry in a small quantity of lard. Mix diced salami or Veronese sausages with mushrooms and heat well together. Add this to cooked rice, add some tomatoes and half of the grated cheese as well, then season with salt and pepper and mix well. Press into a buttered basin, then turn out onto a dish, sprinkle top with grated cheese and pour tomato sauce around it.

Italian Macaroni

Ingredients: 1 lb. macaroni, 3½ oz. butter, 4 oz. grated cheese, small tsp. salt, pinch of ground black pepper.

Boil macaroni in salted water, drain but do not rinse. Put, without rinsing, into a saucepan, salt and break butter into it, add half of the grated cheese, put on lid and shake well together, then dish it; sprinkle with the rest of the grated cheese and serve straight away. Care should be taken not to overcook macaroni or spaghetti.

Milanese Macaroni

Ingredients: 1 lb. macaroni, 1 oz. salt, 2½ oz. butter, 2½ oz. lard, 1 oz. onions, 3½ oz. mushrooms, 5 oz. ham or smoked ox-tongue, 7½ oz. tomato purée, 5 whole black peppers, 1 oz. sugar and 5½ oz. grated cheese.

Cook macaroni in salted water, drain and rinse with cold water. Fry finely chopped onions in lard until light brown, and simmer together with mushrooms sliced finely. Also cut ham or smoked ox-tongue into slices and add, together with tomato purée, to mushrooms; season with salt, pepper and sugar, dilute with soup or gravy and boil well, together with the cooked macaroni. Add half of the grated cheese, mix in butter, breaking it in gradually, and serve hot, sprinkled with the rest of the grated cheese.

Bolognese Macaroni or Spaghetti

Ingredients: 12 oz. macaroni or spaghetti, 3½ oz. butter, 3½ oz. bacon, 14 oz. beef tenderloin fillets, 5 oz. onions, 2 oz. carrots, 2 oz. celery, 2 cloves of garlic, pinch of ground black pepper, 1 oz. salt, 1 oz. tomato purée, ²/₅ pt. brown sauce, 1 small bunch of parsley, 1 bay leaf, 2 blades of thyme, ¹/₅ pt. red wine.

Cook macaroni or spaghetti in salted water, drain and rinse with cold water. Dice bacon finely and fry lightly in half the quantity of butter, then add finely chopped onions, finely diced carrots, celery and crushed garlic; fry them slowly under cover. Add coarsely minced beef, season with salt and pepper, and season with a bouquet of mixed herbs (parsley, bay leaf and thyme). Add tomato purée as well as brown sauce, and dilute with a little stock or water, then boil slowly, together with red wine, reducing well, remove bouquet of mixed herbs. Dip macaroni into hot water in a colander, then drain well; place on the dish, pour mince on top of it, sprinkle with grated cheese and serve hot, placing little dabs of butter on top.

Neapolitan Macaroni

Ingredients: 12 oz. macaroni, 4 oz. butter, 1 oz. salt, ½ lb. onions, 1 lb. fresh tomatoes, pinch of ground black pepper, 1 tsp. sugar, 1 clove of garlic, 5½ oz. grated cheese.

Cook macaroni in salted water and rinse in cold water. Scald tomatoes in hot water, skin them, and cut them in halves: remove seeds, squeeze out juice and cut into squares. Fry finely chopped onions in half the quantity of butter until light brown; add tomatoes, season with salt, pepper and sugar and thicken on open fire. Add boiled macaroni into this sauce, and bring to boil, adding a little soup or gravy. Sprinkle with half the quantity of grated cheese and break in butter gradually, then shake well together. Serve hot, sprinkling top with the rest of the grated cheese.

Macaroni au Gratin

Ingredients: 12 oz. macaroni, 1 pt. milk, 1½ oz. flour, 5½ oz. butter, ⅕ pt. cream, 3 egg-yolks, pinch of nutmeg, 1 tsp. salt, 3½ oz. grated cheese, 1 oz. bread-crumbs.

Make a light roux with 2¼ oz. butter and with the flour, dilute with hot milk and bring to boil. Mix in yolks, season with salt, pepper and grated nutmeg. Cook macaroni in salted water in the meantime, drain and add to sauce, mixing it well together with half the quantity of grated cheese and the cream. Butter fireproof dish well, pour in macaroni, sprinkle top with bread-crumbs and grated cheese, besprinkle with melted butter and bake in hot oven until golden-brown.

Ravioli (Meat Pockets)

Ingredients: 11 oz. flour, 2 eggs, 1 tsp. salt, 5 oz. pork, 5 oz. veal, 3½ oz. calf's brains, 7½ oz. spinach, 2 oz. onions, 3½ oz. butter, 2 eggs, pinch of ground black pepper, pinch of nutmeg, 1 tsp. salt, 5 oz. grated cheese.

Knead a stiff pasta from ½ lb. flour, 2 eggs, ⅓ oz. salt and a little water and roll out until quite thin (as for jam pockets). *Stuffing:* Cook meat, brains and spinach well and cut finely. Chop onions finely and fry in lard until light brown; add mixture, heat well, season with salt, pepper and nutmeg; add half the quantity of the grated cheese and 1 whole egg. When cooled, fill pasta with it. Cut pasta into circles with a fluted pastry cutter (2 inches in size) and put the stuffing in the middle of round pasta forms, placing a small spoonful on each one. Spread pasta with egg, fold them over, so as to make halfmoon shapes, and cook in boiling salted water. When ready, take out of the water, and shake well together with butter and some of the grated cheese, adding salt. Turn out into a fireproof dish, sprinkle top with the rest of the grated cheese and put into a hot oven for a few minutes. Serve tomato sauce or gravy separately.

Pancakes Stuffed with Ham

Ingredients: 14 oz. lean ham, 1 egg-yolk, $^1/_5$ béchamel sauce, $^1/_2$ tsp. red paprika, pinch of ground black pepper, $^1/_5$ pt. sour cream, 2 eggs, 5 oz. bread-crumbs, $7^1/_2$ oz. lard.
For 10 pancakes: 2 eggs, 5 oz. flour, $^3/_5$ pt. milk, $3^1/_2$ oz. lard, a little salt.

Make 10 pancakes from salted batter. Cut ham finely and mix well with béchamel sauce, sour cream, flavour with pepper, red paprika, and with salt, if necessary. Fill pancakes with the stuffing, roll them up, turning in edges, then dip into eggs, dredge in bread-crumbs and fry in hot fat. Tomato or Madeira sauce should be served separately. As an alternative to pancakes, fried in bread-crumbs, they may be prepared without coating; put them in a buttered, fireproof dish, sprinkle with sour cream and melted butter and bake in a hot oven.

Pancakes Stuffed with Mushrooms

Ingredients: 28 oz. mushrooms, 3 oz. butter, 2 oz. onions, 2 egg-yolks, pinch of ground black pepper, 1 tsp. salt, 1 oz. flour, $^2/_5$ pt. milk, 1 small bunch of parsley, 2 eggs, 5 oz. bread-crumbs, $7^1/_2$ oz. lard and 10 pancakes made from salted batter.

Wash mushrooms and cut into small cubes. Fry finelly chopped onions in butter until light brown, add mushrooms and simmer together. When reduced, sprinkle mushrooms with flour, browning a little, then dilute with hot milk and bring to boil. Season with salt, pepper and parsley, and thicken, adding 2 egg-yolks. Fill pancakes with the stuffing described above, fold up the edges; roll them, dip into eggs, and dredge in bread-crumbs; then fry in hot fat. Serve tomato sauce with pancakes, separately.

Pancakes Stuffed with Calf's Brains

Ingredients: 2 calf's brains, 3 oz. butter, 3 oz. onions, 4 eggs, 1 tsp. salt, pinch of ground black pepper, 1 small bunch of parsley, 5 oz. bread-crumbs, $7^1/_2$ oz. lard, 10 pancakes made from salted batter.

Trim and peel off skin from fine, fresh calf's brains, and cut them up finely. Chop onions finely and fry in butter until golden-brown, add brains, flavour with salt, pepper and chopped parsley, then steam. When tender, pour 2 well-beaten eggs on top, to thicken. Fill pancakes with the stuffing described above, fold up edges, roll them, dip into eggs, dredge in bread-crumbs and fry in hot fat. Serve tomato or tartare sauce with pancakes, but in a separate sauceboat.

Pancakes Stuffed with Chicken

Ingredients: 28 oz. chicken, 2 oz. butter, 1 tsp. salt, 3 oz. flour, 2 egg-yolks, pinch of nut-meg, bunch of parsley, pinch of ground black pepper, $1^3/_4$ oz. onions, $5^1/_4$ oz. bread-crumbs, $7^1/_2$ oz. lard, 10 pancakes made from salted batter.

Prepare stuffing with chicken meat. (See: Buttered Paste with Chicken Meat.) Fill pancakes with the mixture, then fold up the edges, dip in eggs, dredge in bread-crumbs and fry in hot fat. Serve tomato or mushroom sauce with it, in separate sauce-boat.

Pancakes Filled with Meat the Hortobágy Way

Ingredients: 1 lb. veal, 3½ oz. lard, 1 pt. sour cream, 1 oz. flour, 7½ oz. onions, 1 tsp. salt, 1 dessertspoon red paprika, 10 pancakes made from salted batter.

Make a stew from the veal, with condiments and finely chopped onions. Take out meat from gravy when tender, and chop finely. Add half of the gravy, 1—2 spoonfuls of sour cream, and simmer until the mixture looks like pasta. Fill pancakes with this stuffing, fold in edges and roll them up, then place in a fireproof dish and heat well in the oven. Thicken sour cream with flour, and dilute with the other half of the gravy, bring to boil and strain. Pour this red paprika sauce over the pancakes and serve them hot.

VEGETABLE DISHES

Asparagus

When preparing asparagus, great care should be taken to prepare them soon after purchase, while quite fresh. The cooking time for asparagus varies between 20 to 30 mins., according to thickness. Must be cooked carefully, because it may lose its pleasant flavour if overcooked. Start cooking asparagus therefore only 30 mins. before serving.

Orly Asparagus

Ingredients: 4 lb. asparagus, 1 tsp. sugar, 1 tsp. salt, pinch of ground black pepper, ½ lemon, 1 tbsp. oil, 7½ oz. lard, 1 pt. tomato sauce.

Cook asparagus and cut off about 2 inches of the stalks. Dry on cloth then marinade with lemon, salt and ground pepper. Dip into batter and fry in hot fat, before serving. Serve tomato sauce with it separately.

Batter: Prepare thick pancake-like batter from ½ lb. flour, ½ tsp. salt, 2 tsp. sugar and 1 tablespoonful of oil, mixing them well with tepid water, and lastly add stiffly beaten white of eggs.

Asparagus with Hollandaise Sauce

Ingredients: 4 lb. asparagus, 1 tsp. sugar, 1 tsp. salt, 1 pt. Hollandaise sauce.

Scrape asparagus, tie them together with string, and boil in hot, salted and sugared water until tender. Drain through a sieve; before serving, remove string and place on a serviette folded over a silver plate. Serve Hollandaise sauce separately.

Asparagus with Buttered Bread-crumbs

Ingredients: 4 lb. asparagus, 1 tsp. salt, 1 dessertspoon sugar, 5 oz. butter, 3½ oz. bread-crumbs.

Cook asparagus, dry on cloth, serve on a plate. Cover asparagus heads with bread-crumbs fried in butter. Buttered bread-crumbs may also be served separately.

Asparagus au Gratin

Ingredients: 4 lb. asparagus, 1 tsp. salt, 1 dessertspoon sugar, 1 tbsp. cream, 1 pt. milk, 5 oz. butter, 2 oz. flour, 4 egg-yolks, 3 oz. grated cheese, 1 oz. bread-crumbs, pinch of nutmeg.

Cook asparagus, dry on cloth and place into a fireproof dish. Make a light roux with 2 oz. butter and 2 oz. flour, dilute with hot milk, whisk until smooth, then bring to boil. Add egg-yolks mixed with cream, take off cooker and break in gradually 1½ oz. of butter, mix well, season with salt and nutmeg. Pour this sauce over the cooked asparagus, sprinkle with cheese and bread-crumbs, besprinkle with melted butter and brown in a hot oven.

Hungarian Asparagus

Ingredients: 4 lb. asparagus, 1 tsp. sugar, 1 oz. salt, 2 egg-yolks, 1 pt. sour cream, 1 tbsp. flour, 2 oz. butter, 1 tbsp. bread-crumbs.

Cook asparagus and dry on cloth. Place into a fireproof dish. Mix sour cream well with salt, sugar, flour and yolks, pour over the asparagus, sprinkle with bread-crumbs, and putting a few dabs of butter on top, brown in the oven.

AUBERGINES

Aubergines Fried in Bread-crumbs

Ingredients: 2 lb. aubergines, 1 tsp. salt, 3½ oz. flour, 2 eggs, 5 oz. bread-crumbs, 11 oz. lard, pinch of ground black pepper, ³/₅ pt. tartare sauce.

Peel aubergines and cut them into slices. Season with salt and pepper, roll in flour, dip into eggs, dredge in bread-crumbs, then fry in hot fat. Serve with tartare sauce in a separate sauceboat.

Stuffed Aubergines

Ingredients: 5 good sized aubergines (about 2 lbs. in all), 3 oz. onions, 1 tsp. salt, 1 tbsp. oil, 11 oz. mushrooms, 7½ oz. rice, 2 eggs, 3½ oz. butter, pinch of ground black pepper, 1 tbsp. bread-crumbs, 2 oz. grated cheese, 1 small bunch of parsley, 1 pt. Madeira sauce.

Cut aubergines in halves, score the inner side and place in an oiled baking tin (with inside down). Bake in a hot oven, when cooked scrape out insides, and chop finely. Place scraped-out halves into a buttered tin. Fry finely chopped onions in butter until light brown, add finely chopped mushrooms, season with salt, pepper and steam well. When mushrooms are tender, mix together with the finely minced inside of aubergines and heat well. Sprinkle with finely chopped parsley, break eggs into the mixture and mix well with 3½ oz. of cooked rice. Fill shells of aubergines with this mixture, sprinkle with grated cheese, bread-crumbs, and besprinkle with melted butter and brown in a hot oven. Place on a bed of rice before serving and pour Madeira sauce around them.

EGG DISHES

ON EGG DISHES IN GENERAL

Egg dishes may be prepared in many ways, with many variations. They are most suitable for entrées, but many varieties may be included in our menus as independent courses. Many dishes have the great advantage of being prepared quickly, almost in a few minutes, and presenting tasty dishes of great nutritive value at the same time.

Eggs spoil quickly and easily and they are susceptible to all sorts of infections, therefore they ought to be prepared with care. Wash the shell of eggs well before breaking, so as to avoid the soiling of the food by impurities sticking to the shells. Break eggs just before use, but if we have to store them for some reason or other, we should keep them on ice, or at least in cold water. If we want to beat the white of egg until foamy, it is advisable to cool the eggs first, because it is easier to beat them up stiffly, when cold. Take great care to separate the whites of eggs to be beaten up properly, because even a small amount of the yolk may prevent the whites from whisking properly.

Casino Eggs

Ingredients: 5 eggs, 1 tsp. salt, 1 tsp. mustard, ½ tsp. anchovy paste, 2 oz. butter, pinch of ground black pepper, 1 tbsp. sour cream, 14 oz. French salad, 1 tsp. chopped chives, 7½ oz. aspic, ½ pt. tartare sauce, 1 roll, small bunch of parsley.

Cut hard-boiled eggs in halves, pass yolks through a sieve, together with the roll, previously soaked in milk. Mix salt, mustard, anchovy paste, butter, pepper, sour cream and finely chopped parsley with it. Beat, until smooth, then fill eggs with this mixture with the help of a forcing bag and nozzle; then place halves or doubles, on a bed of French salad, cover with tartare sauce, sprinkle with finely chopped chives and garnish with diced aspic and lettuce leaves.

Stuffed Eggs with Caviare

May be prepared as for Casino eggs. Place 1 tsp. of caviare on top of each egg. Serve with mayonnaise sauce instead of tartare sauce.

Stuffed Eggs with Anchovies

May be prepared as for Casino eggs, but mix 1 oz. of anchovy paste into the stuffing. Place an anchovy ring on top of each egg. Do not put on a coating of sauce, but serve tartare sauce separately.

Stuffed Eggs with Salmon

May be prepared as for Casino eggs, but decorate eggs with a slice of smoked salmon, instead of caviare. Serve with tartare sauce.

Stuffed Eggs with Goose-liver

Ingredients: 5 eggs, 5 oz. goose-liver, 1 tsp. salt, 2 oz. lard, 2 oz. butter, pinch of ground black pepper, 14 oz. French salad, 2 oz. onions, $1/5$ pt. béchamel sauce, $2/5$ pt. cognac, $4/5$ pt. mayonnaise sauce.

Slice goose-liver, fry together with onions cut into rings, then pass through a sieve, together with egg-yolks, and mix well with butter and béchamel sauce until smooth. Flavour with salt, pepper and cognac, then fill eggs with the help of a forcing bag and nozzle. Place on a bed of French salad and serve with mayonnaise sauce.

Stuffed Eggs with Fillets of Herrings

Ingredients: the same as for Casino eggs, and 5 fillets of herrings in addition.

May be prepared as for Casino eggs, but eggs should be decorated with fillets of herrings, and placed on a bed of herring salad instead of French salad.

Stuffed Eggs with Crayfish

To be prepared as for Casino eggs. Place 2 crayfish tails on top of each egg: Serve with $4/5$ pt. of mayonnaise sauce instead of tartare sauce.

Stuffed Eggs with Asparagus

To be prepared as for Casino eggs. Garnish with 1 lb. of tinned asparagus. Decorate each egg with asparagus heads, and serve with $4/5$ pt. of mayonnaise sauce.

Poached Eggs

Put $1/5$ pt. of vinegar and a little salt into 2 pt. of water. Break the raw eggs into the boiling water, boil for 3 mins. until whites are hard, but yolks remain soft. Lift out with a ladle and dip into cold water to set; dry on a clean cloth, before serving.

Jellied Eggs à la Munkácsy

Ingredients: 10 eggs, ½ lb. boiled, boneless fish, 4 oz. mushrooms, ½ lb. celery, ½ lb. tomatoes, ½ pt. Rémoulade sauce, salt, pepper, 2½ pts. fish jelly, 1 small bunch of tarragon leaves, ¹/₅ pt. vinegar.

Prepare salad from finely chopped boiled fish, mushrooms, celery, tomatoes, together with Rémoulade sauce, and mix in some melted jelly. Poach 10 eggs and place into flat tin moulds filled with jelly, previously garnished with tarragon leaves. Dip moulds into hot water, turn out and serve with fish salad arranged in cone form. Fill gaps between eggs with finely chopped jelly. Garnish with diced jelly and lettuce leaves.

Jellied Eggs in Cups

Ingredients: 10 poached eggs, 11 oz. French salad or 7½ oz. boiled ham, 1 pt. meat aspic, 1 small bunch of tarragon leaves, ¹/₅ pt. vinegar.

Put French salad or slices of ham at the bottom of small cups, and place already poached and cooled eggs on top. Garnish with blanched tarragon leaves and pour melted jelly over them. Put on ice.

Astoria Eggs Poached

Ingredients: 10 eggs, 10 crayfish, ¹/₅ pt. vinegar, pinch of caraway seeds, 1½ lb. fillets of jack salmon, ½ tsp. salt, 3½ oz. lard, 2 oz. bread-crumbs, 5 portions of béarnaise sauce, 20 crayfish tails.

Poach 10 eggs. Cook crayfish in salted water with caraway seeds, and afterwards remove flesh. Form 10 round or oval slices from fillets of jack salmon, salt them, roll in bread-crumbs and fry in hot fat. Place hot eggs on top of fried fish slices. Pour béarnaise sauce over them, and garnish each egg with 2 crayfish tails.

Poached Eggs with Béarnaise Sauce

Ingredients: 10 eggs, 2 oz. butter, ¹/₅ pt. vinegar, 1 small bunch of tarragon leaves, 5 rolls, 5 portions of béarnaise sauce.

Poach 10 eggs. Place warm eggs on slices of rolls, fried in butter, pour béarnaise sauce over them and garnish with blanched tarragon leaves.

Poached Eggs de Bruxelles

Ingredients: 10 eggs, ¹/₅ pt. vinegar, 1 oz. salt, 2 oz. butter, 14 oz. Brussels sprouts, pinch of ground black pepper, 2 oz. grated cheese, 1 oz. bread-crumbs, 5 portions of Mornay sauce.

Poach 10 eggs. Clean Brussels sprouts and wash them well in cold water, then boil in salted water, until tender, rinse with cold water and drain. Heat

2 oz. butter in a frying pan, add Brussels sprouts, drained and squeezed well first, season with salt and pepper. When Brussels sprouts are already hot, place in a fireproof dish and place hot eggs on this foundation. Pour over Mornay sauce, sprinkle with grated cheese and bread-crumbs, besprinkle with a little melted butter and brown quickly in a hot oven.

Turkish Poached Eggs

Ingredients: 10 eggs, 1½ tsp. salt, ¹/₅ pt. vinegar, 3½ oz. liver (poultry), 3½ oz. mushrooms, 3½ oz. butter, 2 oz. lard, 5 rolls, pinch of ground black pepper, ½ lb. rice, 1 small bunch of parsley, 5 portions of tomato sauce.

Poach 10 eggs. Cut liver into small squares and mushrooms into thin slices and fry in butter until brown. Cook rice in butter and a little salt water, add fried liver and mushrooms, season with salt and pepper. Pour risotto into a buttered cone mould for 5 persons, then turn out onto a plate; place slices of rolls fried in lard around it, place hot eggs on top and pour tomato sauce over them. Sprinkle a little chopped parsley on top of each egg.

Poached Eggs with Minced Chicken

Ingredients: 10 eggs, ¹/₅ pt. vinegar, 1½ tsp. salt, 22 oz. chicken, 5¼ oz. puff pastry, 5 portions of supreme sauce, 2 oz. butter, 5 oz. mixed vegetables, 2 oz. onions, pinch of ground black pepper, 1 small bunch of parsley.

Cook chicken with vegetables and onions. Prepare filling from the meat of the boiled chicken, as for omelettes. Poach 10 eggs, bake 10 small basket forms from puff pastry, fill with the mince, place hot eggs on top, pour supreme sauce over them and sprinkle with chopped parsley.

Poached Eggs à la Rossini

Ingredients: 10 eggs, 1 tsp. salt, ¹/₅ pt. vinegar, 2 oz. butter, 2 oz. lard, 7½ oz. goose-liver, 3 oz. heads of mushrooms, ⅓ oz. truffles, 5 rolls, 5 portions of Madeira sauce.

Poach 10 eggs. Cut goose-liver into 10 thin slices and fry, together with the heads of mushrooms. Brown slices of rolls in butter, place 1 slice of goose-liver on each slice, add 1 hot egg on top, and cover with a head of mushroom. Pour Madeira sauce over them and garnish with slices of truffles.

Baked Eggs with Asparagus

Ingredients: 10 eggs, 2 oz. butter, 1 tsp. salt, 1 lb. tinned asparagus, 1 small bunch of parsley, 5 portions of supreme sauce.

Butter fireproof dish well and break fresh eggs into it carefully. (Take care to keep the yolks whole.) Salt the whites of eggs slightly, put into the oven and bake for 2—3 mins., remove while still soft. Pour supreme sauce around eggs and garnish with asparagus heads, fried in butter, and sprinkled with chopped parsley.

Eggs Baked with Vienna Sausages

Ingredients: 10 eggs, 2 oz. butter, 2 oz. lard, 1 tsp. salt, ½ lb. Vienna sausages, 2½ portions of tomato sauce.

Skin sausages, cut them in halves and fry both sides in lard. Butter fireproof dish, place sausages into it, break eggs on top, salt whites slightly and bake in the oven for 2—3 mins., removing them while yolks are still soft. Serve, garnished with tomato sauce.

Eggs Baked with Kidneys

Ingredients: 10 eggs, 3½ oz. lard, ½ lb. mutton or lamb kidney, ⅓ oz. salt, ½ pt. red wine sauce.

Garnish eggs baked in a fireproof dish with roasted mutton or lamb kidneys and pour red wine sauce over them.

Opera Baked Eggs

Ingredients: 10 eggs, 2 oz. lard, 3 oz. mushrooms, 5 oz. liver (poultry), 7½ oz. tinned green peas, pinch of ground black pepper, 1 oz. butter, 1 tsp. salt, ½ pt. Madeira sauce.

Fry sliced mushrooms and finely cut chicken-liver in lard, heat green peas in butter. Bake eggs in a fireproof dish and pour Madeira sauce around them. Garnish alternately with chicken-liver, mushrooms and green peas.

Poached Eggs on Veal Rissoles with Mushroom Sauce

Ingredients: 11 eggs, ⅕ pt. vinegar, 1 tsp. salt, 12 oz. veal, 3 oz. butter, ½ lb. mushrooms, 1½ oz. flour, 1 oz. bread-crumbs, 2 oz. lard, 1 roll, ½ pt. cream, ½ pt. milk, ⅓ tsp. ground black pepper, 1 small bunch of parsley, 2 oz. onions.

Poach 10 eggs. Prepare 10 rissoles from veal and bake them. Make a light roux with butter and flour, dilute with milk and cream and cook for half an hour, stirring frequently. Brown finely chopped onions and sliced mushrooms together in a frying pan; add to the sauce, boil for a few more minutes. Mix yolk with a little cream and add to sauce as well. Do not boil sauce any more. Season with salt and pepper, adding parsley and a lump of butter to it. Place hot eggs on top of veal rissoles, pour mushroom sauce over them, and sprinkle with chopped parsley.

Hunter's Poached Eggs

Ingredients: 10 eggs, 1 tsp. salt, ⅕ pt. vinegar, 4 oz. butter, 7½ chicken-liver, 5 oz. mushrooms, ⅘ pt. brown sauce, pinch of ground black pepper, 1 small bunch of parsley, 5 rolls.

Poach 10 eggs. Dice mushrooms and chicken-liver finely. Brown in a frying pan with a little butter, season with salt and pepper, then bring to boil, together with brown sauce, until thick enough. Toast slices of rolls in butter, and place hot eggs on top; pour hunter sauce over them and sprinkle with finely chopped parsley. May be prepared during the hunting season with game purée as well.

Poached Eggs with Asparagus

Ingredients: 10 eggs, 1 tsp. salt, $^1/_5$ pt. vinegar, 2 oz. butter, 1 tsp. sugar, 1 bunch of parsley, ½ lb. tinned asparagus, 5 oz. puff pastry, 5 portions of supreme sauce.

Poach 10 eggs and prepare 10 basket forms of pastry. Cut asparagus into small pieces, heat them in butter and fill baskets with them. Place hot eggs on top and pour supreme sauce over them. Sprinkle a little chopped parsley on top of each egg.

EGG COURSES

Remark: The following dishes may be served as independent courses, counting 3 eggs for each person. If given for entrées, take 2 eggs and $^2/_3$ of the given quantities.

Plain Omelette

Ingredients: 15 eggs, 1 tsp. salt, $^1/_{10}$ pt. cream, 2 oz. lard or 2½ oz. butter.

Break eggs into a deep bowl, add cream, salt and beat well with a fork. Put lard or butter in a frying pan over an open flame. When hot, pour beaten eggs into it. Mix and shake well, until it thickens, then roll up with a fork, fry for one more second, to brown, and turn out. Take care to keep omelette's middle soft, because it may be properly shaped only while soft.

Omelette with Fine Herbs

Ingredients: 15 eggs, 1 tsp. salt, 1 tbsp. cream, 2 oz. lard or 2½ oz. butter, 1 sprig of parsley, 1 small bunch of chives and 1 sprig of tarragon leaves.

Remove stalks of herbs, chop them finely and mix into well beaten eggs, previously salted, and fry as described above.

Omelette with Liver (Poultry)

Ingredients: 15 eggs, 1 tsp. salt, 4 oz. lard, 7½ oz. liver (poultry), pinch of ground black pepper, 1 tbsp. cream, 1 sprig of parsley, $^1/_5$ pt. Madeira sauce, 1 oz. onions.

Cut liver into small cubes, and fry in lard together with onions. Add salt, ground pepper and chopped parsley, mix well with Madeira sauce, and fill omelettes with liver mixture, before rolling up.

Omelette with Green Peas

Ingredients: 15 eggs, 1 tsp. salt, 7½ oz. cooked green peas, 2 oz. lard or 2½ oz. butter, 1 tbsp. cream, 2 bunches of parsley.

Put cooked green peas, together with chopped parsley into the eggs, previously mixed with cream, salted and well beaten and prepare omelettes as usual.

Omelette with Spinach

Ingredients: 15 eggs, 1 tsp. salt, 1 lb. spinach, 1 tbsp. cream, 2 oz. lard, 1 oz. butter, pinch of ground black pepper.

Cook spinach, pass through a sieve, heat up with butter, flavour with salt and ground pepper. Whisk eggs well, together with cream, salt and 1—2 spoonfuls of spinach purée. Make omelette as usual and fill with the rest of the spinach purée.

Omelette with Mushrooms

Ingredients: 15 eggs, 1 tsp. salt, 3 oz. lard, 7½ oz. mushrooms, pinch of ground black pepper, 1 tbsp. cream, 1 sprig of parsley.

Cut Champignon mushrooms into slices, fry in lard, add salt, ground pepper and chopped parsley; pour eggs, beaten and mixed well, over them and make it in the usual way.

Chicken Omelette

Ingredients: 15 eggs, 1 tsp. salt, 4 oz. lard or butter, 22 oz. chicken, 5 oz. mixed vegetables, 2 oz. onions, 2 oz. flour, 2 egg-yolks, 2 tbsp. cream, pinch of ground black pepper, ½ bunch of parsley.

Prepare fricassee of chicken, strain sauce and flavour with yolks and cream whisked together. Remove meat from bones, mince well, mix together with 2—3 spoonfuls of sauce, season with chopped parsley, pepper and salt; fill omelette with this mixture, roll together and turn out onto a dish. Serve with sauce.

Omelette with Asparagus

Ingredients: 15 eggs, 1 tsp. salt, 1 tsp. sugar, 14 oz. tinned asparagus or 2 lb. fresh asparagus, ½ bunch of parsley.

Cut asparagus into smaller pieces, mix together with some supreme sauce, flavour with sugar, chopped parsley and fill omelette with it. Garnish with some asparagus heads before serving.

Omelette with Ham

Ingredients: 15 eggs, 1 tsp. salt, 5 oz. ham, 1 tbsp. cream, 2 oz. lard or 2½ oz. butter.

Put finely chopped ham into hot lard or butter, pour slightly salted, whisked eggs over it and prepare in the usual way.

Omelette with Calf's Brains

Ingredients: 15 eggs, 1 tsp. salt, 11 oz. calf's brains, 3½ oz. lard, 1 oz. onions, pinch of ground black pepper, pinch of marjoram, 1 tbsp. cream, ¼ bunch of parsley.

Clean calf's brains and cut small; then fry, together with finely chopped onions and parsley; season with salt and ground pepper. Prepare omelettes in the usual way and fill with mixture.

Peasant Omelette

Ingredients: 15 eggs, 1 tsp. salt, pinch of ground black pepper, 3 oz. bacon, 14 oz. potatoes, 2 oz. onions, 2 oz. lard.

Cut bacon into small dices and fry them lightly in a frying pan. Take them out of the pan, and fry diced potatoes in bacon fat until golden-brown, add finely chopped onions and when golden in colour, add bacon too. Season with salt and pepper, pour on whisked eggs and prepare as usual.

Portuguese Omelette

Ingredients: 15 eggs, 1 tsp. salt, 2 oz. lard or butter, 1 oz. onions, 1 tsp. sugar, 1 lb. fresh tomatoes, pinch of ground black pepper, 1 tbsp. cream, 1 oz. butter, ½ bunch of parsley.

Skin tomatoes, dice them and fry in butter, together with finely chopped onions. Season with salt and pepper, sprinkle with chopped parsley and fill omelette with it.

Omelette with Potatoes

Ingredients: 15 eggs, 1 tsp. salt, 4 oz. lard or butter, 1 lb. potatoes, 1 tbsp. cream, ½ bunch of parsley.

Fry finely diced potatoes in a frying pan, salt, pepper, sprinkle with chopped parsley, pour on well-beaten eggs, mixed previously with cream and salt, and prepare in the usual way.

Grandmother's Omelette

Ingredients: 15 eggs, 1 tsp. salt, 1 tbsp. cream, 4 oz. lard, 5 oz. white bread, ½ bunch of parsley.

Remove crust of stale white bread or rolls, and cut insides into small squares. Fry in a frying pan in lard, until golden-brown in colour, add chopped parsley, whisk eggs well with cream and salt, and pour mixture over fried bread and prepare in the usual way.

Omelette with Vegetables

Ingredients: 15 eggs, 1 tsp. salt, 1 tbsp. cream, 2 oz. lard or butter, 2 oz. carrots, 2 oz. green peas, 3½ oz. asparagus heads, 2 oz. French beans, $^3/_{10}$ pt. supreme sauce.

Cut vegetables into small dices, cook them in salted water until tender, then mix together with supreme sauce. Prepare omelette in the usual way and fill with the vegetable mixture.

Spanish Omelette

Ingredients: 15 eggs, 1 tsp. salt, 3½ oz. lard or butter, 5 oz. onions, 11 oz. fresh tomatoes, 3 oz. mushrooms, 3½ oz. green paprikas, pinch of ground black pepper, 1 tbsp. cream, ½ bunch of parsley.

Slice mushrooms and fry together with 2 oz. finely chopped onions; add green paprikas cut in rings, as well as skinned and diced tomatoes. Heat everything well, salt and pepper and sprinkle with chopped parsley. Fill omelette with this mixture and place rings of onions, dredged in flour and fried in fat, on top.

Omelette with Cheese

Ingredients: 15 eggs, 1 tsp. salt, 3½ oz. grated cheese, 1 tbsp. cream, 2 oz. lard or butter.

Grate Parmesan or other dry cheese, mix into eggs, whisked previously with cream and salt and prepare in the usual way.

Whipped Eggs with Crayfish

Ingredients: 15 eggs, 1 tsp. salt, 3 oz. butter, 2 tbsp. cream, 25 crayfish, 2 oz. crayfish butter, ½ tsp. caraway seeds, ½ bunch of parsley.

Cook crayfish with caraway seeds and parsley, in salted water, remove meat from claws and tails. Melt crayfish butter, add crayfish meat and keep hot. Prepare whipped eggs in the above way and serve, garnished with crayfish meat in a fireproof or porcelain dish.

Simple Whipped Eggs

Ingredients: 15 eggs, 1 tsp. salt, 2 tbsp. cream.

Break eggs into a dish, add cream and salt and whisk well. Heat butter in an enamel or metal frying pan, pour eggs into it, and fry, stirring constantly, until done but still soft. (Like slightly underdone scrambled eggs.)

Whipped Eggs with Cheese

Ingredients: 15 eggs, 1 tsp. salt, 3 oz. butter, 3½ grated cheese, 2 tbsp. cream.

Mix into ready whipped and cooked eggs half the quantity of the grated cheese, serve, and garnish with the rest of the cheese, piling it around the dish in small heaps.

Whipped Eggs with Ham

Prepare whipped eggs and mix in finely cut ham. Ham may be heated in butter and served with whipped eggs already prepared, placed in the middle or around the eggs.

Whipped Eggs with Asparagus

Ingredients: 15 eggs, 1 tsp. salt, 3½ oz. butter, 2 tbsp. cream, 1 tsp. sugar, 1 lb. tinned asparagus, small bunch of parsley.

Garnish whipped eggs when ready with asparagus heads, warmed previously in butter, seasoned with salt and pepper and sprinkled with chopped parsley.

Whipped Eggs with Chicken-liver

Ingredients: 15 eggs, 1 tsp. salt, 3 oz. butter, 7½ oz. chicken-liver, 1 oz. lard, 1 oz. onions, pinch of marjoram, pinch of ground black pepper, 2 tbsp. cream, $1/_5$ pt. Madeira sauce.

Cut chicken-liver into small cubes and fry together with finely chopped onions in lard. Season whipped eggs when ready and mix well together with Madeira sauce. Garnish eggs with chicken-liver when serving.

Whipped Eggs with Tomatoes

Ingredients: 15 eggs, 1 tsp. salt, 2 tbsp. cream, 1 lb. tomatoes, 4 oz. butter, pinch of ground black pepper, 1 tsp. sugar, ½ bunch of parsley.

Blanch tomatoes in hot water, skin and cut them in halves, remove cores and seeds. Dice tomatoes and fry in butter, season with salt and pepper, adding a little sugar and some chopped parsley. Garnish whipped eggs when ready with small heaps of tomato mixture.

Whipped Eggs with Green Peas

Ingredients: 15 eggs, 1 tsp. salt, 2 oz. butter, 7½ oz. tinned green peas.

Mix warmed green peas into whipped eggs, when ready.

Egg Croquettes

Ingredients: 12 eggs, ³/₅ pt. milk, 2 oz. butter, 1 tsp. salt, pinch of black pepper, 3 oz. flour, 1 pt. tomato sauce.
For coating: 2 oz. flour, 2 eggs, 5 oz. bread-crumbs, 5 oz. lard.

Remove shells of 10 hard-boiled eggs and dice them finely. Make a light roux with butter and flour, dilute with milk, bring to boil, add 2 egg-yolks as well as diced eggs, season with salt and pepper and put to cool in a flat dish. Make 3 croquettes for each person, roll them in flour, dip into egg and dredge in bread-crumbs, then fry in hot fat. Serve with tomato sauce, separately.

Sour Eggs

Ingredients: 10 eggs, 3 oz. lard, 3½ oz. flour, 2 oz. onions, 1 bay leaf, 1 tsp. salt, 1 oz. sugar, 5 whole black peppers, ¹/₅ pt. vinegar, 2 tbsp. sour cream, ½ lemon, 1 oz. mustard.

Make a light caramel with lard and sugar, add flour and brown further, stirring constantly. Continue until roux is quite brown, then add finely chopped onions, dilute with vinegar and water, season with salt, whole black pepper, bay leaf, mustard and lemon peel and bring to boil. Strain sauce into another saucepan, put over the fire, give appropriate sour taste, and when boiling, break the eggs into it. Boil for some time (but take care not to hard-boil eggs), then add sour cream, shake well together and serve hot.

Ham and Eggs

Ingredients: 10 eggs, 2 oz. lard, 14 oz. ham.

Melt lard in a frying pan, heat well and put boiled slices of ham into it. Break eggs over them and fry for 2—3 mins. Remove from frying pan, sliding them onto a dish with the help of a fork, and salt the whites of eggs slightly

Bacon and Eggs

Ingredients: 10 eggs, 14 oz. bacon.

Put slices of bacon into a frying pan and place on the open fire. Brown bacon and turn over on the other side when golden in colour. Remove frying pan from fire and break in eggs. Bake in a hot oven for 2—3 mins. Salt slightly and remove from frying pan with the help of a fork, sliding onto a dish.

Cold Fogas (Pike-perch) ▷
Grilled Fogas

Eggs in Puff Pastry

Ingredients: 10 hard-boiled eggs, 3 oz. butter, 2 tbsp. milk, 1 tsp. salt, 1 oz. mustard, pinch of black pepper, ½ bunch of parsley, 14 oz. puff pastry, 5 portions of Madeira sauce.

Cut off the bottom parts of hard-boiled eggs, and remove yolks, but keep the whites whole. Prepare stuffing in the same way as for Casino eggs, and fill eggs with it. Roll out puff pastry. Cut pastry into 10 even squares, brush with egg and place one stuffed egg onto each square. Cover up eggs with the pastry by pressing the four corners of the pastry together, above the eggs, and covering them over with small coins of pastry. Brush with egg and bake in a hot oven. Serve with Madeira sauce.

Stuffed Eggs au Gratin

Ingredients: 5 eggs, 1 roll, pinch of ground black pepper, 1 tbsp. sour cream, ½ bunch of parsley, 1 tsp. salt.
For milk sauce: 2 oz. butter, 2 oz. flour, 1 pt. milk, 2 egg-yolks, $^1/_{10}$ pt. sour cream, 2 oz. grated cheese, 1 oz. bread-crumbs, 1 tsp. salt and 1½ oz. butter.

Remove shells of 5 hard-boiled eggs, cut them in halves and pass yolks through a sieve, together with a roll, previously soaked in milk. Mix in butter, salt, pepper, sour cream and finely chopped parsley, beat well, until smooth, and fill halves of eggs with this stuffing.

Make a light roux with 2 oz. butter and flour, dilute with warm milk and bring to boil. Take off the fire, mix in 2 egg-yolks, salt, cream and half the quantity of grated cheese. Butter fireproof dish, put some sauce at the bottom, then place eggs into it and cover with the rest of the sauce. Sprinkle with the rest of the grated cheese, besprinkle with melted butter and brown in a warm oven.

FISH DISHES AND DISHES PREPARED FROM CRAYFISH AND FROGS

There are two big groups of fish: saltwater and freshwater fish. Freshwater fish are those caught in rivers or lakes. Hungary is situated far from the sea, and in consequence Hungarian cooking must be content with freshwater fish. But as already mentioned in the foreword, there are two kinds amongst them that may please even the most discerning palate. These are the sterlet, a river fish, and the excellent fish of Lake Balaton, the pike-perch *(fogas)*.

The *sterlet* (Acipenser ruthenus) is a smaller kind of sturgeon, found in our country in the southern regions of the Danube and the Tisza. It has no scales, its bones are gristle-like, and instead of the backbone it has a notochord. These are properties which render the sterlet especially suitable for cooking purposes.

The *pike-perch* (Lucioperca sandra var. Fogas Balatonicus) is a variety of the sandres, which inhabit European fresh waters, living exclusively in Lake Balaton. Full-grown specimens weigh as much as 24—34 lb. Its flesh is boneless, white and very tasty. Young specimens, 1—4 lb. in weight, are also known as jack salmons. They are served either cold or hot, prepared in the most various ways.

The preparation of fish for cooking purposes requires much attention. Live fish should be killed with a blow on the head, then cleaned with a knife, scraping from tail towards head and thus removing scales. Remove the entrails by cutting the whole length of the belly from vent to head, taking care not to cut into the gall.

Fish dishes figuring most frequently in our menus may be divided in two groups; cold and hot fish dishes.

Cold fish can be prepared in various ways, not only because of variations in size, but quality as well. The most popular cold fish dishes in our country may be prepared from the pike-perch of Lake Balaton, the sheat-fish and the sterlet.

Hot fish can also be prepared in many ways. One of the best fish dishes, well-known abroad, is Szeged chowder ("Szegedi halászlé").

We must be very careful when buying fish. It cannot be too fresh, because whereas meat may be kept at a temperature of 39 or 41° F in fresh condition for days, fish may spoil in unfavourable circumstances within 12—24 hours.

The gills of the fish should be lively red in colour and not slimy to the touch, the bulging eyes should be clear, with transparent cornea, the flesh firm and resilient to the touch, without any smell and the body should sink if put into water.

If the fish is stale, its gills are yellowish grey in colour, and the inner sides of gills have a bad odour, the eyes are lack-lustre, discoloured, rimmed with red, the flesh is flabby to the touch, not resilient, and it does not sink in water, but floats on the surface. Such fish must not be used for human consumption.

COLD FISH

Cold fish are generally boiled or soused, then cooled and served. They may be served whole, with head and tail on the dish as well, but we can fillet fish by removing the flesh from the backbone. The fish may be served in the skin but we can remove the skin, if necessary, and truss it neatly with string. Neat, nice-looking fish are generally served whole (sterlet, tunny-fish), mostly for the purposes of cold buffets. Otherwise cutting fish into pieces is more practical from the point of view of serving, because in this way the bones may be removed more easily.

Fish mayonnaise and fish salad may be prepared from mixed fish. The flesh for this purpose can be detached from the head and from those parts which are not suitable for slicing or filleting. We can also use fish such as pike, barbel and tench which is tasty, but very bony and therefore cheap and less popular, and, which should be cleaned very carefully.

The flesh of pike-perch and jack salmon is most suitable for cold fish dishes. The fish meant for cold plates and fillets, should be rather big in size. Remove flesh from the backbone, remove all the bones as well, truss neatly and in the meantime make a stock, from the parts left after filleting (head, backbone); cook fillets in this stock. When cooked, cool, then place on ice, and clarify stock intended for jelly. The flesh of sheat-fish is also tasty if served cold, and is very popular because of its fine white colour. Tunny-fish and sturgeon should also be cleaned and dressed in the way just described; remove flesh from the backbone, truss up with string, and cook in stock, prepared from bony parts. Their flesh is not quite as white as that of the sheat fish, being a little yellowish or pinkish in parts, but they have a fine flavour, and these fish are generally regarded as delicacies.

Trouts, blanched, to retain blue colour and served cold, are rather tasty; salmons, belonging to the same species, may be prepared in the same way. All fish are very pleasing to the eye when served in a cold buffet together with the pink-fleshed salmon, either whole or in fillets.

Cold Fogas (Pike-perch)

Ingredients: 3 lb. pike-perches (whole), 5 oz. mixed vegetables, 1 oz. onions, pinch of whole black pepper, ½ bay leaf, 1 tsp. salt, ¹/₅ pt. vinegar, 5 portions of French salad, ½ lb. aspic, 2 hard-boiled eggs, 1 pt. tartare sauce.

Always cook fish 1—2 days before serving, and put on ice; it can be sliced more neatly when chilled well. Remove scales of the fogas, wash well, then remove the entrails, cutting the whole length of the belly from vent to head. Cut off head and, using a sharp knife, cut down the centre to the backbone; starting from bone remove flesh all the way, to obtain two fillets. Wash, salt and neatly tie fillets with a string. Put vegetables and onions cut into rings, together with salt and vinegar into water, add bay leaf and a few grains of pepper. Place two fillets of fogas into the water, and bring to boil quickly, pull off the fire and boil slowly for 5—6 mins. Take off the fireplace, cool, and afterwards put on ice. Cut into slices, when chilled, and serve on fish plate, on a bed of French salad; garnish with finely diced aspic and quarter eggs. Serve tartare sauce with it. Can also be served with caviare, crayfish, smoked salmon, etc.

Cold Sheat-fish or Sturgeon

Ingredients: 2 lb. sheat-fish or boned sturgeons, 5 oz. mixed vegetables, 1 oz. onions, ¹/₅ pt. vinegar, 5 whole black peppers, ½ bay leaf, 1 dessertspoon salt, ½ lb. French salad, 2 hard-boiled eggs, ½ pt. tartare sauce.

Truss sheat-fish or sturgeon neatly with a string, and salt. Place into a saucepan, add vegetables and onions cut into rings, and season with pepper and bay leaf: add water, flavour with salt and vinegar, and bring to boil, then cook on a low flame for 15—20 mins. Take off the fireplace, and when cooled, place on ice. Further prepare and serve as for cold fogas.

Cold Sterlet

Ingredients: 3 lb. sterlets, 1 tsp. salt, 5 oz. mixed vegetables, 1 oz. onions, 5 whole black peppers, ½ bay leaf, ¹/₅ pt. vinegar, ½ lb. aspic, 5 portions of French salad, 5 portions of tartare sauce, 2 hard-boiled eggs, 2 oz. butter, ½ bunch of tarragon leaves.

Remove the entrails by cutting the whole length of the belly from vent to head: pull out the fins in the back as well. Cut vegetables and onions into thin slices and rings, put into salted water with vinegar, add pepper, and bay leaf, and bring to boil. Place sterlets into the water and boil slowly for 10—12 mins. Then take off the fireplace, and when cool, put on ice. Skin sterlets before serving, with a small knife, then fill them with French salad. Place on a plate, then decorate the backs with the help of a forcing tube and nozzle with the yolks of hard-boiled eggs, mixed with butter, and sides with blanched tarragon leaves. Garnish with diced aspic and hard-boiled eggs. Serve tartare or green sauce with sterlets.

Tihany Jack Salmon Fillets

Ingredients: 2 jack salmons, about 11 oz. each, ½ lb. mayonnaise sauce, 1 sheet of gelatine, 12 oz. fish jelly, ½ lb. French salad, 3 hard-boiled eggs, 1 oz. smoked salmon, 1 dessertspoon salt, some tarragon leaves, ½ pt. green or tartare sauce.

Remove entrails of jack salmons, cut off heads, and remove fillets from the backbones, skin fish. Remove all the bones, fold back the tail ends and pat them lightly, to form triangles. Make stock from fish heads and backbones. Salt fish slices, place in a baking tin, pour fish stock over them and cook, then take off the fire and cool. Place slices on a rack when cooled. Dissolve gelatine in some fish stock; mix together with mayonnaise sauce and glaze fish slices with it. Decorate with thin slices of smoked salmon and blanched green aspic and hard-boiled eggs cut in four. Serve green or tartare sauce with fish.

Jellied Carp

Ingredients: 4 lb. carp, 1 tsp. salt, 7½ oz. onions, 3½ oz. green paprikas, 1 tsp. tomato purée, ½ tsp. red paprika, whites of 2 eggs, 3 hard-boiled eggs, 1 dessertspoon gelatine, 7½ oz. fresh tomatoes.

Clean carp, remove entrails, wash, cut off the head, then remove the flesh from backbone; cut fillets into neat pieces and salt them. Put head, backbone, the roe or milt of the carp, together with onions cut into rings, salt and paprika into a saucepan: dilute with 2⅓ pt. of water and cook for ½ hr. Add green paprika and tomatoes when in season. Place fillets of carp in a deep saucepan, strain fish stock over them and cook until tender, then put aside and when somewhat cooled, take out fish and remove all bones, if possible, then place on a plate. Garnish with hard-boiled eggs, green paprika, fish roe and milt. Clear fish stock by adding to it the whites of two eggs beaten well together with tomato purée and a little water. Add gelatine and, after a few minutes boiling, strain through cloth, and when somewhat cooled, pour over the fillets and put to cool.

HOT FISH

Boiled Fogas (Pike-perch)

Ingredients: 3½ lb. fogas (pike-perch), 1 tsp. salt, 7½ oz. vegetables, 1 bay leaf, 2 oz. onions, 5 whole black peppers, 5 oz. horse-radish, 1½ lemon, 1 tbsp. vinegar.

Clean fogas and remove entrails; cut off two fillets from the backbone, skin and wash well. Cut cleaned fogas into pieces, salt, slice mixed vegetables finely, and cut onions into thin rings. Put some water into a saucepan to boil, salt and add vegetables, bay leaf, onions, whole black pepper, and vinegar and cook until tender. When vegetables are tender, add fogas pieces, cover and cook. Arrange sliced vegetables on top of fogas when serving, place boiled salted potatoes around fish and sprinkle with chopped parsley. Cut lemons into rings, place small heaps of horse-radish on top, and decorate, i. e. garnish fish plate with them.

Fogas in Butter

Ingredients: 3½ lb. fogas, 1 dessertspoon salt, 5 oz. butter.

May be prepared as for Boiled Fogas. Cook 2 fillets in salted water. When soft, place on a plate, pour hot butter over fish and garnish with salted, boiled potatoes.

Fogas with Hollandaise Sauce

Ingredients: 3½ lb. fogas, 1 tsp. salt, 1 oz. butter, 1 bunch of parsley, 5 portions of Hollandaise sauce.

May be prepared as for Boiled Fogas. Cook 2 fillets in salted water. When cooked, place on a plate, garnish with potatoes prepared with butter, and add Hollandaise sauce separately.

Fogas with White Wine Sauce

Ingredients: 3½ lb. fogas, 1 tsp. salt, 3½ oz. mushroom heads, 1 oz. butter, 1 tbsp. white wine, 5 portions of white wine sauce, 1 bunch of parsley.

Remove fogas fillets from backbone, clean, slice and salt them. Place in a buttered baking tin, add mushroom-heads, pour white wine on them, together with the same quantity of fish stock—made from the fish head and backbone—cover with greased paper, bring to boil and steam in the oven until tender. Place fogas, when cooked, on a plate and put mushroom heads on top. Reduce the juice of fish and mix into the white wine sauce. Pour sauce over the fish and sprinkle mushroom-heads with chopped parsley. Garnish with potatoes in butter.

Fogas à la Meunière

Ingredients: 3½ lb. fogas, 1 tsp. salt, 1 tbsp. flour, 3½ oz. lard, 5 oz. butter, pinch of ground black pepper, 2½ lemons, 1 bunch of parsley.

May be prepared as for Boiled Fogas. Salt fillets, sprinkle with ground black pepper, roll in flour and fry both sides in hot fat in a frying pan until slightly brown in colour. Place fried fish on a plate, decorated with lemon slices, besprinkle with lemon-juice, sprinkle with finely chopped parsley and keep hot. Heat and brown butter in a frying pan and pour over fish when frothy, then serve, together with salted boiled potatoes.

Fogas with Spinach

Ingredients: 3 lb. fogas, 1 tsp. salt, ½ oz. onions, 3 oz. butter, $^3/_{10}$ pt. white wine, pinch of ground black pepper, 1 lb. spinach, 2 oz. grated cheese, 5 portions of Mornay sauce.

Slice and salt cleaned fogas, then place into a buttered baking tin, pour white wine over fish, together with the same quantity of fish stock (prepared from the head and backbone of the fish) and chopped onions, and cover with greased paper, bring to boil and put into the oven to cook, until tender. Remove stalks from spinach in the meantime, clean and wash well and cook in salted water, then rinse with cold water, when cooked. Heat 2 oz. of butter, add spinach leaves squeezed well, salt and pepper and place in a fireproof dish. Drain fish stock and reduce. Mix together with Mornay sauce. Place cooked fish slices on spinach, pour over sauce, sprinkle with grated cheese, and brown in a hot oven.

Mornay Fogas

Ingredients: 3 lb. fogas, 1 dessertspoon salt, 3 oz. butter, $^1/_5$ pt. white wine, 1 lb. potatoes; 1 whole egg, 1 egg-yolk, 1½ oz. grated cheese, pinch of nutmeg, 5 portions of Mornay sauce.

Clean and slice fogas. Salt and place into a buttered baking tin, pour white wine over, and dilute with the same quantity of fish stock. Cover with greased paper and bring to boil, then put into the oven to steam. When fish is cooked, place on a plate or a fireproof dish. Drain liquid and mix into Mornay sauce. Pour this sauce over the fish, sprinkle with grated cheese, and decorate with Duchesse potatoes forced through a forcing bag with star-shaped nozzle; then brown in a hot oven.

Duchesse potatoes: Peel 1 lb. of potatoes and cut into pieces, cook in salted water, drain and pass through a sieve. Add 2 oz. butter, 1 whole egg, 1 egg-yolk, salt, grate nutmeg into it and beat well together.

Bakony Fogas

Ingredients: 3 lb. fogas, 1 tsp. salt, 3½ oz. onions, ½ tsp. red paprika, ½ lb. mushrooms, 3 oz flour, ½ pt. sour cream, 1 small bunch of parsley

Cut up the belly of the fogas and remove entrails, cut off the head, and remove 2 fillets from backbone. Skin with a knife and wash well. Slice, salt and place in a buttered baking tin. Cook head and backbone in a small quantity of water. Brown finely chopped onions in butter, add sliced mushrooms, continue browning, then sprinkle with red paprika, dilute with fish stock and with sour cream, mixed together with flour, bring to boil and salt slightly. Pour this mushroom sauce over fogas slices and cook in the oven until tender. Sprinkle with chopped parsley before serving and garnish with green paprikas cut into rings. Serve with noodles or potatoes in butter.

Jean Bart Fogas

Ingredients: 3 lb. fogas, 1 tsp. salt, 2 oz. butter, pinch of ground black pepper, $^1/_5$ pt. white wine, 1 oz. onions, 1 tbsp. grated cheese, $7\frac{1}{2}$ oz. mushrooms, 1 bunch of parsley, 1 dessert-spoon bread-crumbs, $^3/_5$ pt. white wine sauce.

Remove flesh of cleaned fogas from the backbone, slice, salt and place into a buttered baking tin. Sprinkle with finely chopped onions, sliced mushrooms, chopped parsley and ground black pepper. Pour white wine over fish, and the same quantity of fish stock. Cover with buttered white paper, bring to boil, and steam in the oven until tender.

Place fish on a plate or a fireproof dish. Reduce the remaining liquid a little, and add to white wine sauce. Pour sauce over fish, sprinkle top with grated cheese, bread-crumbs, besprinkle with melted butter and brown in a hot oven. Serve with potatoes in butter.

Russian Slices of Fogas

Ingredients: 3 lb. fogas, 1 tsp. salt, 2 oz. flour, 5 oz. mixed vegetables, $^1/_5$ pt. white wine, $3\frac{1}{2}$ oz. butter, $^2/_5$ pt. cream, 2 oz. onions, pinch of ground black pepper, 1 bunch of parsley, $\frac{1}{2}$ lemon.

Cut up the belly of fogas, remove entrails, and cut off 2 fillets from backbone, then skin, wash well, salt and place into a buttered baking tin. Peel carrots and turnips with a fluted vegetable knife and cut them, together with onions, into thin rings; then salt slightly and adding a lump of butter, simmer, in a small quantity of water. Put cooked vegetables over fish fillets, pour white wine on top, together with the same quantity of fish stock, bring to boil covered up with greased paper, then steam in the oven until tender. Place cooked fillets onto a plate; reduce liquid somewhat, add cream, thicken with mixed flour and butter and bring to boil once more. Season with salt, ground black pepper and with the juice of $\frac{1}{2}$ lemon. Pour this sauce over fish and sprinkle with coarsely chopped parsley. Serve with potatoes in butter.

Portugese Fogas

Ingredients: 3 lb. fogas, 1 tsp. salt, 1 oz. onions, $^1/_5$ pt. white wine, pinch of ground black pepper, 1 tsp. sugar, $3\frac{1}{2}$ oz. butter, 1 lb. fresh tomatoes, $^2/_5$ pt. brown sauce, 1 bunch of parsley.

Clean fogas and remove flesh from the backbone, slice, salt and place into a buttered baking tin. Boil backbone and head with a small quantity of water. Add white wine to sliced fish and the same quantity of fish stock; cover with greased paper and steam in the oven. Blanch and skin tomatoes, and dice finely; put into half the quantity of butter, together with finely chopped onions and simmer until reduced. Add brown sauce, flavour with salt, pepper, chopped parsley and sugar and bring to boil. Take off the fire and mix in the rest of the butter and the fish stock, reduced. Place fish onto a plate and pour sauce over it. Serve with potatoes in butter.

Duglère's Fogas

Ingredients: 3 lb. fogas, 1 tsp. salt, 1 oz. onions, 1 tbsp. flour, 1 tsp. sugar, pinch of ground black pepper, 2 tbsp. white wine, 1 lb. fresh tomatoes, 3½ oz. butter, 1 bunch of parsley, 2 egg-yolks, 2 tbsp. cream.

Clean fogas and remove flesh from backbone; slice, wash, salt and place into a buttered baking tin. Sprinkle with finely chopped onions, peeled and diced tomatoes, ground pepper and parsley. Pour white wine over fish, cover with greased paper and bring to boil, then steam in the oven until tender. Reduce juice of the fish in a separate saucepan; mix half the quantity of butter mixed with the flour into this, and boil for a short time, then add yolks mixed well with cream. Take off the fire, break in the rest of the butter gradually, flavour, and pour over the fish, placed on a plate. Serve with potatoes in butter.

Good Woman's Fogas

Ingredients: 2 lb. fogas, boneless, 1 tsp. salt, 1 oz. onions, pinch of ground black pepper, 2 oz. flour, 2 tbsp. white wine, 7½ oz. mushrooms, 2 tbsp. cream, 3½ oz. butter, 1 small bunch of parsley.

Cut up the belly of the fogas, remove entrails, cut the head off, and remove 2 fillets from backbone. Skin with a knife, wash meat and cut into 10 slices. Place fogas fillets, salted, into a buttered saucepan, pour white wine over them, together with the same quantity of fish stock, made from fish head and backbone. Sprinkle with sliced mushrooms, finely chopped onions, parsley and ground black pepper. Cover saucepan with buttered paper, bring to boil and steam in the oven. When cooked, strain off the juice of the fish into a separate saucepan, bring to boil together with the cream. Mix a small lump of butter with flour, add to this sauce, whisk well and boil for a few minutes; then take off the fire and mix in the rest of the butter. Place fogas fillets onto a plate, pour sauce over them and serve with potatoes in butter.

Fogas with Crayfish Sauce

Ingredients: 3 lb. fogas, 1 dessertspoon salt, 1 oz. butter, 3½ oz. mushroom heads, ⅕ pt. white wine, 1 oz. crayfish butter, 1 pt. crayfish sauce, 20 crayfish, ⅓ oz. truffles, 1 tsp. caraway seeds, 1 bunch of parsley.

Cook crayfish in salted water with caraway seeds, remove flesh from claws and tails. Clean fogas fillets, slice and salt them, then place into a buttered baking tin. Add white wine and the same quantity of fish stock, cover up with greased paper, bring to boil and steam in the oven. Place fish onto a plate when cooked, put mushroom heads braised in butter on top and add crayfish flesh heated in crayfish butter. Mix fish stock—in which the fillets were steamed—into the sauce and boil together. Pour this sauce over the fish, besprinkle with crayfish butter and decorate with slices of truffles. Serve with potatoes in butter. (May be prepared without truffles as well.)

Fogas with Paprika

Ingredients: 3 lb. fogas, 1 tsp. salt, 3½ oz. onions, 3½ oz. lard, 1 tsp. red paprika, 1 oz. flour, ⅕ pt. cream, ⅖ oz. sour cream, 3½ oz. green paprika, 1 oz. butter.

Cut off the head of the cleaned fogas and remove fillets from backbone; skin, wash and salt. Place fillets into a buttered baking tin and steam, covered with greased paper. Lightly brown finely chopped onions in lard, add red paprika, dilute with ⅗ or ⅘ pt. of water, and salt. Add head, backbone and boil for about ½ hr., then remove head and backbone from liquid, pour in sour cream mixed with flour, bring to boil again, and lastly, add cream and pass through a sieve. Place fish onto a plate; pour paprika sauce over and decorate with green paprika cut into rings. Serve with noodles or potatoes.

Keszthely Jack Salmon

Ingredients: 5 jack salmons about 11 oz. in weight each, 1 dessertspoon salt, 5 oz. lard, 2 lb. boiled potatoes, ⅗ pt. cream, 1 tsp. red paprika, 1 bunch of parsley.

Remove scales from jack salmons, cut them up, remove entrails and gills, then wash well. Score skin with knife, salt, rub well with red paprika, place into a well buttered baking tin and put into a hot oven. When partly baked, put boiled potatoes cut into rings into the baking tin and cook until ready. Afterwards pour cream on top and boil for a few mins. Place baked potatoes on the plate first, when serving, put jack salmons on top, pour juice over them and sprinkle with chopped parsley.

Parisian Fogas

Ingredients: 3 lb. fogas, 1 tsp. salt, 2 oz. flour, 3 eggs, 1¼ lemon, 7½ oz. lard, ½ pt. tartare sauce.

Clean fogas, and remove fillets from backbone; slice, salt, roll in flour, dip in whipped eggs and fry in hot fat. Garnish with lemons cut in four, when serving. Serve with tartare sauce and potatoes in butter.

Grilled Fogas

Ingredients: 3 lb. 11 oz. fogas, 1 tsp. salt, 2 oz. bread-crumbs, 3½ oz. lard, ½ pt. tartare sauce, 2½ lemons.

Prepare fogas as for Boiled Fogas, cut in flesh slightly, salt and fry both sides dredged in bread-crumbs until golden-brown. Garnish with potatoes prepared in butter and lemons cut in quarters when serving. Serve tartare sauce separately.

Balaton Grilled Jack Salmon

Ingredients: 5 jack salmons about 11 oz. each, 1 tsp. salt, 5 oz. bread-crumbs, 7½ oz. lard, ½ pt. tartare sauce, 1¼ lemons.

Remove scales from jack salmons, cut them up, remove entrails and gills; then wash, dry and score both sides with a sharp knife. Salt, roll in bread-crumbs and fry both sides in hot lard until golden brown. Garnish with lemons cut in quarters. Serve tartare sauce and baked potatoes with jack salmons.

Carpathian Sterlet

Ingredients: 2½ lb. sterlets, 20 crayfish, 1 dessertspoon salt, pinch of ground black pepper, 3½ oz. butter, 1½ oz. flour, $^2/_5$ pt. cream, $^3/_5$ pt. soup, 5 oz. mushrooms, 1 oz. crayfish butter, ½ tsp. caraway seeds, 1 small bunch of fresh dill.

Clean and cut up sterlets, remove entrails, and pull out fins from the back. Blanch with hot water, skin with a knife, wash and salt. Place in buttered baking tin and stew in the oven, basting frequently. Cook crayfish in salted water with caraway seeds and remove flesh from claws and tails. Cut mushrooms into thin slices and fry in butter; make a light roux with 2 oz. butter and flour, dilute with hot crayfish stock and cream, and bring to boil. Flavour with salt, pepper, and finely chopped fresh dill. Put in the flesh of crayfish, mushrooms, and if sauce is too thick, thin it with a little cream or stock, pour over the cooked sterlets and bring to boil together. Besprinkle with melted crayfish butter before serving and garnish with potatoes in butter. (Fogas or jack salmon fillets may also be prepared in the above way.)

Sterlets in Red Wine

Ingredients: 1 sterlet about 3 lb. in weight (or 5 sterlets about 11 oz. each), 1 tsp. salt, 3½ oz. mushrooms, 3½ oz. butter, $^3/_{10}$ pt. red wine, $^4/_5$ pt. brown sauce, 2 oz. onions.

Clean and dress sterlets (see: Carpathian Sterlet), then follow instructions given for the preparation of carps in red wine.

Boiled Sterlet

Ingredients: 1 sterlet about 3 lb. in weight (or 5 sterlets 11 oz. each), 1 tsp. salt, 7½ oz. mixed vegetables, 1 oz. onions, 1 bay leaf, 5 whole black peppers, 5 oz. horse-radish, 2 lemons.

Clean sterlets, as described above, and prepare, according to method quoted for Boiled Carp.

Hungarian Sterlet

Ingredients: 1 sterlet about 3 lb. in weight (or 5 sterlets 11 oz. each), 3 oz. lard, $^4/_5$ pt. sour cream, 1 tbsp. flour, $\frac{1}{2}$ tsp. red paprika, $3\frac{1}{2}$ oz. onions, 1 tsp. salt, $7\frac{1}{2}$ oz. green paprika.

Clean and wash sterlets and place into a baking tin. Fry finely chopped onions in lard, sprinkle with red paprika, dilute with a small quantity of water, bring to boil, salt, pour over sterlets and steam in the oven until tender. When cooked, pour sour cream mixed with flour on top and boil for a few more mins. Place green paprikas cut in rings on sterlets when serving. Serve with noodles.

Sheat-fish Slices Fried in Bead-crumbs

Ingredients: 2 lb. boneless sheat-fish, 1 tsp. salt, 2 oz. flour, 2 eggs, 5 oz. bread-crumbs, $7\frac{1}{2}$ oz. lard, $\frac{1}{2}$ pt. tartare sauce, $1\frac{1}{4}$ lemon.

Prepare as for Fogas Fried in Bread-crumbs. Serve with baked potatoes.

Grilled Sheat-fish Slices

Ingredients: 2 lb. boneless sheat-fish, 1 tsp. salt, 2 oz. bread-crumbs, $3\frac{1}{2}$ oz. lard, $\frac{1}{2}$ pt. tartare sauce, $1\frac{1}{4}$ lemon.

Prepare as for Grilled Fogas. Serve with baked potatoes.

Sheat-fish with Tomatoes

Ingredients: 2 lb. boneless sheat-fish, 1 tsp. salt, 1 oz. onions, 2 oz. flour, pinch of ground black pepper, 1 tsp. sugar, $^3/_{10}$ pt. cream, 2 tbsp. white wine, $3\frac{1}{2}$ oz. butter, 1 lb. fresh tomatoes, 1 bunch of parsley, whites of 2 eggs.

Slice sheat-fish, salt and place into a buttered baking tin. Sprinkle with finely chopped onions and tomatoes peeled and sliced into rings, salt, ground black pepper and finely chopped parsley. Pour white wine over mixture, cover with greased paper, bring to boil and steam in the oven until tender. Place fish onto a plate. Reduce liquid a little, together with half the quantity of cream, mix half the quantity of butter with flour and add to this liquid, boil for short time, and then mix into it 2 yolks beaten well with the cream. Break in the rest of the butter gradually, flavour sauce and pour over the fish. Serve with potatoes in butter.

Grilled Carp

Ingredients: 4 lb. carp, 1 tsp. salt, $2\frac{1}{2}$ oz. bread-crumbs, 4 oz. lard, $\frac{1}{2}$ pt. tartare sauce, $1\frac{1}{2}$ lemon.

Clean carp and slice, salt, roll in bread-crumbs and fry in hot fat until golden-brown in colour. Garnish with slices of lemon and baked potatoes. Serve separately tartare sauce with it.

Carp Fried in Bread-crumbs

Ingredients: 3 lb. carp, 1 tsp. salt, 2 oz. flour, 2 eggs, 5 oz. bread-crumbs, 7½ oz. lard, ½ pt. tartare sauce, 1½ lemon.

Scale carp, cut up belly, remove entrails, and wash. Cut off the head, cut in two lengthwise, fillet and salt. Roll in flour, egg and bread-crumbs and fry in hot fat. Serve together with potatoes in butter and tartare sauce. May be served with potato salad with onions instead of potatoes in butter.

Carp with Supreme Sauce

Ingredients: 4 lb. carp, 1 tsp. salt, 1 oz. onions, 7½ oz. mushrooms, pinch of ground black pepper, 1 small bunch of tarragon leaves, 1 bunch of parsley, 3½ oz. butter, $^1/_5$ pt. red wine, ½ pt. brown sauce.

Clean carp and slice, salt, then place in a buttered baking tin, add red wine and a small quantity of water. Cover with greased paper, bring to boil and steam in the oven until tender. Prepare sauce: Fry finely chopped onions in butter, add finely chopped mushrooms, tarragon leaves, parsley, salt, pepper, and brown it. Dilute with brown sauce and boil together with the fish stock, somewhat reduced, for 10—15 mins. Take off the fire and break in the rest of the butter gradually, mix and flavour well. Pour this sauce over the carp, sprinkle with chopped parsley and serve with potatoes in butter.

Devilled Carp

Ingredients: 4 lb. carp, 1 dessertspoon salt, 7½ oz. onions, 3½ oz. lard, 7½ oz. bacon, 1 tsp. red paprika, 1 oz. flour, 2 lb. boiled potatoes, 1 pt. sour cream, 11 oz. green paprika, ½ lb. tomatoes.

Clean, wash and slice carp. Score the slices of carp and push thin slices of bacon through cuttings, salt and sprinkle with red paprika. Butter baking tin, arrange sliced boiled potatoes at the bottom, place fish on top, cover with onions, green paprikas and tomatoes, cut into rings, sprinkle with melted lard or butter and put in the hot oven. Mix sour cream with flour and pour over the fish when partly cooked, and bake until ready.

Carp in Paprika Sauce

Ingredients: 4 lb. carp, 1 dessertspoon salt, 7½ oz. onions, 3½ oz. lard, 1 tsp. red paprika, ½ lb. green paprikas, 7½ oz. fresh tomatoes or 5 oz. lecsó (stewed onions, tomatoes and paprika).

Clean carp, cut in pieces and salt. Fry finely chopped onions in lard, sprinkle with red paprika, dilute with a little water. Add green paprikas cut in four, sliced tomatoes (use lecsó in the winter instead) and bring to boil. Place pieces of carp in an enamelled baking tin, pour sauce of stewed paprikas, onions and tomatoes over them and steam in the oven—basting when necessary—until tender. Serve with noodles or boiled potatoes.

Carp Prepared with Red Paprika and Sour Cream

Ingredients: 4 lb. carp, 1 dessertspoon salt, 3½ oz. onions, 3½ oz. lard, 1½ tsp. red paprika, ³/₅ pt. sour cream, 2 oz. flour.

Clean and cut carp in pieces, then salt. Fry finely chopped onions in lard, sprinkle with red paprika, dilute with a little water and bring to boil. Add pieces of carp, cover and steam. Mix sour cream with flour and add, when carp is cooked. Bring once more to boil. Serve with noodles.

Boiled Carp

Ingredients: 4 lb. carp, 1 dessertspoon salt, 5 oz. mixed vegetables, 2 oz. onions, 5 whole black peppers, 1 bay leaf, 1 tbsp. vinegar, 5 oz. horse-radish, 1 lemon, 1 bunch of parsley, 2½ lb. potatoes.

Clean and cut carp in pieces, then salt. Cut mixed vegetables into fine slices and onions into rings. Bring water to boil in a saucepan, salt, and add vegetables, onions, bay leaf, whole black peppers, and vinegar, and cook until tender. When vegetables are tender, add pieces of carp, cover and cook. Arrange vegetables on fish, when serving, put boiled salted potatoes around them and sprinkle with chopped parsley. Cut lemon into rings, place small heaps of horse-radish on each slice and decorate, i. e. garnish fish plate with them.

Carp with Red Wine Sauce

Ingredients: 4 lb. carp, 1 tsp. salt, 3½ oz. butter, 3½ oz. mushroom heads, ²/₅ pt. red wine, pinch of black pepper, 1 bay leaf, 1 oz. onions, 1 oz. flour.

Clean and cut carp to pieces, season with salt, pepper and place into a buttered saucepan. Pour on red wine and some water, add mushroom heads, bay leaf and onions cut small. Cover with greased paper, bring to boil and steam in the oven. Place fish on a plate when cooked. Arrange mushroom heads on fish. Reduce juice a little. Mix flour with 1½ oz. of butter in the meantime, and add this mixture, stirring constantly with a whisk, to the fish stock, bring to boil and strain. Mix the rest of the butter into it, flavour and lastly pour sauce over fish and sprinkle with parsley. Serve with potatoes in butter.

Carp with Sour Cream and Mushrooms

Ingredients: 4 lb. carp, 1 tsp. salt, 1½ oz. flour, 3 oz. butter, pinch of ground black pepper, ²/₅ pt. sour cream, ¹/₅ pt. cream, 5 oz. mushrooms, 2 oz. onions, 1 bunch of parsley, ³/₁₀ pt. white wine.

110

Clean carp and remove flesh from backbone, slice and place into a baking tin. Pour white wine over fish, sprinkle with sliced mushrooms, finely chopped onions and chopped parsley, and with ground black pepper. Cover with buttered white paper, add some water and bring to boil, then steam in the oven until ready. Whip sour cream and cream together with flour and pour over carp when cooked; bring once more to boil, flavour and serve. Give potatoes in butter with carp.

Polish Carp

Ingredients: 4 lb. carp, 1 tsp. salt, 3 oz. butter, pinch of ground black pepper, $^1/_5$ pt. red wine, $^3/_5$ pt. brown sauce, 2 oz. sultanas, 3 oz. peeled almonds.

Clean carp and remove flesh from backbone, cut in pieces and salt. Place in a buttered saucepan, pour red wine over them, together with the same quantity of fish stock, made from backbone, and steam under cover. Place fish on a plate when cooked. Reduce juice and mix in brown sauce, boil well. Add peeled and sliced almonds, sultanas, salt, pepper and boil, then take off the fire and break in the rest of the butter gradually, shake well together and pour over cooked fish. Serve with potatoes prepared in butter and sprinkled with finely chopped parsley.

Fisherman's Soup

Ingredients (for 10 persons): 1½ lb. carp, 1½ lb. sheat-fish, 1 lb. sterlets, 1 lb. jack salmons, 2 tsp. salt, 11 oz. onions, 2 tsp. red paprika, 5 oz. green paprika, 3½ oz. tomatoes.

Prepare soup from fresh (live) fish, if possible, for better flavour. It is very important, however, to use several kinds of fish, because the taste of different fish gives the real flavour to the soup. Clean fish and cut into pieces, about 2 oz. each, then salt. Place heads, backbones and fins separately into a saucepan and boil with onions cut into rings. Sprinkle water with sweet red paprika when boiling and boil steadily for 40 mins., then strain liquid and pour over salted fish. Add roe or milt, green paprikas cut into slices and sliced tomatoes, and boil together for 20 more mins. until ready. Do not stir soup while cooking, merely shake from time to time. Sprinkle with green paprikas cut into rings when serving. (Fisherman's soup may be prepared quite well from carp alone.)

Fish Solyanka in Saucepan

Ingredients: 1½ lb. carp, 5 oz. tomato purée, 7 oz. pickled cucumbers, 2 lb. cabbage, 3½ oz. lard, 2 oz. onions, 3½ oz. butter, 1 oz. flour, 2 oz. bread-crumbs, 2 oz. capers, 1 tsp. salt, pinch of ground black pepper.

Stew the cabbage. Cut fish into 2 oz. pieces, sprinkle it with salt and pepper and turn the slices in flour. Fry in hot butter, together with sliced onions. When ready, add tomato purée, sliced cucumber, capers; lastly a little fish stock. Let it boil for about 10 mins.

Put a layer of the boiled cabbage into a casserole, arrange fish on top and pour the gravy over it. Bake it in a hot oven. Serve with sliced spring onions, sliced cucumbers or beetroots.

CRAYFISH AND FROGS

Freshwater crayfish are in season from May to the end of August, during the months without an "R". Two kinds are known best: one is dark brown-greenish in colour, hard-shelled; the other, the Polish or locust-crayfish, is light green in colour, softer shelled, with long claws. The first has a better flavour, but the advantage of the second one is its softer shell, it may be handled much better in consequence.

Crayfish may be grouped in three sizes and used according to size. They should be used in live state only. Do not use dead crayfish, they may cause very serious poisoning. Tinned crayfish, however, can be substituted for live ones. Other substitutes which can be used when crayfish are not easily obtainable are prawns or shrimps, or lobsters. When lobsters are used the quantities given in the recipes should be varied accordingly.

Frogs' legs may be consumed in the autumn and spring months only; their flesh is considered tasty only during these months, when they cannot feed on flies. The legs of the brown-backed bull-frog are sold cleaned and dressed; the freshness of the meat can be ascertained by its firm and elastic touch.

Crayfish in Paprika Sauce

Ingredients: 50 crayfish, 1½ tsp. salt, ½ tsp. caraway seeds, 1 small bunch of parsley, 5 oz. butter, ½ tsp. red paprika, 1 oz. flour, 2 oz. crayfish butter, $^2/_5$ pt. meat stock or bouillon.

Cook crayfish in salted water with caraway seeds and parsley, remove flesh from claws and tails. Melt and heat butter, and add crayfish flesh, heat up again a little, sprinkle with paprika and flour. Dilute with soup and bring to boil. Take off the fire and salt. Sprinkle with crayfish butter before serving and give a dish of rice separately. Serve hot:

Crayfish Ragout with Fresh Dill

Ingredients: 50 crayfish, 1 dessertspoon salt, ½ tsp. caraway seeds, 1 small bunch of parsley, 5 oz. butter, 1½ oz. flour, $^2/_5$ pt. cream, $^3/_5$ pt. stock, 7½ oz. mushrooms, ½ lb. crayfish butter, 1 small bunch of dills, pinch of ground black pepper.

Stuffed Green Paprikas ▷
Stuffed Vegetable Marrow with Dill

Cook crayfish in salted water with caraway seeds and remove flesh when cooked. Cut mushrooms into small dices and fry in lard. Make a light roux with 2 oz. butter and flour, dilute with hot stock, add cream, bring to boil, flavour with salt, ground black pepper and finely chopped dill, place crayfish meat, together with fried mushrooms, into sauce, bring to boil once more, then take off the fire, break in the rest of the butter gradually, and shake well together. Sprinkle with crayfish butter before serving. Garnish with rice.

Pancakes Filled with Crayfish

Ingredients: 10 salted pancakes, 30 crayfish, 1 dessertspoon salt, ½ tsp. caraway seeds, 1 small bunch of parsley, 2 pinch of ground black pepper, ½ tsp. red paprika, 1½ rolls, 1 tbsp. cream, ½ lb. mushrooms, 4 eggs, 5 oz. lard, 2 oz. butter, $^3/_{10}$ pt. milk.

Cut the flesh of boiled crayfish tails and claws, together with mushrooms, into small dice, and fry with finely chopped parsley in butter. Soak rolls in milk, pass through a sieve and mix well with crayfish and mushrooms, flavour with salt, pepper and red paprika, then add cream. Fill pancakes with this stuffing, fold them, roll in egg and bread-crumbs and fry in hot fat. Serve crayfish sauce separately.

Crayfish Meridon

Ingredients: 50 crayfish, ½ tsp. caraway seeds, 2 oz. onions, 1 small bunch of parsley, 11 oz. rice, 3½ oz. butter, pinch of Cayenne pepper, 2 oz. crayfish butter, 1 pt. soup, 6 portions of crayfish sauce.

Cook crayfish in salted water with caraway seeds, remove flesh from claws and tails when cooked, and rinse them. Lightly fry onions in 2 oz. butter, add rice, brown a little, salt, and dilute with 1 pt. of hot stock. Put into the oven, when boiling and steam—under cover—for 18—20 mins. Use long-grained and brightly polished rice (Carolina). Butter longish or roundish mould and arrange crayfish tails and claws in it. Mix a few spoonfuls of cray-fish sauce into rice, salt smaller claws and bits trimmed off the tails, mix all well together and fill mould with mixture. Put mould in hot water, so as to heat crayfish flesh well. Turn out meridon onto a round dish, when serving, pour crayfish sauce around it and sprinkle with crayfish butter.

The same dish of cooked rice mixed with crayfish claws, if garnished with sliced mushrooms, fried in 7½ oz. of butter and 7½ oz. of cooked green peas, is called Crayfish risotto.

Frogs' Legs with Mushrooms

Ingredients: 25 frogs' legs, 1 tsp. salt, 1 tbsp. flour, 3 oz. butter, pinch of ground black pepper, $^3/_5$ pt. cream, 7½ oz. mushrooms, 2 oz. onions, ½ bunch of parsley, 2 egg-yolks, ½ lemon.

◁ Székely Gulyás
English Larded Rabbit

Cook frogs' legs with finely chopped onions and sliced mushrooms. Make a roux with flour and butter, dilute with the frog gravy, add cream and bring to boil. Flavour with lemon-juice, ground black pepper and chopped parsley. Add 2 egg-yolks, but do not boil after adding yolks. Pour this sauce over frogs' legs and garnish with rice.

Frogs' Legs Fried in Bread-crumbs

Ingredients: 25 frogs' legs, 7½ oz. lard, 1 tbsp. oil, 1 tsp. salt, pinch of ground black pepper, 1 lemon, 1 bunch of parsley, 5 oz. bread-crumbs, 2 eggs, 3½ oz. flour.

Clean frogs' legs and pickle with salt, oil, ground black pepper, chopped parsley and a little lemon-juice. Roll in flour, egg and bread-crumbs and fry in hot fat. Garnish with parsley fried in bread-crumbs, slices of lemon or tartare sauce.

Stewed Frogs' Legs in Paprika Sauce

Ingredients: 25 frogs' legs, 3 oz. lard, ½ tsp. red paprika, 1 tsp. salt, 5 oz. onions, 5 oz. green paprikas, 3½ oz. fresh tomatoes or 5¼ oz. lecsó (stewed onions, green paprikas and tomatoes).

Fry finely chopped onions in lard, sprinkle with red paprika and dilute with a little water. Add green paprikas cut into pieces and diced tomatoes (in winter use lecsó instead), bring well to boil, put in frogs' legs washed well previously, and cook for 10 mins. until ready. Serve with a garnish of rice.

Frogs' Legs in Batter

May be prepared as for Frogs' Legs Fried in Bread-crumbs, but roll in batter (Orly) instead of bread-crumbs, and fry in plenty of hot fat. May be garnished with parsley fried in batter.

MEAT COURSES

THE PREPARATION OF MEAT COURSES

The economical and expert use of meat should be the vital interest of all people concerned with cooking and baking. It is very important when preparing meat courses to distinguish between the various parts and kinds of meat, and according to their quality to decide upon the dishes one can make from them.

It should be mentioned that we ought to use those parts first which deteriorate most readily (offal, thinner meats, scraps). Bigger pieces of meat, and thicker parts may be kept on ice for longer, without the danger of spoiling.

Sirloin and steak can be processed with oil and pepper, a way of conservation to be recommended, as the meat becomes more soft and tender.

Beef should only be used for cooking a few days after slaughter, because even prime fattened beef is tough while fresh. This rule should be respected especially in the case of cuts of meat suitable for serving slightly underdone. This rule, however, should not be applied in the case of veal, pork and mutton, because these meats can already be used a day after slaughtering.

The best cut of beef for soup is the rump, as well as good quality fat brisket and the thicker parts of the chuck. Most suitable for stewing are the round of beef, the aitchbone steak and the topside. For roast beef to be served as a whole joint, or for beef served slightly underdone and sliced (the so-called English meat dish) use fattened sirloin, sirloin cutlets and rump steak. These are also suitable for stewing as well.

The best parts of beef to be boiled, grilled or fried are as follows:

From tenderloin:

about 2	slices	filets mignon
about 3—4 oz.	slices	beefsteak
about 5—6 oz.	pieces	beefsteak
about 6—7 oz.	pieces	Chateaubriand

From sirloin:

about 5—6 oz. slices	sirloin cutlet (upper part)
about 5—6 oz. slices	rump steak (flat part)
about 6—7 oz. slices	entrecôte (flat part)

Gulyás, stew with paprika or pepper, or minced meat may be prepared from spare rib, chuck, thin parts and from small scraps left over after the filleting and boning of the thick meat.

The joints of veal suitable for roasting are the following: brisket, shoulder, fricandeau, leg, fillet and knuckle.

The best cuts of veal for broiling, grilling or frying are as follows: fricandeau, round of veal; from the latter we prepare cutlets, fried in bread-crumbs or rolled in flour; the leg, from which we prepare veal steaks, and from the fillet we make slices and filets mignon: chops, cleaned and dressed, may be used for cutlets (fried in bread-crumbs or in flour). For stews, gulyás, soups and all kinds of stews prepared with pepper and spices, as well as for minced meat we may take the meat from the neck, the shin and all the scraps, left over after the filleting and boning of the meat.

The most suitable parts of pork for roasting are: chops, leg (fricandeau, round of pork, filets mignon), shoulder, spare rib, knuckle, fillet and thin flanks. Cutlets may be cut from long and short chops, and fried, rolled in bread-crumbs or flour. Leg or fillet may be cut into thin slices of filets mignon, and from the spare rib we may prepare the so-called flekken (mixed grill).

For stew and Transylvanian gulyás use knuckle, thin flank and shoulder. For stew, prepared with pepper, minced meat or stuffing use the other smaller parts of meat. Prepare aspic from the head, feet, tail and skin and serve when cooked with horse-radish.

The saddle and leg of a young lamb should be roasted whole. Other, more fleshy parts should be prepared fried in bread-crumbs. From the breast, chuck or neck make stew with paprika with much or little gravy, soup with tarragon leaves, or various other dishes cooked from the scraps.

Saddle of mutton or leg should be hung just like beef and used only after some days. The saddle and leg of fattened mutton should be roasted whole and served slightly underdone, while lean mutton should be stewed. The other parts of mutton may be used for the preparing of stews made with paprika or pepper, and gulyás, Irish stew, mutton with pearl barley or different ragouts.

When roasting meat, care should be taken first of all, to bone all pieces expertly, lest bones needlessly left in the meat should hinder the carving of the roast.

Wash meat first, then rub in salt and place in a baking tin into previously heated fat. Whole joints, slightly underdone sirloin, beef chine or inside steak should be roasted in a hot oven; great care, however, is needed, in order to avoid overcooking, since it may render meat tough and impalatable.

Veal, pork or mutton should be roasted in a not too hot oven, over steady heat and frequently basted with the fat; add a little water only after having browned both sides of the meat first. We may find out whether the meat is done or not by slowly sticking a pointed meat-fork into it. If it goes through the meat easily, and hardly any juice runs out, the meat may be considered to be ready. The time needed for preparing meats can be established only approximately, because it depends on the thickness of the meat, on the age of the animal and on the temperature of the oven.

Quickly fried meat dishes should be cooked over a full gas flame, because slices of veal, for instance, are usually beaten out until quite thin, and ought therefore to be fried in a small quantity of fat and quickly. If we fry meat slowly, it may not brown properly, and, at the same time, it will lose its juice, and may stew instead of frying, and this may involve the risk of its becoming tough.

Quickly fried, slightly underdone, so-called English meat dishes—such as sirloin cutlets, tenderloin steaks, beefsteaks or rump steaks—should also be cooked quickly in a small quantity of fat, over a brisk, full flame, in order to give them a good brown colour speedily, but at the same time leaving them slightly underdone inside. Grilled meat should be brushed frequently with oil or fat, during grilling, and also cooked quickly, in accordance with the thickness of the meat.

All slices, rolled in bread-crumbs or coated in panada just like every other dish prepared with bread-crumbs, should be fried in plenty of fat. Slices, beaten out thin, should be fried quickly; those, however, with a thicker coating, ought to be cooked more slowly, by frying them evenly, taking care to pre-heat the fat first and to put the meat into it only when it is hot.

When preparing different stewed meat dishes, including various kinds prepared with paprika and pepper, do not forget that the liquid may boil away in 15—20 mins. by quick stewing, and a little water or unsalted stock should be added to avoid burning. But take care to add liquid only when really needed to avoid burning, because if the gravy or sauce is too thin, it may spoil the meat-dish, however well and carefully prepared otherwise. The quality of seasonings—especially in the case of dishes prepared with paprika—is very important. If the paprika is too hot, we should reduce the quantity accordingly, because most people dislike dishes prepared with unusually hot spices. We may vary the quantities of other spices and seasonings as well, including salt, according to taste. This is particularly so for dishes prepared with vinegar. Unsuitable garnishes, vegetables, sauces and salads, served with some meat dishes may spoil their pleasant flavour. Stews prepared with pepper and paprika, in plenty of gravy or little gravy, may be garnished with potatoes boiled in salted water or mashed and prepared with fried, chopped onions, dumplings, granulated dried pastry made of flour and eggs (tarhonya), or occasionally with rice. Stewed meat-dishes, served with sauces, may be garnished with macaroni, spaghetti, buttered noodles, various kinds of rice, potato croquettes or potato doughnuts, or possibly with potato hot-pot. Boiled beef may be served with the vegetables cooked with the meat, and also boiled potatoes with fried onions in addition, and various kinds of sauces. We may also serve horse-radish and beetroot seasoned with vinegar, or cold chive sauce instead of other sauces. Roast veal should be served with spinach, spring vegetables prepared with roux, green peas or other greens in addition to potatoes and rice. Roast pork may be served with slightly sour vegetable dishes, in addition to potato garnishings; different kinds of cabbages, in the first place, but vegetable marrow or French beans, prepared with sour cream are also quite suitable. Slightly underdone English roast beef should be served with potato purée or various kinds of potatoes fried in fat, as well as green peas, French beans, Brussels sprouts or spinach, boiled in salted water and besprinkled with butter. For special occasions all roast meat courses may be served with fine mixed garnishings. Quickly fried meats, slightly underdone, are best suited by the garnishes described previously, but they may also be served with béarnaise sauce, served separately in a sauceboat. The different meat dishes included in the various menus may be accompanied by different kinds of sauces. Meats, fried in bread-crumbs, should always be served with fried potatoes, with various green salads or mixed pickles in addition, and occasionally as well with the tender greens and vegetables of the season.

BEEF

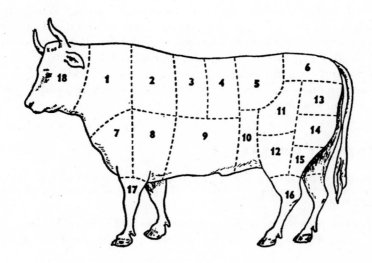

Cuts of beef:

1. Neck or sticking piece
2. Fore ribs
3. Middle ribs
4. Chuck ribs
5. Sirloin
6. Rump
7. Clod
8. Brisket or shoulder
9. Nine holes
10. Thin flank
11. Topside
12. Thick flank
13. Aitchbone
14. Mouse buttock
15. Veiny piece
16. Leg or shin
17. Hough or shin
18. Head including cheek

The most advantageous use of the cuts:

Boiled, braised or stewed
Roasted (underdone), sliced steaks grilled or fried, braised in different ways
Roasted (underdone), sliced steaks fried or grilled, braised in different ways
Roasted (underdone), sliced steaks fried or grilled, braised in different ways
Roasted (underdone), filleted and grilled, fried steaks, braised in different ways
Boiled, braised
Boiled, braised, smoked
Boiled, braised or stewed
Boiled
Boiled, stewed (pörkölt) or braised (tokány)
Boiled, braised or stuffed
Boiled, braised
Boiled, braised
Boiled, braised
Boiled, braised
Paprika stew (pörkölt or gulyás), braised
Paprika stew (pörkölt or gulyás), braised
Tongue: boiled, stewed or smoked

119

Bogrács Gulyás (Cauldron Gulyás)

Ingredients: 1½ lb. beef, 2 oz. lard, 7 oz. onions, 1 clove of garlic, 1 tsp. paprika, pinch of caraway seed, pinch of marjoram, 1 tsp. salt, 2 lb. potatoes, 5 oz. green paprika, 5 oz. tomatoes, 2 oz. flour, 1 egg.

Cut the beef into small cubes, and place in a saucepan; add lard, finely chopped onions, garlic, paprika, caraway seed, marjoram, and salt; stir well, add a little water, cover, and let it simmer, stirring it from time to time and adding a little water every now and then to prevent burning. When the gulyás is half-cooked add the sliced green paprika, tomatoes and diced potatoes and pour in sufficient water to cover it. Simmer till tender. Before serving, knead 6 oz. flour and 1 egg into a stiff paste, tear with fingers into small squares — *csipetke* —and cook in boiling salt water. Strain and add to gulyás.

If fresh tomatoes and green paprika are not available, add 4½ oz. lecsó or 1 tbsp. of tomato purée.

Kolozsvár Gulyás

Ingredients: 1½ lb. beef, 2 oz. lard, 7 oz. onions, 1 clove of garlic, 1 tsp. paprika, pinch of caraway seeds, pinch of marjoram, 1 tsp. salt, 1 lb. potatoes, 5 oz. green paprika, 5 oz. fresh tomatoes, 1 lb. cabbage.

Use beef of prime quality and prepare it as for Cauldron Gulyás, the only difference being that sliced cabbage is added to the meat along with the potatoes.

It is served without csipetke.

Szeged Gulyás

Ingredients: 1½ lb. beef, 2 oz. lard, 7 oz. onions, 1 clove of garlic, 1 tsp. paprika, pinch of caraway seed, pinch or marjoram, 1 tsp. salt, 7 oz. mixed vegetables, 5 oz. green paprika, 5 oz. fresh tomatoes, 2 oz. flour, 1 egg.

Prepare as for Cauldron Gulyás, the only difference being that mixed vegetables cut into cubes and stewed separately in a little water, until they are tender, are added.

Serbian Gulyás

(For 5 people)
Ingredients: 1½ lb. beef, 2 oz. fat, 7 oz. onions, 1 clove of garlic, 1 tsp. paprika, pinch of caraway seed, pinch of marjoram, 1 tsp. salt, 1 lb. potatoes, 5 oz. green paprika, 5 oz. fresh tomatoes and 1½ lb. savoy cabbages.

Prepare as for Cauldron Gulyás using prime beef, the only difference being that besides the potatoes thinly sliced savoys are added; both are added to the gulyás at the same time. Csipetke is not added.

Csángó Gulyás

Ingredients: 1¾ lb. of beef, 4 oz. lard, 5 oz. onions, 1 tsp. paprika, 1 clove of garlic, 1tsp. salt, pinch of caraway seed, 1 lb. sour cabbages, 3 gills sour cream, 2 oz. rice.

Cut the meat into cubes of about 3 oz. each. Heat up the sliced onions (don't fry them) in the lard adding the paprika, garlic and caraway seeds. Stir and pour a little water into the saucepan. Bring to boil, then put in the meat, salt it, cover and let it simmer, adding a little water every now and then to prevent burning. When it is half-cooked add the previously rinsed cabbage (in season 2 sliced green paprikas are added as well) and pour sufficient water over the ingredients to cover. Simmer till nearly ready, then put in the rice and continue the cooking. Add the sour cream when ready, and serve the gulyás in a deep bowl.

Palóc Gulyás

Ingredients: Take the same quantity of mutton instead of beef as used for the preparing of the Gulyás soup, together with 7 oz. tinned green beans and 1½ gill of sour cream.

Cook as for Gulyás Soup, using mutton instead of beef. After adding the potatoes, the tinned green beans are put in, which are cut into one-inch pieces, and cook the whole until tender. Add csipetke a few minutes before serving and finally mix with the sour cream.

Marhapörkölt (Beef Paprika Stew)

Ingredients: 1¾ lb. beef, 3½ oz. lard, 7 oz. onions, 1 tsp. paprika, pinch of caraway seed, pinch of marjoram, 1 clove of garlic, 1 tsp. salt, 5 oz. green paprika, 2 fresh tomatoes.

Use shin of beef, cut into 2 oz. cubes. Heat the finely chopped onions in the fat (don't fry them); add the crushed garlic, paprika, caraway seed and marjoram, stir well and then add a little water. After boiling a few minutes, put in the meat, salt, cover and let it simmer. Stir occasionally adding a little water now and then to prevent burning. When half-cooked put in the sliced green paprika and tomatoes, then continue to braise until ready. Take care to make the gravy thick. We can substitute 5 oz. of lecsó for fresh paprika and tomatoes.

Peppered Tenderloin Stew (Tokány)

Ingredients: 1¾ lb. tenderloin steak, 3 oz. lard, 5 oz. onions, 1 clove of garlic, pinch of ground black pepper, pinch of marjoram, 1 tsp. salt, dessertspoon tomato purée.

Cut the tenderloin steak into strips of ⅛ inch width and 3 inches length. Chop onions finely and fry them in fat until they turn yellow, add crushed garlic and tomato purée; then adding a little water, stir for 2—3 mins. Add meat, salt, pepper and marjoram, cover and let it simmer. Add a little water now and then to prevent burning.

Take care to make the gravy thick because tokány must be served in thick gravy. Garnish with rice, tarhonya or mashed potatoes, pickles can also be served with it.

Transylvanian Tokány

Ingredients: 1¾ lb. of beef, 3 oz. bacon, 2 oz. lard, 5 oz. onions, 1 clove of garlic, 1 dessert-spoon tomato purée, 1 gill white wine, pinch of ground black pepper, pinch of marjoram, 1 tsp. salt, 2 green paprikas.

Cut meat into strips of 3 inches length and ¹/₈ inch width. Cut up bacon into strips of a pencil's width and fry, then take out of pan and lay aside. Fry finely chopped onions in the bacon fat, then add the crushed garlic, wine and tomato purée and cook for a few minutes, stirring all the while. Put the meat into the saucepan together with pepper and marjoram, cover it and allow to simmer. (In season 2 green paprikas can be added also.) Stir from time to time and add a little water to it. When the meat is tender, add fried bacon, bring to boil and then serve it with a thick gravy. Garnish with mashed potatoes mixed with fried onions, or with *puliszka* (hominy or maize-porridge), a paste prepared of maize-flour and water to which lard is added when it is cooked.

Butcher's Tokány

Ingredients: 1½ lb. beef, 2 pairs of Vienna sausages, 3 oz. lard, 5 oz. onions, 2 oz. bacon, 1 dessertspoon tomato purée, 1 gill white wine, pinch of ground pepper, pinch of marjoram, 1 tsp. salt, 2 green paprikas.

It is prepared as for Transylvanian Tokány, the only difference being that Vienna sausage is added skinned and cut into slices of 1½ inch width; fry lightly in lard and add to the already cooked tokány, and boil the whole for 2—3 mins. longer. Garnish it with mashed potatoes mixed with fried onions.

Seven Chieftains' Tokány

Ingredients: 10 oz. tenderloin, 9 oz. shoulder of pork, 9 oz. shoulder of veal, 2 oz. bacon, 2½ oz. lard, 3½ oz. onions, 3½ oz. lecsó, 1 tsp. salt, 1½ gill sour cream, 1 dessertspoon flour, 1 dessertspoon paprika.

Melt lard in a saucepan, add bacon cut in thin strips, fry lightly, then take out of saucepan and put it aside. Then fry the finely chopped onions in the fat, till they are golden-brown. Add the paprika and a small quantity of water. Boil for 2—3 mins. Then put in the tenderloin, cut into strips of

$^1/_5$ inch width and $2\frac{1}{3}$ inches length, salt and cover it, letting it simmer gently for about half an hour. This is followed up with the pork and lastly the veal is added some 20 mins. later. Let the whole simmer, adding a little water from time to time.

When the meat is tender add the lecsó (2 green paprikas and 2 small tomatoes during summer) and the fried bacon and cook the whole until it is ready; then pour sour cream mixed with flour, over it, letting it boil 3—4 minutes longer. Should the gravy be too thick, it can be diluted with water.

Serve with dumplings or steamed rice.

Shepherd's Meat

Ingredients: 1½ lb. beef, 3½ oz. bacon, 7 oz. mushrooms, 3 oz. lard, 4½ oz. onions, 1 tsp. salt, pinch of ground black pepper, small bunch of parsley, 1½ gill sour cream, 1 tsp. flour.

Cut meat into small cubes; then melt the lard in a pan and fry the finely chopped onions; add the paprika, pour 2 tbsp. water into the pan and allow to boil for 2—3 mins. Put in the meat, salt and cover, letting it simmer gently. Stir from time to time and add a little water when necessary.

Wash and slice mushrooms. Fry chopped bacon lightly, add the mushrooms; flavour them with ground pepper and finely chopped parsley, cook the whole a few mins. Add these to meat about 10 mins. before serving. Finally pour the sour cream, mixed with flour, over the whole and bring to boil again. Garnish with steamed rice or mashed potatoes.

Sour Vetrece (Braised) Beef

Ingredients: 1¾ lb. shoulder of beef, 3 oz. lard, pinch of ground black pepper, 5 oz. onions, 1 tsp. salt, 2 gills sour cream, 1 dessertspoon flour, 1 tbsp. vinegar or one lemon.

Cut the beef into strips the width of a pencil. Chop onions finely, fry in lard until they are yellow. Add the meat, salt and pepper, pour on a little water, cover, and let it simmer, stirring from time to time and adding a little water to it. When the meat is tender, pour in the sour cream mixed with flour, add the vinegar or lemon-juice, cook the whole for 4—5 mins. and garnish with rice.

Braised Beef with Mushrooms

Ingredients: 1¾ lb. beef, 5 oz. mushrooms, 3 oz. lard, 5 oz. onions, 1 clove of garlic, 1 dessertspoon tomato purée, 1 gill white wine, pinch of ground black pepper, pinch of marjoram, 1 tsp. salt, small bunch of parsley.

This dish is prepared as for the Transylvanian Tokány, using mushrooms instead of bacon. Wash the mushrooms, slice and fry them in a little lard and add them to the meat about 10 mins. before it is tender. Dish sprinkled with chopped parsley, and garnish with rice or mashed potatoes mixed with fried onions.

Tokány of Debrecen

Ingredients: 1½ lb. shoulder of beef, 4½ oz. smoked Debrecen sausage, 2 oz. bacon, 1½ oz. lard, 5 oz. onions, 1 clove of garlic, 1 tsp. paprika, 1 tsp. salt, 5 oz. green paprika, 1 tomato.

Cut the meat into strips of ⅛ inch width and 3 inches length. Slightly heat the bacon which is also cut into strips, then fry the thinly sliced onions with it until they are yellow. Add the crushed garlic and paprika, pour 1 gill of water into it and cook for 2—3 mins. Add the meat, salt it and cover, allowing it to simmer gently. Stir it from time to time, adding a little water if necessary. When meat is nearly cooked, add the Debrecen sausage sliced and lightly fried in a little lard, the green paprika and tomato, and cook the whole until meat is tender. Instead of fresh paprika and tomatoes, 2½ oz. lecsó or 3 oz. tomato purée may be used.

Garnish with potatoes boiled in salt water, or with rice.

Herány Tokány

Ingredients: 10 oz. tenderloin, 10 oz. shoulder of pork, 7 oz. pork or veal kidneys, 3½ oz. mushrooms, ½ tsp. paprika, pinch of ground black pepper, pinch of marjoram, 1 tsp. salt, 1 clove of garlic, 1½ gill sour cream, 1 tsp. flour, 3½ oz. lard, 5 oz. onions.

Melt 2 oz. lard in a saucepan and fry the finely chopped onions in it, until they are golden-brown. Add paprika and crushed garlic. Stir, then add a little water and let it boil for 2—3 mins. Cut meat into finger-sized strips and put into the gravy; salt it, sprinkle with pepper and marjoram, cover, and allow to simmer for about ½ hour; then add the pork cut into strips and continue to cook. Add the kidneys, cut into small cubes and the mushrooms, previously fried in 1 oz. lard, and stew the whole until tender. Finally pour in the sour cream mixed with flour and let it boil again thoroughly. Garnish with boiled potatoes, rice, or dumplings.

Marjoram Stew

Ingredients: 1¾ lb. beef, 3 oz. lard, pinch of marjoram, pinch of ground pepper, 1 tsp. salt, 1½ gill sour cream, 15 oz. onions, 2½ oz. flour.

Cut the shoulder of beef into strips of ⅛ inch width and 3 inches length. Fry the finely chopped onions in lard until golden-brown, add meat, pepper, marjoram and salt, and a little water, cover and let it simmer. Stir it from time to time, and if the juice evaporates, add a little more water. Pour the sour cream mixed with flour over it. When meat is tender, cook it five minutes longer and dish it garnished with rice or spaghetti.

Sailor's Meat à la Parisienne

Ingredients: 1¾ lb. tenderloin, 3 oz. lard, 2½ oz. butter, 2½ oz. onions, 1 tsp. salt, pinch of ground pepper, 1 tsp. tomato purée, 2 tbsp. red wine, 5 eggs, 1 tbsp. milk, 1 tsp. flour, 2 gills brown sauce.

Trim the tenderloin, dry it with a cloth and cut into strips the width of a pencil. Fry finely chopped onions in lard, taking care that they should retain a light colour; sprinkle meat with flour and pepper and add to fried onions. Put on an open fire and, stirring slowly with a fork, let it fry a few mins. Then take it off the fire, add the tomatoes, red wine, and brown sauce and boil the whole thoroughly. Take off flame and mix it with 1 oz. of butter. Make scrambled eggs with the remaining 1½ oz. of butter, the eggs, milk and a pinch of salt. Place scrambled eggs in the middle of a round dish in the form of a cone, arrange the meat around it. Serve with cooked rice in a separate dish.

Ox-tail with Sour Cream

Ingredients: 4 lb. ox-tail, 5 oz. mixed vegetables, 3½ oz. lard, pinch of ground black pepper, pinch of thyme, 2 bay leaves, 2 oz. onions, 2 tbsp. white wine, ½ lemon, 2 gills sour cream, 1 tbsp. flour, 1 dessertspoon mustard, 1 dessertspoon sugar, 1½ tsp. salt.

Wash ox-tail thoroughly first in warm, then in cold water; dry it with a cloth, then cut into pieces of 1—1½ inch width, and salt it.

Melt the lard in a pan, and add the vegetables, cut into thick slices, onions, pepper, bay leaves and thyme; place the ox-tail on it and roast it in the oven, stirring from time to time. When nicely browned, put the whole into a saucepan, pour wine over it, add the thinly pared lemon peel, and a little stock or water; cover and let it simmer slowly on the cooker for 2—3 hrs. Add a little water from time to time. When meat is tender, add mixture of sour cream and flour, the mustard, sugar and lemon-juice and cook for another 10 mins. taking care that the gravy should be neither too thick nor too thin. Then lift the pieces of meat into another saucepan with a fork, strain the gravy over, then boil once again and serve.

Garnish with dumplings made of rolls or macaroni.

Braised Rump of Beef

Ingredients: 2 lb. rump of beef, 1 tsp. salt, 5 oz. mixed vegetables, 2 oz. onions, 1 clove of garlic, 3 oz. lard, 2 whole black peppers, pinch of thyme, 1 bay leaf, 2 oz. tomato purée, 1 tbsp. sugar, 2 oz. flour, 1 gill red wine.

Salt and fry meat in lard, evenly on all sides, then take out of the fat and put aside. Melt sugar in fat, until it is brown, then add the sliced vegetables, onions, whole clove of garlic, and continue to braise slowly. After a short time add the flour, pepper, bay leaf and thyme. Braise a little longer, then add tomatoes and red wine; pour 2 pt. of water or stock over it. Bring to boil, then put in the oven, cover, and let it simmer in the oven for about 3 hrs. Stir in rice, while it is simmering and add a little water if necessary. Take the meat out of the sauce when it is tender, taking care that the gravy is neither too thick nor too thin. Strain gravy and keep it warm. Cut the meat into rather thin slices, place them on a dish, and pouring the gravy over it, serve.

Garnish with macaroni, casserolled potatoes (see: rakott burgonya), or crisply fried potatoes.

Braised Beef à la Znaim

Ingredients: 2 lb. beef (fillet), 1 tsp. salt, 7 oz. vegetables, 2 oz. onions, 1 clove of garlic, 3 oz. lard, 2 whole black peppers, pinch of thyme, 1 bay leaf, 2 oz. tomato purée, 1 dessertspoon sugar, 2 oz. flour, 1 gill red wine, 5 oz. pickled gherkins, 1 dessertspoon mustard.

Prepared as for Braised Rump of Beef. Cut the pickled gherkins into thin slices, and add to the strained gravy, together with the mustard and cook a few mins. longer. When dishing cover the sliced meat with the gravy.

Garnish with macaroni, or crisply fried potatoes.

Roast Beef à la Burgundy

Ingredients: 2 lb. rump of beef, 1 tsp. salt, 7 oz. mixed vegetables, 2 oz. onions, 3½ oz. button (pearl) onions, one clove of garlic, 5 oz. mushrooms, 3½ oz. streaky bacon, 3 oz. lard, 2 whole peppers, pinch of thyme, 1 bay leaf, 2 oz. tomato purée, 1 dessertspoon sugar, 2 oz. flour, 1 gill red wine.

Prepare as for Braised Rump of Beef. Slice streaky bacon and fry it lightly in a small pan. Add button onions (shallots) cut in halves or slices and the sliced mushrooms. Simmer for a few mins. then add the strained sauce, and boil the whole for another 10—15 mins. Serve the sliced meat covered with the sauce.

Garnish it with freshly made potato chips.

Braised Beef à la Stéphanie

Ingredients: 2 lb. mock rump, 1 tsp. salt, 3 boiled eggs, 7 oz. mixed vegetables, 2 oz. onions, 1 clove of garlic, 3 oz. lard, 2 whole black peppers, pinch of thyme, 1 bay leaf, 2 oz. tomato purée, 1 dessertspoon sugar, 2 oz. flour, 2 tbsp. red wine.

Cut the middle of meat through with a long, sharp knife and press the boiled and shelled eggs into the opening. Bind the end of the meat with string, if necessary. Prepare as for Braised Rump of Beef. Garnish with rice, spaghetti, or noodles in butter.

Braised Beef with Bacon

Ingredients: 1¾ lb. mock rump of beef, 5 oz. bacon, 1 tsp. salt, 7 oz. mixed vegetables, 2 oz. onions, 1 clove of garlic, 3 oz. lard, 2 whole black peppers, pinch of thyme, 1 bay leaf, 2 oz. tomato purée, 1 dessertspoon sugar, 2 oz. flour, 2 tbsp. red wine.

Cut deeply into top of the meat, diagonally in 6—8 places with a small pointed knife, and thread strips of bacon, the length and width of a little finger, into the openings. For the rest prepare as for Braised Rump of Beef. Serve with mashed potatoes.

Tenderloin Prepared Like Venison in Game Sauce

Ingredients: 1¾ lb. trimmed tenderloin, 2 oz. bacon, 1 tsp. salt, 2 oz. lard, 5 oz. mixed vegetables, 2 oz. onions, 2 oz. flour, 5 whole black peppers, 1 bay leaf, pinch of thyme, 1 tbsp. vinegar, ½ lemon, 1 dessertspoon sugar, 1 tsp. mustard, 1 tsp. capers, 3 gills sour cream.

Draw strips of bacon through the tenderloin, then salt it. Melt the lard in a saucepan, add vegetables cut into small cubes, sliced onions, rind of bacon, pepper, bay leaf, thyme and the thin peel of the lemon and lastly the meat. Put it into the oven allowing it to brown. Then place saucepan on the cooker, add vinegar and 4 gills of water or stock. Stir it occasionally, adding a little water if the gravy evaporates. Take the meat out of gravy when it is tender; pour the sour cream mixed with flour into the gravy, add lemon-juice, sugar and mustard, and stirring the sauce once in a while, cook for 12 mins. Strain it, and adding the capers, boil once again.

When dishing, cut the meat into slices and pour the sauce over it. Garnish with spaghetti, or bread dumplings.

Braised Round of Beef

Ingredients: 5 slices of beef weighing 5 oz. each, 3½ oz. lard, 1 tsp. salt, 5 oz. onions, 2 cloves of garlic, pinch of ground black pepper, 1 bay leaf, 2 oz. flour, 1 tbsp. tomato purée, 2 tbsp. white wine, 1 tsp. sugar.

Beat the slices of meat to tenderize them; salt, pepper and flour them on both sides and fry quickly in lard till both sides are golden-brown; then take them out of the fat and put aside, in a saucepan. Fry the finely chopped onions in the fat, add crushed garlic, sprinkle with the flour left over, fry lightly taking care that the onions do not burn, then add tomatoes, white wine, sugar and the bay leaf. Pour on 2—3 gills of water, boil well together, then pour over the meat, cover with lid and let it simmer. Turn it over from time to time, and if necessary add a little more water. When tender, place it in a dish and pour the gravy over it.

Garnish with mashed potatoes mixed with fried onions, creamed potatoes or with any other kind of vegetable.

Braised Sirloin Steaks

Ingredients: 5 slices of steak weighing 6 oz. each, 3½ oz. lard, 7 oz. onions, 2 cloves of garlic, 1 tsp. paprika, pinch of caraway seed, pinch of marjoram, 1½ tsp. salt, 5 oz. green paprikas, 5 oz. tomatoes, 3 lb. potatoes.

Beat and salt the steaks, brown both sides in lard, lift out and put them in a saucepan. Fry the finely chopped onions until they are a light yellow colour, add the crushed garlic, paprika, caraway seeds and marjoram. Mix well, add a little water and cook for a few mins., then pour over the sirloin steaks. Add as much water as will cover the meat and let it simmer slowly, under a lid. Turn the slices from time to time and add more water if necessary. When it is half-cooked, add the green paprika cut into thin slices, the tomatoes and, lastly, the sliced potatoes, adding as much water as is required to cover. Simmer till tender.

We can substitute 4½ oz. lecsó for the fresh tomatoes and green paprikas.

Sirloin Steak with Mushrooms

Ingredients: 5 slices of sirloin steak weighing 6 oz. each, 3½ oz. lard, 2 oz. onions, 1 tbsp. flour, 1½ tsp. salt, 2 oz. tomato purée, 2 tbsp. red wine, pinch of ground pepper, 5 oz. mushrooms.

Beat the slices of steak a little, salt them, and placing them in a frying pan let them brown slightly, then lift out into a suitable pan. Add flour to remaining fat, brown it slightly, then add the finely chopped onions, and stir till onions are golden-brown. Add wine, tomatoes, and pepper and, stirring continually, cook it for a few minutes; then pour this sauce over the slices of steak. Add sufficient water to cover and let it simmer slowly under lid. Turn the meat from time to time and add a little more water if needed. Wash and slice mushrooms, fry them in the remaining lard and also add these to the other ingredients 10—15 mins. before the steak is ready.

Garnish with rice, potatoes and macaroni.

Sirloin Steak à la Csáki

Sándor Csáki, the eminent Hungarian chef was the author of a cookery book, bearing the title: "The Art of Cooking in the 20th Century", and it was in order to honour his memory that this Hungarian dish was created.

Ingredients: 5 slices of sirloin steak weighing 6 oz. each, 3½ oz. lard, 7 oz. onions, ½ tsp. paprika, 2 gills sour cream, 2 oz. flour, 1 tsp. tomato purée, 2 tsp. salt, 1 lb. lecsó, 5 eggs, 3½ oz. streaky bacon, pinch of ground black pepper.

Prepare the following stuffing: cut bacon into small cubes, and fry in a pan till crisp; then add 2 oz. finely chopped onions. Add the lecsó when onions turn golden yellow, salt, and let it simmer for a little while. Pour well-beaten eggs over the lecsó stirring continually, allow to set, then mix in 1 tsp. flour and set aside to cool. Beat the steak into thin slices, salt and pepper them, cover the middle of each with $^1/_5$ of the stuffing. Fold edges of meat over the stuffing, roll them and tie up each roll with string. Melt the lard in a pan, put in steak and roast them in a hot oven for 20 mins. Then take the meat out, and fry the finely chopped onions in the remaining fat, until they are a light brown colour, add paprika and tomatoes, and stir well. Then replace beef, add sufficient water to cover it, and let it simmer under lid till it is tender. Then pour mixture of flour and sour cream over it and cook for another 10 mins. Put large butter dumplings on one side of a deep dish, putting the sirloin steak beside it (removing string first), and finally pour the paprika sauce over the whole.

During the season use green paprika and tomatoes.

Hortobágy Sirloin Steak

Ingredients: 5 slices of sirloin steak, weighing 6 oz. each, $3\frac{1}{2}$ oz. lard, 1 oz. onions, 2 cloves of garlic, 1 tsp. paprika, pinch of caraway seed, pinch of marjoram, 1 tsp. salt, 5 oz. lecsó, 1 dessertspoon flour, 1 dessertspoon tomato purée.

Salt and flour steaks, and fry both sides quickly in lard, then put them into a pan of suitable size; fry finely chopped onions in the fat until they are golden-brown, add paprika, tomato purée, crushed garlic, caraway seed and marjoram. Mix well, add a little water, boil a few mins., and then pour over the steak, adding sufficient water to cover the meat and let it simmer slowly under lid. Turn from time to time, adding a little more water if necessary. When meat is nearly tender, put in the lecsó, and continue cooking. Serve with a layer of galuska (thimble dumplings) over each steak. Instead of lecsó use 5 oz. green paprika and 5 oz. fresh tomatoes when in season.

Bácska Steak with Lecsó

Ingredients: 5 slices of sirloin steak weighing 6 oz. each, $3\frac{1}{2}$ oz. lard, 7 oz. onions, 2 cloves of garlic, 1 tsp. paprika, pinch of caraway seed, pinch of marjoram, $1\frac{1}{2}$ tsp. salt, 1 dessertspoon tomato purée, 1 dessertspoon flour, 10 oz. green paprika, 7 oz. fresh tomatoes, $3\frac{1}{2}$ oz. streaky bacon.

Prepare as for Hortobágy Steak (without the dumplings) with the following variation: cut the bacon into strips of 1 inch length, fry lightly in a pan, add sliced green paprika and tomatoes. Salt it and let it simmer covered, for about 10 mins. Pour this sauce over half-cooked steaks and let it simmer till meat is tender. Garnish with potatoes boiled in salt water, or with tarhonya.

Casino Steak

Ingredients: 5 slices of sirloin steak weighing 5 oz. each, 3½ oz. lard, 7 oz. onions, 1 clove of garlic, 1 tsp. paprika, pinch of marjoram, 1 tsp. salt, 1 dessertspoon tomato purée, 5 eggs, 5 oz. green peas, pinch of caraway seed, 3½ oz. fresh tomatoes, 3½ oz. green paprika.

Prepare as for Fried Steak with the difference that the potatoes are cut into large squares. Serve with a soft-boiled egg on top of each steak and add separately heated green peas just before serving.

Szeged Sirloin Steak

Ingredients: 5 slices of steak weighing 6 oz. each, 3½ oz. lard, 7 oz. onions, 1 clove of garlic, pinch of caraway seed, pinch of marjoram, 1 tsp. paprika, 1 tsp. salt, 5 oz. green paprika, 5 oz. fresh tomatoes, ½ lb. mixed vegetables, 2 lb. potatoes, 2 oz. flour, 1 egg.

Prepare as for Fried Steak with the difference that both the potatoes and vegetables are cut into cubes. Pre-cook the vegetables first then add potatoes and the steak simultaneously. Serve with csipetke on top of steaks.

Petőfi Sirloin Steak

Ingredients: 5 slices of steak weighing 5½ oz. each, 3½ oz. lard, 7 oz. onions, 1 clove of garlic, 1 tsp. paprika, pinch of marjoram, 1 tsp. salt, 7 oz. bacon.

Prepare in the same manner as for Hortobágy steak, excepting that it is served with five pieces of potato griddle cake instead of groat dumplings; place a piece of fried bacon atop of each steak. Nick the slices of bacon with a knife and fry till golden-brown.

Sirloin Steak in Vegetable and Sour Cream Sauce

Ingredients: 5 slices of steak weighing 6 oz. each, 1 tsp. salt, 3½ oz. lard, 7 oz. mixed vegetables, 3 oz. onions, 2 oz. flour, 2 gills sour cream, 1 bay leaf, 1 pinch of ground black pepper, 1 gill white wine, ½ lemon, 1 tsp. mustard, ½ tsp. sugar, 1 tsp. capers, small bunch of parsley.

Beat the steaks a little, salt and pepper them, then fry in the lard quickly on both sides till they are browned slightly; then place them into a saucepan. Add flour to the hot lard, stir till it turns frothy, add 1½ oz. finely chopped onions, fry them lightly. Dilute with the wine and 3 gills of water, boil together well and then pour sauce over the steaks. Add bay leaf and grated lemon peel, cover and let it simmer slowly. Turn the meat from time to time, adding a little water if necessary. Cut the vegetables into strips of 2 inches length and the remaining onions into slices, braise them in 1 oz. of lard and a little water till they are tender. Pour the sour cream over the meat, adding the mustard, vegetables, capers, sugar and lemon-juice and boil the whole once again. Serve sprinkled with finely chopped parsley. Garnish with macaroni, rice or spaghetti.

Stuffed Sirloin Steak

Ingredients: 5 slices of sirloin steak weighing 6 oz. each, 3½ oz. lard, 5 oz. onions, 1 tsp. paprika, 1 tsp. salt, 1 dessertspoon tomato purée, 2 oz. flour, 2 gills sour cream, 5 oz. lean boiled ham, or smoked pork, 1 egg, 2 tbsp. milk.

Prepare the following stuffing: Mix the chopped ham with the egg, milk and 1 oz. flour and cook the whole until it thickens, then set it aside to cool. Beat the steak into thin slices, salt them, cover the middle of each with ¹/₅ of the stuffing. Fold edges of the meat over the stuffing, roll them and tie each roll up with string. Melt lard in a saucepan, put in the steaks and cook them in a hot oven for about 20 mins. Take meat out and fry finely chopped onions in remaining fat, till they are golden-brown; then add the paprika and tomatoes; stir well, put back the steaks, addig sufficient water to cover them, and covering with a lid let steaks simmer till tender. Add a little more water from time to time, if necessary. Finally pour in the sour cream, mixed with flour and let it boil a few mins. longer. Put noodles on one side of a fairly deep dish, place the steaks beside them (take off the string first) and pour the paprika sauce over them.

Bavarian Stuffed Sirloin Steak

Ingredients: 5 slices sirloin steak weighing 6 oz. each, 1½ tsp. salt, 3 oz. lard, 1 oz. butter, 2 oz. onions, 4½ oz. mixed vegetables, 3 oz. cooked ham, 3½ gills sour cream, 2 oz. flour, 3 eggs, pinch of ground black pepper, 1 bay leaf, ½ lemon, 1 tsp. mustard, 1 tsp. sugar, ¾ lb. boiled potatoes.

Prepare the following stuffing: Beat the eggs and butter together till creamy, then add 2 dessertspoons of sour cream, pinch of salt, the boiled and mashed potatoes and the chopped ham. Beat the steaks to make them thinner, salt and pepper, divide the stuffing and put on them; fold the edges over it, roll each into a longish shape and tie together with string. Melt the lard in a saucepan, add the sliced vegetables and the onions, the thinly peeled lemon-rind and bay leaf. Place the steaks on top of the vegetables, put the saucepan into a hot oven, and turning the steaks from time to time, roast them until they are nicely browned. Lift the pan on the cooker, add a little water and let it simmer until meat is tender. Turn meat from time to time, adding a little more water if necessary. When the steaks are quite tender, take them out of the gravy (take off the string) but keep them warm. Mix the remaining sour cream with the flour, pour it into the gravy, squeeze the lemon-juice into it, put in the sugar and mustard and, stirring repeatedly, boil for 15 mins.; then strain it and boil again, taking care not to let it become either too thick or too thin. Heat up the steaks in the sauce again before serving.

Gipsy's Sirloin Steak

Ingredients: 5 slices of steak weighing 6 oz. each, 3½ oz. lard, 5 oz. bacon, 2 oz. onions, ½ lb. mixed vegetables, 1 tsp. salt, 2 oz. tomato purée, 2 tbsp. red wine, pinch of ground pepper, 1 oz. flour, 1 bay leaf.

Fry the lightly beaten salted and peppered steaks letting them colour rapidly; then place into a suitable pan. Fry the flour in the hot lard, then add the finely chopped onions, and fry till onions are golden-brown. Add wine, tomatoes and bay leaf, boil the whole for a few mins. stirring constantly, then pour sauce over the steaks. Add sufficient water to cover them and stew them slowly under lid, turning steaks from time to time. Add a little water or stock if needed. Clean and slice vegetables and cook them in a little stock to which 1 oz. lard is added. Add vegetables to steaks and stew the whole for another 10 mins. Nick with a knife and fry the slices of bacon and serve steaks covered with the vegetable sauce and with cockscombs of bacon on top of the steaks. Garnish with baked potatoes.

Sirloin Steak with Onions

Ingredients: 5 slices of steak weighing 6 oz. each, 1 tsp. salt, 5 oz. lard, pinch of ground black pepper, 10 oz. onions, 1 dessertspoon flour.

Beat the steak a little but do not have them too thin, sprinkle with salt and pepper. Slice onions, sprinkle them with flour and mix thoroughly. Put lard into a frying pan and fry the onions until they are light brown, then strain and keep them warm. Place the steaks into the hot lard, fry them quickly on both sides. Place steaks on a flat dish, arrange grilled onions over them, and add some of the gravy. Garnish with baked potatoes.

Roast Beef

Ingredients (for 10 people): 4 lb. beef, 2 tsp. salt, pinch of ground black pepper, 4 oz. lard.

For this try to obtain the meat of a fattened ox, as lean beef is tough and unpalatable. Trim the cut carefully, then rub salt and pepper over the meat. Melt lard in a pan of suitable dimensions, heat oven thoroughly, put meat in and roast. Baste and turn meat frequently, so that it browns on either side, taking care not to prick the meat, and let blood ooze out. After cooking it for 35—40 mins. let the meat stand for half an hour, in the still warm oven, to set.

The time of cooking depends upon the thickness of the meat. Cut the roast into slices with sharp knife before serving, place slices on the dish in a neat row, pour gravy over them. Garnish with either creamed, or baked potatoes, or French garnish.

Minced Beef

Ingredients: 1 lb. beef, ½ lb. fat pork, 2 bakery rolls, 1 egg, 1 tsp. salt, pinch of ground black pepper, pinch of marjoram, 5 oz. lard, 2 oz. onions, 1 clove of garlic.

Mince both the beef (having cut away the sinews) and fat pork. Add the rolls which have been steeped in water and pressed out, the onions finely chopped, and fried in 1 oz. lard, salt, pepper, marjoram, egg and crushed garlic; knead mixture well together, then, dipping the hands in flour, form 5 large or 10 small rissoles. Fry them in hot lard. Serve with some of the gravy poured over, garnish with creamed potatoes, or any kind of vegetables.

Rump Steak with Béarnaise Sauce

Ingredients: 5 pieces of rump steak weighing 7 oz. each, 1 tsp. salt, pinch of ground black pepper, 3½ oz. lard, 3 gills béarnaise sauce.

For this dish you need prime quality meat. Flatten the steaks slightly, but do not make them too thin, salt and pepper and fry them in lard, over open fire, if possible. The steaks do not need long cooking. After a few mins. test by pressing meat gently with back of fork; if gravy appears take them out of the frying pan at once. Cut each piece into 5—6 slanting slices and arrange pieces of steak into the joint's original shape on a flat dish. Pour gravy over it and garnish with fried potatoes. Can also be served with green peas or French beans. Serve béarnaise sauce separately in a sauceboat.

Larded Steak

Ingredients: 2 lb. steak, 2 oz. bacon, 3 oz. lard, 1 tsp. salt, pinch of ground pepper.

Trim superior quality beef with a sharp knife, and thread with thin strips of bacon with help of larding pin; salt and pepper it. Heat lard in a pan, put in the meat and roast it in a very hot oven, basting frequently. Take meat out, after 25—30 mins. put it on a dish and let stand in a lukewarm place for at least 20 mins.

Cut it into 10—12 slices of equal size when serving and pour gravy over it. Garnish with creamed potatoes, potatoes casseroled or baked potatoes.

Tenderloin in Lace

Ingredients: 1¾ lb. beef, ½ lb. pork lace, 2 oz. lard, 1½ oz. butter, 2 tsp. salt, pinch of ground pepper, 7 oz. mushrooms, small bunch of parsley, 1 dessertspoon chopped onions, a tsp. bread-crumbs, 1 egg.

Trim and skin the middle part of a tenderloin steak of superior quality with a sharp knife; sprinkle it with salt and ground pepper. Heat the lard in a pan of suitable size. Arrange meat neatly in a pan, and roast it in a hot oven for 10 mins., after which put aside to cool. Wash the mushrooms thoroughly, then chop them into small pieces. Fry the finely chopped onions, parsley and the mushrooms in butter, add ½ tsp. salt, the remaining ground pepper and fry mixture for another 4—5 mins. Add well beaten egg and bread-crumbs, and stirring continually let it set a little, then put it in a cool place. Wash pork lace through several times in cold water, then wring the water out of it.

When the meat is cooled, spread mushroom purée on top of it, and fold carefully in several layers of pork lace, tuck lace beneath the meat and bind it loosely round with a string. Replace it in the lard carefully; the side covered with mushroom purée should be uppermost. Put it into the hot oven and basting from time to time, roast it for 20—25 mins. Take meat out of the oven, and let it stand for 20 mins. in a cool place. Remove the string, then cut the meat into 10 slices with a sharp knife, taking care that the lace should not slip off it. Lay slices on dish in a neat row pouring the gravy over them. Garnish with creamed potatoes, fried potatoes and French garnishing.

Boston Tenderloin

Ingredients: 1¾ lb. beef, ½ lb. goose-liver, ½ lb. pork lace, 1½ tsp. salt, good pinch of ground black pepper, 3 oz. lard, 1½ oz. butter, 1 dessertspoon chopped onions, small bunch of parsley, 1 egg, 1 tsp. bread-crumbs, 1 tsp. flour, 3½ gills Madeira sauce.

Prepared as for Tenderloin in Lace, with the following variation: cut the goose-liver into 8 pieces of 1 oz. each, flatten them carefully, salt, pepper and turn them round in flour; fry lightly in 1 tsp. lard, and let them cool. Press the pieces of goose-liver into the mushroom purée spread on the meat, then wrap the whole into the lace. Roast and serve just like Tenderloin in Lace, except that Madeira sauce should be served with it in a sauceboat, instead or gravy. Serve with French garnishing in a separate dish.

Wellington Roast Beef

Ingredients: 1¾ lb. tenderloin, 1 lb. puff pastry, 2 oz. lard, 1½ oz. butter, 1½ tsp. salt, pinch of ground pepper, 7 oz. mushrooms, small bunch of parsley, 1 tsp. chopped onions, 1 tsp. bread-crumbs, 1 egg, 3½ gills Madeira sauce.

Trim and skin the middle of tenderloin with a sharp knife, then sprinkle it with 1 tsp. salt and half of the ground pepper. Heat the lard in a small frying-pan, place meat in it and roast in a hot oven for 10 mins. Take meat out and keep it in a cool place. Wash and chop mushrooms. Fry the finely chopped onions in butter until they are golden-brown, then add the finely chopped parsley, the mushrooms, ½ tsp. salt, and the remaining ground pepper and allow the whole to fry for another 3—4 mins. Stir in a beaten egg and the bread-crumbs; stir till set, keep in a cool place. Roll out puff pastry (see Pastries) to 1 inch thickness, then spread the cold mushroom purée over the cold meat; then place meat on rolled-out pastry taking care that mushroom filling should be uppermost; fold pastry over, first one side, then the other. Place the encased meat in a shallow pan, brush it with egg; cut the remaining pieces of pastry into strips and use for decorating; brush with egg once again and bake in a hot oven for 20—25 mins. then let it stand for 20 mins. on mild heat.

Cut the meat into slices with a sharp knife before serving, place slices on the dish in a neat row, pour a little Madeira sauce along them, and serve Madeira sauce in a separate sauceboat as well. ½ oz. finely chopped truffles may be added to the sauce. Garnish with creamed potatoes or French garnishing.

Colbert Tenderloin

Ingredients: 1¾ lb. beef, pork lace, 2 tsp. salt, pinch of ground black pepper, 2 oz. fat, 1½ oz. butter, 1 tsp. chopped onions, small bunch of parsley, 1 tsp. bread-crumbs, 1½ lb. savoys, 1 egg, 3½ oz. bacon, ½ pt. brown spiced sauce.

Prepare as for Tenderloin in Lace, with the following variation: cut up savoys, boil in salt water (do not overcook), strain through a sieve, dust with pepper when cold, then spread over the mushroom purée. Cut the bacon into thin slices, place them upon the savoy leaves, then encase the whole in the lace as for Tenderloin in Lace. Roasting and dishing are also similar, only in varying that brown spiced sauce is added served separately in a sauceboat, instead of the meat's own gravy. Garnish with potatoes of French garnishing.

Tenderloin with Poached Eggs

Ingredients: 2 lb. of tenderloin steak, 1 tsp. salt, pinch of ground black pepper, 5 eggs, 4½ oz. lard.

Cut the meat into 5 equal pieces after having trimmed it. Flatten slices out with a broad knife to finger's thickness, salt and pepper. Heat 3½ oz. lard in a frying pan and roast the slices rapidly on both sides over an open flame, until they are rosy-brown. When gravy appears on gently pressing the meat, take steaks out of the lard at once; arrange them on a dish, placing a poached egg on each slice. Add a little gravy and garnish with baked potatoes.

Sliced Tenderloin with Spiced Butter

Ingredients: 2 lb. tenderloin, 1 tsp. salt, good pinch of ground black pepper, 3½ oz. lard, 3 oz. butter, ½ lemon, ½ tsp. mustard, small bunch of parsley.

Trim the middle part of tenderloin and cut it into ten equal pieces. Flatten them with the palm of hand, then salt and pepper, using half the pepper.

Then mix the butter with the remaining pepper, lemon-juice, mustard and the finely chopped parsley. Form little pats of 2 inches each, place them into iced water, and chill to harden well. Put lard into a frying pan and fry steaks on either side over a fierce open fire. Take them out of the lard as soon as gravy begins to ooze from them and place on a dish in a neat row. Cut the chilled spiced butter into 10 pieces, placing a piece on each slice of meat and dish at once, garnished with roast potatoes cut in cubes or with French garnishing.

Hunter's Steak (Tournedos)

Ingredients: 1¾ beef, 1½ tsp. salt, ½ tsp. ground black pepper, 4½ oz. lard, 2 oz. butter, 5 oz. chicken liver, 5 oz. mushrooms, 5 rolls, 1 tbsp. chopped onions, small bunch of parsley, 1 tbsp. white wine, 1 dessertspoon tomato purée, 2 gills brown sauce.

Trim and cut the middle of tenderloin into ten equal pieces. Slightly flatten them with hand then salt and sprinkle with half of the pepper. Take five rolls and cut ten round slices of 1 inch thickness, then fry them on both sides in the lard. Wash the mushrooms and liver; cut them into small cubes. Put butter in small frying pan and fry the finely chopped onions in it, till they are golden-yellow; add the finely chopped parsley, the mushrooms and liver. Salt and pepper and continue to fry a few minutes longer. Pour in the wine, add tomato purée, and brown sauce and boil for 2—3 mins. Keep the sauce warm before dishing on the edge of the cooker. Put lard in a saucepan over an open fire and fry steaks in it until they colour rosy-brown, taking care to lift them out as soon as gravy oozes out.

Lay the slices of rolls on a dish in a neat row, and place the half-roasted steaks over them, cover with the sauce, taking care that livers and mushrooms remain on top. Garnish with steamed rice and baked potatoes, or with crisply fried potatoes.

Rossini Tournedos

Ingredients: 1¾ lb. tenderloin steak, 1½ tsp. salt, pinch of ground black pepper, 5 oz. lard, 7 oz. goose-liver, 7 oz. mushrooms, 5 rolls, 1 tsp. flour, 4 gills Madeira sauce.

Trim the middle of tenderloin, then divide it into 10 slices of equal size, flatten slightly with hand, salt and flour on both sides. Cut the stems off 10 mushrooms, wash and salt them, then sprinkle with flour. Cut 10 slices of rolls, 1 inch thick, and fry in lard on both sides. Then fry the goose-liver and mushroom tops, put them into a small pan, add a little Madeira sauce and keep them warm. Place the lard in a frying pan over an open flame, frying steaks rapidly until they are rosy-brown, on both sides, taking care to lift them out of the pan as soon as gravy begins to ooze. Serve as follows: Place a quantity of potato chips on one side of the dish, lay the slices of rolls beside, and put the steaks on them; cover meat with the small slices of goose-liver and mushroom tops. Pour a little Madeira sauce over and serve the rest in a separate sauceboat. Put finishing touch to the steaks, by laying thin slices of truffles over the mushrooms.

Astoria Tournedos

Ingredients: 1¾ lb. middle tenderloin, 1½ tsp. salt, pinch of ground black pepper, 7 oz. fat, 1 calf's brain, 1 lb. tinned peas, 5 rolls, 1 egg, 2 oz. bread-crumbs, 1 dessertspoon flour, 1 oz. butter, 4 gills béarnaise sauce.

The preparation and frying of the meat and slices of roll is similar to that of Hunter's Steak. Further preparations are as follows; Trim and skin calf's brains and cut into 10 round pieces, salt and dip both sides into egg and bread-crumbs, then fry them in hot lard. When serving arrange the fried slices of rolls on a dish in a neat row. Place the steaks on them, then cover each separately with a thick béarnaise sauce. Now put the slices of fried calf's brains carefully on top. Serve with potato chips on one side of the dish and the green peas with small pieces of butter on top, on the other.

Tenderloin Steaks with Mushrooms

Ingredients: 2 lb. steaks, 1½ tsp. salt, 3½ oz. lard, ½ lb. mushrooms, ½ tsp. ground black pepper, 3 oz. butter, 1 bunch of parsley, 2 oz. onions, ¼ lb. rice.

Trim tenderloin and cut it into ten slices. Flatten slices slightly with hand, salt and sprinkle with half of the pepper. Wash and slice the mushrooms. Then fry the finely chopped parsley and onions, add mushrooms, salt and pepper and fry them for 3—4 mins. over an open fire. Keep them warm on the edge of the cooker. Fry steaks rapidly on both sides until rosy-brown, which should take 3—4 mins. Then take them out of the pan at once. Fry rice, arrange it on the middle of the dish placing the steaks on it in a neat row, add fried mushrooms on top. Serve with baked potatoes.

Tenderloin Steaks with Marrow

Ingredients: 1¾ lb. tenderloin, 1½ tsp. salt, pinch of ground black pepper, 4 oz. lard, 5 rolls, ½ lb. bone marrow, 4 gills red wine sauce.

The preparation of the meat and slices of rolls is similar to that for Hunter's Steak. Further preparations are as follows: Take the marrow out of the bone and cut into slices of ½ inch, with a knife dipped into warm water; cook them in broth or salt water for about 5 mins. Set the slices of fried rolls lengthwise in an oblong dish, lay the half-roasted steaks upon them, top with the small pieces of marrow (drained of moisture); then pour on the red wine sauce, using a tablespoon. Serve with baked potatoes.

137

Fried Medals of Tenderloin Steak à la Hungaria

Ingredients: 1½ lb. tenderloin, 10 oz. pork or veal bones, 1½ tsp. salt, 5 oz. lard, 1 tsp. paprika, 1 tsp. flour, 5 oz. onions, 7 oz. lecsó, 2 lb. potatoes, 1 tsp. tomato purée, 5 oz. mushrooms, 7 oz. tinned asparagus-heads, 5 oz. tinned green peas and 2 oz. butter.

Fry the finely chopped onions, in 2 oz. of lard, add the paprika and tomato purée and mix them well; add a little water and boil for several minutes. Chop the bones into small pieces, put them into the gravy and half cover with water. Place a lid over them and cook for 40 mins., then take bones out of the gravy, strain gravy through a sieve and keep it warm. Cut the trimmed tenderloin into pieces, of about 1 oz. each, beat lightly, salt and cover with a little flour, and fry rapidly over an open fire in a little lard. Take them out and put them in the gravy, adding lecsó and the mushrooms, cut into small, thin slices and fried separately in 1 oz. butter. Fry the boiled and peeled potatoes in the lard left over after frying the meat. Slice the potatoes and carefully mix with the sauce and meat; then serve in a deep dish, putting the green peas and heads of asparagus, which have been heated in warm butter, on top. (In season use fresh green paprika and tomatoes instead of lecsó.)

Medici Tenderloin Steaks (Tournedos)

Ingredients: 1¾ lb. tenderloin, 1 tsp. salt, pinch of ground black pepper, 4½ oz. lard, ½ oz. truffles, 2 gills Choron sauce, 5 rolls.

The preparation of the slices of beef and of the rolls is identical with that for Hunter's Steak. Place the ten slices of rolls in the middle of an oblong dish when serving, lay the tenderloin steaks over them, then pour thick Choron sauce over each slice individually, laying a slice of truffle on them on top of the sauce.

Serve with potatoes fried to a crisp brown on both sides of the dish.

Henry IV Tenderloin Steaks (Tournedos)

Ingredients: 1¾ lb. tenderloin, 1 tsp. salt, pinch of ground black pepper, 4½ oz. lard, 1 oz. butter, 10 artichokes, 5 oz. tinned green peas, 2 gills Berne sauce, 5 rolls.

The preparation of the slices of beef and the rolls is identical with that for Hunter's Steaks. After straining, warm the green peas in butter and salt them. Heat tinned artichokes in their own juice. When serving, place the slices of rolls lengthwise in the dish, set the steaks over them, pour a little Berne sauce on each slice individually and put an artichoke beside each and fill their hollows with a teaspoonful of green peas. Decorate with small potato chips on the ends of the dish.

Favourite Tenderloin Steak (Tournedos)

Ingredients: 1¾ lb. tenderloin, 7 oz. goose-liver, pinch of ground black pepper, 5 oz. lard, 1 oz. butter, 1½ tsp. salt, 5 rolls, ½ lb. tinned heads of asparagus, 1 tsp. flour, 3½ gills Madeira sauce.

The preparation and roasting of the meat and roll slices is identical with that for Hunter's Steak. Cut the goose-liver into ten small pieces, salt, turn in flour and fry quickly. Heat the heads of asparagus—after having strained them—in butter; salt a little. When serving place the pieces of rolls in the middle of the dish, lay the slices of steak upon them, decorate with goose-liver slices and pour Madeira sauce over the whole. Put the heads of asparagus on one side of the dish, and fried potato chips on the other.

Godard Tenderloin Steaks

Ingredients: 1¾ lb. tenderloin, 5 oz. goose-liver, 5 oz. sweetbreads, 5 oz. mushrooms, 5 rolls, 5 oz. lard, 1½ tsp. salt, pinch of ground black pepper, 2 oz. butter, 2 gills Madeira sauce.

The method of preparing the slices of beef and rolls is identical with that for Hunter's Steak. Cook the sweetbreads for 10 mins., cool in cold water, and cut it into largish cubes, with the goose-liver, and mushrooms. Fry the mushrooms lightly in a little butter in a frying pan, add the goose-liver and sweetbreads, salt and pepper and after letting the whole fry a few minutes, pour on the Madeira sauce, boiling up quickly and thoroughly. Put the slices of rolls in the middle of the dish when serving, place the slices of tenderloin over them, and with a tablespoon put the ragout—divided equally—on the top. Serve with potato chips on both ends of the dish.

Victor Hugo Tenderloin Steaks

Ingredients: 1¾ lb. tenderloin, 1 tsp. salt, pinch of ground black pepper, 4½ oz. lard, 5 rolls, 10 anchovy rings, 2 gills Berne sauce.

The preparation of the meat and roll slices is identical with that for Hunter's Steak. When serving place the slices of rolls in the middle of the dish, then the steaks; pour a thick coating of Berne sauce over each slice individually, laying the unrolled rings of anchovy across in bars. Serve with potato chips on both sides of the dish.

Villefrance Tenderloin Steaks

Ingredients: 1½ lb. tenderloin, 1 tsp. salt, pinch of ground black pepper, 5 oz. lard, 2 oz. butter, ½ lb. mushrooms, 5 eggs, 2 gills Madeira sauce, small bunch of parsley.

Trim and cut the tenderloin into 5 pieces, flatten them out with the back of the knife to a thickness of 1 inch, salt and pepper, then fry them rapidly in hot lard. Wash and slice mushrooms, fry them in butter, add salt and pepper and finely chopped parsley and keep warm. Break and salt eggs, then whip them well. Make pancake-like flat omelettes, bake them and lay a little mushroom in the middle of each, put a steak on them and wrapping each up, place on an oval dish in a neat row. Serve with Madeira sauce around it.

Smoked or Pickled Ox-tongue

Ingredients: 2 lb. smoked or pickled ox-tongue.

Boil the tongue in plenty of water until it is tender. If it is too salty, pour the water off after half an hour, and set it to boil again in plenty of fresh water. Skin when it is tender, then slice and serve. Pour a little of the stock over it. Garnish with creamed potatoes, creamed peas or lentils.

Ox-tongue with Madeira Sauce

Ingredients: 2 lb. cleaned ox-tongue, 2 oz. onions, 5 oz. mixed vegetables, 5 whole black peppers, 1 bay leaf, 2 cloves of garlic, 1 tsp. salt, ¾ pt. Madeira sauce.

Boil tongue until tender together with the spices and vegetables, then cool and skin it. Make Madeira sauce and cook the tongue in it for another 10—15 mins. Serve sliced and pour sauce over it. Garnish with steamed rice or creamed potatoes.

Ox-tongue in Tomato Sauce

Ingredients: 2 lb. cleaned ox-tongue, 2 oz. onions, 5 oz. mixed vegetables, 5 whole black peppers, 1 bay leaf, 2 cloves of garlic, 1 tsp. salt, 1 pt. tomato sauce.

Boil tongue together with the spices and vegetables until tender, then skin it. Cut the tongue into slices before dishing and serve with tomato sauce, previously thinned with the stock, poured over them. Garnish with steamed rice, or mashed potatoes with fried onions.

Polonaise Ox-tongue

Ingredients: 2 lb. ox-tongue, 2 oz. onions, 5 oz. mixed vegetables, 5 whole black peppers, 1 bay leaf, 2 cloves of garlic, 2 tsp. salt, 5 gills brown sauce, 2 tbsp. red wine, 1 dessertspoon sugar, 1 tbsp. raisins, 2 oz. peeled almonds, 1 tsp. tomato purée, 1 gill vinegar.

Boil the tongue until it is tender along with the spices and vegetables, then skin it. Add the wine, vinegar, tomato purée, sugar, raisins, and the peeled and chopped almonds to previously prepared brown sauce and boil the whole. Lay the skinned tongue into this sauce and boil it slowly for another 10—15 mins. Cut the tongue into slices and pour the sauce over it when serving. The sauce must have a tart flavour. Garnish with steamed rice.

Sholet with Smoked Brisket of Beef

Ingredients: 2 lb. brisket of beef, 3½ oz. goose-fat, 1 dessertspoon flour, 1 lb. large dried beans, 7 oz. onions, ½ tsp. paprika, pinch of ground black pepper, ½ tsp. salt, 3 eggs.

Place the beans, goose-fat, finely chopped onions, crushed garlic, paprika, black pepper and salt in a deep saucepan. Sprinkle with flour and mix the whole thoroughly. Pour water over it and, stirring occasionally, bring to boil; then put in the smoked brisket of beef, the washed uncooked eggs and setting a lid upon the pan let it stew in the oven, taking care that the gravy should cover the sholet. Stew for 3 to 5 hrs. Take the meat out of the saucepan when ready, then slice it. Serve the beans in a deep dish, placing the sliced meat on top of it, and garnish with the eggs shelled and cut in halves. 3½ oz. pearl barley may be cooked with the sholet; in this case omit flour.

Stewed Tripe with Lemon

Ingredients: 2½ lb. tripe, 3½ oz. lard, 2 oz. bacon, 1 tsp. salt, 3 cloves of garlic, 3½ oz. flour, a good pinch of ground black pepper, small bunch of parsley, 1 lemon.

Wash the tripe thoroughly in cold water and set it to boil in plenty of salt water. Take off the cooker after having boiled it for half an hour, cool in cold water and cut into strips of 2½—3 inches length. Put into a pan and pour on sufficient stock or water to cover it well. Salt and let it cook for 3—4 hrs. Melt lard in another pan, add the bacon cut into small cubes, and fry slowly till bacon is crisp. Now add the flour and when it has turned a light yellow, add the crushed garlic, the finely chopped parsley and the grated lemon peel, and stir well. Add a little cold water and stir sauce till smooth with a whisk, then add cooked tripe and lemon-juice to it, pepper to taste and continue to cook it—stirring constantly—for another 15 mins. Garnish with steamed rice.

Tripe in Paprika Sauce

Ingredients: 2½ lb. tripe, 4½ oz. lard, 7 oz. onions, 1 tsp. paprika, 3 cloves of garlic, 1 tsp. salt, pinch of marjoram, pinch of caraway seed, 1 dessertspoon tomato purée, 7 oz. lecsó, 1 tsp. flour, 3 stems of celery.

Wash tripe in several lots of water, then set it to boil in plenty of water. Take scum off with a spoon, while boiling. Take tripe out of cooker after half an hour, cool it in cold water and cut into strips of 2½—3 inches long. Fry the finely cut onions in lard, add the paprika and crushed garlic, marjoram, chopped caraway seeds and the tomato purée and, stirring all the time, fry mixture half a minute longer. Add sliced tripe and salt, stir once again and pour sufficient water on it to cover well and setting a lid upon the pan cook for 3—4 hrs. Stir from time to time, adding a little water if the juice evaporates.

When it is tender, put in the flour mixed with a little cold water, the finely chopped celery leaves and the lecsó and boil the whole for another 15 mins. Garnish with mashed potatoes and fried onions, or potatoes boiled in salt water with parsley and caraway seed.

Ox-heart and Kidney

Ingredients: 1¼ lb. ox-heart, 1¼ lb. kidneys, 3½ oz. lard, 1½ lb. onions, 1 tsp. paprika, pinch of caraway seed, 3 cloves of garlic, 1 tsp. salt, 1 dessertspoon tomato purée, 5 oz. green paprika, 3½ oz. tomatoes.

Cut both the heart and kidneys into one-inch cubes and prepare them as for pörkölt. Garnish with potatoes, dumplings or tarhonya.

Bean Gulyás

Ingredients: ¾ lb. ox-heart, ¾ lb. kidneys, 7 oz. cow's udder, 2 oz. lard, 7 oz. onions, 2 cloves of garlic, 1 tsp. paprika, pinch of caraway seed, pinch of marjoram, 1 tsp. salt, 15 oz. dried beans, 5 oz. green paprika, 5 oz. tomatoes, 2 oz. flour, 1 egg.

Cut the meat into one-inch sized cubes and prepare it as for Gulyás. Instead of potatoes boil beans separately and mix with the gulyás. When meat is tender, serve with csipetke in a separate dish.

VEAL

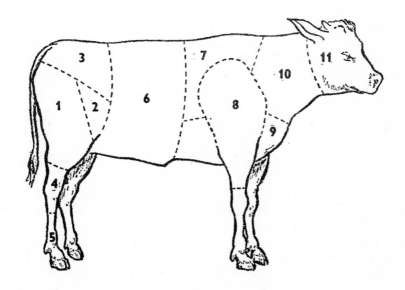

Cuts of veal:	The most advantageous use of the cuts:
1. Leg	Roasted, braised, filleted
2. Veal-nut	Roasted, braised, filleted
3. Fricandeau	Roasted, braised, filleted
4. Knuckle	Roasted, pörkölt
5. Feet	Boiled, steamed and fried in bread-crumbs
6. Loin (kidney end)	Roasted, sliced and grilled
7. Loin (chump end)	Roasted, or sliced and grilled (chops)
8. Shoulder	Roasted, paprika stew (pörkölt), fricassée, braised in different ways
9. Breast	Bonet, stuffed and roasted
10. Neck	Stewed, braised, tokány
11. Head	Scalded, fried in bread-crumbs
	Tongue: Boiled, steamed
	Brains: Fried in bread-crumbs, mixed with scrambled eggs

Offals:	
Liver	Sliced, browned on grill fried
Kidney	With brains and eggs
Lung	Boiled, sour
Glands	Browned
Mesentery	Tripe, pörkölt, fricassée
Tail	Soup, ragout

143

Minced Zrazi (Meat Rissoles)

Ingredients: 1 lb. meat, 3½ oz. onions, 3½ oz. lard, 1 clove of garlic, 1 tsp. salt, 2 oz. bread-crumbs, 2 eggs, 1½ rolls, pinch of ground black pepper.

Soak the rolls and put through mincer together with the meat, add flavourings and knead well together with one egg. Divide mixture into 5 parts and fill each with the following.

Chop finely 1 hard-boiled egg, add the finely chopped fried onions; mix in the bread-crumbs. Flatten out minced meat heaps then put filling in the middle of each and shape them into rissoles. Fry in hot lard. It can be served with any kind of garnishing. Serve with gravy or tomato sauce.

Veal Pörkölt (Paprika Stew)

Ingredients: 2 lb. shoulder or leg of veal, 3½ oz. lard, 7 oz. onions, 1 tsp. salt, 2 cloves of garlic, 1 tsp. paprika, 1 tbsp. tomato purée, 4½ oz. lecsó, 1 tsp. flour.

Cut the meat into fairly large cubes and wash well. Fry the finely chopped onions in lard until they are golden-brown, then add paprika and crushed garlic to it, stir and add the tomato purée and a little water and cook for a few minutes. Put in the meat, salt, and covering the pan with a lid let it cook rapidly. Stir from time to time and add a little more water if necessary. Add the lecsó when meat is half cooked. (In summer use 2 green paprikas and two small tomatoes instead of lecsó.) Let it simmer gently till tender. Dust with flour, stir and cook it for another 3—4 mins., taking care that the gravy should not be too thick. If you want the gravy thin, do not use flour. Garnish with dumplings or potatoes boiled in salt water.

Paprika Veal

Ingredients: 2 lb. shoulder of veal, 3 oz. lard, 3½ oz. onions, 1 tsp. salt, 3½ oz. lecsó, 2 gills sour cream, 1 dessertspoon flour, ½ tsp. paprika.

Cut the meat into fairly large cubes. Fry the finely cut onions until they are a light yellow colour, add the paprika, pour on a little water and cook for 1—2 mins., then add the meat, salt it and let it simmer under cover, stirring from time to time and pouring on a little more water if necessary. Add the lecsó when meat is nearly tender (in summer substitute 2 small green paprikas and 2 small tomatoes) and cook it a little longer; then add the sour cream mixed with flour. Boil the whole for another 3—4 mins. Should the gravy be too thick, add a little water. Garnish with dumpling or steamed rice.

Tokány of Veal

Ingredients: 2 lb. shoulder of veal, 3½ oz. lard, 5 oz. onions, 1 tbsp. tomato purée, 1 tsp. salt, 2 tbsp. white wine, pinch of ground pepper, 1 clove of garlic.

144

Cut the meat into strips of ½ inch width and 2 inches length. Fry the finely chopped onions in the lard, until they turn golden-brown, add the crushed garlic, tomato purée and white wine and cook it for 2—3 mins. Then place the meat in gravy, salt and pepper it and allow to simmer under lid until meat is tender. Stir from time to time, adding a little water if needed. As always when preparing tokány, see that it has sufficient gravy. Garnish with steamed rice or mashed potatoes with fried onions.

Veal Tokány with Mushrooms

Ingredients: 1¾ lb. shoulder of veal, 3½ oz. lard, 5 oz. onions, 1 tsp. salt, 1 dessertspoon tomato purée, 2 tbsp. white wine, pinch of ground black pepper, 2 cloves of garlic, 5 oz. mushrooms, small bunch of parsley, 1½ gill sour cream, 1 tsp. flour.

Prepare as for Veal Tokány, the only difference being that diced mushrooms, grilled with finely chopped parsley, are added to the meat before it is tender; then simmer for another 10 mins., finally add the sour cream mixed with flour and bring to boil again. Garnish with rice, noodles, or spaghetti.

Risotto of Veal with Peas

Ingredients: 1½ lb. veal, 1 tsp. salt, 5 oz. lard, ¾ lb. rice, 2 oz. onions, pinch of ground pepper, pinch of marjoram, small bunch of parsley, ½ lb. tinned peas, 3 oz. grated cheese.

Cut the meat into 1 inch cubes. Fry the finely chopped onions in 2 oz. of lard, till they are golden-yellow, then add the meat, the salt, pepper and marjoram; pour a little water over it and allow to simmer under lid for about 35 mins. Pour on a little water when needed. Fry the rice in 3 oz. lard, add the finely chopped parsley and the meat, pour twice as much water over it as the quantity of rice used, then let the whole simmer slowly under a lid. Stir from time to time—till it is tender and finally mix in the green peas. Sprinkle some of the grated cheese over it, then serve the rest of the cheese separately. Also serve tomato sauce or gravy in a sauceboat.

Veal Stew with Vegetables

Ingredients: 1¾ lb. shoulder of veal, 1 tsp. salt, 7 oz. mixed vegetables, 2 oz. celery, 2 oz. lard, 2 oz. butter, 2½ oz. flour, 1 bunch of parsley, 3½ oz. tinned peas, 2 oz. mushrooms, 1 whole black pepper, 1 tbsp. chopped onions.

Cut the meat into cubes of 1 inch each, and stew in 2 pt. of water. Skim with a spoon as soon as it begins to boil and after boiling for five minutes add the vegetables cut into small cubes, the celery, and salt; add a small muslin bag containing the onions and whole pepper and cook the whole for about 45 mins. Mix flour, lard and butter into a light paste, add a little cold water to it, stirring until smooth and add to the cooking meat. Add the washed and sliced mushrooms, and the finely chopped green parsley and allow to simmer till ready. Take the muslin bag out of ragout before dishing and add the green peas. Garnish with steamed rice. Veal stew can be prepared with asparagus or cauliflower, in this case take out vegetables and celery before serving.

French Veal Ragout

Ingredients: 1¾ lb. shoulder of veal, 3½ oz. lard, 2 oz. butter, 3½ oz. onions, 7 oz. mixed vegetables, 3½ oz. celery, pinch of ground black pepper, 2 oz. tomato purée, 5 oz. mushrooms, 2 cloves of garlic, 5 oz. tinned green peas, 1 tsp. salt, 3 oz. flour, 1 gill white wine, small bunch of parsley.

Dry meat with a cloth, cut it into cubes of 1 inch, salt and pepper, then sprinkle with 1 tbsp. of flour. Heat the lard in a frying pan and add the meat; stir rapidly until it is nicely browned, then put meat into a saucepan. Fry the remaining flour in the lard until light brown, add the finely chopped onions and the tomato purée, then pour in wine and ½ pt. water and bring to boil. Pour this gravy over the meat, cover and stirring it occasionally, let it simmer.

Cut the celery and vegetables into small sized cubes, fry them lightly in half of the butter, then add a little water to cover, and allow to simmer till nearly done. Cut mushrooms into slices and fry them for 5 mins. in the remaining butter. Add the cooked vegetables and mushrooms to the meat and cook till tender. Pour the heated green peas over it when serving, and add fried potatoes. Sprinkle the whole with finely chopped parsley.

Escalopes of Fried Veal à la Hongroise

Ingredients: 1½ lb. leg of veal (fillet), 10 oz. calves' bones, 1 tsp. salt, 5 oz. lard, 1 tsp. paprika, 1 dessertspoon flour, 5 oz. onions, 7 oz. lecsó, 2 lb. potatoes, 1 tsp. tomato purée.

Fry the finely chopped onions in 2 oz. lard, add the paprika and tomato purée, mix thoroughly, thin with a little water and boil for a few mins. Chop the bones into small pieces, put them into the gravy and pour sufficient water over to half cover. Cook under cover for 30—40 mins., then lift the bones out of the gravy, strain through a sieve and keep warm. Trim the meat, cut it into pieces of 1 oz. each, then cut them again into small slices, salt and flour them, then fry them over an open fire till golden-brown, place the little fried escalopes into the previously prepared gravy, add the lecsó and after cooking the whole well through, keep warm on the edge of the cooker. Fry boiled and sliced potatoes in the fat left over from frying the meat, add to the slices of meat in the gravy, and mix the whole carefully. Place it in a fairly deep dish and serve at once. Replace the lecsó with green paprika and tomatoes during the summer. They should be cut into slices and stewed in the gravy of the roast meat.

Fried Veal à la Palatine

Ingredients: 1 lb. veal (sirloin), 10 oz. goose-liver, 10 oz. calf's bones, 1 tsp. salt, 5 oz. lard, 1 tsp. paprika, 1 dessertspoon flour, 5 oz. onions, 7 oz. lecsó, 2 lb. potatoes, 1 tsp. tomato purée, 5 oz. tinned green peas.

Prepared as for Escalopes of Fried Veal à la Hongroise, excepting that small slices of goose-liver are added. Cut liver into slices of 1 oz. salt and flour them and fry lightly in the fat in which the meat was previously fried. Serve with the green peas on top.

Escalopes of Veal with Fried Potatoes

Ingredients: 1½ lb. veal, 1 tsp. salt, 1 tbsp. flour, 4½ oz. lard, 2 lb. potatoes, 2 oz. butter.

Trim meat, then cut slices of 1 oz. and beat them into thin slices; salt and flour them, and fry them rapidly in hot lard over an open fire; then take out of the frying pan and put them aside. Pour part of the lard off into a frying pan, add a little water to the remaining gravy, boil thoroughly, then drawing it to the edge of the cooker, place the meat slices back into the gravy, add the fresh butter and keep it warm. Boil potatoes in their skins, peel, then slice into the frying pan containing the fat poured off from them meat; mix the meat and potatoes carefully together, and serve at once in a deep dish. Serve lettuce with it.

Escalopes of Veal

Ingredients: 1¾ lb. leg of veal, 1 tsp. salt, 1 tsbp. flour, 3½ oz. lard, ¾ lemon.

Cut the meat into five slices, beating it out slightly; nick edges with the point of a knife, salt, turn them in flour; then fry in hot lard over an open fire till golden-brown, and place the slices onto a dish. Pour part of the fat out of the frying pan, boiling what is left with the little water; take off the cooker, then put the meat back and heat it through. Serve with fried potatoes or steamed rice, laying slices of lemon around it in the dish. Can be served with vegetables—according to the season; cut the meat into ten smaller slices if preferred.

Wienerschnitzel

Ingredients: 1½ lb. leg of veal, 1 tsp. salt, 2 oz. flour, 2 eggs, 5 oz. bread-crumbs, 7 oz. lard, ¾ lemon.

Divide the meat into five slices, beat out well, nick edges with the point of a knife, salt; then turn them over first in flour, secondly in the well-beaten egg, and lastly in the bread-crumbs; fry them to a light brown colour in hot lard. (Cut the meat into 10 smaller slices if preferred.) Garnish with fried potatoes and slices of lemon.

147

Parisian Escalopes of Veal

Ingredients: 1½ lb. veal, 1 tsp. salt, 1 tbsp. flour, 3 eggs, 7 oz. lard, ¾ lemon.

Cut meat into five slices, beat them out well, nick edges with the point of a knife, salt and turn them in flour on both sides. Heat lard in a frying pan and put the slices of meat into it after having dipped them into the well-beaten egg. Fry, until they turn a light brown colour. Garnish with slices of lemon, steamed rice and baked potatoes, or any vegetable in season. (Cut the veal into 10 smaller slices if preferred.)

Milanese Veal Cutlets

Ingredients: 2 lb. veal, 1 tsp. salt, 1 tbsp. flour, 2 eggs, 3 oz. bread-crumbs, 3 oz. grated cheese, 1 dessertspoon lard, 1 lemon.

The cutlets are prepared in same manner as for Veal Cutlets with Mushrooms. Beat the cutlets to make them quite thin, and salt them. Beat the eggs well in one dish, placing the bread-crumbs mixed with grated cheese into another. Turn the cutlets on both sides in the flour, then the eggs, lastly in cheese and bread-crumbs and fry them in hot lard. Place macaroni sprinkled with grated cheese on the side of a large-sized dish, arrange the cutlets alongside in a row, and put a slice of peeled lemon on top of each cutlet.

Veal Cutlets with Mushrooms

Ingredients: 2 lb. cutlet of veal, 1 tsp. salt, 1 tbsp. flour, 3½ oz. lard, 1 dessertspoon butter, 7 oz. mushrooms, 1 oz. onions, small bunch of parsley, pinch of ground black pepper, 2 tbsp. white wine, 1 dessertspoon tomato purée.

Clean the cutlets, cutting off spinal bones and leaving only the ribs, besides removing membranes between the ribs. Cut into 10 cutlets of equal size, beat them out slightly, salt and flour them on both sides. Fry in lard heated in a frying pan, until they are nicely browned, then place them into a saucepan. Fry the flour a little in the fat left in the frying pan, add the tomato purée, white wine and 1 gill of water. Let it boil for a few mins., pour over the cutlets and simmer till tender. Fry the onions in butter, until they turn a light yellow, add the finely chopped parsley, the mushrooms washed and sliced, sprinkle with pepper and fry for 4—5 mins. Add cooked mushrooms to the meat when it is half done, and allow to simmer together until ready. Place the cutlets side by side on the dish, and pour the gravy over them. The gravy should be neither too thick nor too thin. Serve with steamed rice, or roasted potatoes.

148

Springtime Veal Cutlets

Ingredients: 2 lb. veal cutlet, 1½ tsp. salt, 1 tbsp. flour, 3½ oz. lard, 1 tbsp. butter, 1 tsp. tomato purée, 7 oz. carrots, 7 oz. cauliflower, 7 oz. green peas, 3½ oz. mushrooms, 7 oz. French beans, small bunch of parsley, ½ tsp. sugar.

The method of preparing the cutlets is similar to that for Veal Cutlets with Mushrooms. Salt and flour them, then place in a frying pan, and fry in hot lard, until golden-brown on either side; put them aside in a saucepan of suitable size. Lightly fry the remaining flour in the fat left in the frying pan, add the tomato purée, stir, then add 2 gills of water, boil for a few mins., then strain gravy over the cutlets, and covering with a lid, cook till tender. Cook the sliced carrots, and all the other vegetables separately, until tender, then strain off water. Place the butter into a frying pan, and fry the thinly-sliced mushrooms in it for 5 mins. Sprinkle them with the finely chopped parsley, add all other vegetables; add salt and sugar and let the whole simmer for 5 mins. Place the cutlets in a dish, add gravy from the meat to the vegetables, bring to boil, then pour the whole over the cutlets. Garnish with fried potato cubes.

Cutlets of Veal au Gratin

Ingredients: 1¾ lb. veal, 2 tsp. salt, 3 oz. lard, 4½ oz. butter, 3 oz. flour, 1 pt. milk. 2 yolks of egg, pinch of nutmeg, 1 tbsp. grated cheese, 1 tsp. bread-crumbs, 1¼ lb. cleaned Brussels sprouts.

The method of preparing the cutlets is similar to that for Veal Cutlets with Mushrooms. Clean the meat and cut it into cutlets, and after beating them out a little, salt and flour them; then place in a frying pan containing hot lard and cook them until nicely browned, then put aside to cool. Boil the Brussels sprouts in salt water, until they are tender, strain and allow them to cool. Mix 3 oz. butter with 2 oz. flour, and make a light roux. Dilute with hot milk and stir constantly with a whisk, till sauce is nice and thick. Add salt, grated nutmeg, and lastly the yolks of egg, stir, and take off the cooker. Butter the inside of a fireproof dish, put the cutlets in it, arrange sprouts over each cutlet. Spread the milk sauce over each cutlet separately, sprinkle with grated cheese and bread-crumbs, and finally cut the butter into small dabs and place them on top of each cutlet. Bake in the oven until top is nicely browned and serve at once.

Financier's Cutlets of Veal

Ingredients: 2 lb. veal, 5 oz. goose-liver, 3½ oz. sweetbreads, 3½ oz. mushrooms, 3½ oz. smoked boiled beef tongue, 1½ tsp. salt, 1 dessertspoon flour, pinch of ground black pepper, 2 oz. butter, 3½ oz. lard, ¼ oz. truffles, 2 gills Madeira sauce.

The method of preparing the cutlets is similar to that for Veal Cutlets with Mushrooms. Salt the cutlets and having floured them lightly, fry in fat until they are slightly browned, then keep them warm until dishing. Cook the sweetbreads for 10 mins., cool in cold water, and cut them into small cubes. Cut the goose-liver, mushrooms, and tongue into cubes of same size. Fry the mushrooms lightly in butter, then add the goose-liver and sweetbreads, salt and pepper; fry a few mins. longer, then pour on the Madeira sauce, add tongue and bring to boil. Place the cutlets in a row upon the dish, pour the ragout over them with a tablespoon and finally lay thinly-sliced truffles on top of them. Garnish with potato-chips at both ends of the dish (see Garnishes).

Veal Cutlets with Asparagus

Ingredients: 1 lb. veal, 1 tsp. salt, 1 tsp. flour, 3½ oz. lard, 1 pt. supreme sauce, 1½ lb. tinned heads of asparagus, 1 oz. butter, ½ tsp. sugar.

The method of preparing this dish is similar to that for Veal Cutlets with Mushrooms. Fry the cutlets in a frying pan, having salted and dipped them into flour first, then put them aside. Pour off part of the fat from frying pan, then add 1 gill of water to the fat left, bring to boil and then pour this gravy over the cutlets; cover with a lid and allow to simmer. Strain water off the heads of asparagus, heat them in butter, adding a little sugar and salt. When serving lay the cutlets side by side on the dish putting a few heads of asparagus on top of each; then pour supreme sauce over them (see Sauces). Garnish with steamed rice, served separately.

Vichy Cutlets of Veal

Ingredients: 2 lb. veal, 1 tsp. salt, 1 dessertspoon flour, 3½ oz. lard, 1 carrot, 3½ oz. butter, 1 tsp. sugar, small bunch of parsley.

The method of preparing cutlets is much the same as that for Veal Cutlets with mushrooms. Salt, flour, and then fry the cutlets until they are nicely browned, then take out of frying pan and let them cool. Pour off part of the fat from frying pan, add a little water to the remaining gravy and boil it thoroughly, then drawing it to the edge of the cooker, replace the cutlets, and add 1 oz. butter. Keep warm until dishing.

Clean the carrot and after cutting in half, cut it into small slices. Melt the remaining butter in a small pan, place sliced carrot in it, salt and sugar slightly, add the finely chopped parsley and pouring on a little water let the whole stew until tender. Place the sliced carrot on the side of the dish when serving, arrange cutlets in a row and pour the gravy over them. Serve with steamed rice in a separate dish.

Veal Steak à la Bonne Femme

Ingredients: 1¾ lb. veal, 1½ tsp. salt, 1 dessertspoon flour, 7 oz. lard, 1 oz. butter, 5 oz. mushrooms, 5 oz. boiled streaky bacon, 2 lb. potatoes, 5 oz. shallots or small onions, small bunch of parsley.

Cut the veal into five equal pieces, beat it slightly, taking care to leave slices thick and round-shaped. Salt, dip them in flour, put them into the melted lard, cover and let them braise slowly, till both sides are nicely browned.
Braise the onions slowly in a little butter, leaving them whole, until they are cooked, then keep them warm. Fry the potatoes cut into cubes in the remaining butter until they are crisp, then taking them out, keep them warm, too. Place the meat in a deep dish. Now put a little flour into the fat left over in the frying pan, fry lightly, add a little water, then boil thoroughly and strain over the veal in the dish. Cut streaky bacon up into small strips of 1 inch length; fry lightly, add the sliced mushrooms, sprinkle with the finely chopped parsley and fry them for 4—5 mins. When dishing mix together the potatoes, onions, beef and mushrooms, salt them and place them on top of the veal steaks. Serve with lettuce.

Steak of Veal à la Creole

Ingredients: 1¾ lb. veal, 1 tsp. salt, 1 tsp. flour, 3½ oz. lard, 2 oz. butter, 5 oz. mushrooms, ½ lb. fresh tomatoes, 3 oz. onions, pinch of ground black pepper, small bunch of parsley.

The preparation of this steak and its roasting is similar to that for Veal Steak à la Bonne Femme. After frying, place the steaks in a row upon a dish and keep them warm on the edge of the cooker. Take the butter and part of the fat left over in the frying pan and fry the finely chopped onions in it, until they are light yellow. Then add the sliced mushrooms, salt and pepper, sprinkle with the finely chopped parsley, and fry for 4—5 mins.; finally add the tomatoes, skinned and cut into fairly thick slices, and continue frying a few mins. longer. Pour this sauce over the meat in the dish and garnish it with rice.

Roast Veal

Ingredients: 2 lb. veal, 3 oz. lard, 1 tsp. salt, ½ tsp. tomato purée, ½ tsp. flour.

Bone the meat, because in this way the joint can be carved better, then salt it. Melt half of the fat in a roasting pan of suitable size, put in the meat and add the chopped bones to make a nice gravy. Then spread the other half of the lard on top of the meat, place it in medium-hot oven and, basting frequently, roast. Add a spoonful of water occasionally to prevent burning. When the veal is tender, take it out of the pan, add tomato purée to the browned fat, and mix well. Sprinkle on flour, and let it brown a little. Dilute with water, boil for 5—6 mins., and strain it into a small saucepan. Slice the meat, place slices on the dish and pour the gravy over it. Garnish with roast potatoes, steamed rice and also any vegetable in season, or with lettuce. If a thick gravy is not wanted prepare it without flour and tomatoes.

Veal Cutlets with Butter and Lemon

Ingredients: 1¾ lb. veal, 1 tsp. salt, 1 tbsp. flour, 3 oz. lard, 2 oz. butter, 1 lemon.

Fry the cutlets according to the procedure employed with steak of veal, then place them into a pan. Fry the remaining flour in the fat left over in the frying pan, pour on 2 gills of water, allow to boil for a few mins., then strain gravy over the cutlets. Sprinkle with grated lemon-peel, add the butter and cook the cutlets until they are tender. Place slices of lemon beside them when dishing. Garnish with steamed rice and creamed potatoes.

Veal with Asparagus

Ingredients: 1¾ lb. veal, 3½ oz. lard, 2 oz. butter, 1 tbsp. flour, ½ tsp. salt, 1 lb. tinned heads of asparagus, ½ tsp. sugar, sprig of parsley.

Divide the meat into 5 large or 10 small slices, beat them a little, nick the edges with a knife, salt and sprinkle with flour. Heat lard in a frying pan and fry the cutlets until both sides are nicely browned; then place them in a saucepan. Fry the remaining flour in the fat left over in the frying pan, pour on 2 gills of water or water from the asparagus, boil for a few mins., then strain over the cutlets; add 1 oz. of butter, cover and let cutlets simmer until they are tender. Melt the remaining butter in a small flat pan, place asparagus in it, add a little salt and sugar, and heat. Place the cutlets in a row upon the dish, pour the gravy over them, arrange the asparagus heads on top and sprinkle with the finely chopped parsley. Garnish with rice, baked potatoes, or with potato doughnuts.

Veal in Paprika Sauce

Ingredients: 1¾ lb. veal, 1 tsp. salt, 3½ oz. onions, ½ tsp. paprika, 3½ oz. lecsó, 2 gills sour cream, 2 oz. flour, 3½ oz. lard.

Divide the meat into 5 large or 10 smaller slices. Beat slices to flatten, nick edges, salt and sprinkle it with a little flour. Fry the cutlets lightly on both sides in lard heated in a frying pan. Lift out and place them into a saucepan and fry the onions, chopped into small pieces, in the fat left in frying pan until they turn golden; put in the paprika and mix well; then add 1½ gill of water, and bring to boil; then pour sauce over the cutlets and allow to simmer covered, for about 20 mins. Finally add the sour cream mixed with the remaining flour, add the lecsó and turning cutlets from time to time, simmer until they are tender. Should the gravy be too thick, thin with a little hot water. Garnish with thimble dumplings (galuska).

Veal Cutlets with Green Peas

Ingredients: 1¾ lb. veal, 3½ oz. lard, 1 oz. butter, 1 tbsp. flour, 1 tsp. salt, 1 lb. tinned green peas, ½ tsp. sugar, 1 gill cream, small bunch of parsley.

Divide the meat into 5 large or 10 small slices, beat them, nick edges with a knife, salt and sprinkle with flour. Fry them in lard, heated in a frying pan, until both sides are nicely browned and lift them into a saucepan. Fry the remaining flour in the fat left over in the frying pan, add 2 gills of water, boil for a few mins., then strain gravy over the cutlets; cover them and let them simmer, until tender. Melt the butter in a small frying pan, add the finely chopped parsley, the strained green peas, and a little sugar and let it boil for a few mins. When meat is tender, pour the cream over it, and bring to boil. Place the cutlets into a deep dish, and pour the green pea sauce over them. The sauce should not be too thick. Garnish with rice, potatoes in butter, or crisply fried potatoes.

Stuffed Breast of Veal

Ingredients (for 6 people): 2½ lb. veal, 2 tsp. salt, 3 rolls, 4 eggs, 2 oz. butter, pinch of ground black pepper, small bunch of parsley, ½ tsp. tomato purée, ½ tsp. flour, 3½ oz. lard, 2 gills milk.

Take the thicker part of breast of veal and bone it. Push knife through meat lengthwise to make pocket for stuffing, taking care not to cut sides open. Beat the butter in a dish till creamy; then add 3 egg-yolks successively, the rolls, with crusts pared off, steeped in milk and well pressed out, salt and pepper and finally the finely chopped parsley. Stuff meat with this mixture, then stitch the ends together with a large needle, gently pressing the stuffing to even it out; salt the meat. Roasting and preparation of the gravy is similar to that for Roast Veal. When it is ready keep the meat in the warm oven for another 20 mins. to let stuffing set; then take out the string, cut meat into equal slices, lay it carefully on the dish and pour on the gravy. Garnish with potatoes in butter and spinach, or any other vegetables.

Minced Veal

Ingredients: 1½ lb. veal, 2 oz. lard, 1 tsp. salt, 1 egg, 1 tbsp. cream, 2 rolls, 1 gill milk, small bunch of parsley, 2 oz. butter, 1 tsp. flour.

Trim the meat, then pass it twice through the mincer, put it in a bowl, salt, add the egg, cream, the rolls steeped in milk and pressed out, and a little finely chopped parsley, previously fried in ½ oz. of butter. Heat lard in a frying pan; form 10—20 round rissoles of the meat with hands dipped in flour, and fry them until golden-brown on both sides. Pour part of the fat out of the frying pan, add a little water to remainder, boil for a few mins, and then, drawing it to the edge of the cooker, mix with 1 oz. butter. Pour the gravy over the rissoles when serving and garnish with rice. This dish can be included in diets, garnished with creamed potatoes, creamed green peas and creamed carrots.

Veal's Pluck in Paprika Sauce

Ingredients: 2 lb. veal's pluck, 4½ oz. lard, 7 oz. onions, 1 tsp. paprika, 3 cloves of garlic, 1 tsp. salt, pinch of marjoram, 1 dessertspoon tomato purée, 7 oz. lecsó, 1 dessertspoon flour, 3 sprigs of celery.

Soak the veal's pluck in cold water, then wash in fresh water several times; parboil for 20 mins., let it cool and then cut into strips. Fry the finely chopped onions till they are a light yellow, add the paprika, tomato purée, crushed garlic, and marjoram, and stir for a min. Then add the veal's pluck, salt, add a little water, cover with a lid, and let it simmer, slowly. Add a little water if necessary. When tender, add the lecsó and the finely chopped leaves of celery. Mix flour with a little water, pour over meat, and cook the whole for another 10 mins. Garnish with mashed potatoes flavoured with fried onion.

Veal Light in Sour Sauce

Ingredients: 1 lung and heart of veal, 1½ tsp. salt, 3½ oz. lard, 3½ oz. flour, pinch of ground pepper, pinch of paprika, 1 bay leaf, pinch of thyme, 1 lemon, 2 oz. onions, 2 cloves of garlic, 2 oz. pickled gherkins, 1 tsp. capers, 1 tbsp. vinegar, 1 tsp. sugar, 1 tsp. mustard, small bunch of parsley.

Cook lights in slightly salted water till tender, then take them out of the stock; when cooled cut into thin strips. Mix onions, garlic, bay leaf, gherkins, capers, parsley, thin lemon peel and thyme and chop all into tiny pieces. Fry the sugar in the melted lard until it is brown; add the flour, stir till dark brown. Put in the mixed and chopped spices, stir and when they are partially fried, add the paprika; pour on the stock and stirring with a whisk boil the whole for 15 mins. It must not be too thick or too thin. Put in the sliced lights, add mustard, lemon-juice and the amount of vinegar required, salt and cook the whole for another 15—20 mins. Place in a deep dish and serve with bread-roll-dumplings.

Veal's Pluck à la Italienne

Ingredients: 2 lb. veal's pluck, 4½ oz. lard or oil, 5 oz. onions, 4½ oz. tomato purée, 2 cloves of garlic, pinch of ground black pepper, 1 bay leaf, 1 tsp. salt, small bunch of parsley, 2 tbsp. white wine.

Soak the veal's pluck in cold water, wash through several times in fresh water, parboil for 20 mins. and when it has cooled, cut into fairly thick strips. Fry onions in lard till they are golden-brown, then add garlic, tomato purée, coarsely chopped parsley, white wine and the bay leaf and boil the whole a few mins. Put in the meat, salt and pepper it and let it simmer under lid till tender. Stir from time to time while cooking; add a little water if necessary taking care to let the gravy remain thick. Garnish with steamed rice.

Braised Calf's Liver

Ingredients: 1¾ lb. calf's liver, 4½ oz. lard, ¼ tsp. salt, 7 oz. onions, pinch of ground black pepper, pinch of marjoram, ⅓ tsp. paprika.

Trim the calf's liver and cut it into slices. Fry the sliced onions in lard, till light yellow, add pepper and marjoram. Fry the liver rapidly, stirring all the while. Then add the paprika. Salt just before dishing and garnish with mashed potatoes flavoured with fried onions.

Fried Calf's Liver Slices

Ingredients: 1½ lb. calf's liver, 1 tsp. salt, 2 oz. flour, 2 eggs, 5 oz. bread-crumbs, 5 oz. lard.

Trim liver, cut into thin slices, flatten them lightly, salt and then turn them in flour, beaten eggs and lastly in bread-crumbs; then fry both sides in hot lard. Serve with roast potatoes and pickles.

Fried Calf's Liver and Bacon

Ingredients: 1 tbsp. flour, 1 tsp. salt, 2 oz. lard, 7 oz. streaky bacon, 1¾ lb. calf's liver.

Trim liver and dry it with a cloth. Cut it into 10 slices; flatten them slightly. Cut the bacon into thin slices of equal size, nicking slices with knife in several places, to make cockscombs. Melt lard in a frying pan and fry the pieces of bacon in it until they are golden on both sides. Then take them out and keep warm. Salt and flour slices of liver, and fry quickly in the same fat over an open fire. Lay them in the dish in a neat row when serving, and place a piece of bacon on top of each slice of liver; add the gravy. Serve with fried potatoes or steamed rice and pickles.

Calf's Kidneys in Spiced Butter

Ingredients: 1¾ lb. calf's kidneys, 3½ oz. lard, 1 tsp. salt, 2 oz. bread-crumbs, 3 oz. butter, ¼ lemon, ½ tsp. mustard, pinch of ground black pepper, small bunch of parsley.

Dry kidneys with a cloth, then leaving the covering of fat, cut them into equal slices and flatten them lightly. Salt and turn kidneys in bread-crumbs,

155

then fry both sides till golden-brown. Place potato chips on the dish, arrange the kidneys beside them, a piece of spiced butter on top of each. Serve with lettuce. *Spiced butter:* mix butter with a little pepper, lemon-juice, mustard, and finely chopped parsley. Form little bars of 2 inches each and chill.

Calf's Tongue in Tomato Sauce

Ingredients: 2 lb. cleaned calf's tongue, 2 oz. onions, 5 oz. mixed vegetables, 5 whole black peppers, 1 tsp. salt, 5 portions of tomato sauce.

Cook the tongue with the vegetables, onions, salt and pepper, until it is tender; skin it when cold. Make the tomato sauce using stock from the tongue. Cut the tongue into slices lengthwise, put in the tomato sauce and boil it once again; then serve. Garnish with steamed rice or boiled potatoes sprinkled with chopped parsley.

Calf's Tongue in Mushroom Sauce

Prepare the calf's tongue as for that prepared with tomato. Place the sliced tongue in mushroom and sour cream sauce, boil and dish sauce and tongue together. Garnish with steamed rice or boiled potatoes in butter, sprinkled with parsley.

Calf's Brains with Eggs

Ingredients: 3 calf's brains, 1 tsp. salt, 3 oz. lard, 2 oz. onions, pinch of ground black pepper, pinch of marjoram, small bunch of parsley, 10 eggs.

Soak brains in cold water for a short time, dry them on a cloth, trim and peel off thin skin, then cut them into small pieces. Fry the finely chopped onions in a frying pan until golden-yellow, add the finely chopped parsley, and the brains; then salt, pepper and sprinkle with marjoram; fry for 5—6 mins. Beat the 10 eggs up thoroughly, pour over the mixture and cook them like scrambled eggs.

Fried Calf's Brains

Ingredients: 3 calf's brains, 1 tsp. salt, 2 oz. flour, 2 eggs, 4½ oz. bread-crumbs, 5 oz. lard.

Soak brains in cold water, dry them on a cloth, trim and skin, then cut each brain in half, salt, dip in flour, beaten eggs, and lastly in bread-crumbs; fry them in hot lard. Serve with rice and tomato sauce, or with tartare sauce.

Calf's Brains with Chicken Sauce

Ingredients: 3 calf's brains, ½ tsp. salt, ¼ lemon, 5 portions of chicken sauce.

Soak brains in cold water. Trim and skin, then cook in salted water, to which the juice of ¼ lemon is added. Strain after cooking. Set them on a dish and serve, pouring the chicken sauce over. Serve with steamed rice.

Lombardy Calf's Brains

Ingredients: 3 calf's brains, 1 tsp. salt, 2 oz. flour, 2 eggs, 2 oz. grated cheese, 5 oz. lard.

Prepare as for Fried brains. Salt the pieces, turn them in flour, then dipping into mixture of grated cheese and eggs, fry them in hot lard. Garnish with risotto (rice and green peas) and serve tomato sauce separately.

Fried Sweetbreads

Ingredients: 1½ lb. sweetbreads, 1 tsp. salt, 2 oz. flour, 4½ oz. bread-crumbs, 5 oz. lard, ½ lemon, 2 eggs.

Trim sweetbreads and cook them in salted lemon water for 5—6 mins. Take out of water and let them cool. Slice and salt them, dip slices first in flour, then beaten eggs, and lastly bread-crumbs. Garnish with green peas in cream or serve with steamed rice and tartare sauce.

Fried Calf's Foot

Ingredients: 3 calf's feet, 1½ tsp. salt, 2 oz. onions, 2 oz. parsnips, 2 oz. celery, 3 oz. flour, 3 eggs, 7 oz. bread-crumbs, 7 oz. lard.

Clean, wash and bone calf's feet, and cook gently in salt water along with the onions and vegetables till tender. Take them out of the stock, salt, turn them in flour, egg and bread-crumbs, and fry them light brown on both sides in plenty of lard. Serve with baked potatoes, adding the tartare sauce separately.

Scalded Calf's Feet with Vinaigrette Sauce

Ingredients: 3 calf's feet, 1 tsp. salt, 2 oz. onions, 2 oz. mixed vegetables, 3 whole black peppers.

Prepare the calf's feet as for Fried Calf's Foot. Cook them in salt water until they are tender, along with the onions, pepper and vegetables. Dish with a little of the gravy, the mixed vegetables and salt potatoes. Serve with vinaigrette sauce.

Fried Calf's Head

Ingredients: 2 lb. calf's head (cleaned), 1½ tsp. salt, 2 oz. onions, 2 oz. celery, 2 oz. parsnips, 2 oz. flour, 3 eggs, 5 oz. bread-crumbs, 7 oz. lard.

Bone and soak the calf's head for half an hour in plenty of cold water; then boil it gently in salted water along with the onions, celery and parsnips, until tender. Then take out of the stock, place on a dish and set in a cool place. Cut into 10 slices lengthwise when cool, salt and turn the slices in flour, egg, and bread-crumbs. Fry in plenty of lard until golden-brown. Serve with baked potatoes and tartare sauce.

Scalded Calf's Head

Ingredients: 2 lb. calf's head (cleaned), 1 tsp. salt, 2 oz. onions, 5 oz. mixed vegetables, 4 whole black peppers.

Prepare the meat as for Fried Calf's Head, boiling it in salt water along with the onions, vegetables and whole peppers until it is tender. Cut the meat into thin slices and dish with a little of its own stock, with salt potatoes, and mixed vegetables. Serve with vinaigrette sauce. The calf's head can also be prepared with mushroom or chicken sauce, but in that case, instead of stock pour sauce over the slices and serve with steamed rice or potatoes in butter

PORK

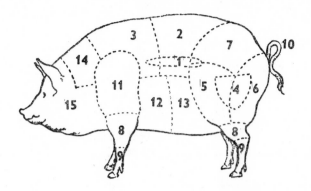

Cuts of pork:	The most advantageous use of the cuts:
1. Tenderloin	Roasted, or filleted and grilled
2. Loin (kidney end)	Roasted, or sliced and grilled (chops)
3. Loin (chump end)	Roasted, sliced to chops and grilled, or fried
	Pickled, smoked and boiled
4—5—6—7. Leg	Roasted, sliced and fried or grilled
8. Hock	Pickled, smoked and boiled
9—10. Feet and tail	Paprika stew (pörkölt), pickled, smoked and boiled, or jellied pork
11. Shoulder	Roast, paprika stew (pörkölt). Boned, pickled, smoked and boiled for rolled ham
12. Spare rib	Braised, paprika stew (pörkölt)
	Transylvanian gulyás
	Pickled, smoked and boiled
13. Belly	Transylvanian gulyás, stuffed cabbage, minced meat, sausages
14. Round chop	Roasted, sliced and grilled or fried, pickled and smoked
15. Head	Boiled. Jellied pork

Pork Paprika Stew (Pörkölt)

Ingredients: 2 lb. shoulder of pork, 3 oz. lard, 7 oz. onions, 1 tsp. salt, 1 tsp. paprika, 1 dessertspoon tomato purée, 4½ oz. lecsó, pinch of caraway seeds, 2 cloves of garlic.

Cut the meat into pieces of 1 oz. each. Fry the finely chopped onions in lard. Add the paprika, crushed garlic and tomato purée, stir well, then, adding a little water, boil for a few mins.; then put in the meat, adding the salt, and the chopped caraway seeds; cover and let it simmer until tender. Stir from time to time during cooking, pouring a little water into the pan if gravy threatens to burn. Add lecsó (or 2 green paprikas and 2 sliced tomatoes when in season) before the meat is quite tender; let it simmer until it is ready, taking care that there should be only as much gravy as covers the meat. Garnish with tarhonya, dumplings, or boiled potatoes.

Székely Gulyás

Ingredients: 1 lb. shoulder of pork, 1 lb. ribs of pork, 5 oz. onions, 1 tsp. salt, 2 oz. lard, ½ tsp. paprika, ¼ tsp. caraway seeds, 2 cloves of garlic, 1 pt. sour cream, 1 dessertspoon flour, 2 lb. sour cabbage.

Cut the shoulder and ribs of pork into 2 oz. pieces. Fry the finely chopped onions lightly in the lard; add the paprika, crushed garlic and caraway seeds; stir well, add a little water, bring to boil, then put in the meat, salt, cover with a lid, and then let it simmer. Cook for about 40—45 mins., then add the previously rinsed cabbage (in season 2 slices green paprikas can also be added); pour sufficient water to cover and—strirring occasionally—cook till meat is tender. Mix ½ pt. of sour cream with the flour, add to the stew and boil for another 4—5 mins.

Hajdú Cabbage

Ingredients: 1½ lb. smoked pork, 5 oz. lard, 1 tsp. salt, 7 oz. onions, 1 tsp. paprika, pinch of caraway seed, 2 lb. sour cabbage, ½ lb. smoked sausage.

Fry 3½ oz. sliced onions in 3 oz. lard, add the caraway seed and the previously rinsed sour cabbage to it; pour in about 1 pt. of water, and let it simmer until tender. Cut the smoked pork into one-inch cubes, heat 2 oz. lard, fry 3½ oz. finely chopped onions till golden, add paprika and pork and cook till meat is tender. Do not forget to put in the sliced sausage about 10 mins. before meat is ready. Finally mix the cooked cabbage with the paprika stew, bring the whole to the boil again and serve.

Cowboy's Tokány

Ingredients: 1¾ lb. shoulder of pork, 3½ oz. bacon, 2 oz. lard, 4½ oz. onions, 1 tsp. salt, 3½ oz. lecsó, 2 gills sour cream, 1 dessertspoon flour, ½ tsp. paprika.

Cut the meat into strips of 2 inches length. Fry the bacon, also cut into strips, for a short time in hot lard; then add the thinly sliced onions and fry till they turn a light yellow colour; put in the paprika, stir well, pour on a little water and cook for 1—2 mins. Add the meat, salt and let it simmer under lid. Stir from time to time, and pour on a little water if necessary. Put in the lecsó (which in season may be replaced by 2 small paprikas and 2 small tomatoes). When the meat is tender, pour mixture of sour cream and flour over it, allowing it to boil for another 3—4 mins. Should the gravy be too thick, thin it with a little water. Serve with dumplings.

160

Butcher's Tokány

Ingredients: 1¾ lb. shoulder of pork, 4½ oz. bacon, 2 oz. lard, 5 oz. onions, 1 dessertspoon tomato purée, 2 cloves of garlic, 1½ gill white wine, 4½ oz. pickled gherkins, pinch of ground pepper.

Cut the meat into strips of 2 inches length. Melt lard and lightly fry chopped bacon in it. Then add the finely chopped onions and fry till golden-brown, add the tomato purée and crushed garlic, stir, then pour in white wine and cook for another 1—2 mins. Add the meat, salt and pepper, cover with lid and let it simmer. Stir it from time to time and add a little water if necessary. Chop gherkins into strips and add to stew 5—10 mins. before serving. Take care that the tokány's gravy is thick. Garnish with tarthonya or with boiled potatoes, sprinkled with finely chopped parsley.

Frankfurt Tokány

Ingredients: 1½ lb. shoulder of pork, 3½ oz. lard, 5 oz. onions, 1 dessertspoon tomato purée, 2 cloves of garlic, 1 tsp. salt, pinch of ground black pepper, 2 tbsp. white wine, 7 oz. Vienna sausages.

Cut the meat into strips of 2 inches length. Melt the lard and fry the finely chopped onions in it until they turn golden-yellow; then add tomato purée and crushed garlic and stir. Pour in the white wine, cook for 1—2 mins. then put in the meat, and pepper, adding a little more water at the same time if necessary. Let it simmer gently. Skin the Vienna sausages, cut them into slices, then fry them lightly in ½ oz. of lard; add to the tokány when it is ready and boil the whole for another 2—3 mins. Serve with mashed potatoes and fried onions or with steamed rice.

Szeged Pork with Tarhonya

Ingredients: 1½ lb. shoulder of pork, 1 tsp. salt, 5 oz. lard, 1 tsp. paprika, 3½ oz. onions, 7 oz. lecsó, ¾ lb. tarhonya.

Cut the meat into cubes of ½ inch. Then fry the finely chopped onions in 3 oz. lard, until they are golden-yellow; mix in the paprika and pour on a little water. Bring to boil, then put in the meat, salt it, cover with lid and let it simmer for about 50 mins. Pour a little water onto stew if necessary. Fry tarhonya to golden-brown, in 2½ oz. of lard, add it to the meat together with the lecsó; add twice the amount of the tarhonya in water, then cook it slowly, stirring occasionally until it is tender.

Bácska (Serbian) Meat in Rice

Ingredients: 1½ lb. shoulder of pork, 1 tsp. salt, 5 oz. lard, 1 tsp. paprika, 3½ oz. onions, ½ lb. lecsó, ¾ lb. rice.

Cut the meat into cubes. Fry the finely chopped onions in 3 oz. lard, till golden-yellow, add the paprika and pour on a little water. After boiling a short time add the meat and cook for 50 mins. Pour on a little water while cooking, if necessary. Fry the rice lightly in 2½ oz. lard, add it to the meat together with the lecsó, add twice the amount of rice in water, then cover with lid, and cook slowly, stirring occasionally till tender. In the season add 3 green paprikas and 2 tomatoes in place of lecsó.

Stuffed Green Paprikas

Ingredients: 1 lb. minced pork, 10 green paprikas, 3 lb. fresh tomatoes, 3½ oz. lard, 2 oz. onions, 2 oz. flour, 2 oz. sugar, 1 tsp. salt, pinch of ground black pepper, pinch of marjoram, 1½ eggs, 3½ oz. rice, 1 clove of garlic, small bunch of parsley.

Wash and core paprikas. Parboil the rice, strain, and put it aside to cool. Place the minced meat in a bowl, add the rice, 1 oz. chopped onions fried in 1 oz. of lard, the finely chopped parsley, one whole egg and one yolk, salt and pepper and sprinkle with marjoram. Fry other half of the onions lightly with crushed garlic, add to stuffing and knead the whole well together. Stuff the paprikas with meat and cook them slowly in the tomato sauce, until ready. If the paprikas are too hot, pour boiling water over them, and rinse with cold, before stuffing. Serve with boiled potatoes.

Stuffed Vegetable Marrow with Tomato Sauce

Ingredients: 1 lb. minced pork, 2½ lb. vegetable marrow, 1 oz. butter, pinch of ground black pepper, 1½ rolls, 1½ gill milk, 1 tsp. salt, small bunch of parsley, 1 egg, 2 pt. tomato sauce.

The method of preparation is similar to that for stuffed vegetable marrow with dill sauce, only pour tomato sauce instead of dill sauce over it, when marrow is cooked.

Stuffed Vegetable Marrow with Dill Sauce

Ingredients: 1 lb. minced pork, 2½ lb. vegetable marrow, 1 oz. butter, pinch of ground black pepper, 1½ rolls, 1½ gill milk, ½ tsp. salt, small bunch of parsley, 1 egg, 2 pt. dill sauce with sour cream, 1 tbsp. vinegar.

Peel the vegetable marrow, cut into 2-inch slices, and remove seeds. Parboil the slices in water to which salt and vinegar are added, strain through sieve and let them cool. Soak the rolls in milk, then press out well and add to the minced meat, together with the egg, ground pepper and finely chopped parsley. Salt and mix well. Fill the cooled slices of vegetable marrow with this stuffing, place them in rows in a pan greased with butter, pour 2 gills broth or water over them and cook them in the oven until they are done. Pour thick dill sauce over the cooked vegetable marrow and let it cook a few minutes longer. Serve in a deep dish, and garnish with rice.

Stuffed Kohlrabis

Ingredients: 10 kohlrabis, 1 lb. veal or pork, 1½ rolls, 1 gill cream, 2 tbsp. milk, 2 oz. flour, pinch of ground black pepper, ½ tsp. sugar, 3½ oz. butter, 1 egg, 1 bunch of parsley, 1 tsp. salt.

Peel the kohlrabis, scoop out the inside, and parboil them in slightly salt water. Put aside to cool. Mince the meat, add pepper, rolls soaked in milk and then pressed out, one egg, add finely chopped parsley; knead together with half of the cream, then stuff the kohlrabis with it. Chop the scooped-out inside of the kohlrabis into tiny pieces and the leaves into strips. Butter the inside of a saucepan, place the kohlrabis with the chopped leaves inside, add salt and sugar and broth or water and, covering with a lid, let it simmer until kohlrabis are tender. Then place in a dish and keep them warm. Thicken their gravy with a light roux. Add the cream, pour it over the kohlrabis, and serve hot.

Stuffed Cabbage with Ribs of Pork

Ingredients: 1 lb. minced pork, 2 lb. sour cabbage and leaves, 3 oz. lard, 3½ oz. onions, 1 clove of garlic, 1 tsp. salt, pinch of ground pepper, pinch of marjoram, 1 egg, 3½ oz. rice, ½ pt. sour cream, 2 oz. flour, ¼ tsp. paprika, ¾ lb. ribs of pork.

Place the minced meat in a dish, add the half-boiled and cooled rice and the egg, spice it with pepper, marjoram and a pinch of paprika and finally also add 1½ oz. finely chopped onions fried in 1 oz. lard, together with the crushed garlic. Mix the whole throroughly. Place the stuffing on the middle of cabbage leaves, folding their edges and rolling them up tightly. Grease the bottom of a pan with 2 oz. lard; place the previously rinsed sour cabbage in it, add salt and fried onions together with the remaining paprika. Lay the stuffed leaves on top of the cabbage, put the ribs in the middle and pour on sufficient water to cover. Cover with lid, and let the cabbage simmer for about an hour and three quarters. Stir it very carefully now and again, adding water if required. When tender, take out the ribs of pork and the stuffed cabbage leaves, and place them in a dish. Pour the 2 gills of sour cream, mixed with flour, onto the cabbage in the pot and boil it for another ten minutes. Serve cabbage in a deep dish and put the stuffed cabbages and the ribs on the top; sprinkle with 2 tbsp. of sour cream and serve hot.

Kolozsvári Stuffed Cabbage

Ingredients: 1 lb. minced pork, 7 oz. smoked sausage, ¾ lb. pork cutlet or smoked pork, 2 lb. sour cabbage and whole leaves, 4½ oz. lard, 3½ oz. rice, 1 pt. sour cream, ½ tsp. paprika.

Prepare as for Stuffed Cabbage. Instead of the ribs, however, cook smoked sausage with the cabbage. The sausages need less cooking. Dish, laying 5 slices of roast pork and 5 pieces of smoked sausage beside the stuffed cabbage. If prepared with smoked pork, it can be cooked with the cabbage, and dished, sliced beside the stuffed cabbage. Pour a generous amount of sour cream on top.

Transylvanian Cabbage

Ingredients: 1¼ lb. minced pork, 3½ oz. bacon, 5 oz. smoked sausage, 3½ oz. lard, 2 lb. sour cabbage, 5 oz. rice, 2 oz. onions, 2 cloves of garlic, ½ tsp. paprika, 1 tsp. salt, pinch of ground black pepper, ½ pt. sour cream.

Fry the finely chopped onions in 2 oz. lard until they turn pale yellow; add crushed garlic, the minced pork, salt, and pepper and dust with paprika. Then fry the whole slowly for 10—12 mins. Cut the bacon into small cubes of ¼ inch, heat them slightly in a frying pan, then add the sliced smoked sausages, and fry for 2—3 mins. Cook the rice until it is half-done, then set it aside. Then boil the cabbage for 20 mins: in salt water; drain off water. Grease the inside of a pan of adequate size or a fireproof dish with 1 oz. of lard, place one third of the cabbage on the bottom, cover it with a layer of bacon and sausages, lay another third of the cabbage over it, sprinkle with a little sour cream, then put on the half-cooked rice, and then adding a layer of the fried minced pork, cover with the remaining cabbage. During the season a few sliced green paprikas and tomatoes can be added. Sprinkle the top of the cabbage with the remaining sour cream, dust a little paprika over it, then sprinkling with 1 oz. melted lard, let it stew for 1¼ hrs. in a warm (not hot) oven.

Pork Djuvets

Ingredients: 1¾ lb. shoulder of pork, 1 lb. potatoes, 3½ oz. onions, 2 cloves of garlic, 3½ oz. rice, 7 oz. green paprika, 7 oz. fresh tomatoes, 7 oz. aubergines, 1 tsp. salt, 3½ oz. lard, ½ tsp. paprika.

Cut the meat into 2 oz. cubes. Dice and fry onions in 2 oz. of lard, add the paprika, garlic and the meat and stew it under cover for 12—15 mins. Slice the aubergines, potatoes, green paprika and tomatoes; then take a pan of suitable size, or a fireproof dish, and grease the inside with 1 oz. of lard; then lay the sliced potatoes and half of the aubergines in the bottom, next add a layer of rice, then the stewed meat, a layer of green paprika and tomatoes, the other half of the rice, and finally the remaining aubergines and potatoes. Salt each layer. Pour sufficient water to cover entirely, and let it stew under lid in the oven for about an hour and a half. Serve it in a fireproof dish or the pan.

Torda Savoy Pie

Ingredients: 1¼ lb. minced pork, 3 lb. savoys, 3½ oz. rice, 3½ oz. bacon, ½ lb. pork lace, 2 oz. onions, 2 cloves of garlic, pinch of ground black pepper, pinch of marjoram, ⅓ tsp. paprika, 1 gill sour cream, 1 tsp. flour, 1 tsp. salt, 2 eggs, 1 roll, 2 oz. lard, 2 tsp. milk.

Trim savoys, cut out thick stalks and boil in salt water until half-cooked; drain through a sieve then put in a cool place. Pass meat through mincer, several times, put into a dish, spice with marjoram and pepper, salt, then add the finely chopped onions and crushed garlic—fried previously in 1 oz. of lard—add the eggs and the soaked and well squeezed-out roll, the boiled and cooled rice and mix all the ingredients thoroughly. Grease the inside of a small pan with 1 oz. lard and lay one third of the flattened-out leaves in the bottom of it, spread on them the meat stuffing, cover it with one-third of the leaves, then make another layer of the meat and finally cover with the remaining third of savoy leaves. Shape with hands into the form of a small cake and cutting the bacon into very thin slices, cover the top. Finally envelop it in pork lace, tucking it neatly beneath the pie. Bake it in a moderate oven, for about 1¼ hrs. basting occasionally. Add a little water, if necessary. When it is ready, lift the pie onto a flat dish and cut it, like a cake, into 10 slices of equal size. Shake the flour into the lard left over int the pan, and after frying a short time add the paprika, pour the sour cream mixed with a little water over it and boil for a few minutes. Strain and pour it over the pie.

Pork Sausage in Lace

Ingredients: 1¾ lb. pork, 1 tsp. lard, 1 tsp. salt, ⅓ tsp. paprika, pinch of ground black pepper, pinch of ground white pepper, 10 oz. pork lace, 1 roll, 1 gill milk, 1—2 cloves of garlic.

Put the coarsely ground fat meat into a dish, salt and spice it, adding to it the roll steeped in milk, together with the milk, and the crushed garlic. Mix this sausage stuffing thoroughly and put in a cool place or an ice-box for an hour. Wash the pork-lace in several different lots of water, then spreading it out, cut it into ten piece of equal size. Divide the stuffing into equal parts, lay them over the pieces of pork lace, then roll them up tightly in the shape of a sausage.

Grease the inside of a pan of suitable size with lard, place the sausages in it in a neat row, and bake them brown in a hot oven. Garnish with mashed potatoes, and stewed cabbage.

Pork Lace Sausage with Lemon

Ingredients: 1¾ lb. pork, 1 tsp. lard,[1 tsp. salt, pinch of ground white pepper, 1 lemon, 1 roll, 1 gill milk, 10 oz. pork lace.

Prepare it as for Pork Sausage in Lace, the only difference being that the stuffing is only spiced with ground white pepper and thinly grated lemon peel. Boil the grated lemon peel in a little water and mix it with the meat when it cools. Garnish with creamed or fried potatoes.

Pork Fillets in Paprika Sauce

Ingredients: 1½ lb. pork, 2 tsp. salt, 3½ oz. onions, ½ tsp. paprika, 3½ oz. lecsó, 2 gills sour cream, 1 tbsp. flour, 3½ oz. lard.

Trim and skin tenderloin of pork. Cut into neat, round slices, weighing about 2 oz. each. Salt and flour fillets and fry lightly in lard. Put them aside in a saucepan. Fry the finely chopped onions in remaining lard till yellow, add paprika and 1 gill of water, bring to boil and pour over the meat. Cover and stew for 20—25 mins. Mix the remainder of the sour cream with flour, add the lecsó (fresh tomatoes and green paprikas in season) and turning them occasionally, stew the fillets until they are ready. Thin the gravy with a little water if it should be too thick. Serve with rice or dumplings.

Roast Pork in Lace

Ingredients: 1½ lb. fillet of pork, ½ lb. pork lace, 2 oz. lard, 1 oz. butter, 1 tsp. salt, pinch of ground black pepper, 7 oz. mushrooms, small bunch of parsley, 1 tsp. chopped onions, 1 tsp. bread-crumbs.

Trim the meat and salt it. Heat lard in a small pan, straighten out the meat and laying it in the pan, roast in the oven for about 20 mins., then lift out, and put in a cool place. Fry the finely cut onions in butter until they are golden, add the chopped parsley, the washed and minced mushrooms, salt and pepper, and fry for 4—5 mins., then mix in the bread-crumbs and put aside to cool. Wash the pork lace in several lots of water, and wring it out well. Spread the cold mushroom purée evenly over the pieces of cold meat, wrap them into the pork lace, and tie around with string. Replace fillets in pan, taking care that the mushroom mixture should remain on the top. Roast it for about 20 mins., adding a little water occasionally. Remove the string before carving; cut the meat into slightly slanting slices carefully, keeping them whole. Place meat on the dish in its original shape and pour the gravy over it. Serve with baked potatoes, or rice and green peas.

Roast Pork in Savoys (à la Colbert)

Ingredients: 1½ lb. pork, 10 oz. pork-lace, 1 lb. savoy cabbages, 3½ oz. bacon, 2 oz. lard, 1 oz. butter, 1½ tsp. salt, pinch of ground black pepper, 7 oz. mushrooms, small bunch of parsley, 1 tsp. chopped onions, 1 tsp. bread-crumbs.

It is prepared as for Roast Pork in Lace, differing only as follows: trim savoys, parboil the leaves in salt water; then strain through a sieve. Flatten the savoy leaves, dust with pepper, cover them with the prepared mushroom purée and meat, top with thinly sliced bacon and wrap the whole in pork lace. Roasting and dishing are similar to that for Roast Pork in Lace.

Round Steaks of Pork with Green Peas

Ingredients: 1½ lb. pork, 3 oz. lard, 1 oz. butter, 2½ oz. flour, 1 tsp. salt, 1 lb. tinned or fresh green peas, ½ tsp. sugar, 1½ gill cream, small bunch of parsley.

Trim meat, cut into 2 oz. slices, flatten and shape them into round steaks. Further preparation is similar to that for Veal Cutlets with green peas.

166

Roast Pork with Cream Sauce

Ingredients: 1½ lb. pork (tenderloin), 2 oz. bacon, 1 tsp. salt, 2 oz. lard, 4½ oz. mixed vegetables, 2 oz. onions, 1 oz. flour, 5 whole black peppers, 1 bay leaf, ½ lemon, 1 tsp. sugar, 1 tsp. mustard, 2 gills sour cream.

Lard meat with thin strips of bacon, trim and salt it. Melt the lard in a saucepan, and add the thinly sliced vegetables and onions, bacon rind, pepper, bay leaf and very thin slices of lemon peel, and finally the flattened steaks and roast the whole in the oven. When browned lift the meat out of saucepan and put aside. Sprinkle the vegetables remaining in saucepan with flour, stir, and add sour cream together with 1 gill stock or water. Let it boil briskly for a short time stirring constantly; replace meat in the pan, cover and stew till tender. Take meat out again, and add to remaining sauce the sugar, mustard and lemon-juice; boil thoroughly and then strain sauce through a sieve. Cut the meat into small slices, place them in a row on a dish and serve, covered with the sauce. Garnish with macaroni, noodles in butter or rice.

Round Steaks of Pork with Morels

Ingredients: 1½ lb. pork (tenderloin), 3 oz. lard, 1 tsp. salt, ¾ lb. morels, 1 oz. bacon, 2 gills sour cream, pinch of ground black pepper, 2 oz. flour, 2 oz. onions, small bunch of parsley.

Trim steaks, then cut them into 2 oz. pieces and flatten them giving a medal-like shape if possible. Heat the lard in a saucepan, salt and flour the slices of steak and fry till golden-brown, then taking out of the fat, put them into a pan of suitable size. Pour part of the remaining lard into another pan, add 1 gill water to the remaining fat, boil and then pour it over the meat, and covering it with a lid, stew for about 20 mins. Clean the morels, wash thoroughly and drain them. Cut bacon into small cubes, fry lightly; then add the finely chopped onions, mushrooms and parsley, salt and pepper slightly and covering with a lid let sauce stew for 15 mins. Mix the sour cream with the remainder of the flour; pour it over the mushroom sauce and stirring occasionally cook for a few minutes; then pour over the meat and let the whole boil several minutes. Garnish with steamed rice.

Bakony Pork Slices

Ingredients: 1½ lb. leg of pork, 1 tsp. salt, 3½ oz. lard, ½ tsp. paprika, 1½ lb. mushrooms, 2 oz. flour.

Cut pork into 5 large, or 10 small slices; beat them out well, salt, and turn them in flour; fry them lightly on both sides, then lay them in a pan of moderate size. Fry the thinly sliced onions in part of the remaining fat, until they turn yellow, adding paprika and stirring well; then put 1½ gill of water into the pan, boil for 2—3 mins., pour over the cutlets, and braise them under lid. Wash and slice mushrooms and fry for 3—4 mins. in the fat left over; then add to the meat, and simmer them together. Finally mix the flour with the sour cream, pour it over the meat, and continue cooking for another 5 mins. Garnish with dumplings.

Pork Cutlets au Naturel

Ingredients: 1¾ lb. pork cutlets, 1 tsp. salt, 1 dessertspoon flour, 3 oz. lard.

Cut out the backbone, leaving only the rib-bones on the cutlets, then cut into 10 pieces. Flatten them out a little, then, having salted and turned them in flour, fry them rapidly. Place the cutlets into a dish; pour off one half of the fat left over in the frying pan and, adding a little water to the remainder, boil thoroughly, and pour it over the meat. Garnish with baked potatoes, pickles, or vegetables of any kind.

Pork Cutlets in Paprika Sauce

Ingredients: 1¾ lb. pork cutlets, 3½ oz. lard, 5 oz. onions, 1 tsp. salt, 1 tsp. paprika, 1 dessertspoon tomato purée, pinch of caraway seeds, 2 cloves of garlic, 5 oz. green paprika, 4½ oz. fresh tomatoes, 2 lb. potatoes, 1 tsp. flour.

Take the meat and divide into 10 slices; flatten slices slightly, score, and turn them lightly in flour. Fry cutlets quickly, then put them into a pan of suitable size. Fry the thinly sliced onions in the remaining fat until yellow and add the paprika, the crushed garlic, and the finely chopped caraway seed; then stir the whole well, put in the tomato purée, and adding a little water boil for 1—2 mins. Pour this gravy over the cutlets and stew them under a lid slowly until they are half-done, then add the sliced potatoes, green paprika and tomatoes; pour on sufficient water to cover, and salt slightly. Stew the whole until meat is tender. If fresh tomatoes and paprika are unobtainable, use 4½ oz. of lecsó.

Debrecen Pork Cutlets

Ingredients: 1¾ lb. pork, 3 oz. lard, 5 oz. onions, 4½ oz. Debrecen sausages, 2 oz. bacon, 1 tsp. salt, 1 tsp. paprika, 1 dessertspoon tomato purée, pinch of caraway seed, 2 cloves of garlic, 1 tsp. flour, 5 oz. green paprika, 4½ oz. fresh tomatoes, 1½ lb. potatoes.

The method of preparation is similar to that for Pork Cutlets au Naturel, the only difference being that Debrecen sausage and bacon are added to it. The bacon is cut into slices of 1 inch length and ¼ inch breadth; fry them lightly in a frying pan, then add the sliced Debrecen sausage and, having fried that also, add both to the cutlets.

168

Bácska Pork Cutlets

Ingredients: 1¾ lb. pork cutlets, 3 oz. lard, 5 oz. onions, 2 oz. bacon, 2 oz. smoked sausages, 1 tsp. paprika, pinch of caraway seed, 10 oz. green paprika, 7 oz. fresh tomatoes, 2 cloves of garlic, 1 tsp. flour, 1 tsp. salt.

Prepare it as for Pork Cutlets au Naturel, the difference being that we don't put in potatoes. Cut the bacon into cubes, and fry lightly, then add the sliced sausages, and a few minutes later the sliced green paprika, and tomatoes, and simmer until half-tender. Mix this lecsó with the meat, and let it simmer till tender. Garnish with boiled potatoes or tarhonya.

Temesvár Pork Cutlets

Ingredients: 1¾ lb. pork, 1 tsp. salt, 3½ oz. onions, ½ tsp. paprika, 2 cloves of garlic, 1 lb. tender green beans, 1 oz. flour, 3 oz. lard, 2 gills sour cream, 2 oz. bacon, 5 oz. lecsó.

Divide the pork into 10 cutlets of equal size, flatten them slightly, salt and having dipped into flour, fry them for ten minutes in a frying pan. Then place the cutlets in a pan, cut bacon into strips and fry in fat, add finely chopped onions and fry till golden-yellow. Mix with paprika and crushed garlic, pour on 1½ gill of water, boil the whole thoroughly then pour over the cutlets and stew until meat is tender. Cut the green beans through the middle, and boil them in slightly salted water; strain off when ready. Mix the sour cream with 1 tsp. flour, pour it over the meat, add the green beans and the lecsó, then let the whole boil for a few minutes. Use 2 green paprikas and 2 tomatoes instead of lecsó, when in season.

Swiss Pork Cutlets

Ingredients: 1¾ lb. pork, 1 tsp. salt, 3 oz. lard, 1 oz. flour, 1 dessertspoon tomato purée, 2 tbsp. white wine, 2 lb. potatoes, 1½ gill sour cream, 3 oz. butter, 2 eggs, 3 oz. gruyère cheese, 1 tsp. bread-crumbs.

Divide the pork into 10 cutlets of equal size, flatten them slightly, then salt and dip them into flour; fry cutlets in a frying pan, until they brown nicely. Place them in a pan of suitable size. Fry the tomatoes in the fat, then pour the white wine and 1½ gill water over them. When thoroughly boiled, pour the sauce over the cutlets, and stew under lid until they are tender. Skin the boiled potatoes, and slice into pieces of equal size. Beat 2 oz. of butter, add 2 yolks of egg one by one; add the sour cream, and mix the potatoes and 2 oz. cubed gruyère cheese to the whole with a sufficient amount of salt. Lastly, beat the whites of 6 eggs and mix carefully with the potatoes. Butter the inside of a small pan, and sprinkle with bread-crumbs, pour the potato mixture into pan, sprinkle 1 tsp. of grated cheese, and some bread-crumbs on top, and bake in the oven. Place the potatoes on one side of the dish and the cutlets alongside and pour gravy over them, when serving.

Alsatian Pork Cutlets

Ingredients: 1¾ lb. pork, 1 tsp. salt, 3 oz. lard, 1 dessertspoon tomato purée, 2 lb. sour cabbage, 2 oz. onions, pinch of caraway seed, 3½ oz. smoked sausage, 2 oz. bacon.

Cook cutlets, according to the process employed when preparing Swiss Cutlets. Use sour cabbage instead of potatoes, and prepare as follows: Cut the bacon into strips of 1 inch length, and fry lightly in a pan; add sliced onions, and fry till they are light yellow; pour a little water into the pan, put in the caraway seed, and the cabbage which has been washed previously; add salt and let it simmer till tender. Place the cutlets on a dish, putting the cabbage on top of them; pour on the gravy and lastly lay the smoked sausage which has been fried in a little fat, on top of the cabbage. Garnish with potatoes and fried onions.

Peasant Pork Cutlets

Ingredients: 1¾ lb. pork, 1 tsp. salt, 1 dessertspoon flour, 5 oz. lard, 2 lb. potatoes, 5 oz. bacon, 5 oz. small onions, small bunch of parsley.

The preparation of the pork cutlets is similar to that for Pork Cutlets au Naturel. Lay cutlets in a pan, after frying; pour off part of the fat, then put 1—2 gills of water into the fat remaining in the frying pan, boil well, pour it over the cutlets, and, covering with a lid, let them stew, until they are tender: Then fry the bacon a little in the fat left over, add the small onions quartered, and strain off the fat when they are pale yellow. Fry cubed potatoes in the fat strained off the onions. When ready, add the fried bacon and onions. Sprinkle with finely chopped parsley, and mix well. Lay the cutlets on the dish in a neat row, cover with the potato mixture and pour gravy over when dishing. Garnish with pickles.

Székely Pigs' Trotters in Sour Cabbage

Ingredients: 2 pairs of pigs' trotters, 5 oz. onions, 1 tsp. salt, 2 oz. lard, ½ tsp. paprika, pinch of caraway seed, 2 cloves of garlic, 1 pt. sour cream, 1 dessertspoon flour, 2 lb. sour cabbage, 1 bunch of fresh dill.

Wash and salt pigs' trotters; then melt the fat in a pan, put in the pigs' trotters, and roast them in the oven, for about 20 mins. till light brown. Take the pigs' trotters out of the pan, fry the finely chopped onions in the left-over fat; then add garlic, caraway seed and paprika, pour on a little water and stew for a few minutes. Replace the pigs' trotters in the gravy, add water and covering the pan with a lid, boil for about 40 mins.; then add sour cabbage and stew the whole. Pour in the sour cream mixed with flour when meat is tender; add the finely chopped dill and boil the whole a few minutes longer. When serving, cut each of the pigs' trotters into three pieces and place them on the cabbage, which is laid in a deep dish.

Ormania Stuffed Belly of Pork

Ingredients: 2 lb. pork belly, 3½ oz. lard, 5 oz. fat bacon, 2 rolls, 2 eggs, 5 oz. pork liver, 2 oz. onions, 1 clove of garlic, pinch of ground black pepper, pinch of marjoram, ⅓ tsp. paprika, 1½ tsp. salt, 1½ gill milk.

Cut the bones off the meat, then cut meat open in the middle with a sharp knife. Prepare the following stuffing: place the rolls, which have been previously soaked in milk and then squeezed out well, into a dish; beat the eggs into it, add coarsely minced liver and bacon, the onions, which have been fried in 2 oz. of fat, garlic, 1 tsp. salt, and the spices, and mix them thoroughly. Put this stuffing into the pocket cut in the meat, sew the end up with string, and press the stuffing until it is even. Then salt and roast slowly in the remaining fat, until brown and crisp. Dish in its own gravy, thinned with stock. Remove the string before serving. Serve with potato and onion salad.

Roast Pork

Ingredients: 2 lb. leg or loin of pork, 2 oz. lard, 1 tsp. salt, 1 tsp. tomato purée, 1 tsp. flour.

Strip off the back bone of the loin, leaving only the ribs. Bone the leg of pork. Having prepared the joint, wash and salt it. Melt the fat in a suitable sized pan, put in the meat and roast it, basting frequently, in a warm oven, until it is tender. Should it brown too rapidly on the bottom, while roasting, pour a little water round it. Take the meat out of the pan, when it is ready, and put the tomato into the fat; mix it well, sprinkle on the flour and fry a little; then pour on a little water, boil 5—6 mins. and finally strain it into a small pan. Slice the meat when serving, place the slices on a dish, and pour gravy over them. Serve with stewed cabbage, vegetable marrow with dill or stewed green beans, as well as mashed or baked potatoes. If we don't want the gravy to thick, it can be prepared without flour and tomato.

Roast Loin of Pork

Ingredients: 2 lb. pork, 1 tsp. salt, 1 oz. lard.

Boil water in a pan, place the joint in it, skin downward, and boil for a few minutes. Having taken it out of the water, score skin with knife, if possible in the same direction as the ribs; then salt the meat except the skin. Melt the fat in a pan, place in the meat, taking care to leave the crackling uppermost; then roast until crisp. Pour a little water onto the fat remaining in the pan, boil well, and pour this gravy round the sliced pork when serving. Serve with braised red cabbage and baked potatoes, or mashed potatoes with onions.

Torda Laci Roast (Torda Barbecue)

Ingredients: 2 lb. leg of pork or cut of sucking pig, with skin, 1 tsp. salt, 1 dessertspoon flour, 3 oz. lard.

Cut the meat into 10 slices of equal size, flatten them well, and score skin with a sharp knife. Salt and dip slices into flour and fry them rapidly, until they turn brown and crisp. Serve with baked potatoes, beetroots and paprika salad.

Braised Leg of Sucking Pig

Ingredients: 2 lb. leg of sucking pig, 3 oz. lard, 1 tsp. salt, 1 dessertspoon tomato purée, 3½ oz. mixed vegetables, 1 oz. onions, pinch of caraway seed, 1 tsp. flour, 1 clove of garlic, 2 tbsp. white wine.

Bone the leg of sucking pig, then roll and tie it tightly with string, and salt it. Melt the lard in a pan of suitable size; put in the sliced vegetables, the onions and clove of garlic, placing the meat on top of them, together with the chopped bones, and sprinkling with caraway seed, place it in the oven. When both meat and vegetables are browned, sprinkle with flour, and add the tomato purée and white wine, then add 1—2 gills of water, and, covering with a lid, let the whole braise in the oven until tender. Remove the string from the meat before dishing, slice and lay it on a dish, pouring strained thin gravy over it. Serve with mashed or creamed potatoes.

Crisp Roasted Sucking Pig

Ingredients (for 10—12 people): 6—7 lb. sucking pig, 2 tsp. salt, pinch of marjoram, 2 oz. bacon, 1 oz. lard, 1½ gill beer.

Clean the pig, then cut off its feet, cut deeply into the backbone at the neck, rub the inside over well with salt and a little marjoram, and put it aside for an hour, back downward, letting the salt penetrate the meat a little. Put several wooden laths crosswise into a pan of suitable size, lay the pig upon them back upwards, wrap paper around its ears and tail and covering it with cold lard, place it in a medium-hot oven. Rub the pig over occasionally with bacon dipped into beer, while it is roasting to give it a nice colour. If crackling blisters, prick with a fork. When, after roasting for about 2 hrs., the pig turns crisp and brown, lift it out onto a board, cut off its head with a sharp and heavy knife, cut it open lengthwise, and then cut the whole into suitably sized pieces, placing the pieces together on the dish in their original shape. Garnish with braised cabbage, or a head of cabbage stewed in wine.

172

Sucking Pig Paprika Stew

Ingredients: 3 lb. tender sucking pig, 4 oz. lard, ½ lb. onions, 1 tsp. salt, 1 tsp. paprika, pepper, 1 tbsp. tomato purée, ¼ lb. lecsó, pinch of caraway seed, 1 clove of garlic.

Cut the meat into 2—3 oz. pieces. Further preparation according to Pork Paprika Stew.

Sucking Pig in Paprika Sauce

Ingredients: 2½ lb. sucking pig's trotters and offal, 1 tsp. salt, 2 oz. onions, 3 oz. lard, 2 oz. flour, pinch of ground black pepper, 1 tsp. sugar, 1 bay leaf, 1½ gill sour cream, 1 tsp. mustard, 1½ gill vinegar, ½ lemon.

Cut the pigs' pluck and trotter into 1 oz. pieces, and having washed them carefully, set to boil in 2 pt. of water. Skim when boiling, salt and add the bay leaf; allow to cook until tender. Fry the flour in fat, until it is light brown; fry the finely chopped onions and thin lemon-peel, add a little cold water, then pour on the cooked trotters and plucks. Add the mustard, sour cream, sugar, ground pepper and lemon-juice. Boil the whole for another 8—10 mins., garnish with steamed rice.

Robber's Meat (Kebabs)

Ingredients: 6 oz. pork, 6 oz. veal, 6 oz. tenderloin steak, 6 oz. goose-liver, 6 oz. bacon, 7 oz. onion, 1 lb. potatoes, 1 tsp. salt, 2 oz. flour, 7 oz. lard, pinch of ground black pepper.

Trim pork, veal and tenderloin; then cut all three into ten pieces of equal size each, flatten them and shape them into round slices. Cut the goose-liver into 10 pieces, and the bacon into 20 tiny slices. Cut the onions into 15 thick slices, and the potatoes into 20 thickish slices. Thread the slices on to skewers, dividing equally, beginning and ending with the potatoes. Salt and pepper them, then turning in flour, fry them in plenty of hot fat until they are crisp. Serve meat on the skewers and garnish with mixed pickles.

Transylvanian Mixed Grill on a Wooden Platter

Ingredients: 10 oz. pork, 10 oz. veal, 10 oz. tenderloin, 7 oz. bacon, 1 tsp. salt, 2 oz. flour, 5 oz. lard, 5 portions of mixed salad.

Cut the various pieces of meat into slices of 2 oz. each, flatten, and salt them, turn them in flour and fry quickly until slices are rosy-brown. Cut the bacon into slices of 1 oz., nick bacon rinds with a sharp knife and then fry until crisp. Then take a wooden platter of suitable size, decorate its edge with previously prepared red cabbage, paprika, tomato, cucumber and beet-root salad; put a pyramid of potatoes fried in fat into the middle of platter, then lay the roast meat around it, putting bacon on top.

Pork Flekken

Ingredients: 1¾ lb. loin of pork, 1 tsp. salt, 1 dessertspoon flour.

Skin, and cut the meat into five slices; flatten them, then salt and turn them in flour, roast rapidly over a bright flame until brown. Dekorate the edge of a suitably sized wooden platter with head of sour cabbage, finely sliced, small, pickled cucumbers, pickled paprika sliced through the middle, with green tomatoes preserved in vinegar and with beetroot. Pile baked potatoes in the middle of the platter and lay the slices of meat on top of them. Serve the following paprika sauce with it: 1 tsp. paprika, a little salt, pinch of ground black pepper stirred smooth in sufficient red wine to make the sauce thick. Flekken can also be prepared with tenderloin of beef.

Boiled Ham

Ingredients (for 10 people): 1 ham, weighing 5 lb., 10 portions of creamed potatoes.

Bone and roll up ham, tie round tightly with string, and boil until tender. Should the ham be too salty, steep it in plenty of water overnight. Putting it in fresh water next day, boil ham for about 20—25 mins., pour off water again, boiling ham in a third lot of water till tender. Slice when ready, pouring some of the gravy over it. Garnish with creamed potatoes or peas, and with grated horse-radish.

Prague Chine of Pork

Ingredients: 2 lb. smoked back, 5 portions sour cabbage, 10 small dumplings.

Chine the back, boil till tender, then cut into 10 slices, and pour some of the gravy over it, when serving. Garnish with sour cabbage prepared with sour cream, setting the dumplings on top.

Brain and Kidneys

Ingredients: 1 lb. pork kidneys, 10 oz. brains, 1 tsp. salt, 3½ oz. lard, pinch of paprika, pinch of ground black pepper, pinch of marjoram, 2 oz. onions.

Cut kidneys through the middle after skinning them, then cut out gristle and slice thinly. Soak brains into cold water, peel off the membranes, drain and cut into small pieces. Fry the finely chopped onions in a saucepan, until they are light yellow, add kidneys, fry for a few minutes, then add spices and chopped brains, and fry the whole for a few minutes longer. Remove from cooker, salt and dish at once. Garnish with mashed potatoes, or with steamed rice.

Jellied Pork

Ingredients: 3½ lb. pig's trotters and ears, 5 oz. mixed vegetables, 4½ oz. onions, 1 oz. garlic, 1 oz. salt, ¼ tsp. whole black pepper, pinch of paprika.

Scald and clean the pig's trotters and ears thoroughly, and bring to boil in plenty of fresh water. Pour off water, and put meat on again in fresh water. Skim it while boiling, salt, add vegetables, onions, garlic and pepper, and boil slowly on low heat. Strain the stock off through a sieve or linen cloth, when meat is tender, skim off fat and allow it to cool. Bone the meat and cut into fairly large cubes; place them in a deep dish, cover with the stock when it has cooled, and lightly sprinkling the top with paprika, set in a cold place The meat can also be placed into 5—6 soup plates. Should the stock be reduced too much, add sufficient water while boiling, to have about 3 pt. when ready.

Boiled Pork with Horse-radish

Ingredients: 3½ lb. pig's head and trotters, 7 oz. mixed vegetables, 3½ oz. onions, 2 cloves of garlic, 1½ tsp. salt, 6 whole black peppers, ¼ tsp. paprika, grated horse-radish.

Cut the cleaned pig's head and trotters into fairly large pieces, put them into 4 pt. of water, and boil; skim while boiling. Salt, and add spices, onions, garlic, and continue cooking on low heat. Add the coarsely chopped mixed vegetables after cooking for half an hour, and let it simmer till tender. Serve in a deep dish with some of the stock and the vegetables. Serve grated horse-radish, or horse-radish in vinegar, separately.

Russian Pork Tokány

Ingredients: 2 lb. pork, 1 tsp. salt, 3½ oz. onions, 2 tbsp. white wine, 1 dessertspoon mustard, 2 oz. tomato purée, small bunch of parsley, 2 gills sour cream, 1 tsp. flour, 2 oz. mushrooms, 5 portions of rice.

Fry the finely chopped onions in lard; add tomato purée and a little water. Cut meat into cubes, and add to onions, together with the cubed carrots and mushrooms and, flavouring with ground pepper, let it simmer until meat is almost tender. Mix with the washed and cleaned rice, add some water, and covering with a lid, stew until ready.

Black Pudding

Ingredients: 2½ lb. belly of pork, 1¾ lb. bath chaps, 3 lb. pig's blood, 8 rolls , 1 tsp. salt, ¾ lb. lard, ¾ lb. onions, 1 tsp. ground black pepper, pinch of white pepper, pinch of marjoram, 1 tsp. paprika.

Cook the pig's belly and the bath chaps in slightly salted water, until nearly tender. Cut the rolls into small cubes, and toast in the oven. Cut pork chap into small cubes. When cool mince the meat coarsely, and place in a large bowl. Add diced rolls, salt and spices, and mix well with the finely chopped onions, fried in part of the fat, the strained blood, and the fat skimmed off the top of the stock. Fill sausage skins loosely and tie ends. Place in boiling water and cook slowly, then lifting pudding onto a board, set to cool. Prick the pudding with a needle or a pointed wooden skewer and if gravy appears instead of blood, then it is ready. Put puddings into a greased pan and roast carefully in a medium-hot oven. Serve with mashed potatoes and fried onions, and with braised cabbage.

Liver Sausage
(For 5 people)

Ingredients: 2 lb. pig's liver, 4 lb. pig's lungs and heart, 2 lb. bath chaps, ¾ lb. skin, 1 lb. rice, 5 oz. salt, ¾ lb. onions, 1 tsp. ground black pepper, pinch of white pepper, pinch of marjoram, 1 tsp. paprika, ¾ lb. lard.

Cook the lungs and bath chaps in slightly salted water, until they are nearly done, and cook the skin in the same stock, until it is quite tender. Take the whole out of the stock, and when cold, put through mincer, along with the raw liver and place in a large bowl. Add boiled rice, salt and spices, mix with the onions, fried golden in part of the fat, and the fat skimmed off the water whilst it was boiling. Fill sausage skins loosely with mixture and tie ends securely. Place sausages into water when in begins to boil and, lowering heat, cook slowly, taking care to keep the water below boiling-point. When ready, lift them onto a board, and leave to cool. Fry the sausages in a well-greased pan pricking them first with a needle in several places. Serve with potatoes and fried onions, and with braised cabbage.

Fried Pork Sausages
(For 5 people)

Ingredients: 2 lb. fat pork, 1 oz. lard, 1 tsp. salt, ¼ tsp. paprika, pinch of ground black pepper, pinch of white pepper, about 3—4 yards of sausage skin, 1—2 cloves of garlic.

Place the coarsely minced meat into a dish, salt and spice it; pour on 2 tbsp. of water boiled with crushed garlic and strained; then mix the whole thoroughly. Wash the sausage skins well in cold water. Fill with stuffing, twist ends, then place in a well-greased pan and roast in a hot oven. Serve with mashed potatoes and braised cabbage or with pickled cucumbers.

Lemon Sausage
(For 5 people)

Ingredients: 2 lb. fat pork, 1 oz. lard, 1 oz. salt, pinch of ground white pepper, 1 lemon, 1 roll, 1½ gill milk, about 3—4 yards of sausage skins.

Place the coarsely minced meat in a dish, salt and pepper it. Add the roll soaked in milk and crumbled well, along with the milk itself, and the thinly cut and grated lemon-peel (boiled in a little water) then mix the whole thoroughly. Wash sausage skins in cold water, fill with the stuffing and roast in a well-greased pan till golden-brown. Serve with mashed potatoes or pickles according to taste.

Pork Brawn

Ingredients: ½ pig's head, 1 lb. fresh pork skin, 1½ lb. fat pig's cheek, 1 pig's tongue, 1 knuckle, salt, ground black pepper, white pepper, garlic.

Boil the head, tongue, skin, cheek and knuckle slowly in slightly salt water, for about 2 hrs.; then take out of the stock, cut into cubes of about 1 inch cutting the meat off the bones; put skin through mincer. Place the ingredients in a large bowl, salt, and spice, according to taste, flavour with 2—3 crushed and finely chopped cloves of garlic, and pour on sufficient of the fat, skimmed off while boiling, to keep mixture soft and moist. Stuff into thoroughly cleaned pig's stomach, sew together, put into water beginning to boil, and cook it on low heat (keep the water below boiling-point) for 2—2½ hrs. Then take out carefully, prick it slightly. Place between two light wooden boards, and press until cold.

Pork's brawn may also be smoked; in that case, however, 1½ gill of pig's blood must be added and mixed with the rest; it can also be spiced with a little paprika.

Meat Pockets in the Russian Way

Ingredients: 1 lb. pork-hearts, 3½ oz. butter, 3½ oz. lard, 2 oz. onions, 1 lb. flour, 1½ tsp. salt, pinch of black pepper, small bunch of parsley, 2 eggs, 2 gills sour cream.

Cook hearts till tender, then put through mincer. Add finely chopped fried onions, salt and pepper, and knead it well together. Prepare paste as for Ravioli, fill it with the mixture and boil in salt water. Strain and add butter just before dishing. Serve sour cream separately.

Meat Doughnuts in the Russian Way

Ingredients: 1 lb. pork-hearts, 6 oz. lard, ½ lb. flour, ½ tsp. sugar, ½ oz. yeast, 1 tsp. salt, 1 gill milk, 2 eggs, pinch of ground black pepper, 2 oz. onions, small bunch of parsley, 1 gill sour cream.

Prepare raised dough and stamp it out with round cutter. Cook hearts till tender, then put through mincer and flavour with finely chopped fried onions, parsley, salt and ground black pepper. Fill the doughnuts with this mixture, then fry them in hot lard. Serve with sour cream.

Stuffed Dumplings in the Russian Way

Ingredients: 1½ lb. pork-hearts, 1 oz. lard, small bunch of spring onions, small bunch of parsley, pinch of ground black pepper, 1 egg, 2 gills béarnaise sauce, 3½ oz. rice.

Put hearts through mincer, add cooked rice, egg and flavourings, mix well together and shape small dumplings of it. Bake in well-greased baking tin together with sliced spring onions, pouring the sauce over it. Serve with buttered noodles, steamed rice or macaroni. For béarnaise sauce see Sauces.

Shashlik (Fried Mutton)

Ingredients: 1 lb. pork, veal or mutton tenderloin, 7 oz. onions, 2 oz. butter, 3½ oz. spring onions, 7 oz. tomatoes, 1½ tsp. salt, pinch of black pepper, 2 tbsp. vinegar, small bunch of parsley.

Cut meat into small slices, salt and pepper it, sprinkle with finely chopped onions. Put the slices of meat into a china or earthenware dish, sprinkle with the vinegar and add some parsley or celery tops. Cover the dish and let it stand for 2—3 hrs. Spear the slices of meat on toothpicks alternatively with slices of onions and fry them in hot fat. Take meat and onions off toothpicks when ready, and dish, pouring melted butter over it. Garnish with spring onions, tomatoes cut in four and steamed rice.

Piroskhi (Meat Pastry)

Ingredients: 1 lb. flour, yolks of 3 eggs, ¼ tsp. salt, 1 tsp. sugar, 2 oz. butter, 1 oz. yeast, 3½ gills milk.
For the stuffing: 7 oz. pork, 7 oz. beef, 5 oz. lard, 2 oz. onions, 1 tsp. salt, pinch of ground black pepper, 1 egg.

Make a light raised dough of the flour and ingredients given above for pastry. Roll it out, cut into squares and fill with the following mixture.

Mix the minced meat with finely chopped hard-boiled eggs and onions, braise the mixture in hot lard and flavour to taste. When filling is cold, fill the squares of dough with it. Let the doughnuts rise again, then fry them in hot fat.

Shredded cabbage may be used instead of meat if preferred.

MUTTON

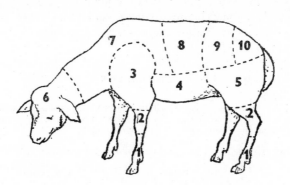

Cuts of mutton:

The most advantageous use of the cuts:

1. Trotters
2. Shank or Haunch   Roasted or braised
3. Shoulder   Roasted, braised, paprika stew (pörkölt), gulyás
4. Breast   Roasted, braised, paprika stew (pörkölt), gulyás
5. Leg   Roasted or braised
6. Head   Boiled, paprika stew (pörkölt)
7. Neck (best end and scrag end)   Paprika stew with short or long gravy (pörkölt, gulyás)
8. Saddle (two loins)   Roasted, braised, sliced and grilled or fried (chops)
9. Loin (best end)   Roasted, braised, sliced and grilled or fried (chops)
10. Loin (chump end)   Boiled, paprika stew (pörkölt)

Roast Saddle of Lamb

Ingredients: 3 lb. saddle of lamb, 1 tsp. salt, 2 oz. lard, 1 dessertspoon flour, 1 dessertspoon tomato purée, 5 portions rice, 5 portions stewed plums.

Wash and salt the saddle of lamb, place in a baking tin, put fat over it, and roast in the oven until tender. Then lift the meat out of the tin, fry the tomato purée and the flour in the fat, add 1½ gill of water, and boil thoroughly. Slice before dishing, and pour the gravy (strained) over it. Serve with rice and stewed plums.

Leg of Lamb à la Boulangère

Ingredients: 1 leg of lamb, 1 tsp. salt, 1 tsp. flour, 1 tsp. tomato purée, 7 oz. onions, 3½ oz. lard, 3 lb. potatoes, small bunch of parsley.

Wash the leg of lamb, salt and put it into a baking tin with 1 oz. lard, and roast in the oven until tender. Wash the potatoes and quarter them length-

179

wise; clean the onions and cut into fairly large cubes. Salt both, put in a pan, with 2 oz. of lard and roast in the oven. Take the meat out of the pan, fry flour and tomato purée in remaining fat, pour on 1½ gill of water, and boil thoroughly. Slice the roast before dishing, and pour gravy—strained—over it. Serve roast potatoes and onions separately.

Leg of Lamb à la Printanière

Ingredients: 1 leg of lamb, 1 tsp. salt, 1 tsp. flour, 1 tsp. tomato purée, 2 oz. lard, 3 oz. butter, ½ lb. carrots, ½ lb. tinned peas, ½ lb. tinned green beans, ½ lb. Brussels sprouts, ½ lb. tinned asparagus, 3½ oz. mushrooms, small bunch of parsley.

Wash the leg of lamb, salt and lay it into a baking tin putting fat on top, and roast in the oven until tender. Clean the carrots, wash and cut them into thin strips. Cut the washed mushrooms into cubes, clean Brussels sprouts, then braise all vegetables in butter. When tender, add green beans, green peas and asparagus (minus juice) and the finely chopped parsley. Take out the meat, fry the flour and tomato purée in the fat, add 1½ gill of water, boil well, and then strain over the mixed vegetables. Slice the leg of lamb before dishing, and garnish with the braised vegetables.

Neapolitan Leg of Lamb

Ingredients: 1 leg of lamb, 2 oz. lard, 1 tsp. salt, 1 tsp. tomato purée, 1 tsp. flour, 5 portions of Neapolitan macaroni.

Wash and salt the leg of lamb, put lard on top and basting frequently, roast until it is tender. Then take meat out of the pan, and fry the tomato and flour in the fat; add a little water, boil well, and strain. Slice the meat before serving; place it on a dish, pour the gravy over it, and serve with macaroni sprinkled with grated cheese.

Stuffed Breast of Lamb

Ingredients: 2½ lb. breast of lamb, pinch of marjoram, 2 oz. butter, 3 rolls, pinch of ground black pepper, 1 tsp. tomato purée, 1½ tsp. salt, 3½ oz. lard, 1½ gill milk, 3 eggs, ½ tsp. flour, small bunch of parsley, 5 portions of steamed rice.

Remove bones carefully from the breast, cut open through the middle with a knife, salt and fill pocket with the following stuffing: beat up the butter with 2 whole eggs and the yolk of a third, flavour with salt, marjoram and pepper, and the finely chopped green parsley, add the rolls soaked in milk and well squeezed out; mix the stuffing thoroughly. Stuff the breast, sewing the open end together with string and place it in a pan. Put fat and a little water beneath it, and roast slowly in the oven which must not be too hot. Baste meat occasionally, so that it browns evenly. Take the joint out of the fat when it is ready. Add tomato purée to remaining fat, brown a little, shake flour over it, fry 1—2 mins. longer, add a little water, boil and strain it. Stuffed lamb should be ready 20—25 mins. before serving, giving time for stuffing to set; this facilitates carving. Slice meat with a sharp knife, pour gravy beside it; serve steamed rice separately.

Fried Lamb

Ingredients: 2 lb. lamb (boneless), 1 tsp. salt, 2 oz. flour, 2 tbsp. milk, 7 oz. bread-crumbs, 7 oz. lard, 5 portions of potato salad.

Cut the lamb into 10 pieces of 3 oz. each, flatten and salt them. Dip the slices into flour, then into egg beaten up with milk; turn them in bread-crumbs and fry them in hot fat on both sides, until slices are light brown. Take out of fat and dish at once. Serve with potato salad.

Lamb Steaks with Fried Potatoes

Ingredients: 2 lb. leg of lamb, 1 tsp. salt, 1 dessertspoon flour, 3½ oz. fat, small bunch of parsley, 1 tsp. tomato purée, 3 lb. potatoes.

Slice the leg of lamb, flatten, then salt the steaks; turn in flour, fry them in 1 oz. fat, until brown, then place them into another pan. Fry the tomatoes and flour in the fat, add 2 tbsp. water; boil then strain over the steaks. Wash and boil potatoes in their skins, peel and cut into slices; salt and fry them in hot fat with finely chopped parsley, until they are nicely browned.

Paprika Lamb Stew with Potatoes

Ingredients: 2½ lb. forequarter lamb, 7 oz. onions, 5 oz. lard, 1 tsp. flour, ½ tsp. paprika, 1 clove of garlic, 3½ oz. tinned lecsó, 5 portions of boiled potatoes, 1 tsp. salt.

Fry onions in fat, until they are light yellow, add paprika and finely chopped garlic, then the meat washed and cut into large cubes, and stew until tender. When meat is tender, add lecsó, and sprinkle with flour. Thin gravy with a little water, and boil a few minutes longer. Serve with boiled potatoes.

Lamb in Paprika Sauce with Thimble Dumplings (Galuska)

Ingredients: 2½ lb. forequarter lamb, 1 tsp. salt, 1 tsp. flour, 2 oz. lard, 3½ oz. onions, ½ tsp. paprika, 3½ oz. lecsó, ¾ pt. sour cream, 5 portions of thimble dumplings.

Fry the finely chopped onions in lard until they turn yellow, add red paprika. Cut the meat into large cubes, and fry lightly with onions; add a little water, and salt, and let it simmer till tender, then mix in the lecsó. Mix the sour cream with flour and stir it into the paprika sauce; boil well, and serve with dumplings.

181

Lamb in Tarragon Sauce

Ingredients: 2½ lb. forequarter lamb, 1 tsp. salt, 2 oz. onions, 2 oz. butter, 1 oz. flour, 1½ gill sour cream, 1 tbsp. sweet cream, ½ oz. tarragon, some tarragon vinegar, yolk of one egg.

Cut the lamb into large cubes, and cook together with the cleaned onions in 2 pt. of water until tender. Make a light roux with butter and flour, dilute it with a small amount of water, add to the meat and cook till meat is tender. Mix the sour cream with finely chopped tarragon, some tarragon vinegar, yolk of egg and sweet cream; add to meat, taking care that the sauce should not boil after this.

Lamb's Tokány with Green Peas

Ingredients: 2 lb. shoulder of lamb, 3½ oz. lard, 5 oz. onions, 2 dessertspoon tomato purée, 1 tsp. salt, 2 tbsp. white wine, pinch of ground pepper, 1 clove of garlic, ½ lb. tinned green peas.

Cut meat into strips of 2 inches length. Fry finely chopped onions in lard, until they turn yellow; add the crushed garlic, tomato purée and white wine, boil a few minutes. Put in the meat, salt and pepper, and stew under lid until meat is tender. Stir occasionally and, if gravy is too thick, add a little water, taking care, however, not to make gravy too watery. Add the strained peas, when meat is tender, and boil once again. Garnish with steamed rice.

Bretonne Leg of Mutton with Beans

Ingredients: 2 lb. leg of mutton, 7 oz. tomato purée, 5 oz. mixed vegetables, 3½ oz. onions, 3 cloves of garlic, 1½ tsp. salt, 3½ oz. lard, 1 gill red wine, 2 oz. flour, pinch of ground black pepper, 1 lb. dry haricot beans.

Melt lard in a pan, put in the sliced vegetables, onion and crushed garlic; bone meat, tie it round with string, salt and pepper it, and roast in the oven with the vegetables until brown. Sprinkle with flour, and a few minutes later add the tomato purée, wine, and about 1 pt. of water, and stew under lid until meat is tender. Pour on water, if necessary, whilst stewing, taking care not to let the gravy get too thick. Cook the beans in salt water until soft, then strain. Take the meat out of the gravy, and remove string. Strain the gravy through a sieve, pour over the beans, and continue cooking for 10—15 mins. longer. Place the beans into a deep dish when serving, laying the sliced leg of mutton on top.

Braised Leg of Mutton with Garlic

Ingredients: 2 lb. leg of mutton, 1 tsp. salt, 5 oz. mixed vegetables, 3 oz. onions, 5 cloves of garlic, 3 oz. lard, pinch of pepper, pinch of thyme, 1 bay leaf, 2 oz. tomato purée, 1 dessert-spoon sugar, 2 oz. flour, 1 gill white wine.

Remove bones, then with a sharp knife make 10 narrow slits in the leg of mutton, and push a piece of garlic into each slit. Preparation is then similar to that for Braised rump of beef. Garnish with steamed rice or macaroni.

Mutton Cutlets with Berne Sauce

Ingredients: 10 cutlets of 3½ oz. each, 1 tsp. salt, 1 oz. lard, 5 portions of Berne sauce, 5 portions of potato chips, 1 tsp. tomato purée, 1 oz. bread-crumbs.

Salt cutlets, dip into bread-crumbs and fry on both sides until they turn light brown, then take them out of the fat. Heat up remaining fat and the tomato purée; stir, dilute with a little water, boil, then strain gravy, and pour over meat. Serve with potato chips and Berne sauce.

Mutton Chops with Soubise Sauce

Ingredients: 2 lb. loin of mutton, 1 tsp. salt, 3 oz. lard.

Trim meat with a sharp knife, cut into 5 equal chops, flatten them and, rolling in their edges, pin each together with a short skewer. Salt and grill in a frying pan or under grill until done. Serve at once, garnished with potato chips, and tender green peas with butter. Serve Soubise sauce separately (see Sauces).

Lord Chamberlain Loin of Mutton

Ingredients: 2 lb. loin of mutton, 1 tsp. salt, 3 oz. lard, 3 oz. butter, ¼ lemon, ⅓ tsp. mustard, pinch of ground black pepper, small bunch of parsley.

Trim and grill meat as for Mutton chops with Soubise sauce. Lay two pats of spiced butter on each chop when dishing, and garnish with potato chips and green beans with butter. Spiced butter is prepared as follows: Mix butter with pepper, lemon-juice, mustard and a little finely chopped green parsley; shape into bars of 2 inches each and place into iced water till serving.

Hungarian Mutton Gulyás

Ingredients: 2 lb. mutton, 2 oz. lard, 7 oz. onions, 1 tsp. paprika, 2 cloves of garlic, pinch of caraway seed, 1½ tsp. salt, 3 oz. flour, 1 egg, 2 lb. potatoes, 3½ oz. lecsó or green paprikas and 2 tomatoes. Cut the meat into pieces of about 1 oz.

Skin onions and chop them finely; clean garlic, and crush well, together with the caraway seeds. Heat fat in a pan; fry the onions, adding paprika and a little water; add the meat, garlic, salt and caraway seed, boil slowly under lid. When meat is half-tender put in cubed potatoes, green paprika and tomato or lecsó; pour on sufficient water to allow for about 1½ gill of broth for each person, and cook until meat is tender. Lastly make csipetke with eggs and flour, and cook them in the Gulyás.

183

Mutton with Tarhonya

Ingredients: 2½ lb. shoulder of mutton, 7 oz. onions, 3 oz. lard, 1 tsp. paprika, 1 clove of garlic, 5 oz. tinned lecsó, 1 tsp. salt.

Cut meat together with bones into fairly large cubes. Further preparation is similar to that for Paprika lamb stew. Garnish with tarhonya.

Turkish Mutton Pilaff

Ingredients: 2 lb. shoulder of mutton, 3½ oz. lard, 2 oz. butter, ¾ lb. rice, 3½ oz. tomato purée, pinch of ground black pepper, pinch of ginger, 1 tsp. salt, 7 oz. onions, 1 clove of garlic, 1 pt. stock.

Cut the meat into cubes of 1 inch each. Fry the finely chopped onions in a pan till golden-brown, add the crushed garlic. Put in the meat, salt, and sprinkle with pepper and ground ginger, and let it stew slowly beneath a lid, stirring occasionally. Then add tomato purée with ½ gill of water, and let it simmer until tender. Should the gravy reduce too much, add a little water, but only a small amount as the gravy should remain thick. Meanwhile fry the washed rice in butter; pour double the amount of stock on it, and stew under cover until tender. Serve pilaff in middle of a round dish surrounded with rice. Pilaff and rice can be dished separately if preferred.

Irish Stew

Ingredients: 3 lb. mutton, 1½ tsp. salt, 3½ oz. onions, 2 lb. savoy cabbage, 2 lb. potato, 7 oz. carrots, 3½ oz. parsnips, 2 cloves of garlic, 5 peppercorns.

Cut the meat into pieces of about 1 oz. each, and cook in a pan with 4 pt. of water. Add the cleaned carrots cut into broad slices, parsnips, onions, garlic and peppercorns. When the meat is half cooked, add the cleaned and quartered savoys, and the potatoes cut into cubes. Serve in individual soup-plates.

Mutton with Millet Porridge

Ingredients: 2 lb. shoulder of mutton, 4½ oz. lard, 7 oz. onions, 1 clove of garlic, pinch of ground black pepper, pinch of marjoram, ⅓ tsp. paprika, salt, 1 lb. millet.

Wash meat thoroughly, cut into 1-inch cubes, then boil in ample water, straining the water off afterwards. Place the meat in a pan, adding the finely chopped onions, garlic, salt and spice; mix the whole with the melted fat and a little water, then stew under cover. Add the washed millet when meat is nearly tender, pour sufficient stock or water to cover it, and cook under lid on low heat until meat is tender.

GAME AND WINGED GAME

ON GAME IN GENERAL

Hare or rabbit, venison and wild-boar's meat are frequently used in the Hungarian cuisine. Game is rather tough when prepared fresh, and should be hung in its skin for about 6—8 days after killing, thus rendering it more tender and palatable. We can buy hare or rabbit frequently. There are several methods of preparation and all parts of the hare or rabbit can be used very economically. The whole back and the hind legs should be larded or stewed in a sauce prepared with sour cream, but it has an excellent flavour if prepared with fine red wine sauce (jugged). If we fillet, slice and lard the flesh from the backbone and fry quickly, we can produce excellent fillets of hare, similar to tenderloin steaks, to be served with different garnishes and sauces. Hare or rabbit stew with paprika, ragout, patties or hash, may be prepared from the animal's shoulders, neck and liver, and from other parts as well. If the hare or rabbit is old, marinade it for a few days before cooking in order to soften the fibres of the meat. The marinade should be prepared as follows; put enough water on to boil to cover the meat. Add sliced onions, mixed vegetables, a little salt, 1—2 bay leaves, a few grains of whole black pepper and a small quantity of tarragon vinegar. Simmer for about an hour, then cool, and when cold pour over the hare or rabbit, larded previously with fat bacon. Keep the pickled hare in a cold place. We can also marinade the hare or rabbit in case we have more than can be used for one meal. Only wooden, enamelled or porcelain dishes kept properly clean should be used for marinading.

Everything said about the preparation of hare may be applied more or less for venison as well, with the difference that there are more variations to be found in the recipes. The flesh from the backbone may be roasted whole and served cold or hot, or filleted and fried in slices, and served together with different kinds of garnishings and sauces. The leg can be roasted or stewed in one piece, but may be carved into slices when still raw, and prepared in various ways by stewing as venison steaks. Venison can be marinaded just like the meat of the hare.

Wild-boar's meat should usually be boiled in pickle made from vinegar seasoned with onions, mixed vegetables, pepper, juniper berries, thyme and red wine, and served hot, together with horse-radish, or rose-hip jam, or cold, with horse-radish in vinegar.

Our choicest winged game are the pheasants, partridges, quails, woodcocks and wild-ducks. Winged game should be generally larded with fat bacon, fried in lard and garnished with apple sauce, rice and lentil purée. If prepared with skill, they can represent the chef-d'oeuvres of culinary art; for example, jellied pheasant pie, partridge stewed with kohlrabis, wild-ducks garnished with orange sauce, woodcocks on toast. Winged game should also be left to hang for a few days before use. Do not scald feathers, just pluck them dry, singe afterwards and wash well before cooking.

Hunter's Hare or Rabbit

Ingredients: One whole back and legs of hare or rabbit, 2½ tsp. salt, 1 tbsp. vinegar, 7 oz. carrots, 3½ oz. parsnips, 2 bay leaves, 6 peppercorns, 2 oz. onions, 5 oz. bacon, 3 oz. lard, 1 oz. sugar, 1 lemon, 1 tbsp. mustard, 1½ gill white wine, 3½ oz. flour, 2 gills sour cream, 5 roll dumplings or 5 portions of boiled macaroni.

Prepare marinade as follows: Take sufficient boiling water with which to cover meat, put sliced onions, mixed sliced vegetables, a little salt, 1—2 bay leaves, peppercorns and a little tarragon vinegar into the water, boil for an hour, cool, and pour it over the hare, and keep in a cold place for 2 days. Take hare out of the marinade, and lard well with thin strips of bacon. Take mixed vegetables out of marinade, and put into a pan with a little fat; put in the hare, and roast until half ready; then take out the hare, sprinkle vegetables remaining in pan with a little flour, brown, and add cream, white wine, a little of the marinade and water. Flavour with sugar, mustard, and vinegar, and boil for 20 mins., and then rub sauce through a sieve. Put in the juice and thin peel of a whole lemon, add the hare and stew until tender. Dish with roll dumplings or with macaroni.

English Larded Hare or Rabbit

Ingredients: 2 whole backs of hare, 2 tsp. salt, 2 oz. lard, 3½ oz. bacon, pinch of black pepper, 3 portions of Duchess potatoes, 3 portions of mushrooms and rice.

Trim the hare's back with a sharp knife, lard with bacon, sprinkle with salt and pepper, and roast it English fashion in a hot oven. Cut off the two fillets from backbone slice, and replace meat before dishing. Serve with potatoes, and with mushrooms and rice. Cranberry sauce is served separately in a sauceboat.

Larded Steaks of Hare or Rabbit

Ingredients: 2 whole backs of hare, 2 tsp. salt, 5 oz. bacon, 2 oz. lard, 1 tbsp. tomato purée, 1 tsp. flour, 7 oz. cranberries, 5 oz. carrots, 2 oz. parsnips, 2 bay leaves, 1 oz. onions, pinch of ground black pepper, 5 portions of rice.

Prepare marinade as for Hunter's hare, cut all meat off backbone, lay in cold marinade and keep in a cold place for 2 days. Taking meat out of marinade, slice and lard slices with strips of bacon; sprinkle with salt, and pepper and fry in hot fat. Take meat out of pan and put tomato purée into the remaining fat; brown slightly, add flour, stir, thin with little water, boil, then strain gravy and pour round the steaks when dishing. Serve with steamed rice and cranberry sauce.

Ragout of Hare or Rabbit

Ingredients: 2 legs and 2 shoulders of hare, 3 oz. lard, 2 oz. flour, 2 cloves of garlic, 1 onion, 1 bay leaf, small bunch of thyme, 1 bunch of parsley, 25 small button onions, 7 oz. mushrooms, salt, pepper, ¾—1 pt. white wine.

Cut the meat of shoulder and legs into 1—2 oz. pieces. Fry in hot fat, until meat is a nice brown colour; sprinkle with flour, add finely chopped onions, and crushed garlic; stir it a few times, add salt and pepper. Dilute with wine mixed with the same amount of water and bring to boil. Add bouquet garni of green parsley, 1 bay leaf and thyme to ragout. Then add the peeled button onions and mushrooms, cut into quarters, and, covering with lid, simmer the whole until meat is tender. Remove bouquet garni before dishing, and serve with steamed rice in butter or spaghetti.

Larded Roast Venison

Ingredients: 4 lb. loin of venison, 1½ tsp. salt, 4½ oz. bacon, 5 oz. carrots, 2 oz. parsnips, 3 oz. onions, 1 bay leaf, 6 peppercorns, 1 clove of garlic, 2 oz. tomato purée, 3 oz. flour, 2 oz. lard, 1½ gill red wine, 5 portions of rice, 5 portions of cranberry sauce.

Marinade the venison after trimming, as for hare, and let is stand 2 days in a cool place. Then take it out, and lard with thin strips of bacon. Clean carrots, parsnips and onions. Cut them into slices and pack into pan, around the venison; add lard, bay leaf, garlic and pepper, and roast till nicely browned. Then take venison out of pan and add tomato purée to the remaining vegetables; then add flour, and fry for a few minutes; dilute with wine and a little water; boil gravy for 15 mins., then strain through sieve, pour over venison, and cook very slowly until tender. Cut meat into 5 slices, serve with steamed rice and cranberry sauce.

Braised Leg of Venison

Ingredients: 2 lb. leg of venison, 1½ tsp. salt, 3½ oz. bacon, 5 oz. carrots, 3 oz. parsnips, 6 oz. onions, 1 bay leaf, 2 peppercorns, 1 clove of garlic, 2 oz. tomato purée, 3 oz. flour, 2 oz. lard, 1½ gill red wine, 5 portions of cranberry sauce, ½ orange, 2 oz. red currant or cranberry jelly.

Lard venison with bacon cut into strips and roast it in hot fat. Take meat out; clean carrots, parsnips, and onions, slice and fry them in the remaining fat; add flour and tomato purée, fry, then add crushed garlic, bay leaf, and pepper; put back the meat, adding at the same time 1½ gill red wine, ½ orange, 2 oz. red currant-jelly and salt; cook very slowly till meat is tender. Strain sauce through a sieve, dish with steamed rice and cranberry sauce.

Small Steaks of Venison à la Kedvessy

Ingredients: 4 lb. loin of venison, 4½ oz. lard, ten large mushrooms, 2 oz. butter, 1 gill sweet cream, 1½ tsp. salt, 1 gill white wine, 1 glass of brandy, pinch of ground black pepper, ½ lemon, 1 tsp. of flour, 5 oz. white bread, 5 portions of steamed rice, bunch of parsley, 1 tsp. meat extract.

Trim with a sharp knife, cut meat off the bone, and divide into 10 small steaks of equal size. Flatten a little, salt slightly, and pepper them. Cut small slices of white bread of equal size and quantity as the venison steaks, and fry them in hot fat. Fry the venison steaks in the same fat, leaving them underdone *à l'anglaise;* lastly fry the mushrooms, then place everything on a plate, and keep it in a warm place. Pour the white wine and brandy into the frying pan, in which the venison steaks were fried, boil slightly, add sweet cream, meat extract, ground pepper, and boil a few minutes. Thicken with 1 oz. butter mixed with flour; boil again, stirring it smooth with a whisk. Take sauce off heat flavour with lemon-juice and lastly add the remaining butter, broken into small pieces. Lay the rice, shaped like a mushroom into the middle of the dish; place the slices of bread around it, putting a small steak of venison over each, and placing mushroom on top of steaks; cover with sauce, and lastly with finely chopped parsley.

Seville Stag Steaks

Ingredients: 2 lb. stag's tenderloin, 4½ oz. bacon, 3½ oz. carrots, 3 oz. parsnips, 1 onion, 1 clove of garlic, 2 oz. tomato purée, 2 oranges, 1 bay leaf, 2 oz. flour, 2 oz. lard, 1 tablespoonful red currant jelly, 1½ gill red wine, 12 mushrooms, 1 small glass of brandy.

Slice tenderloin, lard with the bacon, salt and pepper, and roast in hot fat; then place in a pan. Clean carrots, parsnips, onions; cut into slices, and fry in the fat remaining after steaks were roasted; add tomato purée and flour and fry lightly; pour on red wine and a little water, add garlic and bay leaf; boil, pour gravy over the steaks, and cook until meat is tender. Remove meat to another pan, flavour sauce with juice of half an orange, and red currant jelly; then boil again, strain through a sieve and put in the orange peel cut into thin strips and previously boiled. When serving, place a slice of peeled orange over each steak, put a mushroom in the middle of each, pour hot sauce flavoured with brandy over it, and serve rice separately.

Venison Pörkölt

Ingredients: 2 lb. venison, 1 tsp. salt, 1 tsp. paprika, 2 clove of garlic, 2 oz. green paprika, 2 oz. tomatoes, 2 oz. lard, 5 oz. onions, 5 portions of stewed rice.

Fry finely cut onions in fat, add crushed garlic and red paprika, then put in the venison, cut into cubes. Salt, add a little water and cook slowly under lid; then put in the chopped green paprika, and tomatoes; stew until tender, and dish with steamed rice.

Roasted Partridge

Ingredients: 5 young partridges, ½ lb. bacon, 1½ tsp. salt, 2 oz. lard, a little marjoram, 5 portions of lentil purée.

Clean partridges, cutting them open while dry, wash and salt them and sprinkle insides with marjoram. Wrap each bird in thin rashers of bacon, tying it round partridges with thin string, and roast slowly in hot fat in the oven until tender. Dish with steamed rice and lentil purée.

Bácska Partridge

Ingredients: 3 partridges, 7 oz. lean bacon, 2 onions, ½ tsp. paprika, 2 cloves of garlic, a little caraway seed, 1 lb. potatoes, 5 green paprikas, ½ lb. fresh tomatoes, 2 lb. cabbage, rice.

Halve the partridges after cleaning and washing them. Cut bacon into cubes and render it, fry finely chopped onions in fat, add minced garlic, paprika and a little caraway seed; lay partridges into pan, after salting them, cover with lid and stew.

When the partridges begin to soften, add potatoes cut into cubes, sliced green paprika, tomatoes cut into pieces, cabbage cut into strips and lastly the washed rice. Add a little water, bring to boil, then stew in the oven until ready.

Partridge with Savoys

Ingredients: 5 partridges, 1½ tsp. salt, ½ lb. streaky Kolozsvár bacon, 5 oz. smoked sausage, 7 oz. carrots, 3½ oz. parsnips, 2 onions, 4 cloves, pinch of ground black pepper, 3 lb. savoy cabbages, 2 oz. lard, 2 oz. butter.

Clean partridges while dry, salt, and roast them for 5 mins. in hot oven. Clean savoys, quarter, cut out centre stalk, wash well and boil a few minutes; then strain, sprinkle with salt and pepper. Butter the inside of a pan, lay half of the savoy leaves on the bottom, arrange partridges, bacon and sausage on them, cover with the sliced carrots and parsnips, add onions stuck with cloves, then cover the whole with the other half of the savoys. Add the fat in which the partridges have been roasted, 1—2 gills of stock or water, and pour over partridges. Cover and placing it in the oven, cook for 40—50 mins. Lay half the savoys into the bottom of the serving dish; arrange the partridges (halved) on top, cover with remaining savoys and garnish with sliced bacon, sausage and carrots. Serve hot, with gravy poured round it.

Provençale Partridge

Ingredients: 5 partridges, 3½ oz. butter, 2 oz. flour, 1 lb. tomatoes, 1 onion, 1½ gill white wine, 2 cloves of garlic, salt, pepper, 1 bunch of parsley, small bunch of thyme, 1 bay leaf.

Quarter partridges, salt, fry in butter, covered with lid. Lift partridges on a plate when they are tender. Fry the finely chopped onion a little in the butter remaining in pan; add flour, the crushed garlic and tomatoes cut into cubes. Add stock or red wine; add bouquet garni, and bring gravy to boil. Flavour with chopped parsley and pepper, place partridges into the pan, and boil up once again.

Serve with rice stewed in butter. Always tie bouquet garni with string, then it is easier to remove.

Roast Pheasant

Ingredients: 2 young pheasants, 1½ tsp. salt, a little marjoram, 2 oz. lard, 5 oz. bacon, 5 portions of steamed rice, 5 portions of apple sauce.

Clean and cut open pheasants, and lard them with bacon, cut into thin strips; roast in a slow oven. Serve with steamed rice and creamed apple sauce. Cut the breast meat into very thin slices.

Roasted Field-fare

Ingredients: 10 field-fares, 10 oz. bacon, 1½ tsp. salt, 7 oz. lard, 7 oz. goose-liver, 1 oz. onions, pinch of ground black pepper, 1 tbsp. wine, 10 rolls, 2 eggs, 2 oz. butter, 10 slices of ham, 1½ gill gravy, 5 portions of lentil purée.

Clean field-fares while dry, singe, then open and draw. Remove heart, liver and gizzard and chop up the remaining intestines with the goose-liver. Fry this mixture in butter and fat yielded by diced bacon, together with finely chopped onions; salt, flavour with a little pepper, add yolks of eggs, mix well, and stuff the birds with this stuffing. Salt, pepper, then wrap them in thin slices of bacon, pick out their eyes, pierce legs with the beaks and tie field-fares round with thin string. Roast rapidly with a little fat in a saucepan, over a high flame for 15—20 mins., basting frequently. Slice rolls, stamp slices into round or heart-shaped pieces and fry them in fat. Fry the slice of ham in hot fat, then lay it aside. Remove string when birds are ready, and put the bacon wrapping aside. Halve the birds, take out stuffing and spread it over the croutons. Arrange the birds on a dish, together with the slices of bacon and ham, and surround with croutons spread with stuffing.

Prepare sauce with red wine, gravy, a little lemon-juice and peel, and flavour with salt and pepper. Serve it separately in a sauceboat. Dish lentil purée separately.

Wild Boar with Rose-hip Syrup

Ingredients: 2½ lb. haunch of wild boar, 2 tsp. salt, 7 oz. carrots, 3½ oz. parsnips, 2 oz. onions, 5 peppercorns, 5 juniper berries, 1 bay leaf, 1½ gill red wine, 5 oz. horse-radish, 7 oz. rose-hip syrup.

Cook boar in salt water until half done; add carrots cut into strips, parsnips, onions, garlic, and red wine; flavour with pepper, bay leaf and juniper berries and cook until meat is tender. Slice and serve with grated horse-radish and rose-hip syrup.

Wood Snipe

Ingredients: 10 snipes, 10 oz. bacon, 1½ tsp. salt, 3½ oz. lard, 5 oz. chicken-liver, 1 oz. onion, pinch of ground black pepper, pinch of marjoram, 1½ gill brandy, 5 rolls, 2 oz. butter, 2 oz. rice, 1½ gill gravy.

Clean snipes dry, without cutting open; singe a little, salt, pepper and wrap them in thin slices of bacon, so that, tying legs back, each bird is fully covered. Don't cut off either neck or head. Prick eyes out, and pierce legs with the beak so that birds may retain their original shape while roasting. Roast the birds rapidly over bright flame, or in the oven for 20—25 mins., having placed them into a saucepan with a little fat; baste frequently with their own gravy. When ready add a little good stock and a little brandy, cover and lift off the fireplace, letting them stand and steam for a few minutes, then remove bacon wrapping, and put it aside. Cut open the birds, remove gizzard, heart and liver, cutting up the remaining intestines together with the chicken-liver, then fry with chopped bacon, butter and finely chopped onions, salt and flavour with pepper, marjoram and a little brandy. Slice rolls, fry, and spread them with this mixture (salmi).

Quarter the snipes and place them nicely round the pyramid of rice in the middle of dish, surround them with the croutons, spread with salmi, and slices of bacon. Boil gravy, flavour again with pepper, and brandy, and dish, pouring gravy over the snipes.

Wild Duck with Sour Cream Sauce

Ingredients: 2½ wild ducks, 1½ tsp. salt, 7 oz. mixed vegetables, 5 oz. onions, pinch of pepper, 5 oz. bacon, 1 bay leaf, 3½ oz. flour, 1½ gill white wine, 1 clove of garlic, ½ lemon, 1½ gill sour cream, 1 dessertspoon mustard.

Clean the wild ducks, then salt, and sprinkle with pepper. Grease the inside of a pan of suitable size, put in the sliced vegetables and onions, the bay leaf, bacon, garlic and pepper. Lay the ducks in it, and roast for 15—20 mins. Take out of oven, and when cool, cut off the legs and meat on the breast. Cut the rest into small pieces, and put back into the pan. Sprinkle with a little flour, brown, together with the vegetables in the oven, add the white wine and about ½ pt. stock or water in order to obtain a thin sauce.

When the sauce boils, put in the legs and breast, and covering with a lid, stew them slowly in the oven, stirring occasionally. Take meat out of sauce when it is tender. Add the peel of half a lemon and the sour cream, let them boil a few minutes. Strain gravy through a sieve, put in the meat and serve. (Remember: wild duck has a strong, gamey taste, use flavourings accordingly.) Serve with rice, dumplings, or macaroni.

POULTRY

The flavour and nutritive value of poultry compare well with the flavour of any other meat. Poultry can be prepared in various ways and is, therefore, excellently suited to lend variety to our diet. When buying poultry, we should take care to purchase only young and fresh birds. Always keep poultry in the ice-box or refrigerator, but clean them before storing, because their flesh is more liable to deterioration than other kinds of meat. Chicken should be scalded before plucking, while geese and ducks can be plucked dry. Singe the bird turning over an open flame after plucking, then wash, changing water several times. If geese, ducks, turkeys and chicken are older, and the feathers cannot be removed easily by scalding, pull out the stubs one by one.

Care should be taken when drawing, not to break the gall-bladder on the liver, because this may give the liver a bitter taste, rendering it quite unpalatable.

Young chicken are generally fried in bread-crumbs, but they have an excellent flavour, if grilled or roasted on the spit or sautéed. If the chickens are a little bigger—about $1\frac{1}{2}$—2 lb. in weight—we may roast, lard or stew them, or use for the preparation of stew with paprika, or chicken fricassée, while older birds are more suitable for soup.

It should be mentioned here that the Hungarian cuisine recommends the larding of the breast, when preparing poultry for roasting. At the same time, the method of covering the bird with salt pork or slices of fat bacon, is generally applied in the case of winged game.

Young geese are most suitable for roasting. They should be roasted whole, until crisp. Older, fattened geese ought to be jointed first and roasted only afterwards. The fat should be removed from the meat and melted, and the cracklings served cold or hot. Serve goose-liver roasted in goose-fat, or make patties or slices fried in bread-crumbs, stewed, grilled, sautéed or in risotto. The legs can be roasted, stewed or smoked; the breast can be stewed, minced or prepared with brown sauce, or in the Transylvanian way or braised in a pan. Giblets may be used for soup, or boiled and garnished with rice. Ducks are prepared in the same way.

If the breast of turkey is roasted it should previously be larded with fat bacon, to give better flavour to the meat and gravy. Legs may be used for stews, soups or fricassée, while the flesh, removed from the breast, and sliced, gives excellent fillets, whether fried in bread-crumbs or prepared rolled and fried in flour, or in any other way.

Poultry ought also to be served carefully. First of all, the bony parts (back, wings, etc.) of goose, duck or turkey should be placed on the dish and

Larded Pheasant ▷

the legs and the neatly sliced breast arranged nicely on top of them, as if on a foundation. Do not pour the gravy over roast chicken or the sliced breast-meat of roast turkey when serving, but pour some under the meat, or, better still, serve gravy in a separate sauceboat, in order to keep the fine white colour of the meat.

CHICKEN

Fried Chicken

Ingredients: 2 young chickens (weighing about 1½ lb. each), 1 tsp. salt, 3 eggs, 10 oz. lard, 2½ oz. flour, 7 oz. bread-crumbs, 1 bunch of parsley, 5 portions of fried potato chips.

Use tender spring chickens, clean thoroughly, wash and drain, then cut into serving portions. Wipe with clean cloth and salt. Place livers and gizzards beneath wings. Turning pieces first in flour, then in beaten egg, and lastly in bread-crumbs, fry in ample fat, until they are crisp and golden. Dish as soon as ready, with parsley and fried potatoes. Take care not to let the fat grow too hot, while frying, as the bread-crumbs on the outside would then burn to cinders in a few minutes, while the chicken would remain raw inside. Don't try to fry in fat which is not hot enough, as the chicken would become saturated and lose its natural juice, and the dressing of crumbs would fall off. If frying several chickens at one time, fry thicker pieces separately, and for a longer time than the rest.

Keep pieces together in this manner after taking out of frying pan, because this facilitates dishing and portioning.

Grilled Chicken

Ingredients: 2 young chickens (weighing about 1½ lb. each), 1½ tsp. salt, 5 nice fresh tomatoes, 5 fine large mushrooms, 3½ oz. lard, 3 portions of potato chips.

Clean and wash chickens, then halve them, cutting lengthwise. Cut slightly into the muscles and sinews beneath the wings and at the bend of the legs so that neither wings nor drumsticks may turn upward while grilling. Place liver and gizzard beneath wings, salt, dip pieces into melted fat, and grill until brown. Dish with grilled tomatoes and mushrooms. Do not pour gravy over grilled chicken.

Braised Chicken

Ingredients: 3½ lb. chicken, 1½ oz. flour, 2 tbsp. gravy, small bunch of parsley, 1 tsp. salt, 3½ oz. lard, 2 oz. butter, 5 portions of potato chips.

Clean and wash chicken, then cut into pieces. Salt and flour, then fry chicken in lard, heated in a saucepan, until the pieces turn brown. Then pour off fat, add gravy to chicken, and braise it, covered with a lid, over an open

◁ Beefsteak with Egg
Veal Stew with Sour Cream

flame for 4—5 mins. until meat is tender. Then place chicken on a dish; add butter to the gravy, mix well, boil again, and pour over chicken. Serve with potatoes fried in fat and sprinkle with finely chopped parsley. Small, stuffed, fresh tomatoes, and mushroom heads may also be grilled and served with the chicken.

Place the mushrooms and tomatoes neatly around the chicken when dishing.

Hungarian Braised Chicken

Ingredients: 3½ lb. chicken, 3½ oz. fat, 1 dessertspoon tomato purée, ½ tsp. paprika, 1 tsp. salt, 2 oz. bacon, 3½ oz. tinned lecsó, 2½ oz. onions, 5 portions of sauté potatoes.

Clean chicken, wash thoroughly, cut it into pieces and salt it. Heat fat in frying pan, fry the pieces in it rapidly, until they turn brown. Then pour fat into another pan, cover the chicken and set it aside. Put the bacon, cut into small cubes, into the fat, fry till pale yellow, then add finely chopped onions, and fry again. Add red pepper, tinned lecsó and tomato purée, salt, stir, then pour over the chicken. Replace chicken over the open flame, and braise —covered with lid—over a hot flame for several minutes, until the chicken is tender. Dish with sauté potatoes. Use fresh tomatoes and green paprika instead of lecsó, during the summer; taking ¾ lb. fresh tomato and 1½ lb. fresh green paprika, in which case, tomato purée and even bacon can be dispensed with.

Hunter's Braised Chicken

Ingredients: 3½ lb. chicken, 3½ oz. fat, 5 oz. mushrooms, ⅓ tsp. ground black pepper, 5 oz. fresh tomatoes, 2 oz. butter, 2 gills ready-made brown sauce, 1 tsp. salt, 1 oz. onions, 7 oz. chicken-liver, ½ tsp. tarragon leaves, 2 tbsp. white wine, 1 bunch of parsley, 5 portions of steamed rice.

Clean chicken, wash and cut it up into pieces, then clean and slice onions and chop them finely together with mushrooms. Chop parsley and tarragon leaves separately. Dip fresh tomatoes into hot water for a moment, skin and remove pips, and cut into small pieces. Lastly cut the chicken-liver into small cubes. Having prepared everything, heat fat in a saucepan, fry the chicken in it rapidly over a brisk flame, turning, so that it may fry evenly. Then pour off fat into another pan, and covering the chicken with a lid, set it aside. Heat fat again, put in the chopped onions, fry till light yellow, add sliced mushrooms, the chicken-liver cut into small cubes and the tomatoes. Salt, pepper, and holding the whole a few minutes over a full flame, fry stirring occasionally. Pour off surplus fat, when it is ready, thin it with white wine, and boil thoroughly, until almost all the juice evaporates. Then add the brown sauce, stir well and pour over the chicken. Sprinkle with chopped parsley and tarragon, replace over the fire, and braise beneath a lid for a few minutes, until chicken grows tender and sauce is sufficiently thick. Break up butter and stir it in well, before dishing. Serve with steamed rice.

Marengo Fried Chicken

Ingredients: 3½ lb. chicken, 2 oz. flour, 3½ oz. oil. 1 lb. fresh tomatoes, 2 oz. onions, pinch of ground black pepper, 1 gill white wine, 5 eggs, small bunch of parsley, 1 tsp. salt, 3½ oz. lard, 2 oz. butter, 1 clove of garlic, ½ tsp. sugar, 2½ rolls, ½ lb. mushrooms, 1 tbsp. gravy.

Clean chicken, wash and cut into pieces. Clean onions and garlic and chop them separately. Put the fresh tomatoes into hot water for a moment, skin, remove pips, and cut into small cubes. Heat oil in saucepan, fry pieces of chicken, which have already been salted and turned over in flour, add chopped onions and the mushrooms, cut into cubes, and fry the whole for a minute or two, over an open fire. Then pour off oil, put in tomatoes, cut into cubes, (or 3½ oz. tomato purée), the chopped garlic, salt and pepper; flavour with a taste of sugar, and continue roasting for a few minutes. Then add white wine and the gravy; cover with a lid, and cook rapidly for 4—5 mins., over a bright flame, until chicken is tender. Meanwhile, fry eggs in ample fat, frying them in the pan separately, until they are nicely brown, and also fry the slices of rolls (croutons). Set the pieces of chicken upon the dish, crumble butter into the sauce, sprinkle chicken with finely chopped parsley, and pour the hot sauce over the chicken while hot. Lay fried eggs over it, and surround with croutons (pieces of fried roll).

Stuffed Chicken

Ingredients: 3 chickens weighing 1¼ lb. each, pinch of marjoram, 3 oz. butter, 3 rolls, pinch of ground black pepper, 1 dessertspoon tomato purée, 1½ tsp. salt, 3½ oz. lard, 1½ gill milk, 3 eggs, small bunch of parsley, ½ tsp. flour, 5 portions of sauté potatoes.

Cream butter well, with 2 whole eggs and the yolk of a third; salt the rolls soaked in milk, then well squeezed out, pepper and flavour with marjoram and finely chopped parsley, and knead the whole together. Clean chickens thoroughly, wash them, and then loosen skin with finger on the breast and the legs, taking care not to tear skin. Place stuffing beneath the skin, pressing with hands, so that it may be divided equally, then shape slightly so that the chickens are nice and round. Tie legs to hind part with string, so that the chickens keep their original shape whilst roasting, and bend back the wings. Salt, pour hot fat over chicken, and roast basting frequently. Take care, however, that the stuffed chicken is ready 20—25 mins. before serving, in order to let stuffing set, thus facilitating carving.

Dish with sauté potatoes.

Roast Poulard with Fine Garnishing

Ingredients: 2½ chickens, weighing about 1¾ lb. each, 1½ tsp. salt, 3½ oz. fat, 1 tsp. tomato purée, small bunch of parsley, pinch of marjoram, 2 oz. butter, ½ tsp. flour, 5 portions of fine garnishing.

Clean poulard, wash thoroughly, bend back wings, and tie the legs to rump with string, so that the chickens retain their shape, while roasting. Salt, then place a pinch of salt, marjoram and finely chopped parsley inside each. Place in pan, put in fat and a little water and roast in hot oven until brown and tender. Turn over and baste birds occasionally, so that they brown evenly; when roasted, lay the chickens in another pan; heat fat remaining in first pan, then put in tomato; fry until brown, sprinkle on flour, continue cooking for another 1—2 mins.; add a little water to it, to prevent gravy being too thick. Boil well and mix thoroughly, strain and then pour gravy over the chicken; cover and keep warm until dishing. Remove string and parsley before serving. Slice, and arrange daintily on dish.

Never place chicken into a cold oven, because it loses its gravy and becomes dry and unpalatable. It is important that the oven should be hot when the chicken is set to roast, to give a good colour to the meat. We may roast over a slow, even heat later on. Should the chicken be a little tough, fry until brown, then place into pan, cover over with lid, and stew in a warm oven, adding a little water to it occasionally, until it is tender. Dish daintily with fine garnishing (see French garnishing).

Strasbourg Stuffed Chicken

Ingredients: 3 chickens weighing 1¼ lb. each, 3½ oz. lard, 5 oz. goose-liver, 3 oz. mushrooms, pinch of marjoram, 2 eggs, 1 tsp. tomato purée, 1½ tsp. salt, 2½ oz. butter, 2 oz. bacon, pinch of ground black pepper, small bunch of parsley, 2 rolls, ½ tsp. flour, 5 portions of potato chips.

Cut bacon into small cubes, fry lightly, then add goose-liver cut into small cubes, the cleaned and well-washed mushrooms, also cut into small cubes, and fry the whole. Beat butter well with 2 eggs, add soaked and squeezed-out rolls, sprinkle with finely chopped parsley. Salt, pepper, flavour with marjoram, mix with fried goose-liver and the mushrooms. Knead this mixture well and stuff chicken with it. For the rest proceed as for Stuffed chicken. Serve with potato chips, or with steamed rice.

Chicken in Paprika Sauce

Ingredients: 3½ lb. chicken, 1 tsp. flour, ½ tsp. paprika, 1 pt. sour cream, 3½ oz. canned lecsó (or 3½ oz. green paprika and 3½ oz. fresh tomatoes), 1 tsp. salt, 3½ oz. onions, 3½ oz. lard, 1 tbsp. cream, 5 portions of thimble dumplings (galuska).

Clean chicken, cut it into pieces, take out liver and gizzard, and wash them thoroughly. Clean onions, chop finely and fry in hot fat, until they turn a pale yellow. Add paprika, mix with a little water. Add chicken, salt, cleaned, washed and minced green paprika, fresh tomatoes (or the canned lecsó) and stew it under a lid, stirring occasionally, and adding a little water to it, let is simmer gently in thick gravy until half-done; then mix sour cream with flour and a little cold water; stir until smooth, add it to chicken, stir once again, pour on a little more water and stew until tender. Add cream before dishing, boil again, and serve while hot, along with the dumplings.

During the summer, garnish with sliced green paprika and fresh tomatoes.

Larded Capon

Ingredients: 1 capon (weighing 4 lb.), pinch of marjoram, 3 oz. lard, 1 tsp. tomato purée, 2—3 portions of stewed apples, 1 tsp. salt, 3½ oz. bacon, 5 portions of steamed rice.

Clean capon, wash well, bind both wings, and truss so that it retains its original shape while roasting. Cut bacon into thin strips, and lard capon with them. Salt, then sprinkle inside with salt and marjoram. Place in a pan, add fat, pour a little water round it, and roast in a hot oven turning frequently, until brown, basting occasionally with its own gravy. Add a little water, should it roast too quickly, and cook until tender.

Should the capon be old, place it in another pan, place a lid over it, and stew until tender. Then take it out of the fat, fry the tomato purée in the fat, sprinkle with flour, brown, continue cooking a little longer, then pour on only as much water as will prevent the gravy becoming too thick; stir and boil gravy thoroughly, then strain through sieve and pour over the capon. Keep warm under a lid until dishing. Cutting the capon into neat pieces, place bony parts underneath, slice breast, and lay it on top when dishing. Serve with steamed rice, and apple sauce in a separate dish.

Broiled Paprika Chicken

Ingredients: 3½ lb. chicken, 1 tsp. flour, 1 tsp. paprika, 3¼ oz. fresh tomatoes, 1 tsp. salt, 5 oz. onions, 7 oz. green paprika, or 5 oz. canned lecsó, 1 clove of garlic, 3½ oz. lard, 5 portions of tarhonya.

Wash chicken and cut into pieces, adding liver and gizzard. Clean onions, chop finely and fry in heated fat until they turn yellow; add red paprika, mix well, and dilute with a little water. Put in the pieces of chicken, salt, add the cleaned and crushed garlic, the cleaned tomatoes cut into tiny pieces, and the green paprika (or canned lecsó). Place under lid, set upon low flame, stir occasionally, and constantly adding a little water, stew until half-done (don't boil in too much water, but broil it in a small amount of gravy); then reduce the fat, sprinkle with flour, pour on as much water as is sufficient to make the gravy neither too thick nor too thin. Cook until tender.

Serve hot and garnish with dumplings or tarhonya. If you prefer a thin gravy, do not add flour, but add only as much water to the broiled chicken, as will yield a good and substantial gravy. Garlic is optional.

Chicken with Rice

Ingredients: 3½ lb. chicken, 3½ oz. lard, 5 oz. mixed vegetables, pinch of ground black pepper, 2 oz. butter, 10 oz. rice, 1 tsp. salt, 2 oz. onions, 2 oz. celery, 7 oz. mushrooms, 1 bunch of parsley, 1 lb. tinned green peas.

Clean chicken, cut into pieces along with liver and gizzard, and wash thoroughly. Clean mixed vegetables and celery, and cut them into small cubes. Then put chicken and vegetables in a saucepan, pour on sufficient water to cover, then salt, add onions (whole), and boil until half-done. Clean, wash and slice mushrooms. Heat lard in a saucepan, fry mushrooms and add the rice; sprinkle finely chopped parsley over it, heat together for 10 mins. over brisk flame stirring occasionally (do not fry), and then mix with half-boiled chicken. Sprinkle with ground pepper, add canned green peas, cover and stew in the oven for 20—25 mins., until both rice and chicken are tender. Then lift out, remove onion, crumble in butter, stir carefully to prevent the meat breaking, and serve hot. When cooking chicken with rice, care must be taken that the gravy in which they are stewed should be double the quantity of the rice.

Bácska Chicken with Rice

Ingredients: 3½ lb. chicken, 3½ oz. lard, 2 oz. bacon, ½ tsp. paprika, 10 oz. fresh tomatoes, 1 lb. green paprika (or 1 lb. canned lecsó), 1 tsp. salt, 5 oz. onions, 10 oz. rice, small bunch of parsley.

Clean chicken, cut into pieces, and wash well along with liver and gizzard. Cut bacon into tiny cubes, add 2 oz. lard, and heat together; fry chopped onions in it until yellow, add red paprika, stir and thin with a little water. Place chicken in sauce, salt, and cover with lid; stir occasionally, pouring on a little water each time, and cook until chicken is half-tender. In the meantime clean and core green paprikas, and cut into pieces—as when preparing lecsó—also wash and slice tomatoes. Then take rice, wash and let water drain off it well; stir about in the remaining fat (do not fry!) over a brisk heat; add to the half-tender chicken, and tomatoes and paprika or the tinned lecsó; stir well. Dilute with 1 pt. of water, salt and bring to boil, then covering with a lid, stew for 20—25 mins. over a medium heat until both rice and chicken are tender. Then take out of pan carefully, so that the tender meat of the chicken does not break. Sprinkle with chopped parsley and serve hot.

During summer, garnish with thin slices of tomato and green paprika.

Szeged Chicken Gulyás

Ingredients: 3½ lb. chicken, 7 oz. mixed vegetables, 2 cloves of garlic, 1 tsp. paprika, 3½ oz. flour, 1½ lb. potatoes, 3½ oz. fresh tomatoes (or 3½ oz. canned lecsó), 1½ tsp. salt, 5 oz. onions, small bunch of parsley, pinch of caraway seed, 3½ oz. lard, 1 egg, 7 oz. green paprika.

Clean chicken, cut into pieces together with liver and gizzard, and wash thoroughly. Clean onions, chop finely; clean garlic, crush and chop it finely, together with the caraway seed. Clean mixed vegetables, chop into tiny cubes, and set to boil in sufficient water to cover them. Melt fat, and half-fry onion in it; add paprika and a little water, stir it, then put in the jointed chicken and crushed garlic. Salt and cover with lid; stir it occasionally, and add a little water when necessary. Cook until half-ready, then reduce gravy. Add tomatoes and green paprika or lecsó, washed and cleaned, the washed and peeled potatoes, cut into small cubes, and the cooked vegetables. Add water, measuring out about 2 gills for each person. Then cook until chicken, potatoes and vegetables are tender. Knead flour and eggs into csipetke, cook them in the gulyás, shortly before serving. Dish while hot, in a soup-tureen, sprinkling parsley over it. Cut into smaller pieces, when preparing Szeged gulyás, than when preparing broiled (pörkölt) chicken or chicken with paprika, as Szeged chicken gulyás is served like soup.

Chicken with Tarhonya

Ingredients: 3½ lb. chicken, 5 oz. onions, 7 oz. green paprika or 5 oz. canned lecsó, 1 tsp. salt, 1 tsp. paprika, 3½ oz. fresh tomatoes, 1 clove of garlic, 3½ oz. lard, 5 portions of tarhonya garnishing.

Prepare chicken with tarhonya, as for paprika chicken, the only difference being that the chicken is half-stewed first, then the gravy is reduced, without being thickened. Add half-boiled tarhonya (garnishing), stir the whole, then covering with a lid, casserole chicken together with tarhonya in the oven, until tender. Stir again carefully before dishing to prevent meat from being broken. Then setting it into a dish, place tarhonya beside it. Chicken and tarhonya may also be prepared separately and only mixed when dishing.

During the summer garnish with small slices of fresh tomato and green paprika.

Chicken in Lecsó

Ingredients: 3½ lb. chicken, 1 tsp. salt, 1 clove of garlic, 2 lb. green paprika, 1½ lb. fresh tomatoes (or 1 lb. canned lecsó), 5 oz. onions, ½ tsp. paprika, 2 oz. bacon, 3½ oz. lard, 5 portions of boiled potatoes.

Cut chicken into pieces, and wash thoroughly. Clean onions, and chop finely, frying in 2 oz. lard; add red paprika, pour on a little water, and put in chicken. Salt, then add cleaned and chopped garlic and cook under lid till meat is half-done, stirring occasionally; then reduce gravy. Cut out seeds of paprika in the meantime, and if, very strong, blanch in hot water; then slice and wash thoroughly, and laying on a sieve, let water drain off. Also clean, wash and cut up fresh tomatoes; cut them up as for lecsó. Cut bacon into small cubes, fry it lightly, adding the remaining fat; heat together, put in the remaining onions, fry them, then add green paprika and fresh tomatoes. Stew under lid for a few minutes, stirring occasionally, and when lecsó is half-ready, put it in the pan beside chicken, being careful to place it so that chicken remains on one side, and lecsó on the other. Stew both together, under lid, stirring occasionally.

Put lecsó over meat when dishing. Pour gravy over it, and serve while hot with potatoes boiled in salt water and sprinkled with parsley.

Chicken Tokány

Ingredients: 3½ lb. chicken, 3½ oz. lard, 1 tsp. salt, pinch of ground black pepper, 1 dessertspoon tomato purée, 5 oz. onions, ½ tsp. flour, 1 clove of garlic, 2 tbsp. white wine, 2 oz. bacon, pinch of thyme, 5 portions of steamed rice.

Clean chicken, cut into pieces, take liver and gizzard, and wash the whole thoroughly. Cut bacon into tiny cubes, half-fry in pan, add fat, then heat the whole. Put in the onions, cleaned and chopped, and fry until brown. Add washed and cut up chicken, the cleaned and chopped garlic, salt and pepper, and stirring, add a little water to it occasionally; cover with lid, and stew until meat is tender, then reduce gravy. Sprinkle with flour, add tomato purée (fresh tomato during summer) and thyme, pour in white wine, stir, and let it simmer beneath a lid until quite tender. The gravy should be neither too thick nor too thin.

Serve hot, with steamed rice.

Chicken with Mushrooms

Ingredients: 3½ lb. chicken, 2 oz. onions, 1 tsp. salt, 2 oz. butter, 3½ oz. lard, 1 bunch of parsley, 1 tsp. flour, pinch of ground black pepper, 2 gills sour cream, ½ lb. mushroom, 5 portions of steamed rice.

Clean chicken, wash and cut into pieces. Heat fat in a frying pan, put in the pieces of chicken, salted and dipped into flour, and turn them about in the frying pan over a brisk fire, but only until the meat is of a pale golden colour. Avoid cooking chicken fully; the frying serves to seal the meat so that it retains its flavour. Place chicken into another pan. Put finely chopped onions into fat, fry till golden-brown, then add sliced mushrooms, and the finely chopped parsley; fry together for a few minutes, then pour over the chicken, salt, pepper and cover with lid. Stew over a moderate fire, stirring occasionally, and adding a little water when necessary, until nearly tender. Reduce gravy, sprinkle with flour, stir, add sour cream and a little more water if necessary, so that gravy is neither too thick, nor too thin. Stew until tender, crumble butter into gravy before serving, and mix thoroughly.

Dish while hot, and garnish with steamed rice.

Chicken with Green Peas

Ingredients: 3½ lb. chicken, 1 tsp. salt, 1 oz. flour, 2 tbsp. cream, 1½ lb. fresh shelled peas (or 1 lb. tinned green peas), 1 tsp. sugar, 1 oz. onions, 1 bunch of parsley, 2 oz. butter, 2 oz. bacon, 5 portions of steamed rice, 3½ oz. lard.

Clean chicken, cut into pieces, and wash thoroughly. Heat lard in a frying pan, salt chicken, dip into flour, and fry lightly. Cut bacon into tiny cubes, and fry it, add finely chopped onions, fry a little, and add to the chicken. Salt and cover, add a little water and stew until half-ready. Then reduce gravy, sprinkle with a little flour, add the green peas (which in the meantime have been half-cooked in sugared, salt water), or canned green peas, strained through a sieve; sprinkle with finely chopped parsley, and let it simmer until tender.

Should gravy be too thick, thin with a little water. Put in cream and crumble butter into gravy before dishing, and serve hot, with steamed rice.

Chicken Fricassée

Ingredients: 3½ lb. chicken, 7 oz. mixed vegetables, 1 tsp. salt, 2 oz. flour, 2 tbsp. cream, small bunch of parsley, 2 oz. celery, 2 oz. onions, 5 whole peppercorns, 2 oz. butter, 2 oz. lard, 5 portions of steamed rice.

Clean chicken and cut into pieces. Clean vegetables, cut into tiny, even cubes. Place chicken in saucepan along with the vegetables, pour 2 pt. of water over it, if a spring chicken; should it be an older bird, use 3 pt. Skim top with straining spoon, salt, put in cleaned onions whole, the cleaned and chopped celery, and the pepper, and cook until almost tender. Make a light roux from lard and flour, dilute with stock or water and when chicken and vegetables are almost soft, take out the whole onion and pepper and add sauce. Continue cooking more slowly over an even heat until quite ready. Then add cream, finely chopped green parsley and boil the whole once again. Crumble butter into sauce, mixing it in well, just before dishing. Serve with steamed rice.

The sauce should be of the consistency of cream soup.

Chicken Fricassée with Cauliflower

Ingredients: 3½ lb. chicken, 2 oz. celery, 1 tsp. salt, 2 oz. flour, 2 tbsp. cream, 2 lb. cauliflower, 5 portions of steamed rice, 7 oz. mixed vegetables, 2 oz. onions, 2 whole black peppers, 2 oz. butter, 2 oz. lard, small bunch of parsley.

Clean cauliflower, soak well, wash in several lots of water, until clean, divide into sprigs and boil in slightly salted water until nearly soft. Strain through sieve, then put the cleaned and jointed chicken in the cauliflower's stock. Add cleaned and washed mixed vegetables, onions, celery, and pepper. Salt, and cook until chicken is nearly tender. In the meantime prepare roux with lard and flour, dilute with stock from chicken and stir until smooth with a whisk. Put in the pieces of chicken, add half-cooked cauliflower and cook over a gentle heat until both chicken and cauliflower are tender. Don't stir the fricassée, only shake from time to time to prevent cauliflower breaking. Add cream, also the finely minced parsley, boil the whole once again, and dish hot with steamed rice. Crumble butter in before serving.

Chicken Fricassée with Asparagus

Ingredients: 3½ lb. chicken, 2 oz. celery, 1 tsp. salt, 2 oz. flour, 2 tbsp. cream, 7 oz. mixed vegetables, 2 oz. onions, 5 whole black peppers, 2 oz. butter, 2 oz. lard, 1 lb. tinned asparagus, or 1 lb. fresh asparagus, 1 bunch of parsley, 5 portions of steamed rice.

Prepare as for Chicken ragout, the only difference being that the celery and mixed vegetables are cooked whole, and are removed along with the onions and pepper. Then put in the chicken, cut into pieces, the canned asparagus, and mix with roux diluted with a little water. Vegetables, celery and onions are only put in to give a flavour to the sauce. Serve with asparagus only and use the juice of asparagus for thinning sauce. If using fresh asparagus, clean first, wash, cut into pieces and boil in slightly salted and sugared water. For the rest proceed as with canned asparagus.

Serve with steamed rice.

Chicken Fricassée with Lemon

Ingredients: 3½ lb. chicken, 2 oz. celery, 1 tsp. salt, 7 oz. mixed vegetables, 2 oz. onions, 5 peppercorns, 2 oz. flour, 2 tbsp. cream, 1 lemon, 3½ oz. butter, 2 yolks of egg, 5 portions of steamed rice.

Clean chicken, cut into pieces, wash well and set to boil in about 2 pt. of water. Clean mixed vegetables, celery and onions, and add to chicken without chopping up. Add pepper, a little lemon peel, and covering with lid, cook until meat is tender. Make a light roux with 2 oz. butter and flour. Strain stock of chicken through sieve, pour over roux, stir until smooth and squeezing in the lemon-juice, boil for ten mins. Then mix sweet cream and yolk of egg with a whisk. Take sauce off the heat and add to it the cream and egg-yolk mixture, stir until smooth, and put in the chicken. Do not boil after putting in cream and yolks of egg to prevent curdling. Crumble the remaining 1½ oz. of butter into fricassée, before serving.

Serve with steamed rice.

Fried Chicken Fillet

Ingredients: About 4 lb. breast of chicken, 2 oz. flour, 5 oz. bread-crumbs, 5 portions of green peas in butter, 1½ tsp. salt, 2 eggs, 5 oz. lard, 5 portions of steamed rice.

Cut meat off breast-bones of chicken, taking care not to spoil the shape, leaving only the bones of the wings on it. Draw skin off, cut sinews, then flatten and shape piece. Sprinkle with salt, then turn meat in flour, yolk of egg and lastly bread-crumbs, and fry in ample fat until light brown.

Serve with steamed rice and green peas in butter.

Parisian Fillet of Chicken

Ingredients: (see Fried Chicken Fillet)

Prepare as for Fried Chicken Fillet, the only difference being, that the meat after salting is only dipped in flour and yolk of egg. Instead of steamed rice and green peas, it may be served with potato chips and apple sauce.

Fillet of Chicken in Butter

Ingredients: About 4 lb. breast of chicken, 2 oz. flour, 3½ oz. butter, 5 portions of potato chips, ½ tsp. salt, 2 oz. lard, 5 portions of green peas and butter, 1 tbsp. gravy.

Trim breast of chicken off bone carefully, so that meat remains intact, leaving only the bones of wings on them. Skin, then cut sinew and flatten pieces into the shape of leaves. Salt, dip into flour, and fry until both sides turn a pale yellowish brown. When fried pour off fat, pour gravy over it whilst hot, crumble the butter into it, and setting it on low heat, stew under lid for 2—3 mins.

Serve while hot; garnish with tender green peas and potato chips. (See Garnishes.)

Fillet of Chicken with Sweet Cream and Asparagus

Ingredients: About 4 lb. breast of chicken, 2 oz. flour, 2 oz. butter, ²/₃ tsp. salt, 3½ oz. lard, 5 portions of asparagus sauce with cream.

Trim meat off breast of chickens, leaving only bones of wings upon it. Skin, then cut sinews, so that pieces do not shrink while cooking. Flatten, then shape meat into leaves, salt, dip in flour on both sides, and putting into hot fat, in a frying pan, fry the fillets of chicken over a brisk flame, until both sides turn golden-brown. Then remove from cooker and pour off fat; add butter, while still hot; pour on the asparagus sauce, boil and serve. (See Asparagus Sauce under Sauces.)

203

Kiev Breast of Chicken

Ingredients: About 4 lb. breast of chicken, 2 oz. flour, 5 oz. bread-crumbs, 2 oz. grated cheese, pinch of grated nutmeg, $^2/_3$ tsp. salt, 2 eggs, ½ lb. lard, 2 oz. butter, 5 portions of creamed potatoes.

Trim off chicken breast, taking care not to injure the meat, and leaving the wing-bones on. Cut out sinews with a thin sharp knife, taking care not to cut into the thick flesh; then, using the same knife, cut a narrow slit lengthwise into the meat. Salt the butter a little, flavour with grated nutmeg, and adding the grated cheese knead it together. Divide this stuffing into five; stuff each portion into the pockets made in the meat, press the edge of slits well together, and shape into round form with hands. Salt, turn in flour, egg and crumbs, and fry in hot fat until golden-brown. Take care that the fat is very hot when fillets are placed in it, so that the bread-crumbs turn crisp rapidly, as this prevents the stuffing of cheese and butter from oozing out. It takes longer to fry than fried fillet of chicken, as the meat is thicker, but don't cook too long, or the butter will melt. Serve at once when ready, with creamed potatoes.

Minced Breast of Chicken

Ingredients: 2½ lb. breast of chicken, 1 egg, 2 oz. butter, 1½ rolls, 2 tbsp. cream, 1 tsp. salt, 1 lb. lean veal, 3½ oz. lard, small bunch of parsley, 1½ gill milk, 2 oz. bread-crumbs, 2 tbsp. gravy, 5 portions of spinach with cream.

Soak rolls in milk, then squeeze out well. Trim meat off bones and cut into pieces together with the veal adding rolls, and put through mincer. Chop parsley finely, fry it a little in butter, then add to the minced meat, together with the cream; salt, beat eggs into it, and knead together firmly. Divide into 10 equal pieces, shape into rissoles, turn them in bread-crumbs, then fry them in a saucepan, in hot fat, until they are crisp and brown.

Pour gravy over the rissoles when dishing, and serve spinach, prepared with cream, separately. Instead of spinach the rissoles can also be served with tender green peas or with creamed potatoes.

Chicken Giblets in Paprika Sauce

Ingredients: 1 lb. chicken-liver, 1 lb. chicken-gizzard, 2 oz. bacon, 5 oz. onions, 7 oz. green paprika, 1 tsp. salt, ½ tsp. paprika, 3½ oz. fresh tomatoes (or 5 oz. canned lecsó), 1 clove of garlic, 3½ oz. lard, 5 portions of dumplings.

Clean chicken gizzards thoroughly, remove thick skin and cut them into pieces of moderate size, then wash them in several lots of water, until clean.

Heat fat in a pan, half-fry the finely chopped onions in it, adding a little paprika, and thinning it with a little water. Put in the gizzards, salt, add the crushed and finely chopped garlic, then stew under lid, adding a little water, occasionally, until nearly tender, then reduce gravy. Cut bacon into tiny cubes;

fry lightly. Add the well washed chicken-livers cut into fairly large pieces, and cook for another 2—3 mins. Then core paprikas, wash thoroughly and cut into pieces. Mix fried livers, tomatoes and paprikas (or canned lecsó) with the gizzards, and stew the whole, until meat is tender.

Should gravy be too thick, thin with a little water. Serve hot, together with thimble dumplings. In summer, garnish with finely sliced tomatoes and paprikas.

GOOSE

Roast Goose

Ingredients: Goose, weighing 6—8 lb., 1½ tsp. salt, pinch of marjoram, 1½ gill gravy, 5 portions of backed potatoes.

Clean goose, cutting off neck, feet and wings; cut open, and draw; wash giblets thoroughly until clean. Salt both inside and outside, strew inside with a little marjoram, and roast in a hot oven. Baste frequently. Turn the bird in the oven so that it roasts brown and crisp evenly on all sides. Take out when tender; halve first, then quarter, cut off wings and legs and slice the breast. Lay bonier pieces on the bottom of the dish when serving, setting the sliced breast and legs on the top; pour gravy over it, and a little of its own fat; garnish with baked potatoes and braised cabbage. Roast liver of young goose separately, slice and place beside roast goose when dishing.

Goose Legs with Garlic

Ingredients: 3½ lb. legs of goose (5 pieces), 4 cloves of garlic, pinch of marjoram, 2 oz. lard, 1½ gill gravy, 1 tsp. salt, pinch of ground pepper, 1 tsp. tomato purée, 2 oz. onions, 5 portions of cabbage stewed in red wine.

Clean legs thoroughly, singe and stub out with small knife. Wash, then salt and pepper, sprinkle with marjoram and roast legs on both sides in hot fat, and place in another pan or casserole. Put the sliced onions and the crushed garlic into the fat, in which the legs were fried, and cook slowly for a few minutes, then pour this over the meat; add tomato purée, and a little water, cover with a lid, and basting occasionally, casserole them in the oven, until they are almost tender; then taking off the lid, roast until brown. Place the legs into a dish with cabbage stewed in red wine, add gravy and serve with creamed or baked potatoes.

Stewed Breast of Goose

Ingredients: About 4 lb. breast of goose, 1 tsp. salt, 1 tsp. flour, 2½ oz. lard, 2 oz. bacon, 4 whole black peppers, 1 bay leaf, 4 cloves of garlic, 3½ oz. onions, 3½ oz. mixed vegetables, 1 dessertspoon tomato purée, 2 tbsp. white wine, 5 portions of roast potatoes.

Remove the fat from the breasts of goose, wash and salt them; then heat 2 oz. lard in a saucepan, fry the meat in it a little over a brisk heat, so that the hot fat seals the meat, then place in a pan, and set aside. Cut bacon into tiny cubes, half-fry them in fat; then add cleaned onions cut into small pieces, cut into slices the cleaned and washed mixed vegetables and the crushed garlic, and fry the whole for a few minutes; then pour over the meat. Add bay leaf, tomato purée, pepper, then salt, white wine, and a little water; then cover with lid, stew until meat is almost tender, stirring and adding a little water occasionally. Prepare a thin roux with 1 oz. lard and flour, add to the gravy under the meat, and let it simmer until tender. Then taking the meat out, strain the gravy through sieve, stir with whisk until smooth, then boil again. Cut meat carefully off bone in slices, then replace neatly on the bone before serving. Dish while hot; pour the gravy over and garnish with roast potatoes.

Minced Goose Breast

Ingredients: 1½ lb. skinned breast of goose, 7 oz. fat pork, 1 tsp. salt, 2 oz. lard, 2 oz. onions, 2 cloves of garlic, pinch of ground black pepper, 2 oz. bread-crumbs, 1½ rolls, 2 oz. bacon, 1½ gill gravy, small bunch of parsley, 5 portions of stewed cabbage with tomatoes.

Trim meat of goose breast, and cutting the bones into 5 pieces, set them aside. Cut goose and fat pork meat into pieces and put through mincer twice together with the soaked and squeezed-out rolls. Cut bacon into tiny cubes; fry, then add the cleaned and finely chopped onions; fry a little longer, and add crushed garlic, and finely chopped parsley. Fry the whole for 1—2 mins., then add to minced meat. Salt, pepper, flavour with marjoram, beat in one egg, sprinkle with crumbs, and knead the ingredients firmly together. Break the other egg onto a plate, and beat up with fork. Salt bones slightly, then dipping hands into beaten egg, shape goose breasts out of the minced meat, placing each one back upon a bone. Then brush with the remaining egg, put a little fat on top of each, and roast them in the oven. Baste meat frequently, while roasting, so that it browns evenly. Take meat off bones when roasted, slice, replace neatly, and pouring gravy over it, dish while hot. Serve with cabbage stewed with tomato; but creamed tomatoes, baked potatoes, etc., can also be served with it.

Stewed Goose Legs with Viennese Richette

Ingredients: 3½ lb. goose legs (5 pieces), 1 tsp. salt, 3½ oz. lard, 5 oz. onions, 2 cloves of garlic, 1 lb. pearl barley, ½ tsp. paprika, pinch of ground pepper, small bunch of parsley, 1 lb. tinned green peas, 3½ oz. mixed vegetables, 2 oz. celery, 1 bay leaf.

Wash pearl barley in several lots of water, parboil in sufficient water to cover it; then strain; rinse and put on again in fresh water; salt, and let it simmer under lid, until it is tender.

Clean goose legs, wash them and sprinkle with salt and pepper. Heating the fat in a frying pan, fry the legs in it, until they are brown on both sides. Put meat into a casserole; fry the washed and chopped vegetables, the celery, crushed garlic, and the bay leaf, in the fat left over in the pan. Pour this over drumsticks, salt, pepper and add red paprika; add a little water, and covering with a lid, stew it in the oven, stirring occasionally, until nearly tender. Take meat out of casserole, strain gravy and pour it over the cooked pearl barley; add canned green peas, salt again, adding pepper if necessary. With the meat on top, put back in the oven again; sprinkle top with finely chopped parsley, and cook in the oven until tender.

When serving place Viennese richette on the dish first, put meat on top of it, and serve hot.

Goose Legs in Lecsó

Ingredients: 3½ lb. goose legs (5 pieces), 1 tsp. salt, 5 oz. onions, ½ tsp. paprika, 2 cloves of garlic, 2 oz. bacon, 2 lb. green paprika, 1 lb. fresh tomato (or 1 lb. canned lecsó), 3½ oz. lard, 5 portions of boiled potatoes, 1 bunch of parsley.

Clean legs thoroughly, singe and stub them. Wash well, salt, then heat the lard in frying pan, and fry meat over a brisk fire until brown. Then place in another pan, and fry the finely chopped onions in the fat; add paprika, thin with a little water, and pour it over the legs. Add crushed garlic and cook, adding a little water occasionally to make a thick gravy and covering with lid, stew until nearly tender.

Clean onions, and cut into thin slices. Wash and core green paprika, and cut into pieces; also wash and cut up the tomatoes. Cut bacon into small cubes, half-fry them in a frying pan, add the remaining fat and heat together; add thinly sliced onions, fry a little over a brisk flame, then adding green paprika and fresh tomatoes (or canned lecsó) cook beneath a lid, stirring occasionally.

When the meat is almost tender, put with lecsó, and covering with lid cook until quite tender. Serve while hot, with potatoes boiled in salt water, and sprinkled with finely chopped parsley.

Breast of Goose with Székely Cabbage

Ingredients: 4 lb. breast of goose (about 2½ pieces), 3½ oz. lard, 1 tsp. salt, 3½ oz. onions, ½ tsp. paprika, 2 cloves of garlic, pinch of caraway seed, 1 tsp. flour, 2 lb. sour cabbage, 1 pt. sour cream, 5 oz. green paprika, 3½ oz. fresh tomatoes or 3½ oz. canned lecsó, 2 oz. bacon, small bunch of parsley.

Wash breast of goose well; salt, then fry in saucepan for a few minutes until it browns slightly; wash cabbage, changing water twice, so that it is not too sour; place in pan, adding enough water to cover it, and covering with a lid, cook until it is half-done. Cut bacon into tiny cubes; fry them in a pan, with 1 oz. lard, and finely chopped onions. Put in paprika, thin with a little water, stir, salt and put in breasts of geese, the crushed garlic, caraway seed, the cored, washed and sliced green paprika, and the tomatoes, washed and cut in pieces, or canned lecsó.

Stew until half-done, covering with lid, adding a little water to it occasionally, so that the gravy remains thick. Then add cabbage to meat, cover and cook until it is nearly done.

Then take meat out of cabbage; mix sour cream with flour and a little water, stir smooth with a whisk, and thicken cabbage with it, stirring constantly. Replace meat, and cook till tender. Cut meat off breastbones, when dishing, slice and then replace them neatly; pile cabbage on top, pour on gravy together with the sour cream. Serve hot.

Braised Goose Legs

Ingredients: 3½ lb. goose legs (5 pieces), 3½ oz. lard, 2 cloves of garlic, pinch of caraway seed, 2½ lb. potatoes, 7 oz. green paprika, 3½ oz. fresh tomatoes or 5 oz. lecsó, 1 tsp. salt, 7 oz. onions, 1 tsp. tomato purée, 1 tsp. paprika, small bunch of parsley.

Clean legs, wash and salt; then fry them in hot fat until brown. Take meat out of fat, and place in another pan. Fry chopped onions in the same fat, until they are yellow; add the paprika, stir thoroughly, add a little water, salt and pour over the meat.

Crush garlic, then mince it with a knife, along with the caraway seeds; add to the meat, with a little water and bring to boil. Cover with lid, stir occasionally, and add a small quantity of water if gravy is too thick.

Stew until half-done, then reduce gravy. Peel potatoes, wash them and cut them up lengthwise. Wash fresh tomatoes and cut into pieces; core green paprikas, and cut up. When gravy is reduced, place meat on one side of the pan, add potatoes and tomato purée, put the sliced green paprika and fresh tomatoes (or the canned lecsó) on top, then salt, and covering with lid, stew until tender. Dish while hot, sprinkled with minced green parsley.

In summer, serve garnished with sliced fresh tomatoes and green paprika.

Goose Legs with Richette

Ingredients: 3½ lb. goose legs, 2 oz. pearl barley, 1 clove of garlic, ½ tsp. paprika, pinch of ground black pepper, 1 lb. haricot beans, 5 oz. onions, 3½ oz. lard, 1 tsp. salt, small bunch of parsley.

Clean beans, wash well, and soak in plenty of water for several hours. Wash pearl barley in several lots of water until quite clean, and strain off through sieve. Chop onions finely and crush garlic.

Clean legs, wash and then salt them, and fry in hot fat, until they brown

Carnival Doughnuts ▷
Poppy-seed and Nut Rollo

nicely on both sides. Strain the well-soaked beans, place them in a pan, adding pearl barley, salt, pepper and paprika; then mix thoroughly. Lastly put in the meat, packing beans well around. Pour on sufficient water to cover them amply, cover with lid, and stew in a moderate oven until tender. When beans and meat are both tender, take out meat, stir the richette and flavour it again if necessary.

Serve richette in a deep dish, put meat on top. Sprinkle with finely chopped parsley. Hard-boiled eggs may also be added. Peel and halve them, and arrange neatly around the dish.

Stuffed Neck of Goose

Ingredients: 3 necks of goose (about 2½ lb.), 1 lb. goose meat, ½ lb. pork, 1 roll, 3 hard-boiled eggs, 1 raw egg, pinch of marjoram, pinch of ground black pepper, 1 tsp. salt, 2½ oz. onions, 1 clove of garlic, 3½ oz. tomato purée, 1 tsp. flour, 3 oz. lard, small bunch of parsley, 5 portions of risi-bisi garnishing.

Skin neck of goose carefully, taking care not to injure skin; remove gullet, clean very thoroughly, washing in several lots of water.

Cut pork and goose into pieces, adding the soaked and squeezed-out rolls, and pass the whole twice through the mincer. Shell 3 hard-boiled eggs, cut them into cubes. Heat 1 oz. fat, and fry finely chopped onions, crushed garlic, and also finely chopped parsley, and mix the whole with the minced meat. Salt and pepper it, sprinkle with marjoram, add the raw egg, and knead the whole together. Lastly, mix in the hard-boiled eggs. Fill the 3 necks of geese evenly with this stuffing, sewing their ends together with string. Don't stuff too full, else skins will burst while roasting. Salt again, and then fry them in lard, previously melted in a frying pan, turning them about occasionally, until browned nicely. Then pour the fat into another pan, and fry 1 oz. sliced onions, the cleaned and sliced vegetables and crushed garlic in it; put in the half-roasted necks of geese, cover with lid, then stew in the oven until soft, pouring on a small quantity of water occasionally. Baste and turn frequently. Then take out necks of geese, reduce gravy, put in tomato purée and continue frying; then sprinkle with flour, fry a minute longer, then add sufficient water to it, to thin into a succulent but not too thick roast gravy. Boil it well, then strain through sieve. Slice necks of geese, pour gravy over them, and dish with risi-bisi. Remove string, with which the ends were held together, before dishing.

Goose Cracklings

Ingredients: 2 lb. goose fat, ½ tsp. salt, 5 portions of mashed potatoes.

Clean fat, cutting it carefully off the breast, drumsticks and all other parts of the goose, singe, stub and scrape, and wash thoroughly. Cut into long pieces. Place in pan, pouring on enough water to barely cover it. Cover

◁ Dobos Cake
Ice-cream with Whipped Cream and Fruits

with lid. Stir occasionally. Leave over brisk flame, until water has evaporated, and crackling rises to the surface of fat. Then take lid off, and continue frying until fat becomes quite clear and transparent. Then take it off the cooker, shake a few drops of water on it with your fingers, and cover with lid at once. This will make cracklings crisp.

Strain off fat before it cools, salt and serve cracklings hot with mashed potatoes.

Roast Goose-liver

Ingredients: 2 lb. fattened goose-liver, $2/_3$ tsp. salt, 2 whole black peppers, 1 oz. lard, 2 oz. onions, 1 pt. milk, 5 portions of baked potatoes.

Wash liver well, then soak in milk for an hour. Then take it out, dry with clean cloth and sprinkle with salt. Heat fat in a pan, and fry goose-liver in it for a few minutes, until it browns a little, then pour on enough water to half cover it, put in the whole onion, the pepper, and salt again. Stew in the oven, covered with a lid, until gravy is reduced. Then take off lid, and leave in the oven, until liver is brown on all sides. Set a bed of mashed potatoes in the middle of the dish, and lay the thinly sliced goose-liver over it, when dishing. Strain fat through sieve, and pour some over the liver. Serve hot. A little garlic is optional, and the fat may be given colour with the addition of a little paprika, shortly before the liver is ready.

Fried Goose-liver Slices

Ingredients: 1¼ goose-liver, 2 oz. flour, 5 oz. bread-crumbs, 1 tsp. salt, 2 eggs, 5 oz. lard, 5 portions of risi-bisi garnishing.

Remove heart from goose-liver, then cut liver into 15 slices of equal size, flatten them a little, taking care not to break them in the process. Salt, then turn slices in flour, beaten egg and bread-crumbs, and fry in hot fat, until they are nicely browned. Place fried goose-liver on a clean napkin to drain off surplus fat. Serve hot. Garnish with risi-bisi.

Lyonnaise Goose-liver Slices

Ingredients: 1¾ lb. goose-liver, 1 tsp. salt, 7 oz. onions, 7 oz. lard, 2 oz. flour, 2 tsp. gravy, 5 portions of roast potatoes.

Clean onions and cut into thin slices, plucking slices apart into rings. Salt, sprinkle with a little flour and mix well. Melt fat, and when hot, put in the prepared onions, and stirring constantly, fry over a brisk heat in ample hot fat, until onions become crisp and brown. Then strain and put in a warm place. Cut goose-liver into 15 equal pieces, flatten them with care, so that

210

they do not break. Salt and dip both sides into flour, and fry in the fat in which the onions were cooked, until they are nicely browned. Pour gravy over the slices, and dish while hot. Put the crisply fried onions on top of the slices of goose-liver, and garnish with roast potatoes.

Sliced Goose-liver au Naturel

Ingredients: 1¾ lb. goose-liver, 1 tsp. salt, 5 portions of steamed rice for garnishing, 2 oz. flour, 3½ oz. lard.

Cut goose-liver into slices weighing 5 oz. each, flatten a little, taking care not to break them, salt, and turn them in flour. Heat fat in frying pan, fry slices of goose-liver in it, until they are brown. Take care that the flame is not too brisk as goose-liver might easily scorch and taste bitter, while the inside remains raw. On the other hand, if temperature is too low, the liver will be soggy. Serve hot with steamed rice, sprinkled with its own fat.

Goose-liver Slices with Madeira Sauce

Prepare as for Sliced goose-liver au naturel, but dish with Madeira sauce, served separately in a sauceboat.

Fried Goose-liver

Ingredients: 1¾ lb. goose-liver, pinch of marjoram, ½ tsp. paprika, 4½ oz. lard, 1 tsp. salt, pinch of ground black pepper, 5 oz. onions, 5 portions of fried potatoes.

Cut the goose-liver (which should not be too fat) into equal strips of 1—2 inches length, and ½ inch thickness. Clean and then chop onions finely. Heat fat in frying pan, and fry onions in it over a brisk flame, until they are half-done. Add pieces of goose-liver, salt, and sprinkle with marjoram and ground pepper; fry 1—2 mins. over a brisk fire, stirring carefully, and shaking frying pan, so as not to break the liver. Add red paprika and stir. Serve hot, garnished with roast potatoes.

Goose Stew

Ingredients: 1 lb. goose, 4 lb. giblets, 1 tsp. salt, 2 cloves of garlic, 5 oz. onions, ½ tsp. flour, 3½ oz. fresh tomatoes, 7 oz. green paprika (or 5 oz. canned lecsó), 2 oz. lard, ½ tsp. paprika, 1 tsp. tomato purée, 5 portions of tarhonya garnishing.

Clean giblets very carefully, and cut up into fairly large slices, with the goose meat, then wash both thoroughly. Chop onions and fry in hot fat, until they are golden-brown. Add paprika, stir, and thin with a little water.

211

Put in the meat, salt, then add crushed garlic, and cover with lid. Stir occasionally, adding a little water when necessary, so that there is not too much gravy. Wash fresh tomatoes, and cut to pieces, and core green paprikas, and cut into pieces. Add cut-up tomatoes, and green paprikas (or the canned lecsó) when the goose is half-ready, and stew until it is nearly done. Then reduce gravy, sprinkle with flour, add tomato purée, and pour on sufficient water to make a substantial gravy. Continue stewing until meat is quite tender, and dish while hot, garnishing with tarhonya. Omit the flour if very little gravy is desired.

Fricassée of Goose Giblets

Ingredients: 2—3 sets of giblets (about 6 lb.), 2 oz. onions, 3½ oz. mixed vegetables, pinch of ground black pepper, 5 portions of dumplings, 1½ tsp. salt, 2 oz. celery, 2 oz. mushrooms, 1 bunch of parsley, 2½ oz. flour.

Clean giblets carefully, cut into pieces (avoid cutting through bone, or splinters will get into the meat), wash thoroughly and set to boil in as much water as will cover. Clean mixed vegetables and celery, wash and cut into even cubes. Add to the giblets. Add onions as well, and salt; cover with lid, and continue boiling until meat is tender.

Prepare a light roux of flour, and lard. Clean and slice mushrooms. Remove onions, as soon as meat has become tender, replace them with mushrooms, and boil. Mix roux into fricassée, add pepper and half of the minced parsley; let it boil again. Serve hot, adding brain dumplings (boiled separately in salt water) to the fricassée and besprinkle with remaining parsley. Sauce should be neither too thick nor too thin. Steamed rice can be served instead of dumplings, but must be dished separately.

Goose Giblets with Rice

Ingredients: 2—3 sets of giblet (about 6 lb.), 3½ oz. lard, 5 oz. mixed vegetables, 1 bunch of parsley, 3 oz. mushrooms, 1 tsp. salt, 2 oz. onions, 2 oz. celery, pinch of ground black pepper, pinch of marjoram, 10 oz. rice.

Clean giblets well, cut into pieces, and wash until clean. Clean mixed vegetables, and celery, wash and cut into even cubes. Set the meat and vegetables to boil in a pan, with as much water as will barely cover them; salt, add cleaned onions, cover with lid, and cook until nearly tender. Clean mushrooms, wash thoroughly and slice. Remove onions when meat and vegetables are nearly soft. Heat fat in a frying pan, put in the rice (washed and drained through a sieve), the sliced mushrooms, and minced parsley and mix with the meat. Mix thoroughly, salt, pepper, flavour with marjoram, and boil. Stew covered with lid, for about 20—25 mins., over a medium fire until meat is tender, and the rice is cooked.

Taking it from the oven, dish it whilst hot. Add some fresh goose cracklings and a small slice of fried goose-liver when serving, and pour a little of the gravy over it. Sprinkle with finely chopped parsley. Do not overcook rice or use too much liquid. The amount of water used must only amount to twice as much as the rice in volume. In season, add some sliced tomatoes and green paprikas.

DUCK

Roast Duck

Ingredients: 1 duck weighing 6—7 lb., 1½ tsp. salt, pinch of marjoram, 1½ gill gravy, 5 portions of braised cabbage.

Prepare as for Roast goose, only roasting the liver with it. Cut into pieces when ready, and serve breast sliced, and garnished with stewed cabbage. Time roasting, so that duck will be ready 10—15 mins. before dishing; it will be easier to carve.

Duck with Rice

Ingredients: 2 lb. duck (minus fat), 3 lb. giblets, 1 tsp. salt, pinch of ground black pepper, 5 oz. mixed vegetables, 2 oz. celery, 2 oz. onions, 3½ oz. lard, pinch of marjoram, 3 oz. mushrooms, 3½ oz. canned green peas, 1 bunch of parsley, 10 oz. rice.

Clean meat and giblets thoroughly, cut into pieces and wash well. Clean mixed vegetables and celery, wash and cut them to cubes. Heat 2 oz. lard in a pan, half-fry chopped onions in it, put in the meat, cut into pieces the mixed vegetables and celery; salt, then cover with lid, adding a little water to it, when necessary, and stirring occasionally, cook meat until half-done; then reduce gravy. Wash rice thoroughly, and drain; wash the parsley and chop it finely. Then heat the remaining fat in a frying pan, put in the rice and sliced mushrooms, and stir for 1—2 mins. over an open fire. Add the finely chopped parsley, then mix rice with meat. Pour 1 pt. hot water over it, and salt; flavour with ground pepper and marjoram, add canned green peas, stir, bring to boil, then cover with lid; stew for 20—25 mins., in a medium oven, until meat is tender.

Dish while hot, sprinkled with the remaining parsley. May be garnished with cracklings and fried slices of liver.

Alsatian Duck in Sour Cabbage

Ingredients: 7 lb. duck, 2 lb. sour cabbage, 3½ oz. onions, 3 cloves, 2 tbsp. white wine, pinch of ground black pepper, small bunch of parsley, 7 oz. streaky bacon, 2 tbsp. gravy, 1 tsp. salt.

213

Put sour cabbage to boil, after having washed it, and squeeze it out well; put in the bacon whole, the cleaned onions stuck with cloves, salt and pepper, and pour white wine over it; covering with a lid, boil for 2 hrs. over a low fire. Clean duck, cut off neck, wings and feet, and cut open. Draw and skin it, and cut into fairly large pieces; wash thoroughly and salt. Remove onions and cloves from the cabbage; also remove bacon, if already tender, and set it aside.

Lay the pieces of duck into the cabbage, pour a little water beneath it, cover with lid, and cook for an hour over a low fire. The juice of the cabbage must be evaporated, by the time the meat is tender. Take duck out of cabbage, which must be quite tender and rich, no water remaining beneath it in the pan. Salt and pepper once again. Place cabbage in dish, lay duck meat over it, surround neatly with sliced bacon and sprinkle with gravy, and finely chopped parsley. Serve hot.

Garnish with potatoes boiled in salt water if preferred.

Duck Stew

Ingredients: 2 lb. of duck, 3 lb. duck's giblets, 1 tsp. salt, 2 oz. lard, 2 cloves of garlic, ½ tsp. paprika, 5 oz. onions, 1 tsp. tomato purée, 1 tsp. flour, 7 oz. green paprika, 3½ oz. fresh tomatoes or 5 oz. canned lecsó, 5 portions of tarhonya garnishing.

It is prepared like Goose stew, and can be served with dumplings or boiled potatoes instead of tarhonya.

Duck's Legs with Lecsó

Take 3½ lb. duck's legs, and prepare like Goose legs in lecsó.

Duck's Breast in Székely Cabbage

Take 4 lb. duck's breast and prepare like Breast of goose with Székely cabbage.

Braised Duck's Legs

Take 3½ lb. duck's legs, and prepare like Braised goose legs.

Fried Liver of Duck

Prepare like Fried goose-liver, taking care that liver is lean.

Larded Roast Turkey

Ingredients: 7 lb. turkey, 1½ tsp. salt, 3½ oz. bacon, 3½ oz. lard, pinch of marjoram, 1½ gill gravy, 5 portions of steamed rice garnishing, 2½ portions of stewed prunes.

Clean turkey, cutting off neck, feet and wings. Cut open, and draw, and wash thoroughly. Remove sinews from drumsticks while still raw. Cut bacon into strips with the help of a larding pin, lard turkey thoroughly, especially its breast and legs. Salt both inside and out. Sprinkle the inside with a little marjoram. Truss turkey in the usual way, so that it retains its original shape, while roasting. Place in frying pan, pour on hot lard, add a little water, and roast in a moderate oven for about 1½—2 hrs., until ready, basting frequently and turning it about so that it is crisp and tender, and nicely browned on all sides, when ready.

Should turkey be a little older and its flesh tough, place in a pan when it is brown, cover with a lid, and braise, pouring a little water under it occasionally until it is quite tender. Then reduce gravy and take turkey out of pan 10—15 mins. before serving; this facilitates carving.

Halve and then quarter, when dishing, placing the bony parts on the bottom of the dish; put the legs cut into equal pieces around them, then cut the breast into thin slices, and place neatly on the top. Serve hot, garnished with steamed rice.

Don't pour gravy over the meat, but serve separately in a sauce-boat, or pour it around the roast. Stewed prunes are also dished separately.

Remove string before serving.

Roast Turkey with Chestnut Stuffing

Ingredients: 1 turkey (weighing 5 lb.), 2 tsp. salt, 3½ oz. lard, ½ lb. bacon, pinch of marjoram, ¾ lb. pork, 1 gill milk, 1½ lb. chestnuts, 3½ oz. butter, 2 eggs, pinch of ground black pepper, pinch of grated nutmeg, 1½ rolls, 1 tsp. tomato purée, ½ tsp. flour, 5 portions of fried potatoes.

Wash chestnuts, cut into them with knife, and roast a little in the hot oven, so that they can be easily peeled. Then clean and set them to boil in water. Add milk, when chestnuts are nearly cooked, continue until they are quite soft, then put aside to cool. Soak rolls, squeeze them out, then cut pork into cubes and put through mincer twice together with rolls. Add eggs, salt, flavour with marjoram, grated nutmeg, and ground pepper, add melted butter and the chestnuts, now quite soft and cold, then knead this stuffing together firmly.

Clean turkey, cut off its neck, wings and feet, and remove sinews from legs. Cut open, draw, and wash turkey thoroughly.

Take out breast, taking care not to injure the skin, then salting turkey's inside slightly once again, put in chestnut stuffing. Sew the gash, through which turkey was stuffed with a thread, and truss turkey in the usual way, with a thin string, so that turkey may retain its original shape while roasting.

Shape breast also, so that stuffing is divided equally in it.

Salt the whole turkey, envelop it in the sliced and flattened bacon; place into a pan, add lard, and cover with a lid. Cook until almost tender in a warm oven pouring on a little water when necessary. Then lift off the lid, remove slices of bacon, baste turkey with its own gravy, and roast it until it turns brown, without adding any more water.

Remove thread and string when ready and set turkey aside for 15 mins. before dishing, to let it dry a little; this facilitates carving. Fry tomato purée in fat, in which the turkey was roasted, add flour, and continue frying; adding a little water to it, boil well, in order to obtain gravy of medium thickness; lastly strain it through a sieve. Cut off legs, and cut them into pieces before placing on the dish; then slice the stuffed breast with a sharp knife, and place slices neatly on the top. Serve hot with fried potatoes, and with its own gravy.

Fried Escalopes of Turkey's Breast

Ingredients: 3½ lb. breast of turkey, 1 tsp. salt, 2 oz. flour, 2 eggs, 5 oz. bread-crumbs, 5 oz. lard, 5 portions of roast potatoes.

Cut meat off breastbones, pull off skin, and remove sinews. Cut meat into equal sized slices, counting two for one portion. Flatten them until they are thin. Salt, turn slices in flour, beaten egg, and bread-crumbs, and fry in ample fat until they are golden-brown. Serve with roast potatoes. Stewed prunes can be served separately.

Parisian Slices of Turkey

The method of preparation is similar to that for Fried escalopes of turkey's breast, but they are cooked without bread-crumbs; therefore the slices are only turned in flour and eggs before frying.

Buttered Slices of Turkey's Breast

Ingredients: 3½ lb. turkey's breast, 1 tsp. salt, 2 oz. flour, 2½ oz. lard, 2 oz. butter, 1 tbsp. gravy, 5 portions of steamed rice, 2½ portions of stewed apples.

Cut flesh off turkey's breastbone carefully, pull off skin, and remove sinews from meat, taking care not to injure it. Cut into steaks of equal size, counting two slices for each portion; flatten them, until they are thin, salt, turn them in flour on both sides, and placing in a saucepan containing hot fat, fry them over a brisk fire, until they turn golden-brown on both sides. Then pour off fat, crumble butter over meat, pour gravy over them, and covering with a lid, cook for 2—3 mins. over a low fire.

Serve hot pouring buttered gravy over them, and garnish with steamed rice.

Dish apple sauce separately.

216

Steaks of Minced Breast of Turkey with Butter

Ingredients: 2½ lb. breast of turkey, 1 egg, 3½ oz. lard, 2 oz. butter, small pinch of parsley, 2 rolls, 1½ gill milk, 1 tbsp. cream, 2 oz. bread-crumbs, 1 tsp. salt, 2 tbsp. gravy, 5 portions of risi-bisi garnishing.

Soak rolls in milk, and squeeze them out. Cut flesh off turkey's breast-bone, skin it, remove sinews and cut into pieces; then pass meat and the rolls twice through mincer.

Wash parsley, chop finely, and fry in 1 oz. butter; add to minced meat, salt, beat egg into it, add cream and knead the whole firmly together. Shape into 10 flat steaks of equal size; turn them in bread-crumbs, fry in hot fat, until steaks turn golden-brown on both sides. Boil gravy, add remaining butter to it, and pour over the steaks just before serving.

Garnish with risi-bisi.

Braised Legs of Turkey

Take 3½ lb. turkey's legs and prepare as for Braised legs of goose.

Turkey Fricassée with Brain Dumplings

Prepare as for Chicken fricassée dishing with brain dumplings instead of steamed rice.

Turkey Stew

Ingredients: 1 lb. turkey meat, 4 lb. giblets of turkey, 1½ tsp. salt, 1 tsp. flour, 5 oz. onions, 1 tsp. tomato purée, 7 oz. green paprika, 3½ oz. fresh tomatoes or 5 oz. canned lecsó, 5 portions of thimble dumplings.

Method of preparing is similar to that for Goose stew.

GUINEA-FOWL

Larded Guinea-fowl

Ingredients: 5 lb. guinea-fowl, 3½ oz. bacon, pinch of marjoram, 1½ tsp. salt, 3½ oz. lard, 1 gill gravy, 5 portions of braised red cabbage.

Clean guinea-fowl thoroughly, bend back wings, and truss in the usual way with thin string, so that it retains its original shape while roasting. Cut bacon into thin strips, and lard the guinea-fowl.

Salt and strew a little marjoram inside the fowl. Place in roasting pan, put lard over it, add a little water and roast in a hot oven, turning over frequently, and basting with its own gravy, until it becomes tender and golden-brown on all sides. Then take fowl out of pan and put it aside, keeping hot, until serving. Reduce the gravy, add prepared gravy, boil well, then strain through sieve.

Halve guinea-fowl when dishing, place bony pieces on the bottom of the dish, place drumsticks beside them, and top thinly with the sliced breast. Dish with gravy and braised red cabbage.

Should guinea-fowl be tough, braise it in a pan, under lid, in its own gravy, until it grows tender, pouring on a little water occasionally.

Guinea-fowl Stew

Prepare as for Chicken stews. Dish with dumplings, steamed rice, or boiled potatoes and parsley.

Guinea-fowl in Paprika Sauce

Prepare as for Chicken in paprika sauce. Dish while hot with dumplings:

VEGETABLES AND GARNISHES

ON VEGETABLES AND GREENS IN GENERAL

Vegetables and greens may be served as entrées, main courses or garnishings. In Hungary they are usually prepared with roux or thickened with sour cream, but we can stew them in butter, stuff and boil them as well.

Since most of the vegetables and greens in Hungarian recipes are prepared with roux, we should discuss it briefly. It is important to use exactly as much as is needed for the thickening of vegetables. Too much roux may spoil even the best vegetables. If we add onions to the browned and hot roux, it is not necessary to leave it on the fire, since the onions will brown by themselves, without any further heating. The vegetables must be boiled for 10—15 more mins. after having been thickened with roux. It is not enough to bring them to boil and put them aside too quickly. Warm sauces should be diluted with cold water, and when cooled, they should be thinned by warm water, then mixed well. Take care to mix the thinned roux until smooth, before adding to the dish. We can avoid the roux curdling in the food, if we use semolina flour.

VEGETABLES

Dried Beans (in the Hungarian Way)

Ingredients: 1 lb. white or haricot beans, 1 tsp. salt, 1 oz. lard, 1 dessertspoon chopped onions, 1 clove of garlic, 1 bay leaf, 1 oz. plain flour, 1 tsp. paprika, ½ tsp. sugar, 1 tbsp. vinegar, 2 tbsp. sour cream.

Clean and wash beans and soak in cold water overnight. Put in cold water, salt, add bay leaf, and simmer slowly until tender. The flavour will be improved if bacon or smoked pig's trotters are cooked with the beans. Make a light roux of flour and lard, with finely chopped onions and paprika, adding water. Add roux to the cooked beans, bring it to boil, and flavour with the sour cream, sugar and vinegar. Cook a little longer and set aside until serving. Do not forget to take out the bacon or smoked pig's trotters before adding the roux.

Bean Purée

Make in the same way as for Dried beans, but sieve beans when tender.

Purée of Dried Peas

Ingredients: 1 lb. split peas, 1 tsp. salt, 1 oz. onions, 1 clove of garlic, 2 oz. flour, 1½ oz. lard, 1 pinch of black pepper.

Clean and wash peas and soak in cold water overnight. Cook in cold water (the addition of smoked pork will improve flavour) until tender. Make roux of flour and lard, with finely chopped onions and a clove of garlic, adding cold water, and add roux to peas; bring to the boil, put through sieve and flavour with ground pepper.

Lentils (in the Hungarian Way)

Ingredients: 1 lb. lentils, 1 tsp. salt, 2 oz. lard, 2 oz. flour, 1 oz. onions, 1 clove of garlic, 1 dessertspoon sugar, ½ tsp. prepared mustard, 1 tbsp. vinegar, dash of paprika, 1 bay leaf, ¼ lemon.

Clean and wash lentils in several lots of water, soak in cold water overnight, and put to cook in cold water. Add bay leaf, salt and simmer until tender. Make light roux of flour and lard with finely chopped onions and the garlic, sprinkling in the paprika. Add roux to cooked lentils and simmer a little longer. Flavour with vinegar, mustard, sugar and juice of ¼ lemon.
Smoked pork or bacon will improve flavour if cooked with the lentils.

Potatoes in Sour Cream Sauce

Ingredients: 3 lb. potatoes, 1 oz. lard, 2 oz. flour, 1 tsp. salt, 1 bay leaf, 1 oz. onions, ½ tsp. sugar, 1 tbsp. vinegar, 2 tbsp. sour cream, pinch of black pepper.
Peel raw potatoes, slice and cover with water. Salt and add bay leaf and cook until tender. Make light brown roux of flour and lard, adding finely chopped onions, cold water and liquid drained off potatoes. Mix and pour on potatoes. Add sour cream, sugar, vinegar and pepper and bring to boil.

Potatoes in Marjoram Sauce

Ingredients: 3 lb. potatoes, 1 oz. lard, 2 oz. flour, pinch of marjoram, 1 tsp. salt, 1 oz. onions, 2 tbsp. sour cream.

Peel and slice raw potatoes, salt and cook with enough water to cover them. Make light brown roux of flour and lard with the finely chopped onions, adding cold water. Add diluted roux to cooked potatoes. Flavour with marjoram, add sour cream, bring to a good boil and set aside until serving.

Potatoes in Tomato Sauce

Ingredients: 3 lb. potatoes, 1 oz. lard, 2 lb. fresh tomatoes or 5 oz. tomato purée, a handful of celery leaves, 2 oz. flour, 2 oz. sugar.

Wash and cook potatoes in their jackets. Make light roux of flour and lard with finely chopped onions. Add tomato purée and celery tops to roux, thin with water or stock, salt and bring to boil. Add the cooked, peeled and sliced potatoes and cook together. If the sauce is made of fresh tomatoes, cook the cleaned and washed tomatoes with celery tops and put through sieve when tender. Proceed as when using tomato purée. Flavour with sugar.

Potato Casserole

Ingredients: 2½ lb. potatoes, 3½ oz. lard, 2 oz. butter, 1 tsp. salt, pinch of black pepper, 1 pt. sour cream, 2 oz. bread-crumbs, 5 hard-boiled eggs, 3 raw eggs.

Cook potatoes in their jackets, peel and slice when cooled. Slice 5 hard-boiled eggs. Beat up yolks of 3 eggs with the lard and the sour cream, adding the salt and ground pepper, and folding in whisked whites of 3 eggs. Add sliced potatoes and eggs, and arrange in a casserole greased with butter or lard and dusted with bread-crumbs. Sprinkle top with bread-crumbs and pats of butter. Bake in hot oven till top is golden-brown.

Sometimes the casserole is made with sliced smoked sausages or chopped ham in which case the 5 hard-boiled eggs are omitted.

Swiss Potato Casserole

Ingredients: 2½ lb. potatoes, 3½ oz. butter, 1 tsp. salt, 3 eggs, 2 gills sour cream, 3½ oz. grated cheese, 1 tsp. bead-crumbs.

The preparation differs from that of the ordinary potato casserole only in as much as grated cheese replaces the 5 hard-boiled eggs, and the top is sprinkled with grated cheese before baking. It is always made without the ham or smoked sausages.

Potatoes with Dill Cucumbers

Ingredients: 3 lb. potatoes, 1 oz. lard, 2 oz. flour, 1 tsp. salt, 1 gill sour cream, 3½ oz. dill cucumbers, 1 tsp. chopped onions, 1 tsp. sugar, pinch of black pepper, bunch of fresh dill, small bunch of parsley.

Cook potatoes in their jacket and peel. Make roux of flour and lard with finely chopped onions, and when lightly browned, season with finely chopped parsley and dill. When these have also browned, dilute with stock or water, season with salt and pepper, and bring to boil. Peel dill cucumbers and slice thinly, slice peeled potatoes and mix both with sauce. Add sour cream and bring to boil.

Carrots

Ingredients: 2½ lb. carrots, 2 oz. lard, 2 oz. flour, bunch of parsley, 1 tsp. salt, 1 dessert-spoon sugar, 1 gill milk.

Quarter cleaned carrots lengthwise and then slice. Melt lard in saucepan, add sliced carrots with salt and finely chopped parsley, and stew till tender. Dredge with flour and thin with milk, water or stock. Sugar to taste and bring to boil.

Mixed Vegetables

Ingredients: 2 lb. mixed vegetables (carrots, parsnips, celery), 5 oz. kohlrabi, 3½ oz. fresh or tinned green peas, 1 tsp. salt, 2 oz. lard, 2 oz. flour, 1 tsp. sugar, 2 tbsp. milk, bunch of parsley.

Clean and dice vegetables, salt and cook in enough water to cover. Make a light roux of flour and lard, add finely chopped parsley and dilute with cold water or milk. Add roux to the cooked vegetables, sugar to taste and boil. If tinned peas are used, add only when the other vegetables are almost tender.

Kohlrabi

Ingredients: 4 lb. kohlrabi, 1 oz. lard, 2 oz. flour, 1 tsp. salt, 1 tsp. sugar, 2 tbsp. milk, pinch of black pepper, small bunch of parsley.

Dice cleaned kohlrabi and cook in boiling salted water. Make a light roux of lard and flour, adding finely chopped parsley and cold water. Add to cooked kohlrabi. Cook a little longer and season with sugar and ground pepper.

Sweet Cabbage

Ingredients: 2½ lb. cabbage, 1 oz. lard, 2 oz. flour, 2 tbsp. sour cream, 1 tsp. salt, 1 oz. onions, a good pinch of caraway seeds.

Clean and dice cabbage, and cook in boiling water with salt and caraway seeds. When it is tender, thicken with a roux of flour and lard made with finely chopped onions. Finally add the sour cream and boil again. Flavour with finely chopped fresh dill according to taste.

Sour Cabbage (Sauerkraut)

Ingredients: 2½ lb. pickled cabbage, 2 oz. lard, 2 oz. flour, 2 tbsp. sour cream, 1 oz. onions, 1 clove of garlic, pinch of paprika, pinch of caraway seeds.

If the pickled cabbage is too sour, rinse it first, then put in a saucepan with just enough water to cover it. Salt, add the caraway seeds, bring to boil and cook slowly. (Bacon or ham bones may be added.) Make a well-browned roux of flour and lard adding finely chopped onions, the garlic and the red pepper; mix it with cold water. When the cabbage is tender, thicken with the roux, put in the sour cream and bring to boil. In summertime fresh tomatoes and green peppers may be added, or, if preferred, a bunch of finely chopped fresh dill.

Cabbage in Gravy

Ingredients: 2½ lb. cabbage, 1 oz. lard, 2 oz. flour, 2 tbsp. sour cream, 1 oz. onions, 1 tsp. salt, 1 oz. streaky bacon, pinch of ground black pepper, pinch of caraway seeds, 1 clove of garlic.

Cut the cleaned cabbage into strips, put it with the salt and caraway seeds into boiling water. Dice and fry bacon, strain off the fat and use it for making light brown roux with finely chopped onions and garlic. Thin roux with cold water, mix in some cream, put in cabbage and bring to boil. Let it simmer a while, season with ground pepper and add the fried bacon. Pig's trotters, ears or head improve the flavour if cooked with the cabbage, and can be served with it.

Cabbage in Tomato Sauce

Ingredients: 2½ lb. cabbage, 2 oz. flour, 1 oz. lard, 1 tsp. salt, 2 lb. fresh tomatoes or 5 oz. tinned tomato purée, 2 oz. sugar, 1 oz. onions.

Clean, wash and cut the cabbage into strips and cook in boiling salt water. Make a light roux of flour and lard, adding the finely chopped onions, fry till golden-yellow, then put aside. When the cabbage is tender, drain off part of the water, add the tomato purée, bring it to boil and thicken with the roux. If fresh tomatoes are used, cook, put through sieve and boil again, until a purée of the right consistence is obtained. Then proceed as above.

Savoys in Gravy

Ingredients: 2 lb. savoys, 1 lb. potatoes, 1 oz. lard, 2 oz. flour, 1 oz. onions, 1 clove of garlic, pinch of caraway seeds, pinch of paprika, pinch of ground black pepper, pinch of marjoram, 1 tsp. salt.

Clean, wash and halve the savoy cabbages, slice and parboil them. Drain the water off. Pour fresh water or stock into which the seasoning has been added over the savoys. When savoys are half-done, add the peeled and diced potatoes; cover and cook till tender; make a light roux of flour and lard, add the finely chopped onions, garlic and red pepper. Thin roux with cold water and add to tender savoy cabbages. If the cabbage is too watery, pour some of the water off before adding the roux.

Boiled Lettuce in Sharp Sauce

Ingredients: 3 lb. lettuce, 1 oz. lard, 2 oz. flour, 1 tsp. salt, 1 gill sour cream, 1 oz. sugar, 1 tbsp. vinegar, 1 clove of garlic, small bunch of fresh dill.

Wash, clean and quarter the lettuces. Parboil a few minutes in boiling salt water, strain, put lettuces in fresh cold water or stock and boil gently till tender. Make a light roux adding the finely chopped garlic, dill and parsley and thinning with cold water, pour over the lettuce. Add the sour cream, bring to boil, add sugar and vinegar to taste.

Green Peas (in the Hungarian Way)

Ingredients: 5 lb. unshelled or 1½ lb. shelled green peas, 1 oz. lard, 2 oz. flour, 1 tsp. salt, 1 oz. sugar, small bunch of parsley.

Clean and wash the green peas, simmer gently in water to which the sugar and salt has been added. Make a light roux of flour and lard, adding the finely chopped parsley, and the liquid drained off the peas. Mix roux with the cooked green peas, bring to boil. Do not use too much liquid.

There is another way to cook tender young peas: Stew in lard with chopped parsley, when tender dredge with a little flour, pour on a little stock or water, season and bring to boil.

Vegetable Marrow in Tomato Sauce

Ingredients: 4 lb. whole marrow or 2½ lb. shredded, 1 oz. lard, 2 oz. flour, small bunch of celery top, 2 lb. fresh tomatoes or 5 oz. tomato purée, 1 tsp. salt, 1 oz. onions, 1 tbsp. sugar.

Clean, shred and salt the marrow. Make a thin roux, adding and slightly browning the finely chopped onions. Add the marrow from which the salty liquid has been well squeezed out, and the tomato purée. Add a little stock or water, sugar, bring it to boil. If using fresh tomatoes, simmer them with the celery tops first, put through a sieve and then add to the marrow.

Vegetable Marrow with Fresh Dill

Ingredients: 4 lb. whole vegetable marrow or 2½ lb. cleaned and shredded, 1 oz. lard, 2 oz. flour, 1½ tsp. salt, 1 oz. onions, 1 tsp. sugar, 1 tbsp. vinegar, 1 gill sour cream, small bunch of dill.

Sprinkle the cleaned, shredded marrow with salt; let it stand for a while. Make a light roux of flour and lard, add the finely chopped onions and fresh dill, and lastly the vegetable marrow, with the salty liquid well squeezed out, and sprinkle with vinegar. Cook marrow with roux for a little while, stirring often and thinning with stock or water. Bring it to boil, add the sour cream and sugar and let it simmer a little longer.

Another way to prepare vegetable marrow: Fry the finely chopped onions, add the shredded marrow having squeezed out the salty liquid well. Mix the sour cream with a teaspoonful of flour and add to the marrow: bring it to boil, season it with paprika.

Spinach Purée

Ingredients: 2½ lb. spinach, 1 oz. lard, 2 oz. flour, 1½ gill milk, 1 tsp. salt, pinch of ground black pepper, 1 clove of garlic, dash of bicarbonate of soda.

Clean and wash spinach thoroughly, put into a colander and let it drain well. Put the bicarbonate of soda into boiling water, add the spinach. When tender, strain, rinse with cold water, squeeze, then put through sieve. Make a light brown roux of flour and lard, add finely chopped garlic and the spinach, thin it with a little stock, water or milk. Season with salt and ground pepper, and let it simmer for a quarter of an hour.

Creamed Spinach

Ingredients: 3 lb. spinach, 1 tsp. salt, 2½ oz. butter, pinch of bicarbonate of soda, pinch of ground black pepper, 1 gill cream.

Cook and pass spinach through sieve as above. Heat the butter, add the purée, season with salt and pepper, and bring to boil. Mix in the cream just before serving.

Sorrel with Sour Cream

Ingredients: 2 lb. sorrel, 1 oz. lard, 2 oz. flour, 1 tsp. salt, 1 oz. onions, 2 oz. sugar, 1½ gill sour cream.

Clean, wash and strain sorrel. Fry the finely shredded onions to a golden-brown, add sorrel, cover, and let it stew. Mix the sour cream with flour, add to the sorrel and let it simmer for quarter of an hour. If too thick, thin with stock or water. Put through sieve, add sugar and let it simmer for another. 15 mins.

French Beans with Sour Cream

Ingredients: 3 lb. fresh or 2 lb. tinned French beans, 1 oz. lard, 2 oz. flour, 1 tsp. salt, 1 oz. onions, 1 tbsp. vinegar, pinch of paprika, 1 oz. sugar, 1½ gill sour cream, 1 clove of garlic, small bunch of parsley.

Clean, string and wash beans, cut into one-inch pieces, cook in boiling salt water. Make a light golden roux, add finely chopped onions; stir for another two mins. to brown onions. Add finely chopped garlic, parsely and paprika. Thin roux with cold water, mix in the cooked beans, boil and season with salt, sugar, vinegar and sour cream, then let it simmer for a short time.

Cauliflower in Sour Cream Sauce

Ingredients: 3 lb. cleaned cauliflower, 1 oz. lard, 2 oz. flour, 1 tsp. salt, 1 oz. sugar, 1½ gill sour cream, 1½ gill milk, small bunch of parsley.

Trim and wash cauliflower, break into flowerets, cook in boiling salted water. Make a light roux of flour and lard, add the finely chopped parsley and some liquid drained off the cauliflowers; bring to boil, stirring all the while. Add the cooked cauliflower, sour cream and milk, flavour with salt and sugar. Bring to boil. Take care not to break the tender sprigs of the vegetable.

Lecsó

Ingredients: 2 lb. green paprika, 1½ lb. fresh tomatoes, 2½ oz. lard, 5 oz. onions, 1 tsp. salt, ½ tsp. paprika, 1 oz. streaky bacon.

Scald the tomatoes, skin and quarter. Core the green paprikas and cut lengthwise into strips. Dice bacon, fry in lard till golden-brown, add finely chopped onions, stir for a minute, add paprika and then green paprika and tomatoes. Stew over a slow fire. If the paprikas are too hot, scald them first.

GARNISHES

Mashed Potatoes

Ingredients: 3 lb. potatoes, 1 tsp. salt, 1 pt. milk, 2 oz. butter.

Boil peeled potatoes in salt water. Mash through sieve, add butter in pats, pour the milk in gradually, beating vigorously all the while. Pour a little milk on top and keep the purée hot over hot water till serving. Mash the potatoes while hot to avoid lumps.

Potatoes with Fried Onions

Ingredients: 3 lb. potatoes, 1 tsp. salt, 2½ oz. onions, 2 oz. lard.

Wash and boil potatoes in their jackets, peel and grate or chop. Fry finely chopped onions in lard to a golden-brown, mix in grated potatoes and brown in pan greased with lard.

Potato Chips

Ingredients: 3 lb. potatoes, ½ lb. lard, 1 tsp. salt, small bunch of parsley.

Peel and cut raw potatoes into pieces of finger length and thickness; dry on clean towel. Heat up lard and fry chips till golden-brown. Serve hot sprinkled with salt and finely chopped parsley.

Potatoes Sauté

Ingredients: 3 lb. potatoes, 1 tsp. salt, 3 oz. lard, small bunch of parsley.

Cook potatoes in their jackets, peel. When cold, cut into thin slices, salt and fry in fat turning occasionally. Serve sprinkled with finely chopped parsley.

Potato Crisps

Ingredients: 3 lb. potatoes, 1 tsp. salt, ½ lb. lard.

Peel and cut raw potatoes into very thin slices, wash and dry on clean cloth. Fry potatoes in hot fat till golden-brown and crisp. Salt just before serving. Do not put too many sliced potatoes in the lard at one time as it is apt to boil over.

Potato Straws

Ingredients: 3 lb. potatoes, 1 tsp. salt, ½ lb. lard.

Peel and cut potatoes into straws. Wash and dry on clean cloth. Fry in hot lard till crisp; salt just before serving.

Potato Croquettes

Ingredients: 2½ lb. potatoes, 1 oz. butter, 1 tsp. salt, pinch of grated nutmeg, 2 oz. flour, 3 eggs, 5 oz. white bread-crumbs, 5 oz. lard.

Peel and cut potatoes into fairly large pieces of about equal size. Boil in salt water. Strain well, then dry potatoes by shaking the saucepan a few times over flame. Mash through sieve, add butter, 2 egg-yolks, grated nutmeg and salt, and beat till fluffy. Cool and shape into croquettes. Roll croquettes in flour, then in the well-beaten egg, lastly in bread-crumbs. Fry in hot lard.
Mash potatoes while hot, to avoid lumps.

Potato Dumplings

Ingredients: 2½ lb. potatoes, 4½ oz. flour, 1 tsp. salt, 3½ oz. streaky bacon, 1 oz. onions, 2 eggs, pinch of ground black pepper.

Boil potatoes in their jackets, peel and when cold put through mincer. Dice and fry bacon, drain off fat and add fried bacon to potatoes. Fry the finely chopped onions in the fat drained off the bacon. Add two whole eggs, salt, ground pepper and flour and mix well. Shape small balls of the dough, drop them into boiling salted water. When dumplings rise to top of water, strain and serve hot.

Potato Fritters (Doughnuts)

Ingredients: 2 lb. potatoes, 1 tsp. salt, 1 oz. butter, pinch of grated nutmeg, 5 oz. flour, 3 eggs, 5 oz. lard, 1 tbsp. sour cream.

Peel, boil and strain potatoes: dry by shaking saucepan over fire. Put through sieve, add butter, sour cream, eggs, flour, and seasoning. Mix thoroughly. Make small doughnuts of the dough and fry them in hot lard. Potato fritters can be made with yeast if preferred.

Potato Paprikash (Paprika Potato Stew)

Ingredients: 4 lb. potatoes, 3½ oz. lard, 5 oz. onions, 1 clove of garlic, 1 tsp. salt, 1 tsp. paprika, 3½ oz. lecsó, pinch of caraway seeds.

Fry the finely chopped onions in the fat till golden-brown; add finely chopped garlic, caraway seeds, and paprika; stir and fill up with a little water. Cut the peeled raw potatoes into longish pieces, add to the above paprika sauce together with lecsó and cover with water. Salt and let it stew over a slow fire. In season fresh tomatoes and green peppers may be substituted for the lecsó.

Cook sausages or Vienna sausages in potato paprikash if you want an especially tasty dish.

Szeged Potato Paprikash

Ingredients: 3 lb. potatoes, 3½ oz. lard, 5 oz. onions, 1 clove of garlic, pinch of caraway seed, 1 tsp. paprika, 1 tsp. salt, 4½ oz. tarhonya, 7 oz. green paprika, 3½ oz. fresh tomatoes.

Fry finely chopped onions in 2 oz. lard, add finely chopped garlic, caraway seeds and paprika; mix and fill up with a little water. Peel and dice potatoes, add to paprika sauce together with fresh tomatoes and green paprikas. Fry the tarhonya in hot lard till golden-brown, add to half-cooked potatoes and simmer slowly. Salt to taste before serving.

Cauliflower with Bread-crumbs

Ingredients: 5 lb. cauliflower, 7 oz. butter, 7 oz. bread-crumbs, 1 tsp. salt.

Trim and wash cauliflower, cook in boiling salted water, turning head with flowerets down. Drain tender cauliflower well, arrange it on a dish. Fry bread-crumbs in butter to a golden-brown and pour over cauliflower. Serve immediately.

Baker's Potatoes

Ingredients: 3 lb. potatoes, 1 tsp. salt, 5 oz. onions, 7 oz. lard, 1 tsp. flour.

Peel and cut potatoes into longish pieces and fry in hot lard. Dredge sliced onion rings with flour, fry, and mix with potatoes. You can roast the potatoes and onions in the oven with a leg of lamb or knuckle of veal.

Cauliflower au Gratin

Ingredients: 5 lb. cauliflower, 2 oz. butter, 1 tsp. salt, 1 pt. béchamel sauce, 2 oz. grated cheese.

Wash, boil and drain cauliflower. Grease a fireproof dish with part of the butter, put in cauliflower, pour béchamel sauce on top, sprinkle with grated cheese and add the remainder of the butter. Bake in a hot oven till top is golden-brown.

Fried Cauliflower

Ingredients: 5 lb. cauliflower, 1 tsp. salt, 10 oz. flour, 2 eggs, 5 oz. bread-crumbs, 7 oz. lard.

Clean, wash and then boil cauliflower in salt water till tender; strain. Roll sprigs of cauliflower first in flour, next in beaten egg, lastly in bread-crumbs. Fry quickly in hot lard. The fried cauliflower may be used as a vegetable, with meat, or as a savoury, when it is served with tartare sauce.

Green Peas with Butter

Ingredients: 6 lb. unshelled or 2 lb. shelled green peas, 2½ oz. butter, 1 tsp. salt, 1 tbsp. sugar.

Clean and wash tender green peas, simmer in boiling water seasoned with salt and sugar. Drain and serve hot with pats of butter.

French Green Peas

Ingredients: 6 lb. unshelled or 2 lb. shelled peas, 2½ oz. butter, 1 oz. flour, small bunch of parsley, 1 oz. sugar, ½ tsp. salt, 2 oz. pickling or button onions, 1 lettuce.

Stew the shelled green peas in butter with small pickling onions or shallots. When half-done, add the finely chopped parsley. Wash and quarter lettuce, add to peas and cook slowly. Sprinkle with flour when tender, add some stock, bring to boil and flavour with sugar.

French Beans with Butter

Ingredients: 2½ lb. fresh or 2 lb. tinned French beans, 1 tsp. salt, 2½ oz. butter.

Clean, string and cut beans lengthwise; boil them in salt water till tender. Strain and serve with pats of butter on top.

French Beans with Bread-crumbs

Ingredients: 2½ lb. fresh or 2 lb. tinned French beans, 3½ oz. butter, 1 tsp. salt, 3 oz. bread-crumbs.

Clean, string and wash beans. Boil in salt water. Melt the butter, add bread-crumbs, fry till golden-yellow. Strain cooked beans, arrange on a vegetable plate, and pour the fried bread-crumbs and butter over them just before serving.

Brussels Sprouts

Ingredients: 2½ lb. Brussels sprouts, 3½ oz. butter, 1 tsp. salt, pinch of ground black pepper.

Clean and wash sprouts, parboil them in salt water, drain. Melt the butter, add the Brussels sprouts, a pinch of salt and a little stock. Cook under lid till tender. Instead of butter, bacon fat may be used.

Brussels Sprouts with Bread-crumbs

Ingredients: 2½ lb. Brussels sprouts, 5 oz. butter, 1 tsp. salt, 5 oz. bread-crumbs.

Clean and wash sprouts, cook in salt water till tender. Melt the butter, add bread-crumbs and fry till golden-yellow. Drain sprouts, arrange on a vegetable dish, dredge with the bread-crumbs and butter.

Brussels Sprouts Continental

Ingredients: 2½ lb. Brussels sprouts, 1 tsp. salt, 2 oz. butter, 2 oz. streaky bacon, 2 oz. bread-crumbs, 1 gill sour cream, 1 oz. onions, pinch of ground black pepper.

Clean, wash and cook sprouts in boiling salted water. Slice bacon, fry and add finely chopped onions. Add drained sprouts, salt, ground pepper and sour cream. Grease a fireproof dish, dredge it with bread-crumbs and pour in the prepared Brussels sprouts. Put pats of butter on top and sprinkle with bread-crumbs. Bake till top is a nice golden-brown.

Vegetable Marrow au Gratin

Ingredients: 4 lb. vegetable marrow, 1 tsp. salt, 3½ oz. butter, 2 oz. flour, 1 tbsp. vinegar, 2 gills milk, 3 eggs, 1 oz. sugar, 2 oz. bread-crumbs, small bunch of fresh dill.

Peel and trim marrow, cut into two-inch cubes, and cook in salt water to which a little vinegar has been added. Drain well. Prepare a light roux with flour and butter, add finely chopped fresh dill, dilute with milk, bring to boil, stirring all the while. Add the yolks of the eggs, sugar and cooked marrow; beat up egg-whites and fold in carefully. Grease a fireproof dish with butter, dust with bread-crumbs, pour in prepared marrow, sprinkle top with bread-crumbs, pat on dabs of butter. Bake till top is nicely browned. Serve hot.

Fried Vegetable Marrow

Ingredients: 3 lb. vegetable marrow, 1 tsp. salt, 5 oz. lard, 1 oz. flour, 2 eggs, 5 oz. bread-crumbs.

Clean and slice marrow, sprinkle slices with salt. Put aside for half an hour, then roll each piece in flour, beaten egg, and bread-crumbs, and fry in hot lard. If marrow is tough, parboil first in salted water to which a few drops of lemon-juice have been added. Serve with tomato sauce.

Fried Savoy Cabbage Cutlets

Ingredients: 2½ lb. savoys, 5 oz. lard, 2 oz. flour, pinch of caraway seeds, 1 tsp. salt, 3½ oz. bread-crumbs, pinch of ground black pepper, 2 eggs.

Clean and cut savoys in four or six slices, soak in salt water with a few caraway seeds. Drain and squeeze out water. Sprinkle with salt and pepper and shape into cutlets. Dip cutlets in flour, beaten eggs and lastly in bread-crumbs. Fry in hot lard.

Savoy cutlets with mushroom stuffing are very tasty. For stuffing stew trimmed and chopped mushrooms in a little fat, to which chopped onions and paprika may be added.

French Savoury

Ingredients: ½ lb. fresh French beans, 7 oz. shelled green peas, 10 oz. carrots, 5 oz. mushrooms, 3½ oz. rice, pinch of black pepper, 7 oz. butter, 1 tsp. salt, 2 oz. bread-crumbs, ½ tsp. flour, ½ lb. fresh asparagus, ½ lb. cauliflower, 1 lb. potatoes, 10 oz. spinach, 2 oz. ham, 5 oz. lard, 1 tsp. sugar, small bunch of parsley, 1 egg.

Clean and cut French beans and carrots lengthwise into two or three; cut asparagus crosswise, in three or four pieces; keep cauliflower whole. Cook each and peas and spinach as well in separate saucepans in salted water; drain. Salt and pepper mushrooms, dip them in flour, then beaten egg, then fry. Steam rice, mix with minced ham. Put cooked vegetables into melted butter, add seasoning and let them simmer for a short time. Make potato straws. Fry bread-crumbs in butter till golden-brown; pour over cauliflower and asparagus.

Serve on a large round dish in the following way: put the rice mixed with the ham in the middle of dish; arrange around it the potato straws, mushrooms and the vegetables. Serve very hot. For variety, hot stuffed tomatoes, stuffed mushrooms, fried vegetable marrow, buttered Brussels sprouts, potato fritters, etc. may be added.

Stewed Tarhonya

Ingredients: 10 oz. tarhonya, 1 tsp. salt, 3 oz. lard, 1 oz. onions, ½ tsp. paprika.

Fry tarhonya in lard till golden-yellow, add finely chopped onions, paprika and just enough hot water to cover it. (Add water sparingly to prevent tarhonya from getting soaked. It is better to fill up again when needed.) Bring it to boil then stew till tender and water has evaporated. One or two fresh tomatoes and green paprika may be stewed with the tarhonya.

Buttered Macaroni

Ingredients: 10 oz. macaroni, 1 tsp. salt, 2 oz. butter.

Break macaroni in two, cook in boiling salt water. Strain, rinse, add dabs of butter. Serve very hot.

Steamed Rice

Ingredients: 10 oz. rice, 1 tsp. salt, 2 oz. lard, 1 oz. onions, small bunch of parsley.

Add the lard, the finely chopped onions and salt to 1 pt. of water. Bring to boil, add washed rice, bring to boil again. Put into oven and steam for 18—20 mins. Take out of oven, stir with fork, add butter and finely chopped parsley. The onion may be added whole if preferred, in this case it should be taken out of rice before serving.

Steamed Cabbage

Ingredients: 3 lb. red or white cabbage, 1 tsp. salt, 2½ oz. lard, 2 oz. onions, 1 tbsp. sugar, good pinch of caraway seed, 1 tbsp. vinegar, 2 tbsp. red wine.

Trim and shred cabbages. Sprinkle with salt and let stand for at least half an hour. Fry sliced onion rings in lard till golden-brown, add the vinegar, a little water, the shredded cabbage, salt, sugar and caraway seeds. Steam under lid until tender, add wine. (Wine may be omitted.)

Fried Tomatoes

Ingredients: 2 lb. fresh tomatoes, 5 oz. flour, ½ clove of garlic, 1 gill milk, 1 tsp. salt, 5 oz. lard, 2 eggs, pinch of ground black pepper, small bunch of parsley.

Pick large and not too firm tomatoes. Wash, dry and slice; sprinkle slices with salt and pepper. Mix two thirds of flour with 2 eggs; add milk, finely chopped garlic and parsley, ground pepper and salt. Dip tomatoes first in flour, then in butter and fry in hot lard. Serve with tartare sauce or with vegetables.

232

SALADS

Before describing the preparation of a variety of salads we give the recipes for three different salad dressings.

Plain Vinegar Dressing

Mix 1 gill vinegar, 1 gill water, 2 oz. finely shredded onions, a little sugar and a dash of salt and pepper. Let it stand for half an hour, then mix 2 lb. lettuce with dressing and let it stand a little longer in a cool place to absorb flavours. Sprinkle with a little oil before serving. The onions are optional.

Sour Cream Dressing

Mix $1\frac{1}{2}$ gill sour cream with yolk of one egg, 2 tbsp. of prepared mustard (French), salt to taste, a little sugar and a few drops of vinegar or lemon-juice. Beat till smooth, adding a little milk if too thick. Tomato or paprika purée and a pinch of ground pepper may be added.

Whipped Dressing

Mix well yolks of two eggs with 1 oz. butter, 2 tbsp. of French mustard, teaspoonful of flour, pinch of salt and 2 gills milk. Cook in double saucepan beating till mixture is smooth and creamy. Continue beating while it cools and then season to taste with sugar, ground pepper and vinegar or lemon-juice. If too thick, dilute with a little milk. Mix with salad and serve chilled.

Lettuce Salad

Ingredients: 5 heads of lettuce, 1 tsp. salt, 1 tsp. sugar, 2 tbsp. vinegar, a little onion, 1 tbsp. oil.

Clean and wash lettuces. Dilute the vinegar with water, season with sugar, salt and a little finely shredded onion. Pour dressing on lettuce and sprinkle with oil just before serving. Onions are optional.

Scalded Lettuce Salad

Ingredients: 5 heads of lettuce, 3½ oz. streaky bacon, ½ tsp. salt, 1 tbsp. vinegar, ½ tsp. sugar.

Slice bacon and fry. Dilute the vinegar with water, season with salt and sugar and add this liquid to fried bacon. Mix lettuce with above dressing and serve immediately. A little sour cream may be added.

French Lettuce Salad

Ingredients: 5 heads of lettuce, ½ tsp. salt, 1 tsp. sugar, ½ pt. vinegar, 4 eggs, 1 tbsp. oil, pinch of ground black pepper, 1 tsp. French mustard.

Trim, wash and drain lettuce. Take the yolks of two hard-boiled eggs, mash and mix with yolks of two raw eggs. Add ground pepper, vinegar, oil and French mustard, and mix well. Pour dressing over lettuce and serve.

Green Paprika Salad

Ingredients: 1½ lb. green paprikas, 2 tbsp. vinegar, 1 tsp. salt, 1 tsp. sugar.

Wash and core paprika and cut into crosswise rings. Scald. Mix the vinegar with water, add salt and sugar, mix with sliced paprikas, and let it stand for two hrs. The sugar may be omitted.

Dill Cucumber

Ingredients: 1¾ lb. cucumbers, 2 oz. toasted bread, 2 tsp. salt, 1 clove of garlic, half a bunch of fresh dill.

Wash and score cucumbers, remove the two ends. Put trimmed cucumbers into a large preserving jar with garlic, toasted bread and fresh dill on top. Cover with boiling water and let the jar stand in a warm place for three or four days. Chill before serving.

Cucumber Salad

Ingredients: 2 lb. cucumbers, 1 tsp. salt, 1 gill vinegar, ½ tsp. sugar, 2 tbsp. oil, pinch of ground black pepper.

Peel the cucumbers and cut into thin slices. Salt. Let salted cucumbers stand for half an hour. Mix vinegar and water, flavour with sugar. Squeeze out cucumbers well, then mix with dressing. Add oil before serving, sprinkle with paprika and ground pepper. Some crushed garlic may be added. Taste cucumbers before slicing and do not use bitter ones.

Beetroot Salad

Ingredients: 2 lb. beetroot, 2 tbsp. vinegar, 1 tsp. salt, 1 oz. sugar, pinch of caraway seed, 1 oz. horse-radish.

Wash and cook beetroots in skins. Mix vinegar with a little water, add salt, sugar, caraway seed, and sliced horse-radish for dressing. Peel beetroots, slice, add salad dressing and let stand for three hrs. before serving.

Celery Salad

Ingredients: 2 lb. celery, 1 tsp. salt, 1 tsp. sugar, 1 tbsp. vinegar, 1 tbsp. oil, half a lemon, pinch of ground black pepper, half a bunch of parsley.

Wash, peel and slice celery. Boil it in water to which salt and lemon-juice have been added. Do not overcook. Mix vinegar with water, add salt, sugar and ground pepper and dress celery, sprinkle with finely chopped parsley, pour oil on top. Let it stand an hour before serving.

Potato Salad

Ingredients: 3 lb. potatoes, 2 oz. onions, 1 tsp. sugar, 1 tsp. salt, 2 tbsp. vinegar, pinch of ground black pepper.

Wash and boil potatoes in their jackets; peel and slice. Peel onions and cut into rings. Mix vinegar with water, add salt, sugar, ground pepper and let potatoes and onions stand in this dressing for an hour. More onions may be added, according to taste.

Potato Mayonnaise

Ingredients: 3 lb. potatoes, ½ tbsp. salt, ½ lemon, 1 gill mayonnaise sauce (see under Sauces).

Wash and boil potatoes in their jackets, peel and slice. When cool, mix with mayonnaise sauce, flavour with salt and lemon-juice. You may sprinkle top with chopped chives before serving.

Cabbage Salad (Coleslaw)

Ingredients: 2 lb. white or red cabbage, 2 tbsp. vinegar, 1 tsp. salt, 1 tsp. sugar, pinch of caraway seed.

Clean and shred cabbage. Scald with boiling water, drain well. Prepare vinegar dressing with a little water, salt, sugar and caraway seed and pour over cabbage. Let it stand for at least three hrs. May be served with sliced onions on top if liked.

Tomato Salad

Ingredients: 2 lb. tomatoes, ½ tsp. salt, 1 tbsp. vinegar, chives, pinch of ground pepper, 1 gill oil, 1 tsp. sugar.

Scald tomatoes, peel and slice. Prepare dressing of vinegar, adding a little water and season with sugar, salt and pepper. Scatter finely chopped chives and sprinkle oil on tomatoes and mix with dressing. Chill before serving.

Potato and Mushroom Salad

Ingredients: ½ lb. mushrooms, ¾ lb. potatoes, 1 tsp. chopped onions, 1 gill sour cream dressing, chives.

Trim, wash and slice mushrooms. Parboil for 3 mins. in water to which salt and a few drops of vinegar or lemon-juice have been added. Boil, peel and slice potatoes, cut onions into rings. Arrange cooked potato slices with onions in bottom of salad bowl, put mushrooms on top. Pour sour cream dressing over it and sprinkle with chopped chives.

Endive Salad

Ingredients: 1½ lb. endives, yolks of 2 hard-boiled eggs, 1 tbsp. oil, 2 tbsp. vinegar, 1 tsp. French mustard, a little sugar, salt, pepper and parsley.

Put yolks of hard-boiled eggs through sieve, add oil, vinegar, finely chopped parsley and seasonings. Pour salad dressing over cleaned and washed endives. This salad may be prepared with plain vinegar dressing if preferred.

Boiled Bean Salad

Ingredients: ¾ lb. dried beans, 1 tsp. salt, 3 oz. onions, 2 tbsp. vinegar, 1 tsp. sugar, pinch of ground black pepper.

Clean and wash dried beans, cook in salt water till tender, drain. Mix vinegar with a little water, add salt, sugar and ground pepper for dressing and mix with beans. Arrange sliced onions on top and let it stand for two hrs. A little oil may be added.

Károlyi Mixed Salad

Ingredients: ½ lb. cooked potatoes, 3½ oz. dill cucumbers, 3½ oz. green paprikas, ½ lb. fresh tomatoes, 2 heads of lettuce, 2 hard-boiled eggs, 2 gills tartare sauce, 1 bunch of parsley.

Slice potatoes, cucumbers and hard-boiled eggs, cut green paprikas into strips and dice peeled tomatoes. Slice one head of lettuce as well. Mix with tartare sauce, arrange in salad bowl, sprinkle with finely chopped parsley and garnish with other head of lettuce.

Mushroom Salad

Ingredients: 1 lb. mushrooms, 2 gills vinegar, ½ lemon, 1 tbsp. oil, pinch of ground black pepper, 1 tsp. salt, 3 portions of vinaigrette sauce (see under Sauces).

Wash and trim mushrooms, braise in oil, flavour with vinegar, salt and ground pepper. When cool, mix with vinaigrette sauce and allow to stand for two hrs. Chill before serving.

Mushroom Salad with Tomato Dressing

Ingredients: 1 lb. mushrooms, 3½ oz. tomato purée, 1 tsp. salt, 1½ gill oil, 1 bay leaf, 1 lemon, pinch of ground black pepper, 1 tsp. chopped onions.

Fry finely chopped onions in oil, add tomato purée and trimmed and washed mushrooms. Flavour with salt, lemon-juice, ground pepper and bay leaf. Let it simmer for 20 mins. and chill before serving.

Waldorf Salad

Ingredients: ¾ lb. celery, 10 oz. apples, 3½ oz. fresh young walnuts, 1½ gill mayonnaise sauce, 2 heads of lettuce.

Clean celery, cut into slices, cook in salt water, drain and cool with cold water. Mix with peeled and chopped raw apples, skinned young walnuts and mayonnaise sauce. Garnish with lettuce hearts.

Vegetable Marrow Salad

Ingredients: 2 lb. young vegetable marrow, 1 tsp. salt, 1 bunch of fresh dill, 1½ gill sour cream dressing, 7 oz. fresh tomatoes.

Shred the cleaned, young marrow into thin strips. Salt and let it stand for half an hour, then mix with sour cream dressing. Sprinkle top with finely chopped fresh dill, and garnish with sliced tomatoes.

Mixed Salad

Ingredients: ½ lb. tender vegetable marrows, 4 green paprikas, 7 oz. tomatoes, 3½ oz. Bologna sausage, 2 oz. onions, ½ tsp. paprika, 1 tsp. salt, 1½ gill plain dressing.

Dice marrows and cook in water seasoned with salt and vinegar till tender but not too soft. Strain, mix in dressing and arrange in middle of flat dish. In the meantime cook four large green paprikas in the oven till they wilt, then cut in rings and arrange round marrows. Peel and slice tomatoes and arrange to form an outer ring. Cut Bologna sausage into thin slices and arrange on tomatoes. Finally decorate edge of dish with thin onion rings. Sprinkle well with dressing, dust with paprika and chill.

237

Vitamin Salad

Ingredients: 3½ oz. kohlrabi, 3½ oz. celery, 7 oz. carrots, 7 oz. fresh tomatoes, 10 oz. green paprikas, leaves of lettuce, 1 tsp. salt, 1½ gill sour cream dressing or whipped dressing.

Grate tender kohlrabi, celery and carrots separately. Peel and slice tomatoes; core green paprikas, and cut into rings and sprinkle with salt. Arrange the grated ingredients and the tomatoes and paprikas tastefully, on a flat dish, serve with sour cream or whipped dressing and garnish with lettuce leaves.

Asparagus Salad

Ingredients: 3 lb. fresh asparagus, 1 tsp. salt, 1 tsp. sugar, 1½ gill oil, 1½ gill vinegar, small bunch of parsley, juice of ½ lemon.

Cut trimmed asparagus into about one-inch pieces, cook and season with salt and sugar. Dilute vinegar with a little water and add oil, ½ tsp. salt, 1 tsp. sugar and the lemon-juice as well as chopped parsley. Put the cooked and cooled asparagus into dressing and set aside for an hour before serving.

French Salad

Ingredients: 3½ oz. carrots, 3½ oz. parsnips, ½ lb. potatoes, 3½ oz. peas, 3½ oz. tinned green apples, 3½ oz. pickled cucumbers, ½ tsp. salt, 2 gills tartare sauce.

Trim, wash, dice and cook carrots and parsnips. Cook washed potatoes in their jackets, peel and dice. Dice peeled apples and pickled cucumbers also. Mix all ingredients, peas included with tartare sauce; season with salt.

Rice Salad

Ingredients: 5 oz. rice, 1 small onion, 7 oz. tomatoes, 3½ oz. green paprikas, vinegar, oil, salt, pepper and a little sugar to taste, parsley, 1 head of lettuce.

Cook rice in plenty of fast boiling water for 20 mins., strain and rinse with cold water. Dice peeled and trimmed tomatoes and cored green paprikas, and finely chop onion and parsley. Mix above ingredients with vinegar, oil and seasoning. Garnish with lettuce leaves before serving.

Cauliflower Salad

Ingredients: 2 lb. trimmed cauliflower, 1 tsp. salt, 1 tsp. sugar, 2 tbsp. vinegar, 1 tbsp. salad oil, small bunch of parsley.

Cook trimmed and washed cauliflower in salt water until tender. Mix vinegar with a little water, season with salt and sugar and add finely chopped parsley and oil. Put cooled cauliflower into dressing and set aside in a cool place for an hour.

Italian-style Salad

Ingredients: ¾ lb. French salad (q. v.), 7 oz. tomatoes, 2 hard-boiled eggs, a few olives, 8 fillets of anchovies, 10 crayfish tails, shrimps or prawns, 1 tsp. capers.

Arrange French salad in a heap, and garnish tastefully with the rest of the ingredients.

Russian-style Salad

Ingredients: 10 oz. French salad (q. v.), 1 tsp. caviare, 2 oz. cooked Champignons, 2 oz. boiled ox-tongue, 2 oz. ham, 10 crayfish tails, shrimps or prawns, 2 tbsp. mayonnaise dressing, 3½ oz. beetroot salad (q. v.), 2 hard-boiled eggs.

Dice ham, ox-tongue, Champignons, and crayfish tails and add to French salad. Mix with mayonnaise dressing, heap on a bed of lettuce leaves, and garnish top with caviare, eggs and beetroots.

American Salad

Ingredients: 10 oz. tomatoes, 10 oz. celery, 7 oz. fresh cucumbers, 2 hard-boiled eggs, 2 oz. Roquefort cheese, a little prepared mustard, juice of ½ lemon, 2 tbsp. cream, a little sugar, salt and pepper, 1 head of lettuce.

Peel and trim tomatoes, half cook the celery and peel raw cucumbers. Cut them all in strips. Rub yolks of hard-boiled eggs together with Roquefort through sieve; add mustard, cream and seasonings. Mix well with ingredients cut into strips. Arrange in a heap over a bed of lettuce leaves.

PASTES, PASTRIES, CAKES AND SWEETS

ON CAKES IN GENERAL

Flour is, generally, the basic material of cakes, and its quality should be carefully chosen, because different kinds of cakes must be prepared with different kinds of flour. We use white flour as a rule, and use brown flour only exceptionally, as in the case of preparing honey-cakes. Kneaded pastries and cakes can be made from wholemeal flour. Wholemeal flour is suitable for the preparing of rétes, while plain flour can be used well for the making of short pastries.

The dough of pastries should be aerated, in order to make it easily digestible and more pliable. We may aerate the dough by mixing or by adding a little extra raising agent: yeast or baking powder.

We can use a great variety of raw materials for the making of cakes, pastries and sweets, such as fat, eggs, sour cream, cream and various fruits. Good flavour and sufficient nutritive value in cakes can only be ensured, just as in the case of all other dishes, by using good quality raw foodstuffs.

Quantities quoted in connection with some cakes are different as compared with the recipes meant for 5 people; in such cases, special attention is drawn to this.

Most of the baked pastries are cut into oblong slieces (e. g. apple tart, curd tart, etc.), some are cut into even squares. (E. g. cream tarts, or pastry filled with cream.)

BOILED PASTES

Potato Dumplings

Ingredients: 1¾ lb. potatoes, 7 oz. flour, 1 egg, 4½ oz. lard, pinch of salt, 7 oz. jam, 3½ oz. white bread-crumbs.

Cook potatoes in their jackets, mash, and allow to cool. When cool, add flour, a lump of lard the size of a walnut, the yolk of one egg and a dash of salt and knead well. Roll out dough to the thickness of about half a finger and then cut into some twenty or twenty-five squares. Put about a teaspoonful of some thick jam—preferably damson or plum—on each square and shape each into a dumpling. Drop dumplings into boiling salt water and cook about 20 or 25 mins. In the meantime brown bread-crumbs in fat. Roll strained dumplings in fried bread-crumbs and leave in warm oven until ready to serve.

Potato dumplings are delicious when filled with fresh plums, damsons or apricots. In this case stone the fruit and fill the cavity with sugar flavoured with cinnamon, and so put on the squares of dough. Make the dumplings as above and dredge with sugar flavoured with cinnamon.

If the dumplings are not served right away, keep them in a covered saucepan over steam to prevent drying out.

Cottage Cheese Dumplings I

Ingredients: 1 lb. cottage cheese, 2 rolls, 3 eggs, 2 oz. flour, $3\frac{1}{2}$ oz. lard, $3\frac{1}{2}$ oz. white bread-crumbs, $1\frac{1}{2}$ gill sour cream, salt.

Peel rolls, dice and dry in warm oven. Put cottage cheese through sieve and mix in a bowl with dried cubes of roll, one whole egg, the yolks of two eggs, one soup spoon of bread-crumbs and a little salt. From this paste shape dumplings with floury hands. Cook dumplings in boiling salt water for about a quarter of an hour, and then transfer to a dish, until ready to serve. Brown the rest of the bread-crumbs in lard, put dumplings into browned bread-crumbs and serve sprinkled with sour cream. (These quantities make twelve dumplings.)

Cottage Cheese Dumplings II

Ingredients: $1\frac{1}{2}$ lb. cottage cheese, 5 oz. semolina, 4 eggs, $4\frac{1}{2}$ oz. lard, $1\frac{1}{2}$ gill sour cream, $4\frac{1}{2}$ oz. white bread-crumbs, salt.

Put cottage cheese through a sieve and mix with the eggs, the semolina and a little salt. Let mixture stand for about an hour and then shape dumplings with wet hands. Cook dumplings in boiling salt water. Roll them in bread-crumbs browned in fat and serve with sour cream. If the cottage cheese is dry, use less semolina.

Cottage Cheese Dumplings III

Ingredients: $1\frac{3}{4}$ lb. cottage cheese, 3 oz. flour, 4 eggs, $4\frac{1}{2}$ oz. lard, $\frac{1}{3}$ pt. sour cream, $6\frac{1}{2}$ oz. white bread-crumbs, salt.

Put cottage cheese through sieve and knead well with flour, yolks of four eggs, 3 oz. bread-crumbs, and a little salt, folding in stiffly beaten whites of the eggs. Make dumplings and cook them in boiling water. Roll in bread-crumbs browned in fat and serve with sour cream.

Plum Dumplings

Ingredients: 1¾ lb. cooked and mashed potatoes, ½ lb. flour, 1 egg, 1 tsp. salt, 5 oz. lard, 10 oz. stoned plums, 4½ oz. sugar, 4½ oz. white bread-crumbs, pinch of ground cinnamon.

See directions for making the dough under Potato Dumplings. Roll dough to the thickness of your little finger and cut squares large enough to hold a plum. Place a plum dipped in sugar flavoured with cinnamon in the middle of every square and then make dumplings. Cook in boiling salt water until done, strain and roll in bread-crumbs browned in fat. Dredge with castor sugar mixed with cinnamon before serving.

Semolina Dumplings

Ingredients: ¾ lb. semolina, 1 quart milk, 2 oz. butter, 6 eggs, 3½ oz. bread-crumbs, 2 oz. sugar, 5 oz. white bread-crumbs, dash of salt, 7 oz. plum jam.

Cook semolina in milk, when cooled beat in the butter, the eggs and the 3½ oz. bread-crumbs. If the paste is too hard, use less bread-crumbs. Mix in the sugar and salt. Make dumplings, cook them in boiling salt water, strain and roll in white bread-crumbs browned in fat. Serve with plum jam.

Cabbage Dumplings

Ingredients: 10 oz. butter, 4 rolls, 1 pt. milk, 2 eggs, yolks of 4 eggs, 3½ oz. flour, 1 tsp. salt, 1 lb. cabbage, 2 oz. lard, 3½ oz. grated cheese.

Dice 2 rolls and fry in 2 oz. butter. Soak the other two rolls in the milk. Cream 7 oz. butter and mix with 2 whole eggs and yolks of four eggs, the flour and the salt. Shred cabbage, stew in lard, and mix with paste. Finally add fried cubes of rolls and the two soaked rolls which you have first put through a sieve. Mix and make dumplings. Cook dumplings in boiling water, strain and serve with 2 oz. melted butter and grated cheese.

Pasta with Ham

Ingredients: 1 lb. flour, 3 eggs, 1½ gill sour cream, 5 oz. ham (or smoked meat), salt and pepper, 2 oz. lard or butter.

Knead a stiff pasta of the flour and one egg with a little water. When dry cut squares about half an inch wide, boil these in salt water and rinse with cold water. Cream lard or butter, with yolks of two eggs and mix in minced ham or smoked meat, a pinch of ground pepper and salt. Add sour cream and the drained pasta. Finally fold in whites of two eggs beaten stiff. Grease a casserole with lard and dust with bread-crumbs. Put in the mixture and bake in a moderate oven till top is nicely browned.

If you use ready-made pasta, cook ¾ lb. of it.

Cabbage Squares

Ingredients: 1 lb. flour, 2 eggs, ½ tsp. salt, 2 lb. cabbage, 3½ oz. lard, ½ tsp. sugar, ½ tsp. chopped onions.

Knead flour with two eggs, a little salt and water into a stiff pasta, shaping two loaves of it. Roll each loaf thin. Grate cabbage, salt, let it stand for 20 mins. and then squeeze dry. Melt lard, brown sugar in it, mix in finely chopped onions, then add grated cabbage and sauté stirring often. Cut the pasta into about half-inch squares and cook in boiling salt water, adding a little lard to the water to prevent pasta from sticking together. Season cabbage with ground pepper and drain pasta; toss with grated cabbage and serve hot.

Onions may be omitted if preferred. If ready-made pasta is used, cook ¾ lb.

Noodles with Cottage Cheese

Ingredients: 1 lb. flour, 1 egg, ½ tsp. salt, ¾ lb. cottage cheese, 1½ gill sour cream, 2 oz. bacon, 2 oz. lard.

Knead and roll pasta as directed in above recipe but cut into strips about a quarter inch wide. Serve hot noodles with crumbled cottage cheese and sour cream strewn with cracklings of bacon. Use drained fat from bacon cracklings on noodles. Use ¾ lb. of ready-made pasta.

Cottage Cheese "Csusza"

Ingredients: 1 lb. flour, 2 eggs, ½ tsp. salt, ¾ lb. cottage cheese, 1½ gill sour cream, 3½ oz. bacon, 1 oz. lard.

Make a stiff pasta of the flour with the eggs, some water and salt. Let it stand for a while and then roll out quite thin. Tear into pieces about the size of a penny with forefinger and thumb, and scatter over the rolling board to prevent sticking together. Drop pieces into boiling salt water to which a teaspoonful lard has been added. When they rise to the surface, rinse in cold water and drain. Serve with crumbled cottage cheese and sour cream, and sprinkle with bacon cracklings and bacon fat.

Pasta Squares with Potato (Grenadier's Delight)

Ingredients: 1 lb. flour, 1½ lb. cooked potatoes, 1 oz. onion, 1 tsp. salt, 3½ oz. lard, pinch of paprika, 2 eggs.

Prepare pasta as for cabbage squares. Dice the boiled potatoes. Chop onions finely, fry in lard, add paprika, diced potatoes and lastly the boiled pasta squares. Toss well.

Semolina Noodles

Ingredients: 1 lb. flour, 1 egg, ½ tsp. salt, 3½ oz. lard, 3½ oz. semolina.

Fry semolina in lard till golden-brown. Add about 1 gill of water, simmer a few minutes till mixture becomes crumbly. Add a pinch of salt. Prepare pasta as for cabbage squares, roll out thinly, cut into noodles about the thickness of a match-stick. Boil in salt water, strain, mix with browned semolina.

If made of dried pasta, use ¾ lb. of noodles.

Noodles with Ground Walnuts

Ingredients: 1 lb. flour, 1 egg, pinch of salt, 2 oz. lard, 3½ oz. shelled, ground walnuts, 3½ oz. castor sugar or honey.

Prepare pasta as for semolina noodles, heat lard, add noodles. Mix with ground walnuts and castor sugar, or honey. If preferred, ground walnuts and sugar may be sprinkled on top just before serving.

If made with dried pasta, use ¾ lb. of noodles.

Noodle Layers

Ingredients: 1 lb. flour, 4 eggs, 2 tbsp. milk, a little salt, 2 oz. butter, 2 oz. lard, 2 tbsp. sour milk, 1 tsp. white bread-crumbs, 3½ oz. walnuts, 3½ oz. apricot jam, 3½ oz. sugar, grated rind of 1 lemon.

Make a pasta of the flour, 1 egg and a little water. Let it dry for a little while. Cut into noodles, and cook in boiling salted water. Rinse and drain in colander. Beat up butter with yolks of three eggs, castor sugar and grated lemon peel; add sour cream, the noodles, and lastly the stiffly beaten egg-whites. Grease a deep fireproof dish, dust with bread-crumbs. Put a layer of cooked noodles on bottom. Sprinkle with ground walnuts and sugar. Cover with another layer of noodles; over this spread apricot jam. Top with noodles, bake in oven till golden-brown. Turn it out and serve sprinkled with vanilla sugar.

Styrian Noodles

Ingredients: 1 lb. cottage cheese, 7 oz. flour, pinch of salt, 4 eggs, 1 oz. butter, 1½ gill sour cream, grated rind of half a lemon, 3½ oz. sugar.

Put cottage cheese through sieve, combine with flour, pinch of salt, teaspoonful sugar, ½ gill sour cream and a whole egg. Knead well together on pastry-board; shape two loaves, roll them out to the thickness of a pencil and cut into half-inch wide noodles. Boil in salt water, rinse and strain. Beat up butter with yolks of three eggs, add 1 gill sour cream, remainder of sugar and grated rind of ½ lemon. Add noodles. Lastly fold in stiffly beaten egg-whites. Turn mixture into a greased fireproof dish, bake in a slow oven till golden-brown.

Jam Ravioli

Ingredients: 1 lb. flour, 2 eggs, 3½ oz. lard, ½ lb. damson jam, 3½ oz. white bread-crumbs, 3½ oz. sugar, pinch of salt, pinch of ground cinnamon.

Make a stiff pasta of the flour, 1 whole egg, 1 egg-yolk, a pinch of salt and a little water. Shape into two loaves, roll out thinly on pastry-board. Mark the middle of rolled-out pasta, then put small heaps of damson cheese or stiff apricot jam, equally spaced, on one half of it. Brush the pasta between jam-heaps with white of egg, and cover with other half of rolled-out pasta. With the edge of the palm press down on top layer of pasta to make it stick to bottom layer along the outlines of a square around every heap of jam. Cut squares with fancy cutter. Cook raviolis carefully in slowly boiling salted water, drain in colander and rinse.

Fry bread-crumbs in lard till golden-brown, add boiled raviolis. Sprinkle with sugar mixed with ground cinnamon before serving.

If served later, keep hot under lid to prevent drying.

Cottage Cheese Ravioli

Ingredients: 1 lb. flour, 4 eggs, 3½ oz. lard, 5 oz. cottage cheese, 3½ oz. white bread-crumbs, pinch of salt, 1 packet of vanilla sugar, 3½ oz. sugar.

Prepare pasta exactly as for Jam ravioli, but use cheese filling instead of jam.

Press cottage cheese through sieve, add yolks of two eggs, a little grated lemon-peel, and a tablespoonful of castor sugar. Mix well and use it for filling. Make squares a little larger than for Jam ravioli. Serve dredged with bread-crumbs sautéed in fat, and with vanilla sugar.

If served later, keep hot under lid to prevent drying.

Pozsony Squares

Ingredients: ¾ lb. flour, 3 eggs, 5 oz. ground poppy-seeds, 2 oz. honey, grated rind of ½ lemon, 2 oz. lard, 2 tbsp. sour cream, 2 oz. sugar.

Make a pasta with the flour, one egg, a pinch of salt and a little water. Shape into two loaves, roll out each thinly and cut into ½ inch squares. Cook in boiling salt water, rinse and drain in colander.

Boil about ½ gill water in a small saucepan with a few lumps of sugar; add ground poppy-seeds, honey and grated rind of half a lemon, stir and put aside. Beat yolks of 2 eggs with 1 oz. lard and blend in sour cream. Add cooked pasta. Beat whites of two eggs with castor sugar till stiff and blend with above mixture.

Grease and dredge a deep fireproof dish with bread-crumbs and put in half the mixture. Spread poppy-seed filling over it and cover with other half of pasta mixture. Bake slowly till golden-brown, turn out on a flat dish when ready. Serve sprinkled with vanilla sugar.

If made of dried pasta, use 10 oz.

Apple Charlotte

Ingredients: 5 stale rolls, 3 gills milk, ½ lb. sugar, 2 tbsp. white wine, 3 eggs, ½ lb. apples, 2 oz. lard, 2 oz. apricot jam, a little ground cinnamon, 1 tsp. sultanas, 1 tsp. ground walnuts, 1 tsp. white bread-crumbs.

Cut stale rolls into thick slices. Beat yolks of eggs with boiled cold milk and 3½ oz. sugar, adding sultanas and lard. Soak sliced rolls in this mixture.

Strew peeled and cored apples with 3½ oz. sugar and cinnamon. Take a deep fireproof dish, grease, dust with bread-crumbs and put in half of the pudding mixture, arrange cooked apples evenly on top and strew with ground walnuts. Cover with the remainder of soaked roll mixture. Bake in a slow oven for about 20—25 mins. Whip the whites of the eggs with 2 oz. sugar and fold in apricot jam. Spread top of the pudding with this meringue, put the dish back to the oven for a few minutes. When the top is nicely browned serve immediately.

Emperor's Delight

Ingredients: 4 eggs, ½ pt. milk, ½ lb. flour, 1 oz. butter, 3 oz. sugar, 3½ oz. jam or preserve, 3 oz. lard.

Beat yolks of 4 eggs well with 3 tbsp. sugar; add flour, milk, melted butter and fold in stiffly beaten whites of 4 eggs. Warm lard in a small baking pan, pour in the mixture; bake. Turn out while hot and chop up into small pieces. Serve hot with jam, preserves or fruit syrup, sprinkled with sugar.

Galuska (Gnocchi, Thimble Dumplings)

Ingredients: 1 lb. flour, 1 egg, 1 tsp. salt, 3 oz. lard.

Sift flour into deep basin, add egg, salt and enough water to make a soft dough. Beat with a wooden spoon until it blisters and leaves the sides of the basin. Cut small pieces out of this dough with a tablespoon and drop them one by one into boiling salt water. When cooked, drain in colander and rinse. Heat the fat in a saucepan, add galuskas. Serve it as a garnish with paprikash, stewed or braised meat; or as a separate dish with eggs and sour cream, or with white cheese mixed with sour cream and cracklings.

246

Galuska with Scrambled Eggs

Ingredients: 1 lb. flour, 6 eggs, 1 tsp. salt, 3 oz. lard, 1 gill sour cream.

Prepare dough and boil as above. Heat lard, add galuskas. Beat five eggs and sour cream well together, pour on the pasta, mix well. Let it stand over heat, occasionally stirring for about five mins. before serving.

Salzburg Galuska

Ingredients: 2 oz. butter, 1 pt. milk, 3 oz. flour, 3 eggs, 1 tsp. vanilla sugar, a little salt, 3 pt. milk.
Cream: 3½ oz. butter, 7 eggs, 2½ oz. sugar.

Mix 2 oz. butter with 1 pt. milk and 3½ oz. flour and cook till boiling, stirring all the while. Remove from heat and mix in 8 eggs, one by one. Also add the vanilla sugar and a pinch of salt. Bring to boil 3 pt. of milk. Cut small pieces out of mixture with a tablespoon and drop them one by one into the boiling milk. When cooked, drain well.

Cream 3½ oz. butter with 7 yolks of eggs, and 3½ oz. sugar, fold in the beaten whites of 7 eggs.

Pour half of cream into bottom of a deep fireproof dish. Add galuskas, pour remainder of cream on top. Bake it in a slow oven for about half an hour.

Strapachka

Ingredients: 1¼ lb. peeled grated raw potatoes, 1 egg, ½ tsp. salt, 3 oz. lard, 10 oz. wholemeal flour, 3½ oz. streaky bacon, 5 oz. curded ewe's cheese.

Make a dough of grated potatoes, flour, egg, salt and fat. Knead well, then cook galuskas of it in boiling water. Drain in colander and put aside. Dice bacon, fry in saucepan till crisp, take out cracklings, add galuskas to fat and mix well. Serve with crumbled ewe's cheese and cracklings on top.

RÉTES

Basic Rétes (Strudel) Pastry
(5 servings)

Ingredients: 10 oz. flour, 1 tsp. lard, 1 egg, a pinch of salt, 1 gill water.

You will need a large kitchen table on which to pull out pastry. Sift flour onto pastry-board and knead well with lard, pinch of salt, one egg, and 1 gill lukewarm water. Make a loaf of the paste, cover it with a warmed dish or basin and let it stand for about 20—25 mins.

Cover the table with a clean cloth, flour it well, place the dough in middle, brush it with a little lukewarm lard, and roll it out rolling with pin to a finger's thickness. Flour your hands, place them under the paste, pulling it gently and evenly towards the sides of the table till paste reaches the thinness of tissue paper. Tear off thick edges of the dough, let dry for a few minutes, sprinkle with lard, spread with filling prepared beforehand, roll up into a roly-poly with the help of the tablecloth. Place into a greased baking pan, brush with egg or lard, bake in a hot oven till crisp and golden-brown.

Rétes with Cottage Cheese

Ingredients: 10 oz. flour, 4 eggs, 3½ oz. lard, 1 lb. cottage cheese, 2 gills sour cream, ½ lb. sugar, grated rind of one lemon, 1 tsp. semolina.

For filling, press cottage cheese through sieve, add sour cream and cream with 2 oz. sugar, grated rind of one lemon and the yolks of three eggs. Fold in the whites of 3 eggs, beaten stiff, to which 2 oz. castor sugar has been added.

Sprinkle the rétes pastry (prepared as above) with melted lard and semolina, spread with filling and roll up. Put into greased baking pan, brush top with an egg mixed with sour cream, bake in a hot oven. Serve hot.

Potato Rétes

Ingredients: 10 oz. flour, 1 tsp. lard, 1 egg, pinch of salt, 4 yolks of eggs, 4 tbsp. potatoes mashed, 4 tbsp. castor sugar, 2 tbsp. sour cream, 3 tbsp. ground almonds, whites of 2 eggs.

Prepare rétes dough, pull it out thin and fill with the following mixture:
Cream the yolks of four eggs with 4 tbsp. mashed potatoes, 4 tbsp. castor sugar, 2 tbsp. whites of two eggs. Cream for about half an hour. Roll up the dough with this filling. Brush with beaten egg and bake. Dredge with vanilla sugar.

Cabbage Rétes

Ingredients: 10 oz. flour, 1 egg, 4½ oz. lard, 2½ lb. cabbage, a little sugar, pinch of ground black pepper, one or two tsp. chopped onion (optional), dash of salt.

Halve cabbage, remove stalk and shred finely. Let it stand in salt for half an hour, and then squeeze. Brown one level tablespoon castor sugar in one tablespoon fat; add finely chopped onions (optional), the shredded cabbage and ground pepper and sauté latter ingredients stirring often. After it has dried, sprinkle rétes pastry with fat and spread the cabbage mixture on it. Roll up and put into a baking pan greased with fat. Brush with fat and beaten egg and bake in hot oven until crisp.

Poppy-seed Rétes

Ingredients: 10 oz. flour, 10 oz. ground poppy-seed, 3½ oz. apples, 10 oz. sugar, 3½ oz. lard, 2 gills milk, grated rind of half a lemon, one egg, a little salt.

Cook sugar in milk, and when boiling pour the sweet milk over the ground poppy-seeds which have been flavoured with lemon peel. Mix and if mixture is too thick, thin with a little water. Spread the above filling combined with grated apples on pulled-out dough and sprinkle with fat. Roll up and put in baking pan, brushing with beaten egg and then baking till crisp. Dust with vanilla sugar.

Apple Rétes

Ingredients: 2½ lb. apples, 2 oz. bread-crumbs, 3½ oz. fat, 2 oz. ground walnuts, 3½ oz. sugar, cinnamon to taste, 10 oz. flour, dash of salt, 1 egg (half for dough and half for brushing).

Pull out rétes dough until thin and when it has dried, dust with fine bread-crumbs and sprinkle with melted fat. Spread pared and thinly sliced cooking apples on the dough and dredge with grated walnuts (or almonds), and castor sugar flavoured with cinnamon. Roll up and put into greased baking pan, brush with beaten egg and bake in a hot oven until crisp. Serve straight from the oven; dredge with vanilla sugar.

Cherry or Morello Cherry Rétes

Ingredients: 10 oz. flour, 3½ oz. fat, 2 oz. bread-crumbs, 2½ lb. cherries (stoned), 7 oz. sugar, 1 egg, 2 oz. ground walnuts, a little ground cinnamon, dash of salt.

Pull out rétes dough and when dry sprinkle with melted fat, fine bread-crumbs and ground walnuts. Spread with stoned cherries and bake in hot oven until crisp. (Morello cherry filling is made the same way, but use 2 oz. more sugar. Morello cherries and sweet cherries may be combined, but in this case use more sweet cherries than morello cherries.)

Vargabéles (Cobbler's Delight)

Ingredients: 1 lb. flour, 1¾ lb. cottage cheese, 1 gill sour cream, 5 oz. butter, 1 dessert-spoon raisins, 7 oz. sugar, 6 eggs, ¼ stick of vanilla.

From 7 oz. flour prepare rétes dough and from 10 oz. flour, one egg and some water make a hard noodle pasta.

Put cottage cheese through sieve and mix with yolks of egg, vanilla sugar and sour cream. Put the raisins, the boiled noodles and part of the melted butter in this mixture. Finally gently fold in the egg-whites beaten up with sugar.

Grease tin with butter and line with three or four layers of the pulled-out and dried rétes dough. Sprinkle every layer with melted butter and spread the top layer with the above mixture. Cover with three or four layers of rétes dough sprinkled with butter. Bake in moderate oven. Serve preferably after it has been out of the oven fifteen or twenty mins.; cut into squares and dust with vanilla sugar.

DESSERTS MADE OF RAISED DOUGH

Raised Dough

Ingredients: 1¼ lb. flour, 2 eggs, 3 gills milk, 1 oz. yeast, 2 oz. lard or butter, 2 oz. sugar, pinch of salt.

Prepare leaven mixing the yeast with three lumps of sugar and 1½ gill lukewarm milk and as much flour as it will take. Let it rise in a warm place. Sift the remaining flour in a bowl; add the butter or lard, castor sugar, the yolks of two eggs and the raised leaven. Knead the dough with an adequate amount of lukewarm milk until it no longer sticks to the bowl. Put the dough— which should be neither too hard nor too soft—into a bowl dusted with flour and let it rise in a warm place for about an hour. It may be filled with jam, poppy-seed or walnut filling. The filling is made as for Pozsony crescents (q.v.) but dilute with cold milk or syrup because the filling needs to be softer for this dough.

The same dough may be plaited to form a longish loaf or shaped into brioches.

Bake in moderate oven.

Carnival Doughnuts

Ingredients: 10 oz. flour, 3 eggs, ½ oz. yeast, 1 oz. sugar, 1 oz. butter, 1½ gill milk, 10 oz. lard, dash of salt, 1 tsp. rum, grated rind of ¼ lemon, 5 oz. apricot jam.

Heat milk till lukewarm and make a batter with 2 oz. flour, the yeast and a little sugar. Set it to rise for 15—20 mins. Cream yolks of eggs with the sugar, mix with the flour and the leavened batter and butter. Beat the dough well with a wooden spoon and set it to rise. When risen, turn carefully onto a well-floured board. Roll and cut the doughnuts to the desired size with biscuit-cutter. Cover with a floured cloth and leave on the board allowing it to rise again. Put the lard into deep frying pan and heat well. Press the middle of each doughnut with thumb and put into hot fat with pressed side down. Fry under cover. When the lower side is a golden-brown turn and fry other side without lid. When done put on rack to drain off fat. Warm apricot jam and dilute with a little water. Serve doughnuts with this diluted jam, dusted with vanilla sugar. Keep dough always at an even temperature, because a draft or chilling will make it heavy.

Jam Fritters

Ingredients: ¾ lb. flour, 1 oz. yeast, 2 eggs, 3½ oz. lard, 1 pt. milk, 3½ oz. sugar, rind of ½ lemon, apricot jam.

Sift flour into a bowl, making a well in the middle. Make a batter of a little lukewarm milk with yeast, 2 lumps of sugar and a tbsp. flour. Set it to rise in a warm place and then pour it into the well in the flour. Knead and add the yolks of two eggs, 1 oz. castor sugar, a dash of salt and enough warm milk to make a soft dough. Grate some lemon rind into the mixture, add 1 oz. lukewarm butter and knead well. Cover with clean cloth and set to rise for about ¾ hr. Then mix in stiffly-beaten whites of two eggs. Heat fat in frying pan and spoon fritters of the dough into the fat, frying on both sides. Serve with apricot jam and sifted sugar.

Russian Fritters
(6—8 servings)

Ingredients: ½ lb. flour, ½ oz. yeast, 2 gills milk, 3 eggs, 1 tbsp. cream, dash of salt, ½ lb. lard, 2 oz. butter.

Make a thin batter of the yeast, a little warm milk and flour, and set it to rise for two hrs. Sift the flour into a bowl and add leavened batter and lukewarm milk. Mix well with wooden spoon. Set it to rise again, about half an hour before frying, mix in yolks of three eggs and a dash of salt and fold in stiffly beaten whites of three eggs, as well as the whipped cream and 1 oz. melted butter. Set to a warm place. About 20 mins. later heat fat in a frying pan and scoop out little heaps of the dough with a ladle, dropping them close to each other in the fat. Fry both sides brown over moderate heat and keep warm in a tin greased with butter. Serve with caviars or smoked fish.

Sandwich Bread

Ingredients: ½ lb. flour, 1 oz. butter, 1 oz. yeast, 1 oz. sugar, dash of salt, 1 egg, 2 oz. potatoes cooked and mashed.

Sieve the flour on the pastry-board, and pour leavening made of yeast dissolved in ½ gill warm sweetened water into a well, scooped-out in the middle of the flour. When leavening in the well has risen, add the rest of the ingredients with the exception of the egg, and knead a hard dough with some lukewarm water. Set it to rise for an hour and then roll into long strips the width of a sandwich-loaf. Brush with beaten egg, put on baking sheet to dry and then brush with beaten egg again. Bake in a warm, but not too hot oven. Only slice when cooled.

Coffee Cake

Ingredients: 10 oz. flour, ½ oz. yeast, ½ pt. milk, 3 eggs, 3 oz. butter, 3 oz. sugar, ¼ lemon, 1 oz. raisins, dash of salt, 1 oz. bread-crumbs, 1 oz. castor sugar for dredging or 7 oz. chocolate glaze for icing.

Make a batter of yeast, 3 oz. flour and 1 oz. castor sugar with 1 gill warm milk and set it to rise for half an hour. Cream butter with 2 oz. castor sugar and yolks of 3 eggs. With a wooden spoon blend into the batter the flour, some more warm milk, lemon peel and raisins and keep beating with spoon till it blisters. Cover with clean cloth and let it rise for an hour. Grease cake tin well and dust with finely sifted bread-crumbs. Put in dough and allow it to rise ½ hr. longer. Bake in a moderate oven. When done turn onto floured board and dust with castor sugar or ice with chocolate glaze.

Poppy-seed Fingers

Ingredients: See ingredients for dough under Raised Dough. In addition 7 oz. ground poppy-seeds, 1 gill milk, 2 oz. honey, 1 oz. lard.

Make raised dough with yeast, and roll noodles or fingers out of it. Roll fingers in flour. Bake in ungreased tin until light brown. Take out of oven and scald with hot water. The dough should soften but must not crumble. Drain and place into a little hot fat and then mix with honey and poppy-seeds boiled in milk.

Chelsea Buns

Ingredients: 1 lb. flour, yolks of 7 eggs, dash of salt, 1 oz. yeast, 8 oz. castor sugar, 2 gills milk, 7 oz. butter, 7 oz. almonds or walnuts ground, 1½ gill cream.

Knead a dough the consistency of rétes dough from the flour, the egg-yolks, a little salt and the yeast (first soaked in a little milk), 1 oz. castor sugar and the rest of milk. Knead well and set aside for half an hour in a warm spot. Then roll out thin, and spread on it a filling made as follows. Cream butter with 7 oz. castor sugar and the ground almonds or walnuts. Roll up like a Swiss roll and cut into slices the thickness of your little finger. Loosely arrange in floured tin and set to rise. Bake in an even and fairly hot oven. When half-done, baste with sweetened cream or sweetened unheated milk.

Plaited Milk Bread

Ingredients: 1¼ lb. flour, 3½ oz. butter, 4½ oz. sugar, 3 eggs, 1 oz. yeast, 2—3 gills milk, dash of salt.

Mix yeast with 1 gill warm milk, two lumps of sugar and a little flour. Then set this batter in a warm place. Sift flour onto pastry-board and scoop out a well in the heap of flour. Put the leavened batter into this well, together with 3½ oz. sugar, a dash of salt and 2 eggs. Add as much warm milk as it will absorb and knead dough well. Add 3½ oz. melted butter, knead a little more and then allow it to rise, placing it in a floured dish covered with thin cloth. When is has risen turn onto floured pastry-board and divide into three equal pieces. Roll each piece into longish strip, plait strips and put plaited loaf into a greased tin. Brush with beaten egg. When sufficiently risen, brush again with egg and bake until well browned. The plaiting should be done carefully rolling the pieces into flour before plaiting to prevent them from running into each other in the oven. Bake in a moderate oven. (The butter may be added together with the other ingredients.)

Raised Golden Cake
(4—5 servings)

Ingredients: 10 oz. flour, 2 gills milk, 3 oz. butter, 2 oz. white bread-crumbs, 4 eggs, ½ oz. yeast, 1 packet of vanilla sugar, 4½ oz. sugar, 1 tbsp. rum, 2 oz. ground walnuts.

Make a batter of the yeast, one lump of sugar, 1 tbsp. warm milk and a little flour. Sift ½ lb. flour into a basin, make a well in middle and put the leavened batter into it. Dredge with flour and let it rise a little. Cream the yolks of two eggs with 1 oz. castor sugar and rum. With a wooden spoon mix the flour and the batter with enough warm milk to make a dough like that of doughnuts. Combine with the creamed mixture and 1 oz. butter and continue mixing with the wooden spoon until the dough blisters and leaves spoon clean. Then dredge with flour, cover with clean cloth and set it in a warm place to rise. When risen, turn onto floured pastry-board, roll out to the thickness of a finger and stamp out pieces the size of a walnut with pastry cutter. Turn each piece in melted butter and arrange close to each other in a tin, greased with butter and dusted with fine bread-crumbs. Sprinkle ground walnuts mixed with sugar between the rows. Brush top with beaten egg, let it rise again and bake in a moderate oven. Serve with the following sauce.

Make a light roux of a little flour and a lump of butter the size of a walnut. Dilute it with ½ pt. hot milk. Beat until smooth. Mix well the yolks of 2 eggs with 2 tbsp. vanilla sugar in top of a double saucepan; add 1½ gill milk, and cook, stirring all the time, until it begins to boil, then add milk sauce. Turn the baked golden cake into a bowl and serve with above sauce.

Wine sauce may be substituted for milk sauce.

PUFF PASTRIES

Basic Puff Pastry

Ingredients: 7 oz. butter, ½ gill flour, juice of ¼ lemon, dash of salt.

Knead butter with 1 oz. flour. Form into a flat square and set it in a cool place. In the meantime knead a harder silky-smooth rétes dough of the remaining flour with cold water, the lemon-juice (or a little vinegar) and salt. Let it rest for 20—25 mins. and roll out to oblong shape (not very thin); place butter in middle and fold edges tightly on (take care that the corners should be free of flour and the thickness of the lower layer and of the four corners resting on each other should be equal), and roll out with rolling pin into an oblong, a little over an inch thick. Now comes the folding, an operation you have to repeat three times. After each folding leave the dough in a cool place for 20—25 mins. Fold pastry in the following way: Fold two ends so that edges meet in the middle and then fold again in the middle like a book, and leave in a cold place. Use it for the preparation of any kind of sweets where puff pastry is required.

Morello Cherry Tart

Ingredients: 4½ oz. butter, ¾ lb. flour, yolks of 2 eggs, 2 tbsp. sour cream, 1 tbsp. sugar, ¼ tsp. salt, 2 tbsp. bread-crumbs, 2 lb. morello cherries, 7 oz. sugar, ¼ stick of vanilla, 3½ oz. walnuts, white of 1 egg, grated rind of one lemon, 1 oz. vanilla sugar.

Crumble flour with butter well. Add yolks of two eggs, sour cream, 1 tbsp. of sugar and a pinch of salt. Knead well and shape into 2 loaves. (Prepare this pastry one day beforehand if possible.)

Roll out to pencil-thickness, put into an oblong baking pan. Sprinkle with bread-crumbs. Mix stoned morello cherries with grated lemon peel, vanilla sugar and ground walnuts; spread mixture evenly on pastry. Dust top with bread-crumbs and sugar, cover with other half of pastry. Brush with beaten egg and decorate with coarsely chopped walnuts. Bake in a medium oven.

Vanilla Cream Tart

Ingredients: 7 oz. flour, 5 oz. butter, ¼ lemon, 1 pt. milk, 7 oz. sugar, 4 eggs, ¼ stick of vanilla.

Make puff pastry (q. v.) of following ingredients: 5 oz. butter, 5 oz. flour, pinch of salt, the juice of ¼ lemon. Fold four times, roll out to pencil-thickness, put on baking sheet. Cut pastry evenly round edges, prick with fork and bake in a hot oven till golden-brown. Take out baking sheet and slide pastry carefully onto the pastry-board. Repeat this with the other half.

To prepare cream: Boil 2½ gills milk with vanilla and 3½ oz. sugar. Put it aside. Mix in a saucepan yolks of 4 eggs, 2 oz. flour and 1 gill cold milk; beat till smooth. Pour boiled milk over it and cook over moderate heat, stirring all the while, till mixture thickens and just begins to boil. Remove from heat and mix in the stiffly beaten whites of three eggs, sweetened with 3 oz. castor sugar, while the cream is still hot. Spread cream evenly over one sheet of pastry, cover with the other one. Cut into squares with a very sharp knife.

Mylady's Whim

Ingredients: Basic puff pastry. *Filling:* Whites of 6 eggs, 7 oz. granulated sugar, 1 oz. castor sugar.

Roll pastry into two sheets, bake to a golden-brown. Filling: Boil granulated sugar with 1 gill water till syrup can be pulled into threads between fingers. Pour hot syrup very slowly into the stiffly beaten whites of 6 eggs, stirring all the time and continuing stirring till it cools. Spread filling evenly over one sheet of pastry and cover with the other one. Cut into squares and sprinkle top with castor sugar.

Cherry and Morello Cherry Tarts

Ingredients: 10 oz. short pastry, 1¼ lb. stoned cherries, 4½ oz. sugar, 7 oz. puff pastry, 2 oz. cake crumbs, 1 egg.

Roll out short pastry, put into baking tin and bake in a moderate oven till half-done. (This is to prevent pastry from turning soggy from the juice of fruit.) Take out of oven, dredge with cake crumbs. Spread evenly with stoned cherries and sugar, cover with rolled-out puff pastry. Prick top with fork, and brush with beaten egg. Bake in a moderate oven. If you make it solely with morello cherries, add more sugar to fruit.

If you use both kinds of cherries, use more sweet cherries and fewer morellos.

Ischl Shortcake

Ingredients: 1 lb. flour, ½ lb. butter, 4¼ oz. hazelnuts, 4½ oz. castor sugar, ¼ tsp. bicarbonate of soda, grated rind of one lemon, a little ground cinnamon, 3½ oz. currant jam, 5 oz. chocolate.

Crumble flour with butter; add ground hazelnuts, sugar, bicarbonate of soda, grated lemon peel and a pinch of ground cinnamon. Knead mixture well and put aside in a cool place for an hour. Roll pastry out to pencil-thickness, cut into rounds with a circular biscuit cutter. Put on baking sheet, bake till just slightly browned. Cool, then stick pairs together with currant or other jam; glaze with chocolate or coloured icing.

Ischl Shortcake with Walnuts

Ingredients: 1 lb. flour, 10 oz. butter, 5 oz. ground walnuts, ½ oz. vanilla sugar, 2 oz. chocolate, grated peel of half a lemon, 3½ oz. jam, 5 oz. sugar.

Rub flour and butter together; combine with ground walnuts, castor sugar, vanilla sugar and grated lemon peel. Knead well. Let it stand for half an hour in a cool place, then roll out to ¼ inch thickness. Cut into rounds with a circular biscuit cutter and bake to a light golden-brown. When cool, spread half of the round with jam, and top each with another shortcake. Melt chocolate in double saucepan, brush over pastry.

Rákóczy Cheese Cake

Ingredients: 3½ oz. flour, 3 oz. butter, 2 oz. castor sugar, 1 egg, 1 tbsp. sour cream, a pinch of bicarbonate of soda.
Filling: 1 lb. creamed cottage cheese, 5 oz. sugar, 1 oz. semolina, 2 yolks of eggs, 2 tbsp. sour cream, the stiffly beaten white of two eggs.
Lattice topping: 3 whites of eggs, stiffly beaten with 3 oz. sugar.

Knead pastry from ingredients given above, roll out to pencil-thickness and bake in a medium oven till half-done. Press cottage cheese through sieve, combine with ingredients for filling, and spread over pastry. Squeeze stiffly beaten egg-whites through icing bag to make lattice topping. Put back to oven for a few minutes, until meringue lattice sets, cut into portions with a wet knife. Sprinkle with vanilla sugar before serving.

Apple Tart

Ingredients: 7 oz. flour, 3½ oz. butter or lard, 1 egg, 2 tbsp. sour cream, 1 tsp. rum, grated rind of ¼ lemon, pinch of salt, 2 oz. bread-crumbs, 5 oz. sugar, a little ground cinnamon, 2 lb. apples.

Knead short pastry with butter or lard, 2 oz. sugar, yolk of 1 egg, a little rum, 2 tbsp. sour cream, pinch of salt and grated lemon peel. Keep in a cold place overnight. Next day divide the pastry in two, roll out each half to pencil-thickness. Put one sheet of pastry in baking tin, prick with fork and bake it till half-done. Then, taking it out of oven, sprinkle with bread-crumbs, top with thinly sliced apples and sprinkle with sugar mixed with ground cinnamon. Cover with other half of pastry, brush top with beaten egg and prick with a fork. Bake in a moderate oven till golden-brown.

Let it stand for a little while before cutting up. Dust with vanilla sugar and serve.

Grape Tart

Ingredients: ¾ lb. flour, ¼ lb. butter, 10 oz. sugar, peel of ½ lemon, 1 tbsp. liqueur, 3½ oz. walnuts, 3½ oz. bread-crumbs, 2 eggs, pinch of ground cinnamon, 2½ lb. grapes.

Rub flour, butter, 4½ oz. castor sugar and grated lemon peel together on pastry-board, then add 1 whole egg and knead quickly together. Let it stand for an hour in a cold place.

Clean, wash and drain grapes, add 4½ oz. castor sugar and liqueur. Put aside for half an hour, but stir carefully every now and then.

Mix ground walnuts with bread-crumbs, 3 oz. sugar and quarter of a tsp. ground cinnamon.

Divide pastry in two, roll each half out to pencil-thickness. Bake one half till half-done, cover with half of ground walnut mixture, arrange grapes on it, sprinkle with other half of walnut mixture and cover with the other half of pastry. Press edges down, brush with beaten egg, prick with fork. Bake in a moderate oven for 45—50 mins. Cut into squares when cool and sprinkle with castor sugar mixed with a little ground cinnamon.

Potato Pastry Slices

Ingredients: 1 lb. baked potatoes mashed, 3 eggs, 3 oz. sugar, 7 oz. jam.

Bake potatoes and put through sieve. Beat three yolks of egg with castor sugar; mix well with potatoes. Knead till it begins to stiffen. Fold in stiffly beaten whites of egg. Bake in a greased tin. Cut into slices and put jam between them.

Cottage Cheese Flan with Fresh Dill

Ingredients: 10 oz. flour, ½ lb. butter, 1 tsp. salt, 5 eggs, 1½ gill sour cream, 2 lb. sweet cottage cheese, a little chopped fresh dill.

Make a light dough of 6 oz. flour butter, a little salt, 2 eggs, and 1 gill sour cream. Roll out to finger's thickness, put into baking tin, shaping and trimming edges. Spread the following filling over it. Put 2 lb. sweet cottage cheese through sieve. Mix it with 2½ oz. butter, yolks of 4 eggs, a pinch of salt and finely chopped fresh dill. Fold 4 stiffly beaten egg-whites into mixture. Brush top with sour cream. Bake it in a hot oven.

Walnut and Coffee Slices

Ingredients: 6 eggs, 7 oz. sugar, 3½ oz. ground walnuts, 2 bars of chocolate, 1 dessertspoon finely ground coffee, 3 oz. flour, 2 oz. butter.

Beat the yolks of 6 eggs well with sugar. Add ground walnuts, 2 bars of grated chocolate and finely ground coffee. Fold in stiffly beaten whites of 6 eggs, and blend in flour. Grease a baking tin with butter, dredge with flour, pour mixture in it and bake in a slow oven.

Tasty Delicious Plum Tart

Ingredients: 10 oz. flour, 7 oz. butter or 5 oz. margarine, 1 oz. castor sugar, 1 tsp. sour cream, yolks of 2 eggs, a little salt.
Filling: 1¾ lb. stoned plums, 2 oz. castor sugar, 1 oz. bread-crumbs.
Top: Yolks of 3 eggs, 3 oz. castor sugar, 1 gill sour cream, 2 oz. flour, whites of 5 eggs.

Mix the flour, fat, 1 oz. castor sugar, yolks of two eggs and 1 tbsp. sour cream to a stiffish paste. Let it stand for a while, then roll out and line bottom of baking tin with it. Prick with a fork. Spread halved plums evenly over it. Sprinkle top of fruit with 2 oz. castor sugar and 1 oz. bread-crumbs. Prepare top layer as follows.

Beat well 3 yolks of eggs, 1 gill sour cream and 2 oz. flour. Beat whites of 5 eggs with 1 oz. sugar and when stiff fold into yolk mixture. Cover the layer of plums with it, and bake in a moderate oven.

Tasty Delicious Cherry Tart

Ingredients: 6 oz. butter, 3 eggs, 5 oz. sugar, 6 oz. flour, 2 lb. stoned cherries.

Cream butter, add one by one the yolks of three eggs and 1 oz. castor sugar and continue beating. Beat whites of eggs till stiff, adding 2 oz. castor sugar by degrees. Fold beaten whites carefully into yolk mixture, adding the flour as well. Line a baking tin with greaseproof paper, pour mixture in, strew with cherries ½ inch thick. Bake in a moderate oven till golden-brown. Let it cool, then slice.

Can be made with morello cherries when more sugar is needed.

Tyrolean Apple Rétes

Ingredients: 10 oz. puff pastry, 5 oz. castor sugar, pinch of ground cinnamon, 2 oz. bread-crumbs, 3½ oz. ground walnuts, 1 oz. sultanas, 2 lb. apples, yolk of 1 egg.

Roll out puff pastry to thickness of a thin pencil. Cut off two half-inch-wide strips from width and put them aside. Dust the middle of rolled-out pastry with bread-crumbs in a strip about 3 inches wide and over this evenly arrange the pared and grated apples combined with the raisins; then sprinkle with sugar mixed with ground cinnamon and ground walnuts. Fold over the two sides of pastry so as to cover filling. Brush top with beaten egg. Put pastry-strips on top in a snake-like pattern. Brush again with egg, and bake. Cut in lozenges and serve dusted with vanilla sugar.

Tyrolean Cottage Cheese Rétes

Prepare pastry as for Tyrolean Apple Rétes, only instead of bread-crumbs use semolina.

Filling: 1 lb. dry cottage cheese pressed through sieve, 5 oz. castor sugar, 1 oz. raisins, 1 oz. flour, pinch of salt, yolks of 3 eggs, grated rind of half a lemon.

Cut into lozenges and serve dusted with vanilla sugar.

Raised Puff Pastry

Ingredients: 5 oz. butter, 10 oz. flour, 1 oz. yeast, 1 oz. lard, 2 eggs, 1½ gill milk, pinch of salt.

Cream butter with 2½ oz. flour. Keep it cold till needed. Mix yeast with 2 lumps of sugar, lukewarm milk and sufficient flour to make a batter; let it rise. Sift flour onto pastry-board, make a well and put in 1 oz. castor sugar, a tsp. fat, yolks of two eggs, the leavened batter, a pinch of salt, and lukewarm milk. Knead well, form into a loaf, put on a well-floured pastry-board and let it rise for a while. Roll dough out, place the butter and flour mixture in middle and proceed as usual with puff pastry; fold three times double, letting pastry rest for 10—15 mins. between foldings. It need not be moved to cool place, but may be left on the pastry-board during this period. After last folding, leave for another 10 mins., then roll out and use. This pastry can be flavoured with a little grated lemon peel or rum to taste. It can be filled with jam or cottage cheese.

Let it rise for a few more mins. before putting into a medium-hot oven.

Berlin Slices

Ingredients: ½ lb. sugar, 10 oz. flour, 7 oz. butter, 3 eggs, grated rind of ½ lemon, 5 oz. ground walnuts or almonds, 1 oz. cocoa, pinch of ground cinnamon, vanilla sugar.

Mix and knead well 3½ oz. sugar, 7 oz. butter, 1 egg and grated rind of lemon. Roll out one third of the pastry and line a baking tin with it. Prick with fork and bake till half-done.

Filling: Mix 5 oz. ground almonds or walnuts with 1 oz. cocoa, 5 oz. sugar, a pinch of ground cinnamon, with 2 or 3 eggs. Brush partly-baked pastry with jam, arrange filling evenly over it. Roll remainder of pastry into thin strips and decorate top with a lattice-work of these strips. Bake in a moderate oven. Sprinkle with vanilla sugar, let it cool. Fill squares between lattice-work of pastry with apricot jam. Cut and serve cold.

Pastry Cornet

Ingredients: 1 lb. flour, 3½ oz. butter, 1 oz. yeast, 2 gills milk, 3 egg-yolks, some salt, 2 oz. sugar, white of 1 egg.

Put 2½ oz. butter and 1 oz. yeast into lukewarm milk. Add 3 egg-yolks and salt as well. Let it rise, then add 1 lb. flour and knead the dough well together and set to prove in a warm place. Knead it again when well risen. Meanwhile melt ½ oz. butter, and grease a large cornet mould with it. Roll out the dough, cut it into ribbons, brush with white of egg and twist each strip round the cornet mould. Sprinkle with a mixture of 2 oz. sugar and 2 oz. ground almonds. Put it into a hot oven and bake till crisp.

Poppy-seed or Walnut Roll

Ingredients: ¾ lb. flour, 5 oz. butter or 4 oz. lard, ½ oz. yeast, pinch of salt, 2 tbsp. sour cream.

Make a light pastry of the following ingredients: ¾ lb. flour, 5 oz. butter or 4 oz. lard, ½ oz. yeast mixed with a tbsp. milk, a pinch of salt and 2 tbsp. sour cream. Let it stand for 15 mins., cut in two and roll out each half to the thickness of match-stick. Fill one with poppy-seed, and the other with walnut filling.

Walnut filling: Make a syrup of 5 oz. sugar and 2—3 tbsp. milk. Add 7 oz. ground walnuts, a little grated lemon peel and two or three spoonfuls apricot or apple jam; alternatively one or two pared and grated raw apples.

Poppy-seed filling: Make a syrup of 5 oz. sugar and 1—1½ gill of milk, add ground poppy-seeds and boil. Remove from heat and stir in grated rind of lemon, one or two spoonfuls of apple jam or alternatively one or two peeled and grated raw apples.

Cover rolled-out pastry with filling, roll up, place in baking tin, brush with beaten egg and prick in a few places with larding pin; allow to stand for 10 mins., then brush again with egg. Bake in a moderate oven.

Pozsony Walnut and Poppy-seed Crescents

Ingredients: 2 lb. flour, 7 oz. butter, 5 oz. lard, 1¼ lb. sugar, ½ oz. yeast, 2 eggs, 1½ oz. milk, ½ tsp. salt, ¾ lb. ground poppy-seeds, ¾ lb. ground walnuts, ¼ tsp. ground cinnamon, grated rind of half a lemon, 1 oz. bread-crumbs.

Rub and crumble well butter and lard with flour, and 3 oz. castor sugar, over pastry-board. Dissolve yeast in lukewarm milk. Combine yeast batter, one whole egg and salt with pastry, knead well and then let it stand for a few hours in a cold place. Afterwards shape 5 loaves of the dough, and roll each out into ovals. Spread walnut filling on three of the pastry ovals, and poppy-seed filling on other three. Cover pastry with filling evenly, roll up and twist into crescents. Put on lightly greased baking sheet, leaving sufficient space between crescents. Brush tops with beaten egg, keep warm for half an hour, brush tops with egg again, and now keep in cool place till egg dries and marbles. Bake in a medium oven for about 35—40 mins.

You can also make the crescents much smaller. In this case make about 25 small-size crescents filled with poppy-seed and about the same number filled with walnut filling.

Poppy-seed filling: Make a syrup of 9 oz. sugar and 2 gills water; scald the ground poppy-seeds with it, then add grated lemon peel and half a teaspoonful ground cinnamon. Let it cool before using.

Ground walnut filling: Boil a syrup from ½ lb. sugar and 1½ gill water. Pour over ground walnuts. Add half a tsp. of ground cinnamon, grated lemon peel and 1 oz. bread-crumbs. Let it cool.

Bake it in a hot oven. Prepare walnut or poppy-seed roll in the same way, but instead of an oval, roll pastry out into an oblong, and after filling roll it up and leave in a straight shape. Take care not to make the filling too thick or too thin because otherwise the pastry breaks.

Love Letters

Ingredients: 9 oz. flour, 4½ oz. sugar, 5 oz. butter, 6 eggs, 1 oz. yeast, 1 tbsp. sour cream, a little vanilla sugar, 3½ oz. ground walnuts, 1½ gill milk, grated rind of ¼ lemon.

Knead a light dough of ½ lb. flour, 5 oz. butter, yolks of 4 eggs, 3 oz. sugar, sour cream, yeast and a little vanilla sugar. Let it stand for a while.

Filling: Boil 1½ gill milk, mixed with 2 oz. sugar, 2 eggs, 1 tsp. flour and grated rind of ¼ lemon, stirring all the time. When mixture has thickened, combine with ground walnuts.

Roll pastry to the thickness of a match-stick and cut into oblongs. Put filling in middle, fold four sides of pastry over it. Bake in a moderate oven and serve sprinkled with vanilla sugar.

Walnut Buns

Ingredients: 5 oz. ground walnuts, 3 oz. sugar, 2 oz. butter, a little ground cinnamon, 1 egg, 1¼ lb. raised puff pastry.

Roll out raised puff pastry to pencil-thickness, brush with melted butter, sprinkle with ground walnuts, and sugar mixed with ground cinnamon. Roll up and cut roll into two-inch slices, but not quite down to bottom. Butter baking tin, put pastry rolls in it. Brush top with beaten egg and let it stand for half an hour. Bake in medium oven till golden-brown.

Cottage Cheese Buns

Ingredients: ½ lb. cottage cheese, 2 tbsp. sour cream, 2 eggs, grated rind of ½ lemon, 3 oz. sugar, a few whole cloves, 1 oz. raisins, 1¼ lb. raised puff pastry.

Press cottage cheese through sieve. Mix it in a basin with sour cream, one tbsp. of castor sugar, the yolks of two eggs, raisins, grated lemon rind and lastly with the whites of two eggs, whipped well with a tbsp. castor sugar.

Roll out raised puff pastry, cut into 3-inch squares. Put a spoonful of filling in middle of each square, and brushing the corners with beaten egg, fold them over filling so as to form smaller squares, stick a clove in middle of each square, as if to "pin" corners which meet in middle. Put buns in a baking tin, brush with egg, and let stand for 20—30 mins., then bake in a hot oven till golden-brown. Serve hot sprinkled with vanilla sugar.

Poppy-seed Buns

Ingredients: 10 oz. ground poppy-seeds, 3 oz. sugar, 3½ oz. honey, 1 oz. bread-crumbs, 2 gills water or milk, 2—3 portions of apple or pear compote, 1¼ lb. raised puff pastry.

Boil milk with sugar. Add ground poppy-seeds, apples or pears cut into small pieces, honey and lastly the fine, white bread-crumbs. Let filling cool. Proceed as for cottage cheese buns. Serve hot.

Jam Crescents

Ingredients: 1 lb. apricot or raspberry jam, 1 egg, 2 oz. walnuts or almonds, 2 oz. granulated sugar, 1¼ lb. raised puff pastry.

Roll out raised puff pastry to usual thickness, and cut into triangles. Put jam on middle of each, and roll triangles into crescent shapes. Put in lightly greased baking tin, brush with beaten egg. Mix coarsely chopped walnuts or almonds with granulated sugar, sprinkle on top of crescents. Let crescents stand for a while, then bake in a hot oven. Serve immediately, dredged with vanilla sugar.

Vienna Squares

Ingredients: 2 oz. ground almonds, 2 oz. sugar, 3½ oz. flour, 3½ oz. butter, grated rind of ½ lemon, a little ground cinnamon, 3 oz. ground walnuts, 3 oz. sugar, a little vanilla, 1 tsp. rum, cream, vanilla sugar.

Make a mixture of finely ground almonds, sugar, flour, butter, grated rind of ½ lemon and ground cinnamon and knead well. Roll out and put on baking sheet. Bake in a slow oven. Divide in two while still hot. Cut one half into small squares. Cover other half with the following mixture: Combine ground walnuts, 3 oz. castor sugar and a little vanilla sugar with a teaspoonful of rum, and add as much cream as necessary for a creamy consistency.

Lay small squares of pastry on top of filling, so that sides touch. Cut bottom layer of pastry into squares along the edges of the covering squares. Sprinkle with vanilla sugar.

Cottage Cheese Wallets

Ingredients: Raised puff pastry (amount: as yielded by basic recipe). Filling: ¾ lb. cottage cheese, 7 oz. sugar, 1 oz. bread-crumbs, 2 tbsp. sour cream, 2 oz. butter, 4 eggs, some grated lemon rind.

Roll out pastry to the thickness of your little finger, cut into squares, and put filling in middle of each. Gather the four corners of pastry, press them together over filling. Brush with beaten egg, bake in a hot oven.

For the filling use sweet, dry cottage cheese creamed with 7. oz. castor sugar, bread-crumbs, sour cream, butter, eggs, and lemon peel.

Almond Wallets

Ingredients: Raised puff pastry (see basic recipe).
Filling: 5 oz. ground almonds, 3 oz. castor sugar, 2 yolks of eggs, 1 oz. butter.

Prepare pastry according to raised puff pastry recipe. Mix ground almonds, castor sugar, yolks of eggs and butter. Roll out and cut pastry, put almond filling in middle of each square and make wallets as above under Cottage Cheese Wallets. Bake and sprinkle with castor sugar before serving.

Plain Fruit Tart

Ingredients: 5 oz. butter, 5 oz. sugar, 5 eggs, 5 oz. flour, 1¾ lb. fruit washed and trimmed, 7 oz. sugar.

Cream butter with castor sugar and yolks of 4 eggs. Add 4 whites and flour; mix thoroughly. Divide in two, roll out and line bottom of baking tin with one half of pastry. Arrange cleaned and stoned fruit on top evenly. The fruit may be of any sort; raspberries, apricots, plums, etc. or preserved fruit carefully drained.

Sprinkle top of fruit layer with 7 oz. castor sugar and cover with other half of rolled-out pastry. Brush top with beaten egg and bake it in a moderate oven. It is advisable to bake first layer of pastry for about 10 mins. before spreading with fruit. In this way the pastry will not become soggy from the juice.

Chelsea Buns (Plain)

Ingredients: 1 lb. flour, 3 eggs, 1 oz. yeast, 7 oz. sugar, 4½ oz. ground walnuts, 7 oz. butter, 2 oz. sultanas, ½ pt. milk, 2 oz. lard, pinch of ground cinnamon.

Make a dough of the flour, eggs, yeast, milk, a pinch of salt and 2 oz. sugar. Let it rise for half an hour in a warm place. Roll it out and cover with filling made of 7 oz. butter creamed with 4½ oz. ground walnuts, 5 oz. castor sugar, 2 oz. sultanas and a little ground cinnamon.

Roll up pastry and cut into two-inch slices. Butter baking tin, lay pastry rolls in it. Let them rise for half an hour, then bake in a hot oven, basting once or twice with a little sweetened cream.

Apples in Their Jackets

Ingredients: 1 lb. puff pastry, 1 lb. apples pared, 7 oz. apricot jam, 2 oz. castor sugar and a little ground cinnamon.

For pastry see Puff pastry recipe. Roll out pastry to pencil-thickness, cut into squares, put grated or chopped apple on middle of each. Sprinkle with mixture of castor sugar and ground cinnamon, dab a teaspoonful of jam on each (optional). Fold corners of pastry squares over mixture, brush with beaten egg and bake in a hot oven.

Leaf-lard Pastry

Ingredients: ½ lb. leaf-lard, ½ lb. flour, pinch of salt, ½ oz. yeast, yolk of 1 egg, ½ lemon.

Soak lard overnight in cold water. Then press through a wire sieve or shred with knife. Take half of flour, add a pinch of salt and with the help of a knife work into lard. Shape into oblong, put aside and chill. Make a pliable dough with other half of flour with yeast, the yolk of one egg, lemon-juice and a little water. If used for sweet pastry add a spoonful of sugar as well. Roll out to an oblong, place lard mixture in middle, fold four sides of pastry over, press together lightly with rolling pin, and roll out to a thick oblong. Keep in a cold place for ¼ hr., then repeat rolling-out operation as above. Repeat three times, leaving pastry in a cool place between times.

Finally roll out pastry to finger-thickness and cut into scones, squares or oblongs, as needed. Bake in a very hot oven.

SCONES

Plain Scones

Ingredients: 1 oz. yeast, 2 lb. flour, 1 gill oil, 2 oz. sugar, pinch of salt.

Mix yeast with a little lukewarm water and sugar; let it rise. Rub oil into flour, add a pinch of salt and leavened yeast batter; knead into a stiffish dough. Put aside for an hour, then roll pastry out, cut into neat rounds with scone-cutter. Place scones on baking tin, brush tops with a little syrup made of sugar and water. Bake in a hot oven till golden-brown.

Lard may be used instead of oil if preferred.

Crackling Scones

Ingredients: 10 oz. flour, 3 oz. pork cracklings, 3½ oz. lard, yolks of 2 eggs, ½ oz. yeast, a small tsp. salt, a little sour cream.

Take flour, chopped cracklings, lard, yolks of 2 eggs, and yeast diluted in 1 gill sour cream and knead into a soft dough. Roll out on pastry-board, three times; roll out again to the thickness of two fingers. Scoring criss-cross pattern on top with a sharp knife, cut out scones, place them on baking-tin and let them rise for about 1—1½ hr; brush with beaten egg and bake in a hot oven. Serve hot.

Sweet Butter Scones

Ingredients: 10 oz. butter, 10 oz. flour, yolks of 2 eggs, pinch of salt, 2½ tbsp. castor sugar, 1—2 teaspoonful of rum.

Rub butter well into flour. Add yolks of 2 eggs, pinch of salt, 2½ tbsp. castor sugar and one or two tsp. rum. Roll out to thickness of a finger, cut into scones, brush top with beaten egg and bake in a moderate oven.

Butter Scones

Ingredients: ¾ lb. flour, ½ lb. butter, 5 eggs, 1½ gill sour cream, 1 gill milk, 1 oz. yeast, 3 lumps of sugar, pinch of salt.

Rub flour into butter. Soak yeast in a little lukewarm milk and knead this and 4 eggs, pinch of salt, sugar and 4 tbsp. sour cream into a light dough. Put on a floured pastry-board, roll out three times at half-hour intervals. The fourth time, roll out an inch thick, cut out with scone cutter, brush with beaten egg and bake in a hot oven. Serve hot.

Puff Pastry Scones

Take equal weights of flour and butter. The flour should be dry and sifted and the butter hard. Take 1 oz. of both the flour and the butter and put them aside. Take the larger amount of butter and knead it well together with the 1 oz. flour. Now take the large amount of flour, knead into a stiffish dough with a little cold water and a dash of salt. Set aside both mixtures and leave for 15 mins. in a cool place. (The pastry itself should be made in a cool place.) Then roll out to the shape of oblong, on a floury pastry-board, thin side towards you. Place the butter and flour mixture on it, fold over all four corners of the dough and roll out again, this time with broad side of oblong towards you. Fold over both sides so as to meet in the middle. Repeat this operation two or three times at twenty-minute intervals. Do not handle pastry unless it is absolutely necessary, otherwise use the rolling pin. Use as little flour as possible for rolling out, and brush off surplus.

Roll out pastry for the last time to about pencil-thickness, stamp out scones and put them in baking pan. Brush top of scones with beaten egg, taking care not to let the egg run down sides of pastry. Bake in a hot oven and serve immediately.

Lard Scones

Ingredients: ¾ lb. flour, 5 oz. lard, 1 gill sour cream, 3 eggs, ½ tsp. salt, 1 oz. yeast, 2 tbsp. milk, 2 lumps of sugar.

Rub flour into lard; add sour cream, the yolks of 2 eggs, a little salt, yeast mixed with milk, and 2 lumps of sugar. Knead well together, put aside for an hour. Roll out to the thickness of an inch. Score top of pastry in lattice pattern and bake in a hot oven.

Potato Scones
(About 25 scones)

Ingredients: 7 oz. flour, 7 oz. butter, 7 oz. baked potatoes mashed, 1 oz. salt, 1 egg.

Bake potatoes in their jacket, mash and weigh out 7 oz., and knead with flour, butter and salt. Chill pastry for about 1 hr., then roll out and fold twice according to puff pastry recipe; roll out again and chill for another hour. Stamp out with scone cutter, put scones on a baking sheet, brush tops with beaten egg. Bake in a hot oven.

The remainder of pastry can be kneaded together folded once and used for more scones. Serve hot.

Potato Griddle Cakes

Ingredients: 10 oz. flour, 7 oz. potatoes (peeled, cooked and mashed), $\frac{1}{2}$ oz. yeast, $\frac{1}{2}$ tsp. salt, 1 tsp. sugar, $2\frac{1}{2}$ oz. lard, 1 gill milk, 1 tbsp. water.

If the weather is cold sieve flour the day before using it and let it stand overnight in a warm spot.

Peel, cook, drain and mash potatoes; let them cool. Mix crumbled yeast and sugar well. When yeast becomes liquid from stirring, add a little flour and lukewarm milk, mix well and put aside to rise. When the yeast has risen sufficiently, make a light dough of the flour, the mashed potatoes, a little lukewarm milk, a little water, salt and the yeast. Keep dough warm till it has risen, then roll it out to pencil-thickness; cut into squares and fry cakes in hot fat or oil. Score cakes with knife in one or two places before frying.

SHORTBREADS AND BISCUITS

Plain Linzer Biscuits

Ingredients: $1\frac{1}{2}$ lb. flour, 7 oz. butter, 5 oz. lard, 7 oz. sugar, 2 eggs, 2 oz. ground hazelnuts, pinch of cinnamon, a half a tsp. bicarbonate of soda, grated rind of half a lemon.

Weigh and put on the pastry-board the flour, butter and lard. Rub well together, add the sugar, ground hazelnuts, 2 whole eggs, bicarbonate of soda, grated lemon ring and a pinch of cinnamon. Knead together lightly, form into a loaf and keep in a cold place for one hr. Roll out to pencil-thickness;

stamp out with different biscuit cutters to various shapes. Put biscuits on a baking sheet, brush tops with beaten egg, sprinkle with coarsely chopped almonds, and bake in a moderate oven till biscuits are of a light golden colour.

Ground walnuts or almonds may be used instead of hazelnuts.

Salt Biscuits

Ingredients: 1 lb. flour, 10 oz. butter, 2 eggs, 1 gill sour milk, ¾ oz. salt, 1 tsp. yeast, 2 oz. grated cheese, pinch of caraway seeds.

Rub butter with flour, yeast and salt, add the yolks of two eggs and the sour milk and knead mixture into a loaf. About 20 mins. later roll out pastry, brush with beaten egg, and fold twice at 15-minute intervals. Roll out third time of half-an-inch thickness and cut different shapes (half-moons, rounds, straws, etc.) of pastry. Put them on a baking tin, brush tops with beaten egg, and sprinkle with grated cheese or caraway seeds (optional).

Bake in a moderate oven till golden-brown.

Savoury Straws

Ingredients: 10 oz. flour, 6 oz. butter, ½ oz. yeast, 2 tbsp. sweet cream, ½ tsp. salt.

Knead flour with butter and salt, adding yeast dissolved in cream. Roll out to the thickness of your little finger, brush with white of egg, sprinkle with caraway seeds and cut into straws. Bake in a hot oven.

Caraway Squares

Ingredients: 4½ oz. butter, 2 eggs, 4 tbsp. sour cream, ½ tsp. salt, pinch of ground black pepper, 10 oz. flour, ½ tsp. caraway seeds.

Knead the butter lightly together with the flour, the yolks of eggs, sour cream, salt and pepper. Roll out to pencil-thickness, brush top with beaten egg, sprinkle with salt and caraway seeds and cut into squares. Bake quickly in a hot oven.

Butter Biscuits

Ingredients: ¾ lb. flour, 3½ oz. butter, 1 egg, 1 gill milk, 3½ oz. sugar flavoured with vanilla, half a tsp. bicarbonate of soda.

Rub the flour, and sugar into butter. Combine with egg-yolk and a little milk and knead into a fairly stiff paste. Roll it out, cut fancy shapes with biscuit cutters. Bake in a moderate oven.

Turn tin during baking so that biscuits bake evenly.

Fine Linzer Shortbread

Ingredients: 1 lb. flour, ½ lb. butter, 4½ oz. castor sugar, 1 packet of vanilla sugar, 2 eggs, 1 tsp. rum, grated rind of ¼ lemon.

Rub flour into butter and add sugar and vanilla sugar, yolks of two eggs, grated lemon rind and rum; knead well together. Leave in a cool place for about an hour. Roll out on well floured pastry-board to pencil-thickness, cut into fancy shapes with biscuit cutters, brush top with whites of egg, and bake to a nice golden colour. (You can stick pairs of the same shape together, using fine apricot jam.)

Vanilla Crescents

Ingredients: 2 eggs, 6 oz. flour, 2½ oz. butter, 2 oz. sugar, 2 packets of vanilla sugar, 1 tsp. rum.

Remove yolks of two hard-boiled eggs, and rub through sieve. Knead together the flour, butter, sugar, vanilla sugar, rum and mashed egg-yolks. Lay greaseproof paper on a baking sheet and with the help of an icing bag, press little crescents onto the greaseproof paper. Bake in a medium oven, let crescents cool, and sprinkle with vanilla sugar.

Tea Crescents

Ingredients: 4½ oz. flour, 3½ oz. sugar, 6 eggs, 1 oz. vanilla sugar, 2 oz. walnuts ground, 3½ oz. raspberry jam or other jam.

Beat well 3 whole eggs and yolks of 3 more eggs with sugar flavoured with vanilla in top of double saucepan until the mixture thickens and becomes warm. Remove from heat and continue stirring until cool. Put back over steam and keep beating or stirring until warm again. Remove from heat and once again stir until cool. Now blend in flour. Line baking sheet with greaseproof paper. Squeeze crescents of the mixture onto paper by means of an icing bag. Strew crescents with coarsely chopped walnuts. Bake in moderate oven till light golden. When cool, stick together pairs of crescents with jam. Dregde with vanilla sugar.

Sweet Chips

Ingredients: 3 oz. sugar, 3 eggs, 3½ oz. flour, grated rind of half a lemon, 2 oz. almonds.

Beat whites of eggs stiffly with castor sugar. Add flour and grated lemon peel, mix lightly.

Put mixture in icing bag and squeeze straws on a greased and floured baking sheet. Then knock tin a few times against the table to get the pastry to flatten. Dredge with chopped almonds and bake in a slow oven. Then take out straws one by one, twist each around handle of wooden spoon and slip off immediately. This should be done while the pastry is still hot, preferably in or close to the open oven.

Raisin Biscuits

Ingredients: 5 eggs, 3½ oz. sugar, 3½ oz. flour, 1 oz. butter, 1 oz. raisins and 4½ oz. chocolate fondant.

Cream 5 whole eggs and sugar in top of double saucepan over the cooker. When it is warm, but not hot take off the cooker and continue beating until it turns into a cold, creamy mass. Then lightly blend in the flour and the butter (melted but not hot); bake in a greased and floured baking tin in a moderate oven and glaze with chocolate fondant.

Glazing may be omitted. In that case dredge biscuits with castor sugar.

Fruit Bread

Ingredients: 9 eggs, 2½ oz. walnuts, 7 oz. candied fruits, a liqueur-glass of rum, 5 oz. sugar, 7 oz. flour, 2½ oz. butter, peel of ½ lemon.

Sprinkle chopped walnuts and the candied fruit with rum and add grated lemon peel. Beat the yolks of 6 eggs and 3 whole eggs with castor sugar, in top of double saucepan over low heat until thick; then remove from cooker and mix until cold. When cold, add flour, then the chopped candied fruit and finally blend in lightly the melted, but not hot butter. Pour into an oblong buttered and floured baking tin and bake in a moderate oven for 40—50 mins. Turn onto floured pastry-board and when cold, cut into slices. Dredge with vanilla sugar.

Almond Crescents

Ingredients: ½ lb. ground blanched almonds, ½ lb. castor sugar, whites of 2 eggs, 4½ oz. chopped or ground almonds.

Blanch almonds, grind and mix with castor sugar and whites of eggs. Then make a smooth paste as in the recipe for walnut marzipan. Form crescents of this paste, roll them in chopped, blanched almonds and bake in a greased tin in a moderate oven until cooked but still moist.

Hazelnut Kisses

Ingredients: 10 oz. sugar, 5 oz. ground hazelnuts, whites of 3 eggs, peel of half a lemon.

Mix hazelnuts with sugar, whites of egg, some grated lemon peel and pound smooth in mortar. Lay greaseproof paper on baking sheet and squeeze mixture from icing bag in little heaps onto the sheet. Bake in moderate oven.

When the pastry has cooled, turn paper and wet underside to remove kisses easily. The kisses may be made with ground almonds or walnuts instead of the hazelnuts.

Hazelnut Grillage

Ingredients: 5 oz. hazelnuts (or walnuts or almonds), 7 oz. sugar.

Lightly roast hazelnuts in oven, rub skin off with a dry cloth and chop roughly. Melt and lightly brown castor sugar in frying pan, add nuts mix and transfer mixture into an oiled tin to keep warm in open oven. Cut into several portions, rolling each to the right thickness on an oiled pastry-board or tin. Cut into smaller pieces while hot, keeping the rest warm in oven. Walnut and almond grillage are made the same way. Then grillage may be used to decorate cakes. Handle with caution as it can get very hot.

If made with almonds, scald almonds, blanch and then wipe dry.

Honey Cake I

Ingredients: 1 lb. honey, 1 lb. flour, 7 oz. ground and roasted hazelnuts or almonds, 4 whole eggs, ¼ cup of rum, a little cinnamon and clove, a pinch of bicarbonate of soda and a few blanched almonds.

Bring honey to boil and taking it off the cooker mix with the flour. Set it aside for ½ day or 1 day. Then add ground hazelnuts or almonds, the eggs, the rum, the seasonings and the bicarbonate of soda. Knead well. Bake in one piece or cut into kisses or other shapes on a floured baking sheet. Before baking cut blanched almonds in half and press half an almond into the middle of every kiss.

Debrecen Honey Cake

Ingredients: 1 lb. honey, 1 lb. flour, ½ oz. potash, 4½ oz. castor sugar, yolks of 3 eggs.

Boil honey and when boiling fast, remove from cooker and mix with half of flour and the potash; knead well. Leave for 2 or 3 hrs. The turn onto pastry-board and add other half of flour, castor sugar and the yolks of 3 eggs; mix and knead well. Roll out this dough to pencil-thickness and cut or stamp to desired shapes. Bake on floured baking sheet in hot oven. To glaze, brush top with sweetened milk while it is still hot.

Nuremberg Honey Scones

Ingredients: 1 lb. honey, ½ lb. white wheat flour, ½ lb. rye flour, yolks of 2 eggs, ¼ oz. potash, grated lemon peel, ground cinnamon and, if desired, clove, 2 oz. blanched almonds.

Bring honey to the boil, take off cooker and add half of both kinds of flour to the honey. Leave for 24 hrs. and then turning onto pastry-board, add the rest of the flour, yolks of eggs, potash, lemon peel and seasoning. Knead well and then put aside for two hrs. Then roll out to pencil-thickness, cut or stamp to desired shapes and bake, first pressing a blanched almond into the middle of each piece.

Honey Cake II

Ingredients: 2 gills honey, 3 oz. sugar, 1 oz. almonds, 1 oz. candied orange peel, ¼ oz. potash, 1 tbsp. rum, 1¼ lb. white flour.

Boil honey with castor sugar in a saucepan. When honey mixture has browned, add the almonds and orange peel—both chopped into longish pieces—and mix with the flour. Flavour with rum. When the dough has cooled a little, mix in a pinch of potash and then leave overnight. The next day lightly grease and dust tin of desired size and shape with flour, put in dough and bake in a moderate oven until brown.

Honey Kisses

Ingredients: 10 oz. flour, 5 oz. sugar, 2 eggs, 2 tbsp. warmed honey, pinch of ground cloves and cinnamon, 1 tsp. bicarbonate of soda.

Knead ingredients well and then leave dough for a day. Roll out to the thickness of a pencil and stamp out with scone cutter. Brush tops with beaten egg, press half a blanched almond into the middle of each kiss and bake in a moderate oven.

Cat's Tongue

Ingredients: 5 oz. flour, 6 eggs, 5 oz. sugar, 2 gills sweet cream, 3½ oz. cream of the kind desired.

Beat the whites of eggs stiff, gradually adding sugar and 3½ oz. flour; then blend in cream. Grease a tin with butter and dust with flour. From icing bag squeeze out flat shapes to look like a modified figure 8 onto tin, and bake in a moderate oven until the edges begin to brown. When cool loosen with the edge of knife. Sandwich together in pairs with some kind of cream. Chocolate cream is recommended for the filling, but any other cream will do.

Sponge Cake

Ingredients: 6 eggs, 4½ oz. sugar, 4½ oz. flour.

Cream the yolks of 6 eggs with 2½ oz. castor sugar with a wooden spoon, or beater. Beat egg-whites stiff, gradually adding 2 oz. castor sugar. Gently fold egg-whites into cream and blend in flour as well. Put into tin lined with greaseproof paper and smooth over evenly. Bake in a moderate oven. Cool in baking tin, then turn out of tin and remove paper.

Swiss Roll

Ingredients: 6 eggs, 4½ oz. sugar, 6 oz. apricot jam, 3½ oz. flour.

Cream the yolks of 6 eggs, 1 oz. sugar in a bowl with egg-beater. Beat whites stiff, gradually adding 2½ oz. castor sugar. Gently fold stiff egg-whites into creamed yolks, gradually mixing in the flour too. Line a tin with greaseproof paper and spread the mixture on it to the thickness of a finger. Bake in a hot oven till light golden. When done turn onto floured paper, remove browned greaseproof paper and immediately fill with jam. Then roll up with the help of the paper under it. When cool, remove paper and slice, dredging slices with castor sugar. Instead of the apricot jam, you can use raspberry, strawberry or any other jam. May be served with wine sauce.

Toasted Sponge Cake

Ingredients: 10 eggs, 4½ oz. castor sugar, 6 oz. flour, 2½ oz. butter.

One day before needed make a sponge cake as follows. Put 5 whole eggs and yolks of 5 eggs into the top of a large double saucepan and mix well with castor sugar, using egg-beater. Then beat over very low heat. Remove from cooker and beat until cool. Then add the flour and 1½ oz. melted, not too hot butter. Grease an oblong tin with butter and dust with flour; then fill it three quarters full with the mixture. Bake in a moderate oven and turn onto a cake-rack. The next day cut sponge cake into slices of the thickness of your finger: Arrange slices on a tin and toast lightly in a hot oven.

Water Sponge Cake

Ingredients: 3 eggs, 5 oz. sugar, 5 oz. flour, 5 oz. apricot jam.

Cream yolks of 3 eggs with sugar, add 3 tbsp. water and mix well with flour. Fold in stiffly beaten whites of eggs. Put into greased and floured tin, and bake in a slow oven. Cut into two layers. Spread bottom layer with apricot jam and cover with top layer. Slice and dredge with sugar.

Tousled Cakes

Ingredients: ¾ lb. flour, 2½ oz. lard, 4½ oz. castor sugar, 2 whole eggs, ½ packet of baking powder, a little vanilla.

Knead ingredients and leave pastry overnight. Attach shaper to mincer and put pastry through. Brush with egg and bake in a moderate oven till light golden.

Meringue Kisses

Ingredients: The whites of four eggs, 10 oz. castor sugar, 7 oz. shelled walnuts.

Beat the whites of the eggs with the sugar in top of a double saucepan over steaming water. Remove from steam and continue beating until quite stiff. Then add roughly chopped walnuts. With the help of a tablespoon arrange little heaps on a greased and floured baking sheet. Dry in a slow oven.

Potato Pastry

Ingredients: ½ lb. potatoes cooked and mashed, ½ lb. flour, 3½ oz. lard, 3½ oz. castor sugar, 1 whole egg, 1 tsp. bicarbonate of soda, dash of salt, 7 oz. apricot jam.

Knead ingredients together and divide pastry in half. Roll out one portion and put in a greased tin, spreading apricot jam on top. Roll out other half and cover the pastry spread with jam in tin. Bake without brushing top. Serve cut in lozenges and dredged with sugar.

Cocoa Slices

Ingredients: 3 eggs, 7 oz. sugar, 7 oz. flour, 2 oz. lard, 1 tsp. cocoa, 1 gill black coffee, 1 packet of baking powder, 1 liqueur-glass of rum, ½ packet of vanilla sugar.

Cream the yolks of three eggs with the sugar and lard. Mix in black coffee, the flour and the baking powder and fold in stiffly beaten whites of egg. Flavour with vanilla sugar. Bake in a greased and floured tin in a slow oven. When cool, cut into two layers and fill with some kind of jam or cream. Cut in slices and dredge with sugar.

Walnut Slices

Ingredients: 3 eggs, 10 oz. sugar, 10 oz. flour, 3 oz. margarine, 1 packet of baking powder, grated lemon peel, 1½ gill milk, 1 oz. ground walnuts, ½ lb. apricot jam.

Cream the yolks of two eggs with the margarine and sugar and then add the flour, walnuts and the baking powder and finally fold in the stiffly beaten whites of three eggs. Bake in a greased and floured tin, in a moderate oven. When cool cut into two layers and fill with apricot or raspberry jam. Cut into slices and dredge with sugar.

Bishop's Bread

Ingredients: 8 eggs, 7 oz. sugar, 3½ oz. ground walnuts, 2 oz. raisins, 5 oz. chopped candied fruits, 2 oz. butter, 7 oz. flour, grated peel of one lemon, ¼ stick of vanilla.

Beat 8 whole eggs and 7 oz. sugar with egg-beater in top of double sauce-pan, over hot water. Remove from cooker when the mixture is warm but not hot. Continue beating until cool and creamy. Mix flour and ground walnuts and gently fold into egg-mixture. Next add melted butter and finally chopped candied fruits, raisins and lemon peel. Bake in a greased and floured tin in a moderate oven. Put the stick of vanilla into the egg mixture when you start beating and leave it until flour is mixed in. (Caution: Do not turn tin too early in oven, because in that case the pastry will not rise properly.)

Biscuits

Ingredients: 1¼ lb. flour, 7 oz. castor sugar, 2 whole eggs, 3½ oz. lard, 1 packet of baking powder, 1 packet of vanilla sugar, a little milk and some ground walnuts or almonds.

Knead ingredients with milk. Leave pastry for 2 or 3 hrs. and then roll out, not too thin, and stamp out with fancy biscuit cutters. Put in tin, brush with beaten egg, sprinkle with ground walnuts or almonds mixed with granulated sugar, and bake in a slow oven.

Walnut Roll with Rum Sauce

Ingredients: 6 eggs, 1 oz. walnuts, 3 oz. sugar, 1 oz. butter, 2 oz. flour, ½ oz. sponge cake crumbs, grated peel of ½ lemon, pinch of cinnamon, 3½ oz. apricot jam, ½ oz. vanilla sugar.

Grind walnuts and pound smooth with one egg in a mortar. Cream well the yolks of five eggs and 2 oz. castor sugar with walnut mixture. Beat the whites of 5 eggs stiff, gradually adding 1 oz. castor sugar, and carefully fold into yolk mixture. Add the flour mixed with the sponge cake crumbs, the lemon peel and the cinnamon, and finally the melted lukewarm butter.

Line a baking tin with greaseproof paper and spread pastry in it to the thickness of your finger. Bake in a brisk oven. Turn onto a floured pastry-board as soon as ready, remove paper, spread with apricot jam and roll up immediately. Wrap into paper and let roll cool. When completely cool cut into slices and dredge with castor sugar. Serve with rum sauce in a separate sauceboat.

Rum Sauce

Ingredients: 3 cups milk, 3 eggs, 2 gills cream, 6 oz. sugar, 1 oz. flour, a little vanilla, ⅓ cup of raspberry syrup and 1 tbsp. rum.

Boil milk with 3½ oz. sugar and vanilla. Mix well 1 whole egg and the yolks of 2 eggs in the top of a double saucepan, carefully adding 1 cupful of hot milk. Then blend in flour, and mix until smooth. Now add the rest of the milk at once, put on the cooker and cook, stirring continuously until sauce thickens into a cream. Put through a sieve and when cool combine with rum, raspberry syrup and the stiffly whipped cream which has been sweetened with the rest of the sugar. Serve this sauce with walnut roll.

SWEETS WHICH NEED NO BAKING

Rum Cherry Balls

Ingredients: 5 oz. chocolate, 5 oz. castor sugar, 5 oz. ground walnuts, 3½ oz. apricot jam, 7 oz. morello cherries preserved in rum syrup, 3½ oz. coarsely grated chocolate.

Grate chocolate and mix with castor sugar, ground walnuts and apricot jam to make a pliable paste. (Do not add all of the prescribed amount of the apricot jam if this would make the mixture too soft.) Stone morello cherries and then make balls of the paste putting a cherry in the middle of each. Roll balls in a coarsely grated chocolate and serve in individual paper cases. The paste may be flavoured with rum or any other liqueur.

Coffee Balls

Ingredients: 1 lb. cake or biscuits crumbs, 1 oz. ground coffee, 5 oz. castor sugar, 2 oz. cocoa and 3½ oz. apricot jam.

Left-overs from any cake or sweet biscuits may be used for this sweet with the exception of raised dough. If no left-overs are available, you can crumble sponge fingers or any kind of inexpensive sweet biscuits.

Crumble left-over cakes and biscuits and sprinkle with strong coffee, made of the ground coffee, so as to get a moist but not saturated mixture. Add half of the sugar and cocoa and as much apricot jam as will turn the mixture into an easily-moulded paste. Shape balls of this paste, roll them in the rest of the cocoa-and-sugar mixture and serve in individual paper cases.

In-law Cake
(You can't spoil it!)

Ingredients: 25 sponge fingers, 2 pt. milk, 2 oz. sugar, 1 tbsp. rum, 3½ oz. raisins or candied fruit, 2 gills cream. For the cream filling: 2 pt. of milk, yolks of 4 eggs, 3½ oz. flour, 1 oz. cocoa, 3 oz. sugar, ¼ stick of vanilla.

Mix boiled milk with rum and sugar and dip sponge fingers in the milk. Arrange a layer of the soaked (but not oversoaked!) sponge fingers in the dish in which you want to serve cake. Spread half of the vanilla cream (which see below) on this layer and cover with a second layer of soaked sponge fingers. Spread second layer with the other half of the vanilla cream, mixed with the cocoa. Cover with a third layer of sponge fingers. Sprinkle every layer of cream with raisins or candied fruits. Decorate cake with whipped cream, using an icing bag.

Prepare vanilla cream as follows: Mix yolks of four eggs and the flour in top of double saucepan with a little milk until smooth. Boil the rest of the milk with the sugar adding the vanilla stick. Quickly pour hot milk into the saucepan containing the yolks and, mixing with beater, cook till it bubbles. Remove from heat and take out vanilla stick. Spread cake with this vanilla cream as explained above, dividing cream into two equal portions and flavouring one portion with cocoa.

Biscuit Cake
(You can't spoil it!)

Ingredients: 1 oz. ground coffee, 1 lb. inexpensive biscuits, 7 oz. currant or morello cherry jam (or any other jam which is not too sweet), 3½ oz. ground walnuts, 2 gills cream. For cream: 1 pt. milk, yolks of 2 eggs, 2 oz. flour, 1 oz. sugar, a little vanilla sugar.

Make strong coffee from the ground coffee. Divide biscuits into three equal portions. Soak one third in coffee and arrange flat on a dish. Spread with vanilla cream made of milk according to the procedure explained under In-law Cake above. Dredge with ground walnuts and cover with second third of biscuits dipped in coffee. Now spread with jam and sprinkle with the rest of the walnuts and cover with third part of biscuits. Decorate cake with whipped cream using an icing bag.

Semolina Pudding I

Ingredients: 1 quart of milk, 3 oz. semolina, whites of eggs, 4½ oz. sugar.

Boil milk and when boiling, cook semolina and sugar in it. Cook for 10 mins., stirring all the time and then gradually fold in stiffly beaten whites of five eggs, while still continuing cooking. Rinse a mould with cold water and pour in mixture. Chill. Turn onto a flat dish and serve with raspberry or strawberry syrup.

Crumb Balls with Jam

Ingredients: 3½ oz. butter, 2 eggs, dash of salt, 2 oz. castor sugar, ½ lb. white bread-crumbs.

Cream 3 oz. butter and add two eggs. Continue creaming and then mix in as much of the bread-crumbs as will turn it into a paste which is easily moulded. Set it aside for 10 mins. and then shape balls with floury hands. Cook balls in fast-boiling water. Roll in bread-crumbs browned in butter, dredge with castor sugar and serve with cherry, morello cherry or currant jam.

276

FRIED CAKES AND SWEETS

Hungarian Pancakes
(15 — 20 pancakes)

Ingredients: 10 oz. flour, 2 eggs, 2½ oz. sugar, 2 gills milk, 2 oz. lard, dash of salt.

Mix a whole egg and the yolk of one egg with flour and a dash of salt. Add milk or soda water and mix well. The batter should be smooth and not too thick. Make thin pancakes, frying both sides lightly in greased pan. Spread pancakes with jam, ground walnuts, ground poppy-seeds, cocoa, or cottage cheese. It is very good to make the batter with one half milk and one half soda water.

Apple Pancakes

Make the batter as for Hungarian pancakes and mix it with finely chopped or grated apples (1—1½ lb.) and fry whole mixture. Fold like a handkerchief and dredge with vanilla sugar.

Cabbage Pancakes

Ingredients: Hungarian pancake batter (q. v.), 2 lb. cabbage, pinch of salt, pepper, ½ lb. lard.

Make batter for Hungarian pancakes omitting sugar. Shred cabbage and brown it in fat; season with salt and pepper. Mix into batter. Fry pancakes of this mixture. If you find that the batter is too thick, thin with soda water.

Apple Fritters

Ingredients: 1 lb. apples, 5 oz. flour, 2 gills white wine, whites of 2 eggs, 2 oz. sugar and 3½ oz. lard.

Peel and core large cooking apples and cut into thin slices. Mix flour with wine and salt into a thick batter. Beat the whites of two eggs stiff, gradually adding 1 oz. sugar and mix with batter. Dip apple slices into this batter and fry golden-brown on both sides in deep fat. Remove from fat and drain. Dredge with sugar and cinnamon mixture and serve with wine custard.

Slipped Pancakes

Ingredients: 2 oz. butter, 5 oz. flour, 1 pt. milk, 3 eggs, 1 packet of vanilla sugar, 5 oz. sugar, 2 oz. lard.

Cream butter with yolks of three eggs and 2 oz. sugar; then add milk, flour and a dash of salt. Finally fold in stiffly beaten whites of 3 eggs. Heat fat in frying pan and when hot pour a tablespoonful of batter in to make a pancake a little thicker than usual. Fry one side over slow heat and then slip onto a dish. Dredge unfried side with vanilla sugar. Continue making pancakes as long as any batter is left, frying each only on one side and slipping over the top of the pancake below. Finally fry both sides of the last pancake and cover the others with it. Put into a hot oven for 10 mins. and serve dredged with vanilla sugar.

Another way to make this dish is to sprinkle sugar, grated chocolate, sweetened ground walnuts, or sweetened roasted and ground almonds between the layers instead of vanilla sugar. You can also whip the whites of the eggs stiff, adding 1 oz. sugar for every egg-white and spread the cake-like affair with this meringue. Decorate top with the help of icing bag. Bake for 10 mins. in hot oven and serve dredged with vanilla sugar.

Layered Pancakes

Ingredients: 10 pancakes, 4½ oz. shelled walnuts, 4½ oz. cottage cheese, 2 tbsp. cream, 1 oz. raisins, 3 eggs, 2 oz. chocolate, ½ lb. sugar, 5 oz. apricot jam, grated peel of ½ lemon, ¼ stick of vanilla.

Grind walnuts, and grate chocolate. Put cottage cheese through sieve and mix with the beaten egg and then flavour with lemon peel and a little sugar. Grease a tin with butter and put in first pancake; spread it with grated walnuts and sugar. Continue putting on pancake layers, spreading alternately with chocolate, apricot jam, raisins and cottage cheese mixture until all the different fillings and all the pancakes are used up. There should be a pancake on top. Put into oven for a short time and then spread with beaten egg-whites sprinkled with sugar. Put back into oven and after a short period of baking, when the meringue has set, take out and dredge with vanilla sugar. Cut like a cake for serving.

Apple Omelette

Ingredients: 1 lb. apples, 10 oz. flour, 2 eggs, 4—5 oz. lard, 3½ oz. sugar, 2 gills milk.

Peel and core cooking apples and cut into thin slices. Melt a little fat in pan and fry both sides of apple slices in hot fat. Make a thick Hungarian pancake batter of the yolks of two eggs, milk, as much water as is needed and the sweetened, stiffly beaten whites of two eggs. Melt a little fat in pan, put in a few of the fried apple slices and pour in a tbsp. batter to produce a thick pancake. Fry both sides. Pile the pancakes on top of each other, sprinkling each with sugar, and if desired with chopped walnuts as well. Serve hot cutting as you would cut a cake.

Omelette Soufflée

Ingredients: Whites of 15 eggs, 5 oz. sugar, 7 oz. jam.

Beat the egg-whites stiff with the sugar and add jam. (Apricot jam is the best.) Place this mixture into fireproof dish in a conical heap and brown quickly in hot oven, then serve. It is customary to press half an egg-shell on top of the heap, pour rum in it and light the rum just before serving.

Omelette Confiture

Ingredients: 15 eggs, 5 oz. sugar, ½ lb. flour, 7 oz. jam.

Separate yolks from the whites of eggs and put into different bowls. Cream yolks with part of the sugar and beat whites stiff with the rest of the sugar. Then fold in beaten whites into yolks, and blend in the flour with a wooden spoon. Put mixture into greased and floured tin and bake in a warm oven until still moist. Remove from oven and while the omelette is still hot, spread jam (apricot jam is best) on top. Fold in half and serve.

Omelette Surprise

Ingredients: 10 eggs, 10 oz. sugar, 1½ lb. ice-cream, 1 tsp. rum, 3½ oz. sponge cake, 3½ oz. candied fruit or compote. For the sponge cake: 2 eggs, 1 oz. sugar, 1 oz. flour.

First make the sponge cake (q. v.). When it has cooled, put part of it in the middle of fireproof dish on which you are going to serve omelette. Heap ice-cream on top and cover the sides of the heap with the rest of the sponge cake. (Generally vanilla ice-cream is used but different flavours may also be used if preferred.) Beat the whites of the 10 eggs stiff with the 10 oz. sugar, coat the ice-cream with part of this meringue; do not spoil shape of mound. Decorate with rest of the stiff whites by means of an icing bag, and with pieces of candied fruit or carefully drained preserved fruits, pressing them into sides. Put half an egg-shell on top. Dust the whole heap with castor sugar and bake quickly in hot oven so as to let meringue set.

Take out from oven and fill egg-shell with rum or cognac, light and serve.

Wafers may be substituted for the sponge cake.

Stuffed Apple Slices in Batter

Ingredients: 5 oz. flour, 2 tbsp. white wine, 3½ oz. sugar, ¼ stick vanilla, grated peel of ½ lemon, 2 gills milk, 1 lb. apples, 2 eggs, 3½ oz. lard.

Boil milk with 12 lumps of sugar and ¼ stick of vanilla. When it begins to boil, add ground walnuts and lemon peel, boil a little longer and set aside. This is the filling and it should be thick. Peel and core apples and cut into thin slices. Pair apple slices and sandwich each pair with the stuffing. Make a rather thick batter of the flour, white wine and a little lukewarm water and fold in the stiffly beaten whites of two eggs. Turn filled apple slices with a fork in the batter and fry in hot fat. Dredge with vanilla sugar or sugar and cinnamon mixture and serve hot with wine sauce in a separate dish.

Wine Sauce (Chaudeau)

Ingredients: 2 gills white wine, 2 eggs, 2 oz. sugar, grated peel of ¼ lemon, 5 oz. flour, ¼ stick of vanilla.

Mix wine, eggs and sugar well and flavour with vanilla and lemon peel. Add the flour, in the meantime stirring the mixture with an egg-beater over slow fire. When it rises remove from range.

Fritters

Ingredients: ½ lb. flour, 1 oz. butter, 2½ oz. vanilla sugar, 1 tbsp. sour cream, yolks of 2 eggs, ½ oz. yeast, dash of salt, 1 tbsp. rum, 7 oz. lard, 5 oz. apricot jam.

Rub flour into butter, add yolks of egg and the yeast dissolved in a little milk, a dash of salt, a teaspoonful of sugar, a tablespoonful of sour cream and a little rum. Knead and shape into a loaf. Set aside in a cool place for half an hour. Roll out to the thickness of a pencil. With fancy cutter cut out squares, about the width of a finger. Heat lard in a saucepan and put in fritters (not too many at once) and fry a golden-brown under lid. Drain on a sieve and serve dredged with vanilla sugar. Serve apricot jam separately.

Chocolate Doughnuts

Ingredients: 2 gills milk, 2 oz. butter, 1 tsp. sugar, 3 eggs, 5 oz. flour, vanilla sugar, 10 oz. lard.

Boil milk with butter, sugar and a dash of salt. Mix in the flour and when the mixture has cooled somewhat, add the eggs one at a time, beating well after each addition. Scoop out lumps of the mixture with a tablespoon and fry a deep golden-brown in hot fat. Dredge with vanilla sugar and serve with chocolate sauce (q. v.).

Cream Puffs
(20 pieces)

Ingredients: 3½ oz. butter, 3½ oz. flour, 2 tbsp. water, 3 eggs, 10 oz. whipped cream, 10 oz. vanilla cream (q. v.), 2 oz. sugar.

Put butter, flour and water into a saucepan and boil, stirring all the time. Remove from cooker and add 3 whole eggs, one by one, mixing well after each addition. Put mixture into icing bag and squeeze about 20 buns of about the same size onto a thinly-oiled baking sheet. Bake in a hot oven. When cool, cut off the top of every bun and put aside. Put vanilla cream through sieve to make it smooth and blend with the sweetened whipped cream. Attach star-shaped funnel to icing bag and fill puffs with a thick layer of cream. Replace tops and dust with castor sugar. Keep on ice if not served directly.

Éclairs
(20 pieces)

Ingredients: 3½ oz. butter, 3½ oz. flour, 2 tbsp. water, 3 eggs, 1¼ lb. coffee of chocolate cream, made with whipped cream (q. v.), 3½ oz. fondant.

The basic pastry is made like the pastry for cream puffs above, except that not buns but fingers are put on the baking sheet. Bake éclairs and glaze with brown or chocolate fondant, dipping them into lukewarm fondant and allowing fondant to set. Cut into top part so that the top should form a lid, and fill with coffee or chocolate cream made with thick cream.

Tipsy Friars

Ingredients: 3½ oz. bakery rolls, a day old, 10 oz. apricot or raspberry jam, ½ pt. white or red wine, 3 eggs, 7 oz. bread-crumbs, 7 oz. lard, 3½ oz. castor sugar.

Grate off crusts of bakery rolls, cut them in two, scoop out inside and fill with apricot or raspberry jam. Pair halves again and dip in red or white wine. Then turn in beaten egg and bread-crumbs and fry quickly, in hot fat. Serve dredged with sugar. Vanilla, chocolate or coffee cream may be substituted for the jam filling.

SWEET SOUFFLÉS

Vanilla Soufflé

Ingredients: 1½ gill milk, 2 oz. sugar, 4 eggs, 1 oz. butter, 1 packet of vanilla sugar, 1 oz. flour, ½ stick of vanilla.

Boil half of milk with ½ oz. sugar and vanilla. Mix flour with 1—2 tbsp. cold milk and add to hot milk. Cook a little, stirring all the time, and then set aside. Mix $\frac{1}{4}$ oz. butter and yolks of 2 eggs into milk mixture and then fold in the stiffly beaten whites of 3 eggs which have been sweetened with $\frac{1}{2}$ oz. vanilla sugar. Butter a fireproof dish and dredge with castor sugar. Put in mixture and bake slowly in moderate oven. Serve immediately dusted with sugar.

Almond, hazelnut, and chocolate soufflés are made similarly. Whichever of these ingredients is used, 1 oz. is needed. Grind almonds or hazelnuts finely before adding to milk. Serve vanilla sauce separately.

Vanilla Sauce: 1 pt. milk, $4\frac{1}{2}$ oz. sugar, 1 oz. flour, 2 eggs and vanilla flavouring are needed. Cook ingredients, stirring all the time, until mixture begins to boil. If not thick enough, thicken with a little flour and serve.

Raspberry Soufflé

Ingredients: 5 eggs, 3 oz. flour, 2 oz. butter, $1\frac{1}{2}$ oz. sugar, 2 tbsp. milk, 1 dessertspoon semolina and 5 oz. strawberry syrup for sauce.

Make as you would make vanilla soufflé and serve hot with raspberry syrup.

Apricot Sauce Made of Fresh Fruit

Stone 12 ripe apricots and put through a fine sieve. Thin the jelly-like substance obtained with $3\frac{1}{2}$ gills syrup made of 7 oz. sugar and 3 gills water. Keep boiling until the sauce begins to stick to the spoon. Keep removing scum with a brush. Put through sieve again and flavour with a tablespoonful of cherry brandy or other liqueur.

English Fried Apricots

Halve and stone 10 ripe apricots and cook in syrup for 8—10 mins. Drain through sieve. Put a dessertspoon of cold rice pudding between two halves of apricots and stick them together with a tooth-pick. Dip apricots in flour and fry quickly in hot butter. Put them on absorbent paper to drain and serve hot with apricot sauce.

Baked Rice Pudding with Apricot

Halve and stone 12 ripe apricots and cook in a vanilla-flavoured syrup for 8—10 mins. Allow to cool in the syrup. Line the bottom of a fireproof dish with sweet rice pudding about an inch thick. Cover with the drained apricot halves so as to fill dish. Beat the whites of 4 eggs stiff with some sugar. Put part of stiff whites into icing bag and cover with the rest the apricots, so as to form a smooth, even topping. Now squeeze little heaps from the icing bag to form a decorative pattern on top. Dredge with castor sugar and bake in a moderate oven. Before serving, brown meringue under grill. When removed from the oven, fill spaces between heaps with apricot and currant jam, forming an attractive pattern with the different coloured jams.

This dish is usually served hot, but it is good chilled, too. Cherries, morello cherries, peaches, pears or apples may be substituted for the apricots. Steam fruit a little before using it, and cut into slices or cubes.

Rice Pudding with Fruit

Make a rice pudding flavoured with vanilla or grated lemon rind. Fill a compote dish level with pudding. Top with apricot halves lightly cooked in syrup and drained. Cover with a few spoonfuls of apricot sauce (q. v.) and serve hot or chilled.

Before adding fruit, you may brown top in hot oven. Other fruits may be substituted for the apricots.

Chocolate Soufflé

Ingredients: 3½ oz. grated chocolate, 1½ oz. flour, 4 eggs, 1½ gill milk, 1 gill sweet cream, 1½ oz. vanilla sugar, 1 tsp. cocoa, 1 oz. butter.

Mix chocolate and cocoa with flour, then add milk and cook until it thickens, stirring all the time.

Remove from heat and if not smooth, put through hair sieve. While it is still warm, blend in 1 whole egg and the yolks of 3 eggs. Stiffly beat whites of 3 eggs, sweetened with tablespoon vanilla sugar, and blend into above mixture. Grease a deep, fireproof dish with butter and dust with flour. Put in mixture and bake for about 25—30 mins. in warm oven. Dredge with vanilla sugar, and serve immediately with chocolate sauce. Put soufflé into oven only half an hour before serving.

Chocolate Sauce

Ingredients: 2 gills milk, 2 oz. chocolate, 3½ oz. sugar, 1 egg, 1 dessertspoon flour.

Mix ingredients in a dish and cook until the mixture begins to boil. If the sauce is too thick, dilute with milk.

Almond Soufflé

Ingredients: 2 oz. butter, 2 pt. milk, 3 oz. flour, 2 oz. almonds, 7 eggs, 1 liqueur-glass of rum, grated rind of ½ lemon.

Prepare as for vanilla soufflé, but add also grated almonds and lemon peel. The rum is used to flavour the sauce.

Semolina Pudding II

Ingredients: 5 oz. semolina, 1 pt. milk, 3 oz. sugar, 1½ oz. butter, 5 eggs, grated rind of ½ lemon, 5 oz. raspberry syrup, ¼ packet of vanilla sugar, 1½ oz. bread-crumbs.

Cook semolina with half the sugar in milk, until soft and fairly thick. Remove from fire and stirring all the time, mix in yolks of the eggs, one by one. Beat whites stiff, adding the rest of the sugar to it and fold into semolina mixture. Mix in grated lemon rind. Steam in a pudding-basin, which has been greased with butter and dusted with bread-crumbs, for 30—35 mins. Test with blade of knife: if the blade is sticky after you have pricked the soufflé, continue steaming a little longer. Remove from hot water and let it stand for 10—15 mins. Invert pudding-basin over serving plate, shake it gently, remove basin carefully and serve pudding with raspberry syrup or wine sauce.

Rice Soufflé

Ingredients: 1½ pt. milk, 7 oz. rice, dash of salt, ⅓ stick vanilla, 1 oz. butter, 3 eggs, 4½ oz. sugar, grated rind of ½ lemon, 1½ gill raspberry syrup.

Cook rice till tender in salted milk, flavoured with vanilla. Allow to cool and remove vanilla. In the meantime, cream butter with the sugar and egg-yolks and add to cooling rice. Beat whites of eggs stiff and fold into rice. Grease a dish and dust with fine bread-crumbs, put in the rice mixture and bake in a moderate oven until top is golden-brown. (If you prefer steaming, you have to use 1—2 more eggs.) Serve with raspberry syrup in a separate dish or with wine or milk chaudeau.

PUDDINGS

Vanilla Pudding

Ingredients: 3 oz. flour, 3 oz. butter, 2 gills milk, 2½ oz. sugar, 1 packet of vanilla sugar, 5 eggs, 2 oz. bread-crumbs.

Heat half of butter in saucepan with half of flour until frothy; dilute with hot milk, stir till thickens, bring to the boil and set aside. When the mixture has cooled, blend in the yolks of eggs. Beat whites stiff with ½ oz. vanilla sugar, fold in carefully. Grease five individual pudding moulds with melted butter, dust with fine bread-crumbs and fill moulds about three quarters full with the above mixture. Set in a saucepan and pour cold water into saucepan about 1 inch deep. Cover saucepan with lid, but leave a little opening for steam to escape. Steam for 25—40 mins. in gently, steadily boiling water. To serve, invert moulds over serving dish or individual glass plates and remove puddings gently, loosening edges with knife. Dredge with vanilla sugar and serve with vanilla sauce, fruit compote, or raspberry syrup, lemon sauce, etc.

Semolina Pudding III
(4 servings)

Ingredients: 2½ oz. semolina, 2 oz. butter, 1 oz. sugar, 2 eggs, 2 gills milk, 1 packet of vanilla sugar, 1 oz. bread-crumbs.

Boil milk with ½ oz. butter. Add semolina and beat smooth with egg-beater. When it has cooked for a little while, cover with lid and steam with yolks of 2 eggs; add cooked semolina and stiffly beaten whites of 2 eggs, the latter sweetened with 1 oz. vanilla sugar and castor sugar mixture. Butter 4 individual pudding moulds and dust with fine bread-crumbs. Fill moulds three quarters with mixture, and set in to steam as for vanilla pudding, but allow a little longer time.

Rice and oatmeal puddings are made the same way, but have to be cooked longer.

Serve with any kind of fruit sauce or milk chaudeau.

Almond Pudding

Ingredients: 3 oz. butter, 3 oz. sugar, 3 oz. flour, 3 oz. almonds grated, 2 gills milk, 4 eggs.

Cream butter with 2 oz. sugar. Blend in the flour and dilute with mixture of milk and grated almonds. Cook until it thickens, then remove from heat. Blend in yolks of eggs one by one, and then fold in stiffly beaten whites sweetened with 1 oz. castor sugar. Butter 5 individual pudding moulds and dust with grated almonds. Fill pudding moulds three-quarters full and steam as for vanilla pudding. Serve vanilla or chocolate sauce separately.

Sponge Cake Pudding

Ingredients: 4 eggs, 10 oz. sponge cake, 1 oz. sugar, little vanilla, 1½ pt. milk, 1½ oz. butter, 1½ oz. bread-crumbs.

Break sponge cake into small pieces and put into a deep bowl. Boil milk with the vanilla sugar and butter, pour over sponge cake pieces and mix with spoon. Add yolks and stiffly beaten whites of four eggs, blend, and pour mixture into individual pudding moulds, buttered and dusted with bread-crumbs, filling moulds three-quarters full. Steam, invert over serving dish, shake pudding out gently and serve with compote.

Chocolate Pudding

Ingredients: are the same as for vanilla pudding, with the addition of 1½ bar of chocolate and 1 tbsp. cocoa.

Prepare as for Vanilla pudding except that the chocolate and cocoa are cooked in the milk.

Flavour the sauce with which it is served with chocolate and cocoa.

Coffee and caramel puddings are made the same way except that coffee pudding is flavoured and coloured with strong coffee and caramel pudding with caramelized sugar. Serve each with a sauce of the same kind: coffee pudding with coffee sauce, and caramel pudding with caramel sauce.

Vanilla Sauce

Ingredients: 4 eggs, 2½ oz. sugar, 2 gills milk, ½ stick of vanilla.

Beat the yolks of three eggs and 1 whole egg with the castor sugar in top of double saucepan. Add hot milk gradually and keep beating with egg-beater over hot water till mixture bubbles a few times. It is very good flavoured with rum. In that case add 1½ gill milk and ½ gill rum to eggs. Do not forget to remove vanilla after boiling. The sauce should be neither too thick nor too thin. The sauce should be prepared just before serving whenever possible.

CREAMS

Vanilla Cream

Ingredients: 1¾ gill sweet cream, 1 gill milk, 2 oz. sugar, 3 sheets of gelatine, ¼ stick of vanilla, 2 eggs.

Soak gelatine in cold water. Boil milk with ¼ stick of vanilla split in half. Mix 1 oz. castor sugar with yolks of 2 eggs in top of double saucepan. Grad-ually add hot milk and beating all the time with egg-beater cook until it begins to boil. Remove from fire and mix in the gelatine from which the water has been squeezed out. When the gelatine has melted, strain cream into a china bowl. Set bowl into icebox or cold water, stir cream a few times, and, when it begins to set, fold in half of the whipped cream, sweetened with 1 oz. castor sugar. Fill 4 or 5 individual pudding moulds with the cream and chill. To serve dip moulds into hot water and turn cream onto a dish, decorating with rest of the whipped cream. May also be served in individual stemmed glasses. Serve with wafers or sponge fingers.

Chocolate Cream I

Prepare as for Vanilla cream, the only difference being that 1 oz. grated chocolate and 1 tsp. cocoa are mixed into hot cream after adding the gelatine. If the chocolate has not dissolved completely, heat a little longer and then strain. May be flavoured with a little rum, but this is optional.

Hazelnut Cream I

Roast 2 oz. hazelnuts in clean frying pan putting it into a hot oven. Rub off skins in a clean cloth. Grind hazelnuts finely. Now proceed as under Vanilla cream, except that ground nuts are blended into strained hot vanilla cream.

Almond Cream and *Walnut Cream* (the latter flavoured with rum) are made the same way.

Coffee Cream I

Cook 1 oz. ground coffee in 1 gill water and add 1 tsp. chicory. Ten mins. later strain through clean cloth and boil down until thick, adding 4 or 5 lumps of sugar. Make Vanilla cream (q. v.) and after straining, mix in the cooled thick coffee and 1 tbsp. rum. Chill, but take out a few times to stir. When it begins to set, blend in whipped cream.

Rice and Fruit Cream

Ingredients: 5 gills milk, 3 sheets of gelatine, 1 tsp. rum, 2 gills sweet cream, 1 lb. fruit or 10 oz. mixed compote, 3½ oz. sugar, 5 oz. rice.

Cook rice until tender in 4 gills milk flavoured with vanilla. Soak gelatine in cold water, and dissolving it in 2 tbsp. boiled milk, pour over cooling rice. When rice has cooled, blend in rum and half of whipped cream. Wipe a mould dry, cover bottom with assorted fruits or mixed compote and put in rice mixture. Chill. When cream has set, dip mould in hot water and invert over serving dish. Decorate with rest of sweetened whipped cream. Serve with fruit syrup. May also be served in individual stemmed glasses.

Basic Butter Cream
(Makes about 2 lb. basic cream)

Ingredients: 1 lb. sugar, 1 lb. butter, ¼ pt. water.

Put sugar with the water into a clean saucepan. Bring to the boil, stirring several times until it begins to boil. Now take a cupful of cold water and a clean brush and with the wet brush wash off grains of sugar from sides of dish, into boiling sugar. Repeat this operation a number of times and keep removing the scum from top with the brush. This is necessary to dissolve all grains of sugar because sugar crystals may turn the whole cream gritty. After cooking for about 5—10 mins. (depending on the heat), test, dipping the handle of the brush or of a clean wooden spoon into cup of water, then into the boiling sugar, and then again into cold water. Mould the sample of sugar sticking to the handle between fingers. It is of the proper consistency when you can shape a soft ball of it. Remove from heat and let it cool thoroughly. In the meantime cream butter in a bowl with egg-beater. Now pour the completely cold thick syrup into the butter gradually, stirring all the time, and mix well.

A simpler way to make this cream is to add castor sugar to the butter and cream the butter with the sugar. In this way, however, tiny grains of sugar are left undissolved and you get a heavy, mudlike cream. Made with boiled sugar, the cream will be light and fluffy. If you want a light and fluffy cream, be sure to cream the butter well.

Parisian Cream
(Makes about 2 lb.)

Ingredients: ¾ lb. sugar, 5 oz. cocoa, 2 gills sweet cream, 10 oz. butter, ½ stick of vanilla.

Cook ingredients in a saucepan over slow heat stirring all the time with egg-beater. When it has come to the boil, remove from heat and let it cool. If you add this mixture in the proportion preferred (about 15—20% is the usual ratio) to the basic butter cream, you will get a delicious chocolate cream.

Rococo Cream is the same thing with a little more Parisian cream and with a little more chocolate. Parisian cream is used chiefly for filling cakes and small fancy cakes.

Chocolate Cream II
(Makes about 2 lb.)

Ingredients: 1¾ lb. basic butter cream, 7 oz. Parisian cream, or 2 lb. basic butter cream and 3 oz. cocoa.

Blend Parisian cream with basic butter cream and beat till fluffy—and there is your chocolate cream. If the cream is too soft, chill and then beat until smooth. If too hard, put over low heat or steam for a very short time.

288

If the cream is made with cocoa, scald cocoa powder with a little hot water or sugar syrup and stir until you get a smooth, fairly thick paste. After this mix with the basic butter cream: The cocoa may be added simply as a powder, but the scalding brings out the chocolate flavour better. Flavouring with a little rum is optional.

Coffee Cream (Mocca Cream)
(Makes about 2 lb.)

Ingredients: 2 lb. basic butter cream, 1 oz. sugar, 1 oz. ground coffee.

Make very strong coffee of the ground coffee with a little water. When the coffee has been strained, add sugar and continue cooking until it thickens. Blend the thick, cooled coffee into the basic butter cream and beat until smooth and fluffy. Boiling down the coffee until it thickens is necessary because the cream can absorb only a limited amount of liquid without becoming watery or curdling. If the butter is of poor quality and has relatively small fat and high moisture content, even less liquid can be blended into it. If butter cream curdles, steam for a few minutes and then beat till smooth. If this does not help, more butter must be added. Cook the coffee with very little water only, for long boiling makes it lose a great deal of aroma.

Walnut Cream
(Makes about 2 lb.)

Ingredients: 1¾ lb. basic butter cream, 5 oz. walnuts ground, 2 tbsp. rum.

Blend the finely ground nuts with basic butter cream and beat until smooth and fluffy.

Hazelnut Cream II
(Makes about 2 lb.)

Ingredients: 2 lb. basic butter cream, 3½ oz. roasted ground hazelnuts.

Blend nuts into basic butter cream and beat until smooth and fluffy.

Almond Cream
(Makes about 2 lb.)

Ingredients: 1¾ lb. basic butter cream, 5 oz. almonds blanched.

Put almonds into hot water. If you strain them a couple of minutes later, inner skin can be pulled off. Dry and grind these blanched almonds. Add to basic butter cream and beat until smooth and fluffy.

Chestnut Cream
(Makes about 2 lb.)

Ingredients: 1¼ lb. basic butter cream, ¾ lb. chestnut purée (q. v.), 2 tbsp. rum.

Blend basic butter cream with chestnut purée and rum. Beat until smooth and fluffy.

Strawberry Cream
(Makes about 2 lb.)

Ingredients: 1¾ lb. basic butter cream, 5 oz. strawberry pulp, juice of ½ lemon.

Wash and hull strawberries. Pass through hair sieve into a bowl. Add lemon-juice and basic butter cream, and beat with egg-beater until smooth and fluffy. For stronger colour a few drops of cochineal or some other harmless vegetable colouring may be added.

Raspberry Cream

Ingredients: 1¾ lb. basic butter cream, 5 oz. raspberry pulp, juice of ½ lemon.

Prepare as for Strawberry cream.

Orange Cream
(Makes about 2 lb.)

Ingredients: 1¾ lb. basic butter cream, juice of 2—3 oranges, juice of 1 lemon.

Beat orange and lemon-juice with egg-beater into basic butter cream until smooth and fluffy. One or two drops of red and yellow vegetable dye will give a good orange colour. If possible substitute the following for 2 oz. basic butter cream: 2 oz. candied orange peel minced fine, or, even better, grate into cream some fresh orange peel to give cream more intensive orange flavour.

Cheese Cream
(Makes about 2 lb.)

Ingredients: 2 cups of sweet cream, ½ lb. grated cheese, yolks of 9 eggs, 4½ oz. butter, a little salt.

Put all the ingredients, except butter into a saucepan and cook, stirring all the while with egg-beater, until it comes to the boil. Remove from heat and cool. Add butter and beat until fluffy. This cream is used for filling savoury biscuits.

Vanilla Cream (Yellow Cream)
(Makes about 2 lb.)

Ingredients: 4½ gills milk, 7 oz. sugar, 5 eggs, 3½ oz. flour, ¼ stick of vanilla.

Bring the milk to the boil with the vanilla and half the sugar, stirring occasionally. Break yolks into a large saucepan, and whites into a bowl. Mix flour into yolks with egg-beater until absolutely smooth. Now add about half a cup of the milk—which should not be hot—to the yolks and mix well to get a smooth and rather thin batter. Beat whites stiff with the rest of the sugar. When the milk has been boiled, put the yolk batter in its place on the cooker over strong heat. Add milk and stirring all the time, cook until mixture begins to boil. Remove from heat and gently fold in stiff whites. (Stir especially round the bottom of pan to prevent the mixture from burning.)

Prepare cream directly before it is needed and use immediately, because after a little while it sets. It is used to lighten the filling for cream puffs and for other creams, butter creams, etc. The amount needed for vanilla cream tarts is given under that recipe. (Do not forget to remove vanilla after cooking the cream.) The quality of the cream may be improved by using sweet cream instead of milk.

Coffee Cream II

Ingredients: 1 oz. coffee, 3 eggs, 1 pt. milk, 3 sheets gelatine, 2 gills whipped cream, 5 oz. sugar.

Cook ground coffee with 1 cup water. Filter through clean cloth and boil down with 4—5 lumps of sugar until coffee thickens. Mix egg-yolks with 3½ oz. castor sugar in a saucepan and gradually add the boiled, hot milk to this mixture. Beat with egg-beater over low heat until mixture boils. When it has come to the boil, remove from heat and blend in gelatine previously soaked in cold water. Strain cream through a sieve into a bowl. Add reduced coffee and chill. Stir occasionally and when it begins to set, blend in half of the whipped cream. Put cream into 1 large mould or 5—6 smaller moulds and chill for at least half an hour. The moulds need not be greased, only wiped dry. Turn out when set and decorate with the rest of the whipped cream. Serve with wafers or sponge fingers. It can also be served in stemmed glasses.

Caramel Cream

Ingredients: 2 gills sweet cream, 5 oz. sugar, 1 pt. milk, 3 eggs, 3 sheets of gelatine.

Brown tablespoon castor sugar well, stirring all the time. Add ¼ cup water and boil down. Mix yolks of eggs with 3½ oz. castor sugar and gradually add hot milk stirring all the time with an egg-beater, until it comes to the boil. Remove from heat and blend in gelatine which has been soaked in cold water.

Strain cream into a bowl through sieve. Put caramel through sieve, too, and mix with cream. Set in a cold place and stir occasionally. When it begins to set, blend in half of whipped cream sweetened with vanilla sugar. Put into stemmed glasses and chill. Serve decorated with the rest of the whipped cream sweetened with vanilla sugar and sponge fingers.

Simple Chocolate Cream Filling

Ingredients: 2 eggs, 1 pt. milk, 2 oz. butter, 1 oz. flour, 1 oz. chocolate, ½ oz. cocoa, ½ stick of vanilla, 3½ oz. sugar.

Bring milk to the boil with the sugar and vanilla. Beat up 1 whole egg and the yolk of another egg in a bowl, and then carefully add 1 tbsp. hot milk. Add the flour and the rest of the milk and cook, stirring all the time, until the mixture thickens. Remove from heat and mix in the grated chocolate, the cocoa and the butter. Beat until fluffy, and use for cold fillings.

Chocolate Cream Filling

Ingredients: ½ lb. butter, 7 oz. castor sugar, 2 oz. chocolate, 1 oz. cocoa, 2 eggs.

Mix well the castor sugar, butter, warmed chocolate and the cocoa with the yolk of 1 egg and 1 whole egg, adding also a little vanilla flavouring, and beat the mixture till fluffy. A little rum improves the flavour.

Wine Cream

Ingredients: 2 cups sweet cream, 6 eggs, 3½ oz. sugar, ½ cup of wine, 1 liqueur-glass of cognac, ¼ lemon.

Mix the yolks of the eggs, the wine, sugar, cognac and juice of ¼ lemon in a saucepan and beat over slow heat until it begins to bubble. Remove from heat and pour into a bowl. Stir occasionally and when completely cool, blend in whipped cream. Put into individual glasses and chill for 2 hrs. Serve with sponge fingers.

Walnut Marzipan I
(Bonbon marzipan; will keep; makes a little over 3 lb. marzipan)

Ingredients: 1 lb. ground walnuts, 2 lb. sugar, 2 gills water.

Cook sugar with water. Cook until you can form a ball of it (for this operation see recipe for fondant). Now immediately pour over the ground walnuts which you have put in a separate bowl. Mix well with a wooden spoon and let it cool. When it has cooled, the mixture becomes stiff. The next operation is refining. In a pastry shop this is done with a special machine: the mixture is put through a pair of granite rollers 2 or 3 times and smooth marzipan is obtained. At home you can do this operation in two ways: with the help of a rolling pin, rubbing the marzipan until smooth over a pastry board or table press; or you can pound it in a mortar. Neither operation gives a perfectly smooth paste. Nevertheless, this marzipan will keep almost indefinitely and can be used for making bonbons and flavouring creams. It is a delicious dessert as it is. Flavour marzipan with rum to taste.

Walnut Marzipan II
(For baking, as it will not keep; makes about 2 lb. marzipan)

Ingredients: 1 lb. ground walnuts, 1 lb. sugar, whites of 3 eggs.

Mix ingredients thoroughly in a bowl. The next operation is refining and is done as described in the recipe above. If marzipan roller is not available, use castor sugar. This marzipan is very good, but will not keep and has to be used within a short time. Use for baking as for sweet biscuits and other pastry.

Almond Marzipan

Almond marzipan can be made according to either one of the two recipes above, with the only difference that almonds are substituted for the walnuts. Remove white inner skins of almonds by scalding, draining after 2—3 mins. and then rubbing almonds in clean cloth. Do not flavour almond marzipan with rum. (Ready ground almonds can of course be used.)

Fondant (Sugar Icing)
(Makes about 2 lb.)

Ingredients: 1¾ lb. sugar, 3½ oz. potato syrup, 2 gills water.

If potato syrup is not available, use 2 oz. more sugar and 1 tbsp. lemon-juice or vinegar.

Boil sugar with syrup and water. When it has come to the boil free from crystals of sugar as follows: Prepare a cup of cold water and a clean brush (a feather or pastry brush will do). As the sugar is boiling, wash off grains of sugar on sides of dish with a wet brush into the boiling sugar.

This operation is repeated three or four times while the sugar is cooking to dissolve all crystals. (If it is omitted the tiny crystals spoil the texture and sheen of the whole icing.) Keep removing the scum which forms on top with brush.

Test fondant for whether it is done as follows: dip handle of clean wooden spoon into cold water and then into boiling sugar and again into cold water.

Now if you remove the sample of sugar which has stuck to the handle with your fingers and it can be moulded into a soft ball between your fingers, it is ready and should be removed from the heat. If the sample is too sticky to form a ball, the sugar needs to be cooked longer. If the ball made of the sample is hard or too crisp, more water should be added. When the sample shows that the sugar is just right, remove from the heat and set in a cold place. Sprinkle top with your fingers dipped in cold water. Let it stand and when it is almost cool stir evenly with a clean wooden spoon which is not used for any other kind of cooking until it whitens and sets. Let it stand covered with a wet cloth and about half an hour later you will find it is soft again.

It is in this condition that the fondant should be used for icing cakes. Put the required amount into a saucepan and warm, stirring all the time until lukewarm. If it is too thick, thin with a little water. The icing may be coloured and flavoured with cocoa, chocolate, thick coffee or vegetable colouring. The addition of a little egg-white when it is being warmed, will give your glaze a better sheen. Coat the cake to be iced first with hot jam diluted with water; in this way the cake cannot absorb moisture from the fondant and your icing will be prevented from becoming dull.

You can keep the fondant for weeks without danger of spoiling, but keep it covered with a wet cloth to prevent top from drying out.

Chestnut Purée with Whipped Cream

Ingredients: 1 lb. chestnuts, 6 oz. sugar and 1 packet of vanilla sugar, 1 tbsp. rum, 2 gills sweet cream.

Cook chestnuts until tender. Drain and halve, scoop out insides and put them through hair sieve. Cool pulp spreading it a little and then knead chestnut paste (it should weigh about 10 oz. at this stage) with 5 oz. castor sugar, flavoured with vanilla sugar and rum. Whip the cream stiff and sweeten with remainder of vanilla sugar. Scoop 2—3 tbsp. whipped cream into centre of serving dish and squeeze chestnuts through mincer around and on top of whipped cream in a neat pile. Decorate with the remainder of the whipped cream, using an icing bag.

Marrons Glacés
(Makes 20—25 pieces)

Ingredients: 1 lb. chestnuts, little less than 1 lb. sugar, 1 tbsp. rum, vanilla flavouring.

Prepare chestnuts as for Chestnut purée above. Now divide paste into 20—25 equal parts shaping chestnuts of each. Stick a cocktail stick through each "chestnut".

Boil 10 oz. sugar in 1 gill water and keep boiling evenly. Remove the scum and the sugar grains sticking to the side of the dish with a brush, first dipped into cold water. Cook sugar until crisp, testing it by dipping handle of wooden spoon into cold water, then into sugar, then again into cold water: if the sugar which has stuck to handle is glassy and breaks easily, it is just right. Remove sugar from heat and dip the "chestnuts" one by one into this glaze, using cocktail sticks as handles. Place on lightly oiled sheet of glass or marble. When cool, remove sticks and put "chestnuts" into individual paper cases.

Caution. Be careful that the hot glaze does not burn your hands.

CAKES

Chocolate Cake
(Makes 20 slices)

Ingredients: 6 eggs, 4½ oz. sugar, 3½ oz. flour, 1 oz. cocoa, ¾ lb. chocolate cream (see under Butter Creams), 7 oz. fondant.

Break eggs over 2 bowls, separating whites from the yolks. Keep whites free of all grease! Beat yolks thoroughly with one-third of the sugar and 1 tbsp. water, then mix in cocoa. Beat whites stiff with the remainder of sugar. Fold in stiff whites to the yolks and gently blend in the flour with a wooden spoon. Pour carefully into cake tin lined with white paper. Gently smooth top— gently, because otherwise it may collapse—and bake in a medium oven for about 35—40 mins. Do not turn cake in oven, unless you have to, because too early handling may cause cake to collapse. The cake is done if, when you gently press top with fingertip, it is springy like a sponge. If it remains indented, it needs more baking. When cake is cool remove from tin and cut into three layers. Fill with chocolate cream (q. v.) and chill. Ice with fondant or with cream, in the latter case using 7 oz. more cream. Flavour cream with a little rum if preferred.

Walnut Cake
(Makes 20 slices)

Ingredients: 6 eggs, 4½ oz. sugar, 3½ oz. flour, 1 oz. ground walnuts, ¾ lb. walnut cream, 7 oz. fondant.

Make walnut cake according to above recipe for chocolate cake except that the ground walnuts should not be mixed in with the yolks but mixed with the flour when the flour is blended in. Otherwise proceed as under Chocolate Cake, filling of course with walnut cream flavoured with rum instead of the chocolate cream.

Hazelnut Cake
(Makes 20 slices)

Ingredients: 6 eggs, 4½ oz. sugar, 3½ oz. flour, 1 oz. ground hazelnuts, ¾ lb. hazelnut cream (see under Butter Creams), 7 oz. fondant.

Make cake as for Walnut cake. See recipe for Hazelnut cream under butter creams. Hazelnut cakes are usually glazed with white icing. Trellis-work decoration on top gives cake a festive look.

Coffee (Mocca) Cake
(Makes 20 slices)

Ingredients: 6 eggs, 4½ oz. sugar, 4½ oz. flour, ¾ lb. coffee cream (q. v. under Butter Creams), 7 oz. fondant.

Make the batter for this cake of eggs, sugar and flour, without using any other ingredients. This is the same batter as for sponge cake. Otherwise proceed as when making chocolate cake. Instead of fondant glazing, cake may be iced with coffee cream in which case 7 oz. more of the cream is needed. If fondant icing is used, colour glaze light brown with a little coffee or caramel.

Almond Cake
(Makes 20 slices)

Ingredients: 6 eggs, 4½ oz. sugar, 3½ oz. flour, 1 oz. blanched almonds ground, ¾ lb. almond cream, 7 oz. fondant.

Make as for Walnut cake. The blanched almonds are cleaned of inner skin. Usually the icing is white fondant.

Orange Cream Cake
(Makes 20 slices)

Ingredients: 6 eggs, 4½ oz. sugar, 4½ oz. flour, ¾ lb. orange cream (q. v. under Butter Creams), 7 oz. fondant.

Make the same kind of sponge cake batter as for Coffee cake. Now proceed as when making chocolate cake. If you want to ice cake with cream, use 7 oz. more orange cream instead of fondant. Decorate top with orange slices dipped in sugar syrup.

Strawberry Cream Cake
(Makes 20 slices)

Ingredients: 6 eggs, 4½ oz. sugar, 4½ oz. flour, ¾ lb. strawberry cream (q. v. under Butter Creams), 7 oz. strawberries, 7 oz. fondant.

Make the same batter as for Coffee cake. Fill with strawberry cream to which fresh or frozen whole strawberries are added. If you want to ice the cake with strawberry cream, substitute 7 oz. more cream for fondant. If you ice it with fondant, colour glaze to light pink. Decorate with whole strawberries.

Rococo Cake
(Makes 20 slices)

Ingredients: 6 eggs, 4½ oz. sugar, 3½ oz. flour, 1 oz. cocoa, 1¼ lb. cocoa cream, 2 oz. granulated chocolate.

The batter is made as for Chocolate cake. This cake is always iced, and preferably is attractively decorated by means of an icing bag. Rococo cream differs from chocolate cream in having a more intensive chocolate flavour, therefore use more cocoa or Parisian cream when making it. The sides are coated with grated chocolate. Chocolate cream contains 15—20% Parisian cream; the rococo cream is made of at least 50% Parisian cream and 50% basic butter cream. If the rococo cream is made with cocoa, use at least 5 oz. cocoa for 2 lb. cream, that is, 2 lb. basic butter cream and 5 oz. cocoa.

Dobos Cake
(Makes 20 slices)

Ingredients: 6 eggs, ½ lb. sugar, 5 oz. flour, 1 lb. chocolate cream, 2 oz. oil.

Use 6 eggs, 4½ oz. sugar and 4½ oz. flour for making the same type of batter as for Coffee cake, but beat longer to make it smoother. Previous to this, lightly oil baking sheet and thinly dust with flour. On the floured baking sheet mark out with round cake tin the circumference of the "Dobos" layers. Six layers are required for a cake, therefore batter should be divided into 6 equal parts. Spread as many of the six parts on baking sheet as it will hold, covering circles marked on floured sheet. Bake in medium oven. When you remove from oven, separate layers immediately from baking sheet with a long knife and stamp out into regular disks with round cake-tin. Set aside the best of the six layers and fill the other five when they are cool with chocolate cream, also spreading top and sides with the cream. Chill.

Now prepare the best layer as follows: if there are any flour or crumbs on it, brush off. Lay out 2 long knives. Lightly grease blade of one knife with oil or butter. Melt 3½ oz. castor or granulated sugar in a saucepan, occasionally stirring with a dry wooden spoon. When the sugar has melted, is a golden colour and smooth, pour over prepared cake-round and spread with clean knife evenly on this top layer. (Caution! This melted sugar is very hot, so be careful not to burn your hands.) Immediately after spreading, take the oiled knife and mark out diameters dividing cake into 18—20 slices cutting through the sugar glaze. Place sixth layer on top of other five and then cut cake according to marking. You will have to slice the knife back and forth, otherwise it sticks. The whole operation from melting until cutting must be done quickly because if the caramel cools it cracks very easily and can no longer be cut neatly.

Russian Cream Cake
(Makes 20 slices)

Ingredients: 6 eggs, 6 oz. sugar, 4½ oz. flour, ¾ lb. whipped cream, 2 oz. raisins or 3½ oz. candied fruits, 1 tbsp. rum, 1 tbsp. Triple Sec, 2 oz. bread-crumbs.

Make sponge cake batter of the eggs, the flour and 4½ oz. of the sugar (see under Coffee Cake). Cut cool cake into three layers and fill with the following cream: Whip cream stiff with 2 oz. sugar. Soak raisins or candied fruit into rum and blend raisins and rum and also Triple Sec into whipped cream. Use this cream for filling between layers and also to spread top and sides. Decorate top with help of icing bag and dot with pieces of candied fruit. The sides are dusted with sweetened bread-crumbs. Cut when chilled.

The most frequent source of trouble in making this cake is that the whipped cream is not stiff enough and collapses after the spirits are mixed in. There are two ways to avoid this: either add to the whipped cream half a sheet or at most one sheet of gelatine, dissolved in a little warm water and then cooled, or make 2 oz. less whipped cream and substitute for it 3 oz. vanilla cream (q. v. under Creams) put through sieve. Fold it into whipped cream gradually.

Stephanie Cake

Ingredients: 6 eggs, 4½ oz. sugar, 5 oz. flour, 2 oz. oil, 1 lb. chocolate cream (q. v. under Butter Creams), 1 oz. cocoa, 1 oz. castor sugar.

This cake is made the same way as Dobos Cake, only its top is different. Use the oil and ½ oz. out of the flour for greasing and flouring the baking sheet. All six layers are pasted together with the cream and the top and side of cake are also spread with the cream. Now mix cocoa and very fine castor sugar and sift this mixture on top of cake to cover it evenly. Chill and then cut.

Chestnut Cream Cake
(Makes 20 slices)

Ingredients: 6 eggs, 4½ oz. sugar, 3½ oz. flour, 2 oz. chestnut purée, 1 lb. chestnut cream (q. v. Butter Creams), 7 oz. fondant.

Prepare a batter of the eggs, sugar and flour as described under Coffee Cake, except for mixing chestnut purée with the creamed egg-yolks. Let cake cool, cut into three layers and fill with chestnut cream. When cream has set, glaze with brown or chocolate fondant. Instead of the fondant, top and sides may be spread with the chestnut cream. In this case 3½ oz. more cream and 3½ oz. more chestnut purée are required and the top is decorated with tiny noodles of chestnut purée (obtained when the purée is put through mincer) and, if you like, with whipped cream as well.

Punch Cake
(Makes 20 slices)

Ingredients: 9 eggs, 11 oz. sugar, 6 oz. flour, 1 gill water, 3½ oz. apricot jam, 2 tbsp. rum, 1 oz. fondant.

Make sponge cake batter of 9 eggs, 6 oz. sugar and all the flour (see under Coffee Cake). Since this is 1 and ½ times the usual amount, bake a usual sized cake and bake the remainder of the mixture in a different tin (shape of tin does not matter because this cake will be cut up to form filling). Cut the cake horizontally into three equal layers. Set aside the middle layer because this also goes with the filling. Spread inner sides of top and bottom with apricot jam and put top with jam side up back into tin in which it was baked. Now cut middle layer and the separately baked part into cubes a little under an inch. Put cubes into a bowl and pour over it the rum (a little more rum may be used than given if you like). Put 5 oz. sugar with 2 tbsp. water in a saucepan and bring to the boil. When it has boiled, pour immediately over cubes and allow to soak through. Blend and place whole mixture on the cake in tin. Spread and press down this filling by hand and cover with bottom side of original cake—jam-spread side inward. Press down by hand and then leave it pressed down with a weight. Let it stand this way for about two or three hrs., then remove side of tin, invert cake—as top side was on bottom—and glaze with fondant coloured pink.

Sacher Cake

Ingredients: 5 oz. butter, 6 oz. sugar, 4 eggs, 2 oz. cocoa, 5 oz. flour, 10 oz. apricot jam, 10 oz. chocolate fondant, pinch of saleratus baking powder.

Cream the butter thoroughly with 3½ oz. castor sugar, and then mix in the cocoa. Beat four whole eggs with 3 oz. sugar in top of double saucepan until lukewarm and then, removing from the heat, continue beating until completely cool. Gently blend butter and yolk-mixtures and fold in flour. A dash of saleratus will make the cake lighter. Put batter into a tin prepared in advance and bake slowly in a moderate oven. Cool and cut into three layers. Fill with jam and glaze with fondant. It can be sliced without chilling.

Goose Foot Cake

Ingredients: 3 eggs, 2 oz. sugar, 3 oz. flour, 1 lb. rococo cream, 3½ oz. morello cherries preserved in rum syrup, 3½ oz. walnuts, 3½ oz. chocolate.

Make a mixture of the eggs, sugar and flour as described under Coffee Cake, and bake in a cake-tin. Mix walnuts into rococo cream and spread thin layer of cake (it should not be thicker than ½—¾ inch) evenly with this mixture. Now press morello cherries into cream distributing them evenly. Smooth top and sides of thick cream layer with a knife and chill. In the meantime melt chocolate over hot water, and coat top and sides with chocolate which should be at about body temperature. When the glaze has set, cake can be sliced. It is customary to cut into much broader slices than ordinary cake.

FANCY CAKES

Cream Roll
(Makes 20 slices)

Ingredients: 6 eggs, 4½ oz. sugar, 4½ oz. flour, 1¼ lb. butter cream.

Prepare cake mixture of the eggs, sugar and flour as described under Coffee Cake. Line bottom of baking tin with greaseproof paper and spread batter on it evenly. Bake quickly in a warm oven taking care lest you dry out cake. When done, remove from oven and lightly dust top with flour. Invert and allow to cool. (Depending on the flavouring preferred, you can substitute ground walnuts, almonds, hazelnuts or cocoa for 1 oz. of the flour.) Lift out cake with a paper under it and spread 1 lb. butter cream (any flavouring you want—see under Butter Cream) evenly on top. Now roll up with help of paper under it and chill, keeping rolled up in paper. When cream has set, take off paper coat, roll with part of the remainder of cream and decorate with the other part with the help of icing bag. Cut with knife dipped in warm water.

Strawberry or Coffee Doughnuts
(Makes 20 pieces)

Ingredients: See under Indian Doughnuts.

You can make strawberry or coffee doughnuts the same way as Indian doughnuts. But if you want strawberry flavouring, use a thick fondant for glazing and fill with strawberry cream (q. v.).

For coffee doughnuts, brown fondant and coffee-flavoured whipped cream are used.

Indian Doughnuts
(Makes 20 pieces)

Ingredients: Yolks of 5 eggs, whites of 8 eggs, 3 oz. sugar, 5 oz. flour, 1 tbsp. water, 3½ oz. jam, 10 oz. chocolate fondant, 1 lb. sweetened whipped cream.

Cream yolk with water in a large bowl and then mix in 1 oz. flour. Beat whites stiff with sugar, blend into yolk and then blend in rest of flour gently with wooden spoon. Cover baking sheet with greaseproof paper and squeeze buns the size of half a doughnut from forcing bag onto sheet—about 40 of them. Bake in a slow oven. Scoop out insides with the point of a knife to make room for filling and pair halves. Spread outside of doughnuts, except bottom, with warmed jam thinned with water. Warm fondant (q. v.), dip doughnuts into it, then dry and cool it on a cake rack. Now separate halves again, put lower parts into paper cases and fill them heaped high with whipped cream, using up all the whipped cream. Put on tops. Keep Indian doughnuts in refrigerator until ready to serve. It is best to fill with the whipped cream directly before serving, to prevent soaking.

Rigó Jancsi
(Makes 20 pieces)

Ingredients: 5 eggs, 3½ oz. sugar, 3½ oz. flour, 1 oz. cocoa, 1 oz. jam, 5 oz. chocolate fondant, 3½ oz. chocolate, 1 lb. sweetened whipped cream.

Make a batter similar to that for Chocolate cake of the eggs, sugar, flour and cocoa. Bake in a large oblong tin instead of round cake tin. When cool cut into two layers, spread inner side of top layer with jam and glaze with fondant. When the fondant has set, cut glazed top layer into about 20 squares which will be the tops of the cakes. Set out lower layer on table. Melt chocolate over hot water until it is warm—a little warmer than body temperature—and then add to stiffly whipped cream, mixing quickly. Unless the mixing is done quickly, the chocolate will stiffen and the filling will not be smooth. Pour cream and chocolate mixture on top of the bottom layer and spread evenly. Let it stand in this way for a few minutes, then cover with top squares and cut with knife dipped in hot water and wiped dry through filling and bottom layer, along outlines of top squares. Keep in refrigerator until ready to serve.

Chocolate Log

Ingredients: 2 lb. sugar, 8 eggs, 3 oz. flour, 3½ oz. chocolate, 2 oz. cocoa, 1 lb. butter, 1 tbsp. milk, ¼ stick of vanilla.

Beat yolks of 8 eggs smooth with 2 oz. sugar. Beat whites of 6 eggs stiff, gradually adding 1 oz. sugar. Fold beaten whites into yolks, add flour and gently blend. Put some of this batter aside to make the "knots" on the log.

Lay greaseproof paper about the size of a newspaper page on a baking sheet and spread remainder of batter on it evenly with broad knife. Bake until golden-brown in a hot oven, and then invert baking sheet together with paper, over a floured pastry-board. Remove paper and prepare the cream.

Chop chocolate, add the cocoa and cook in 1 tbsp. milk until you get a thick paste. Cool. In the meantime cream butter with ¾ lb. vanilla-flavoured castor sugar, 1 whole egg, and the yolk of another. Add chocolate paste to this butter cream, but first take out 3—4 tbsp. of the uncoloured butter cream.

Spread three quarters of above chocolate cream over the cake, roll up and then even bottom with a knife so that "log" does not roll on the cake dish. Chill. Lay on a long platter. Put remainder of cream into forcing bag to which a star-shaped nozzle is attached and squeeze lines lengthwise onto "log".

Squeeze tiny heaps of the remainder of the cake batter onto baking sheet with the help of icing bag and bake. Colour left-over butter cream green. Coat baked heaps with this green cream and stick them on "log" as "leaves". Cut off ends of cake obliquely.

Bohemian Slices
(Makes 15 slices)

Ingredients: Whites of 10 eggs, 3 oz. ground walnuts, 4½ oz. flour, 10 oz. butter, 1 lb. sugar, 3½ oz. chocolate, one whole egg, 1 tbsp. rum, 2 tbsp. oil.

Beat whites of eggs stiff with 5 oz. sugar, and then mix in 1 oz. walnuts and 4½ oz. flour. Grease and lightly flour two baking sheets. With the help of a spatula spread batter evenly and bake until light-brown in a moderate oven. Remove from oven and loosen with the help of knife blade inserted between baking sheet and cake. Cut lengthwise into five or six strips of equal width.

When cool cover half of these strips with the following cream: Cream 10 oz. butter, 10 oz. castor sugar and 1 whole egg until smooth and fluffy. Blend in 2 oz. roasted ground walnuts, 2 oz. melted chocolate and the rum. Sandwich cake-strips and chill in refrigerator. Melt rest of chocolate, mix with 2 tbsp. table oil when it is lukewarm, and glaze top with this mixture. When the chocolate has set, cut with knife dipped into hot water into slices of shape preferred.

Fruit Flan

Ingredients: 3 lb. mixed fruit, 1 liqueur-glass of liqueur, ½ lb. flour, 3½ oz. castor sugar, 7 oz. butter, 1 egg, grated rind of ½ lemon, little vanilla flavouring, 1 oz. grated almonds, 1 sheet of gelatine, 2 oz. apricot jam.

Rub butter into flour with sugar, ground almonds, lemon rind and vanilla flavouring over pastry-board and then quickly knead with yolk of one egg. If it still crumbles, add a little milk or sour cream. Set in a cool place for half an hour, then roll out in a round shape about the thickness of your little finger and put into a cake-tin which has been wiped dry.

Form the remainder of the pastry roll long bars. Brush edge of cake with egg and paste bars over edge. Prick with fork and bake in a moderate oven. When done spread with apricot jam and liqueur mixture and fill pastry case with mixed fruits. If fresh fruit is used, peel and slice first and mix with sugar. Soak 1 sheet gelatine in cold water. Boil ¾ cup syrup of fruit preserves, add squeezed-out gelatine and strain. When the syrup has cooled add a little liqueur and coat fruit slices with this mixture, using a brush. Leave to set and then cut flan into 12 slices with knife dipped in warm water.

Chocolate Mignons

Ingredients: 4 eggs, 2 oz. butter, 3½ oz. sugar, 2 oz. sugar, 2 oz. chocolate, 1 dessertspoon cocoa, 2 oz. flour, 1 oz. ground almonds, 1 liqueur-glass rum, 5 oz. apricot jam, ½ lb. fondant, pinch of ground cinnamon.

Cream butter with 2 oz. castor sugar until fluffy and add the yolks of 4 eggs, one by one, beating well in the meantime. Blend in dessertspoon of cocoa and chocolate, warmed in oven until soft. Beat whites stiff with 1 oz. castor sugar; fold gently into chocolate mixture and blend in the flour and the finely ground almonds. Mix with a wooden spoon and bake in a greased and floured tin. When done invert over floured cake-rack and cool. Mix apricot jam with the rum, cut chocolate cake into two layers, spread top of bottom part with rum and jam mixture and replace top layer. Cut into cubes and dip them into fondant flavoured with chocolate or cocoa. When the icing has set, put into individual paper cases.

Puff Pastry Flan

Ingredients: 7 oz. butter, 7 oz. flour, 3 lb. fruit, 5 oz. sugar, 1 liqueur-glass of liqueur, 1 sheet of gelatine, 2 oz. apricot jam, 1 egg, juice of ½ lemon.

Make puff pastry (q. v. under Puff Pastry) of the butter, flour and sugar. Roll out to thickness of about $1/8$ inch. Cut into a circle with edge of cake-tin, roll remainder of pastry into long stripes and paste them around the edge of pastry, which you have first brushed with egg. Prick with fork and bake. Proceed as in above recipe.

ICE-CREAMS AND PARFAITS

Ice-creams and parfaits contain quite a lot of nutritive materials, which are very important for the human body: fats, vitamins, proteins, mineral salt, sugars and starches. The basic foodstuffs, from which we prepare ice-creams and parfaits, cream, milk, eggs, sugar, fruits, have a high percentage of nutritive value.

It must be remembered that these preparations are highly perishable. We should store all kinds of ice-creams therefore, both in a semi-finished and in a finished state, exclusively in the icebox, in order to avoid the spoiling of the raw foodstuffs. Ices are divided in two groups: ice-creams and water ices. It is important to serve ice-creams, as well as parfaits on a cooled dish, plate or glass and serve with sponge cakes, wafers of various kinds and iced or cooled water. Ice-creams may be served garnished with cream, beaten quite stiff and foamy.

Vanilla Ice-cream (Basic Ice-cream)
(10 servings)

Ingredients: 1 quart milk, 11 oz. sugar, yolks of six eggs, ½ stick of vanilla.

Boil the milk in a saucepan with vanilla, split lengthwise to extract flavour. In another saucepan beat the egg-yolks, add 1 cup of cold milk, bring to boil, and stir until smooth. When the milk begins to boil gradually add creamed egg-yolks stirring vigorously all the time. When the mixture has come to boil, remove from the cooker (be careful, as it boils over very easily!) and strain through hair sieve. You can begin freezing the mixture when it has cooled. If you do not want to freeze for an hour or so, store mixture on ice or in refrigerator until then, because it spoils very easily. Once frozen it can be kept for days at around 0° F.

When the ice-cream is frozen its volume increases by about 25—50 per cent. If you don't have a refrigerator put crushed ice into a large dish. Dredge ice with salt and put a smaller bowl with the ice-cream in it into the ice. Keep turning it around and beat ice-cream. Soon the whole mass will freeze. Do not let the salt water seep into it. Scoop out ice-cream with spoon or scooper first dipped into clean water.

Chocolate Ice-cream
(10 servings)

Ingredients: 1 quart basic ice-cream, 2 oz. cocoa

Mix cocoa with just a little liquid ice-cream mixture until smooth and then add this to the whole mixture; beat well, then freeze. The addition of ¼ or ½ cup sweet cream before freezing improves the quality. Freeze as described under Vanilla Ice-cream.

Caramel Ice-cream
(10 servings)

Ingredients: 1 pt. basic vanilla ice-cream, 7 oz. sugar, 2 cups milk, ½ cup of sweet cream.

Heat and melt sugar in a clean saucepan stirring occasionally. When it is golden-yellow and smooth, gradually add the milk and cream. Bring to the boil, then strain. Mix with basic ice-cream.

You can make it without the basic vanilla ice-cream, in which case use double the ingredients.

Caution! Watch out when melting and diluting sugar because the molten sugar is very hot!

Coffee Ice-cream
(10 servings)

Ingredients: 1 quart basic ice-cream, 2 oz. ground coffee, 2 oz. sugar, ½ cup of sweet cream.

Make very strong coffee using the smallest possible quantity of water. When coffee has been strained, add sugar and continue cooking until coffee thickens. Add thickened coffee and sweet cream to basic ice-cream, mix and freeze. (See Vanilla Ice-cream.)

Punch Ice-cream
(10 servings)

Ingredients: 1 quart basic ice-cream, 1 tbsp. rum, 3 oz. candied fruit.

Chop candied fruit and soak in rum, then mix fruit and rum mixture into basic ice-cream. Raisins should be substituted for part or all of fruit when available. Colour with cochineal. Flavour with rum to taste, but remember that if too much is used, the ice-cream will not freeze.

Walnut Ice-cream
(10 servings)

Ingredients: 1 quart basic ice-cream, 2 oz. roasted walnuts ground, 1 tbsp. rum.

Mix walnuts and rum with basic ice-cream, and freeze.

Lemon Water Ice
(10 servings)

Ingredients: 1 quart water, 1 lb. sugar, 5 medium-sized lemons.

Melt sugar in the water over the fire. When cool add juice of lemons. Strain and freeze. If not sharp enough, add more lemon or some tartaric acid. If you prefer a creamier ice, take 1 cup less water and when mixture is cool add 1 cup of sweet cream.

Raspberry Water Ice
(10 servings)

Ingredients: 1 quart water, 1 lb. raspberries, 1 lb. sugar.

Put raspberries through sieve and add pulp to cool sugar solution (q. v. under Lemon Ice). Strain and if required, colour with a few drops of cochineal. Add lemon or tartaric acid if preferred. If you want creamier ice make sugar solution with 1 cup less water and when you add fruit pulp, add also 1 cup of sweet cream.

Orange Water Ice
(10 servings)

Ingredients: 1 quart water, 1 lb. sugar, juice of 3—5 oranges.

Make the same way as for lemon ice. A little tartaric acid may be added and a few drops of yellow and red colouring.

Strawberry Water Ice
(10 servings)

Make the same way as raspberry ice, using strawberries instead of raspberries.

Red Currant Water Ice
(10 servings)

Make as for raspberry ice, with ripe currants.

Morello Cherry Water Ice
(10 servings)

Make as for raspberry ice, with ripe morello cherries.

Apricot Water Ice
(10 servings)

Make as for raspberry ice, using ripe apricots instead of raspberries. Do not add colour.

Peach Water Ice
(10 servings)

Make as for raspberry ice, using ripe peaches. Do not add colour.

Frozen Fruit Cream (Parfait)

Ingredients: 1 lb. whipped sweet cream, 5 oz. fruit pulp, 5 oz. castor sugar.

Mix ingredients and freeze as for vanilla ice-cream, but preferably in mould. Serve turned out of mould (dip mould in lukewarm water first), garnished with whipped cream and decorated with fruit. Serve wafers or sponge fingers with it.

Cocoa, walnut or coffee may replace fruit pulp, but do not use too much of these flavourings.

CHEESE DISHES

Cheese is made from milk by clotting and by natural souring, and then cured or ripened. It contains fat in varying proportions in addition to the proteins and mineral salts of the milk from which it is made, and thus represents very high nutritive value. Among the cheeses made are the following types: the so-called soft cheeses (e. g. Camembert, Roquefort, etc.), semi-hard cheeses (e. g. Edam, etc.), and very hard cheeses (e. g. Emmenthal, Parmesan, etc.).

Cheeses are consumed raw, but may also be used for the preparation of cheese dishes, as well as for flavouring.

Remove the rind of the cheese before serving, cut into even, neat, not too thin slices and place on a dish. It is usually served with butter. May also be garnished with tender young chives, early small radishes or green paprikas. In the winter black radishes may be served instead, sliced and salted slightly beforehand and occasionally sprinkled with caraway seeds. Many people eat cheese with rye-bread, but it has a very good flavour, when consumed with rolls, as well as with dry toast or slices of bread or rolls, spread with butter.

Special menus may be finished off with, and festive meals supplemented by the so-called mixed cheese plate. Take a suitably sized glass or porcelain plate and arrange tastefully various kinds of sliced, mixed cheeses on it, garnished and decorated tastefully with roses or slices of butter, chives, early small red radishes, sliced St. John's radishes, green paprikas cut into slices. Put soft, semi-hard and very hard cheese on the plate proportionately in order to please all guests by suiting individual tastes. At the same time serve various rolls, toasts, and slices of rye-bread on a separate plate.

Curd-cheese may also be included in the above category. It may be prepared quite simply, mixed with butter, and flavoured—in accordance with taste—with finely chopped chives, young onions, early red radish or green paprika.

Spiced sheep-cheese with butter (körözött) may be regarded as a Hungarian speciality. Pass cheese through a sieve together with half the quantity of butter, then salt, season with red paprika, some caraway seeds and very finely chopped or grated onions, mix well and put, shaping nicely, on a dish. Can be served garnished with young green onions, early red radishes or green paprikas. Anchovy paste may also be added to the sheep-cheese, and it can be flavoured with mustard, and occasionally also with beer. For picnics green paprikas can be filled with the sheep cheese, after having removed the core and seeds of paprikas and washed them well, and should be packed, properly cooled. They should be sliced with a knife, previously dipped into water and consumed this way.

Processed cheese of various forms and in various packings, smoked sheep-cheese, Transylvanian cream cheese and cottage cheese may be included in this category as well. They may be garnished and served just like other cheeses.

Cheese should be stored in a dry, cool place of even temperature (below 50° Fahrenheit). Semi-hard and very hard cheeses, if already cut into pieces, should be kept in a slightly damp, clean cloth, to avoid drying.

Use Parmesan cheese for flavouring. It is best if grated and served separately.

Cream cheeses are not suitable for grilling, or for the preparation of cheese courses.

Fried Cheese

Ingredients: ¾ lb. Emmenthal (Dutch or Edam) cheese, 2 oz. flour, 3½ oz. white bread-crumbs, 2 eggs, 3½ oz. lard.

Cut cheese into even slices, remove outer rind, and turning slices in flour, beaten eggs and bread-crumbs in that order, fry to a golden-brown on both sides in hot fat. The fat must be very hot so as to fry the cheese in a few seconds, otherwise it will melt. Serve hot immediately.

Cheese Roll

Ingredients: 3½ oz. butter, 3½ oz. flour, 3½ oz. grated chesee, ½ tsp. salt, 2 gills milk, 3 whole eggs, yolks of 2 eggs.

Make a light roux of half of the butter and half of the flour, dilute with half of milk and stir quickly until smooth. Salt and removing from heat, mix well with 3 egg-yolks and half of grated cheese. Beat whites of three eggs, and gently fold into egg and roux mixture when the latter has cooled. Butter and flour a shallow baking tin and spread batter on it evenly. Bake in a medium oven, taking care that it should retain moisture for easy rolling.

Fill with the following cheese cream: Make a light roux of the rest of the butter and flour, dilute with remainder of milk, quickly beating smooth with egg-beater. Mix in yolks of 2 eggs, and rest of grated cheese. Spread this cream evenly over baked pastry and roll up like sponge cake roll. Slice, cutting a little slantwise. Serve on a pre-heated dish with mushroom sauce made with sour cream, or mashed potatoes.

The slices of the roll may be served turned in flour and beaten eggs and fried on both sides in hot fat. In this way they make a very good lunch with spinach or green peas.

Crisp Cheese Rolls

Ingredients: 5 bakery rolls, 5 oz. Portsalut cheese, 5 oz. grated cheese, 2 oz. flour, 2 eggs, 2 cups of milk, 5 oz. lard, ½ tsp. salt.

Cut rolls into four fairly even slices. Soak slices in milk and squeeze out. Salt lightly. Cutting cheese into 10 even slices, fill pairs of roll slices with it. Press pairs together and turn in flour, beaten egg and grated cheese so that the sides should be coated too, and the pairs should be prevented from falling apart in the frying pan. Fry in deep fat on both sides. Crisp cheese rolls go best with spinach, but make a pleasant light lunch or supper served with mashed potatoes.

Cheese Pudding

Ingredients: For pudding: 3 eggs, 3 oz. butter, 3 oz. flour, 1 cup of milk, pinch of salt, 2 oz. grated cheese.

For sauce: 1 oz. butter, 2 oz. flour, 2 gills milk, 2 oz. grated cheese, pinch of salt, yolk of 1 egg, ½ cup of sour cream.

Grease 5 pudding moulds with 1 oz. butter and lightly dust with flour. Now make a light roux of 2 oz. butter and 2 oz. flour, dilute with 1 cup of milk, stir until smooth, salt and mix in 2 oz. grated cheese. Remove from fire and blend in yolks of 3 eggs, and then gently fold in stiffly beaten whites of 3 eggs. In the meantime prepare following sauce:

Make a light roux of butter and flour; dilute with hot milk, stir until smooth, and salt. Add grated cheese and sour cream and boil well. Remove from heat and mix in egg-yolks. Strain through fine sieve and serve immediately.

Invert moulds, remove puddings and coat with above sauce.

Hot Cheese and Potato Cakes

Ingredients: 1 lb. potatoes, 3 oz. grated cheese, ½ tsp. salt, pinch of ground black pepper, yolks of 2 eggs, 2 oz. flour, 3½ oz. lard.

Peel and wash potatoes, and cook until tender in mildly salted water. Strain well and put through sieve while still hot. Now add grated cheese, season with salt and pepper, blend in egg-yolks and knead thoroughly. Shape this dough on a floured pastry-board into even slices. Turn slices in flour and fry both sides till crisp and golden-brown. Serve hot. Usually served with spinach or green peas, but is very good with mushroom sauce made with sour cream, mashed potatoes, or just sour cream served in a separate sauce-boat.

Hot Stuffed Cheese Eggs

Ingredients: For stuffed eggs: 5 eggs, ½ bakery roll, 2 oz. grated cheese, pinch of ground black pepper, 1 tbsp. sour cream, small bunch of parsley, little salt.
For sauce: 2 oz. butter, 2 oz. flour, 2 gills milk, 2 eggs, 2 tbsp. sour cream, 2 oz. grated cheese, 1 oz. bread-crumbs, little salt.

Hard-boil eggs, peel and halve lengthwise. Remove yolks and put through sieve together with soaked and squeezed-out roll. Season with salt, pepper and minced parsley, add grated cheese and sour cream and mix well. Fill halves of eggs with this mixture. Make the following sauce to go with it:

Make a very light roux of 1 oz. butter and 2 oz. flour; add 2 gills milk and stir until smooth. Bring to the boil, salt, and add sour cream and grated cheese. Boil again, stirring in the meantime. Remove from heat and then add egg-yolks, and finally blend in stiffly beaten whites of eggs. Put stuffed eggs into buttered fireproof dish and pour sauce over them. Sprinkle top with grated cheese and bread-crumbs and also with melted butter. Bake till top is crisp and golden-brown. Serve straight out of the oven.

Hot Cheese-and-curd Cakes

Ingredients: 1 oz. cottage cheese, 2 tbsp. sour cream, 2 eggs, 2 oz. butter, 2 oz. flour, ¼ tsp. salt, 5 oz. lard, 2 oz. grated cheese.

Put curd (cottage cheese) through sieve, add sour cream, grated cheese, melted butter and egg-yolks; salt and mix well. Add beaten whites of eggs, sprinkle in flour and blend gently. Shape even slices of mixture on a floured pastry-board. Turn slices in flour and fry a crisp golden-brown on both sides in deep hot fat. Serve hot with sour cream in a separate sauceboat.

BREAKFAST DISHES AND SNACKS

Old cookery books usually have little or nothing to say of breakfast, mid-morning and afternoon snacks, although these meals play an important part in nutrition. The good housewife must be just as well versed in the preparation and serving of between-meals snack as in the preparation and attractive serving of dinner and supper dishes. Although breakfast and snacks are not main meals, ingredients must be most carefully selected. The plentiful supply of foodstuffs on the market enables us to make varied delicious and nutritious breakfasts and mid-morning and mid-afternoon snacks. As in the case of the main meals, variety and balance must be stressed, the different dishes served must go well together. Simple but attractive serving is equally important.

Breakfast

For the preparation of breakfast, milk is just about essential. Milk should be handled with great care. It should always be boiled in an absolutely clean saucepan, one that is not used for any other purpose. Boil the milk always over brisk heat, but not on an open fire as it catches easily and is then unpalatable. Use or drink immediately after boiling. If some of the boiled milk is left over, pour out into a meticulously clean jug: cool and keep in a protected cold place, covered with clean cheese-cloth or fine sieve until you use it again.

Milk is used most frequently for making café-au-lait, or cocoa, but served in a glass or cup, it can be offered in itself as a breakfast beverage. It is an important food particularly for children and adolescents. For the children serve it several times a week with bread and butter or something else for breakfast. Serve milk hot in the winter and chilled in summer.

In Hungary coffee is the general choice for breakfast. It can be made of genuine coffee, possibly mixed with chicory, or, if necessary, of malt coffee and chicory. Mix the coffee with the milk directly before serving, filling up the coffee with the required amount of milk. Make light or dark coffee according to taste, adding more milk to light and less milk to dark coffee. You can serve coffee with the scalded cream skimmed off the boiled milk, or strained, without the skin. Mix only as much of the coffee with the milk at any one time as needed because left-over café-au-lait turns sour very easily. Usually café-au-lait is served in large coffee cups, but an attractive way of serving is to put the coffee into a pot and the milk into a separate jug and let every one mix his or her drink to taste. Freshly whipped cream adds a festive touch to café-au-lait. It can be added directly before serving or served in a separate dish. In hot summer weather iced café-au-lait is very refreshing.

Another popular breakfast beverage is tea. Like coffee, tea should be served hot, poured into cups directly after brewing, or straight from the pot. Lemon or rum and milk are often used to flavour tea. Iced tea is a summer favourite.

Cocoa is a favourite breakfast drink with children. To make good cocoa, boil the milk, stir cocoa with a little cold milk and sugar until smooth and add slowly to the hot milk, beating all the time with egg-beater to keep it smooth. Bring to the boil again, strain through fine strainer and serve directly in pre-heated cups or from coffee-pot. Iced cocoa is a gratifying drink in summer. Like coffee, cocoa can also be made darker or lighter according to taste and is extra delicious with whipped cream. It is a very rich and nourishing drink if before serving an egg-yolk mixed smooth with a little heavy cream is blended in with a beater. You must not boil it again with the egg-yolk, or the egg will curdle. Drinking chocolate is made similarly to cocoa, except that melted chocolate is used instead of the cocoa.

A choice of different kinds of bread, rolls and scones lends variety to any breakfast. Even simple café-au-lait will never seem dull if it is served every day with different kinds of bread or rolls. Sliced white bread, French loaf, rye-bread, sandwich-bread, home-made bread, toast or toasted rolls, fried rolls (very good in winter to go with hot tea), crescents, brioches, plaited coffee cake biscuits, scones or melba toast, fresh fried cakes, or tiny teacakes may all be served for breakfast. For a festive breakfast table set out a variety of different breads, rolls, etc. on the same plate to enable every one to choose whatever he prefers.

The beverage sets the tone of the breakfast and the other dishes must be chosen depending on whether we serve coffee au lait, cocoa or tea.

Butter and jam or honey, some egg dishes and ham go with both coffee and cocoa. Chill the butter and serve on a glass plate in pats cut with a knife first dipped in hot water. Jam and honey are also served in attractive glass dishes. Arrange evenly sliced ham and cheese tastefully on a plate.

Breakfast eggs are most often soft- or hard-boiled. Soft-boiled eggs are put in boiling water to cook for $2\frac{1}{2}$—3 mins. if liked very soft (this way both whites and yolks remain soft) or for 4—$4\frac{1}{2}$ mins. in which case only the yolks remain soft. Soft-boiled eggs are served in egg-cups, or are scooped from the shell into a small glass. Hard-boiled eggs are cooked completely (taking about $5\frac{1}{2}$—6 mins. of cooking) and served cooled in shell or peeled.

All the foregoing harmonize with tea, but in addition different kinds of cold cuts, cold roasts, bacon and fried egg dishes also go well with tea and should be served in different combinations every day. Salami, Bologna, smoked sausages and other cold cuts should be attractively arranged on a plate, possibly in combination with slices of cooked and smoked pork and the different kinds of bacon (Canadian, Kolozsvár, smoked, paprika and garlic bacon). Many people occasionally like fresh cracklings and crisp-fried bacon for the first meal of the day. In addition, a few slices of cheese, a little curded ewe-cheese with butter, garnished with attractively trimmed radishes and young onions in season, are appetizing. In the summer, fresh green peppers and tomatoes look decorative on the breakfast table. Select perfect peppers and tomatoes, wash them and arrange tastefully on the table.

Whenever possible serve some kind of fruit at the end of breakfast. In the summer there is a wide choice of fruits, any of which make a delicious conclusion to your breakfast. In winter serve apples and pears, or fruit preserves.

Mid-morning Snack (Elevenses)

When we have had an early breakfast and lunch is not to be served until early afternoon, a mid-morning snack should provide refreshment between the main meals. The "elevenses" should consist of light, easily digestible foods. Usually only one dish is served in the middle of the morning.

Scrambled eggs make a very suitable mid-morning dish. They can be made in a number of ways, scrambled in lard or butter. The eggs can be broken into a bowl and lightly beaten with a fork or broken directly into the hot fat. The fat is heated in a frying pan and the beaten eggs are poured in when the fat is hot. Stir occasionally with fork and scramble until the desired consistency. The fat should be hot, otherwise the eggs will stick to the bottom of the pan, especially if they are fried over heat that is not brisk enough. Eggs can be scrambled soft or hard according to taste. Serve eggs on warmed plate. Always scramble your eggs fresh, just before they are to be eaten because eggs that stand as little as a few minutes will cool and dry out and are not nearly as enjoyable.

Scrambled Eggs with Onions are made with a thinly sliced onion first lightly browned in fat. Scrambled eggs are very good when made with diced bacon. In this case no extra fat is needed as the fat yielded by the frying bacon will be sufficient for frying the eggs. Scrambled eggs with green peppers are a popular dish in Hungary. Trim, core, and wash green peppers, slice into narrow strips, wilt in hot fat and then add beaten eggs and fry. Scrambled eggs are delicious with sausages, or Frankfurters too. Cut sausages across into small rounds, turn or lightly fry in hot fat and then break eggs over them. Frankfurters or Vienna sausages are used the same way, except that they are first scalded and skinned and only then cut. Small pieces of ham turned in fat the same way, are also a delicious addition to scrambled eggs.

Sometimes scrambled eggs are made with a combination of several of the above ingredients. You can put diced bacon, onion rings and green peppers into your scrambled eggs, or make them with a combination of green peppers and sausages. Add ingredients in the order determined by the length of time they take for cooking: first fry bacon, then add onions, and when onions are lightly browned add green peppers, and lastly beaten eggs.

Salt eggs when scrambling and sprinkle them before serving with paprika and pepper according to taste.

Bacon-and-eggs and ham-and-eggs and different kinds of omelettes (q. v. under Egg Dishes) are also popular mid-morning dishes. Frankfurters or Vienna sausages are often served for a between-meals snack. Put washed Frankfurters in hot, simmering, but not boiling water and leave for two or three mins. to heat them through and through. Frankfurter should not be cooked fiercely or kept in hot water for a long time because the skins split and they loose some of their flavour and much of their attraction that way. Serve Frankfurters directly on warmed plates with freshly grated horse-radish or mustard. For a more satisfying snack serve Frankfurters in an onion-and-red-paprika sauce with a few pieces of potatoes stewed in this sauce. Paired Hungarian sausages are also popular for snacks. They can be cooked for about five mins. and are served the same way as Frankfurters.

Some people like Bologna with pickled onion garnishing. Skin Bologna and cut into small even slices. Slice onions and put them into a water and vinegar dressing flavoured with salt, pepper and a few drops of oil. Serve chilled.

Often light lunches are served for really satisfying snacks. A little Hungarian stew (pörkölt or paprikash) with gnocchi, or sautéed liver, sour lungs or stewed kidney and brains, mushroom and eggs are popular light lunches in Hungary.

A glass of milk, sour milk or yoghurt make the most suitable "elevenses" for children and adolescents. Healthy and nourishing snacks are: a little curd mixed with sour cream and flavoured with salt and paprika to taste; a hard-boiled egg with bread and butter or ham, salami or cheese sandwich. Children like semolina and rice pudding for their mid-morning snacks. Fruit or freshly-squeezed fruit juice are healthy non-fattening snacks. In winter an apple or a few pieces of fruit preserves can be substituted for the fresh summer fruits.

A f t e r n o o n T e a — which is not always tea in Hungary

For the afternoon snack similar beverages and foods to the breakfast stand-byes are usually served. Variety should be stressed, however; afternoon snacks which are the same as those served for breakfast make a dull daily menu. When you decide on what to serve for tea think over the two main meals, lunch and supper, and, if they consist of heavier, more filling dishes, serve a light tea; on the other hand, if they are light meals, serve a more satisfying mid-afternoon snack.

Milk, café-au-lait, cocoa or tea are the favourite afternoon beverages.

Some people like fresh fruit juices, lemonade or orangeade for mid-afternoon refreshment. Home-made and bakery rolls, butter, jam, honey, egg dishes, cheese sandwiches, and, in season, radishes, green peppers and tomatoes—as described under breakfast—may be served in the afternoon as well.

Children and those of the "weaker sex" in particular have a weakness for chestnut purée with whipped cream or iced rice pudding with fruit and whipped cream, to break the monotony of an afternoon. (See both in the chapter under Sweets.)

Although they are not breakfast or afternoon beverages, some of those hot drinks which are so well liked on certain occasion and especially on a cold winter evening—should be mentioned here.

Best known of these is the mulled wine made of white wine. Season the wine with cinnamon, cloves and lemon peel and bring to the boil in a clean enamelled dish. Sweeten to taste and serve directly strained in a pre-heated bottle wrapped in a clean napkin.

White wine is the basic ingredient of egg-nog too. Season the wine with cinnamon, cloves and lemon peel and bring to the boil. In the meantime cream yolks of the eggs with the sugar (taking about 2 yolks and 2 oz. sugar to 1 pt. wine, depending on how dry the wine is) and, stirring yolk-mixture all the time with an egg-beater, pour in boiled wine. Put back on cooker and bring almost to the boil again, stirring all the time and taking care not to let it actually boil to prevent yolks from curdling. Strain and serve immediately in pre-heated china cups.

Punch is made as follows: Pour rum into a clean enamelled dish, warm a little and light. When the flame of the spirit has gone out, fill up with hot sweet tea, made in advance. Serve in punch glasses (stemmed glasses) and float a thin, peeled lemon slice on top. Pour rum on top of lemon slices and serve with this rum flaming.

PRESERVATION

ABOUT THE PRESERVATION OF GREENS, VEGETABLES AND FRUITS IN GENERAL

One of the greatest worries of housewives, early in the summer—when the first greens, vegetables and fruits suitable for preservation appear on the market—till late in the autumn, is represented by the question, what and how to preserve for the winter. Preservation has become, in the course of time, quite an art, and there hardly exists a housewife, who does not possess some jealously treasured recipes for various preserves. The rules for preserving may be summarized as follows:

1. All greens, vegetables and fruits, meant for preserving, should be sound, unblemished, healthy and, if possible, freshly picked.

2. Preserve fresh greens, vegetables and fruits without delay.

3. Great care must be taken all the time to ensure cleanliness.

4. It is important that bottles or jars should be hermetically sealed, and adequately sterilized.

If we respect these rules, our work will be successful, and our preserved fruits and pickles will not spoil.

It is necessary, first of all, that vegetables and fruits should be fresh, uncut, unblemished and sound. It is only possible to prepare, and to keep for a relatively long time, good and wholesome preserves and pickles from unblemished specimens. Soft, mouldy or squashed greens, vegetables or fruits offer good breeding ground for bacteria, and thereby endanger the success of preservation. Buy only as much as can be bottled within the shortest possible time. Take care not to squash specimens. Always pick through the greens, vegetables and fruits carefully before preserving. Squashed or over-ripe specimens should be discarded and only unblemished and sound ones used for preservation.

Great care should be taken to clean and wash well. Cleanse as quickly as possible, so as not to squash specimens. Wash them, in plenty of clean water, changing it several times, but take care not to bruise or blemish skins.

Start further preparation of the washed foodstuffs straight away, so as not to let them go stale because of the delay, and pack them into scrupulously clean, clear white bottles or jars, cleansed beforehand. Cook marmalades and jams, scald pickles, etc. Many greens, vegetables and fruits should be blanched in the course of preservation. These too ought to be packed straight away after blanching, into clean bottles or jars.

All bottles and jars should be perfectly clean. Wash them in hot water, until quite clean and rinse well, changing the hot water several times while doing so. Do not use cloth for drying, but leave jars to drain, upside down. Bottles and jars with tightly fitting glass caps and rubber band are best; they keep out bacteria and thus prevent decay. Keep caps of patent-bottles and jars in boiled clean hot water and take out only before use. Rubber bands should be boiled well and used afterwards for closing bottles and jars. Preserving tablets are not necessary in case of patent-bottles. Pre-heat cleaned jars for marmalades and jams, and pour hot marmalade or jam into them afterwards, to prevent the glass from cracking, because of the great difference in temperature.

All equipment used for bottling must be spotlessly clean. For the cooking of syrup, marmalade or jam, and the preparing of pickling vinegar, use a thick, enamel saucepan in good condition. It is best to keep a separate saucepan for this purpose which is not used at all for other cooking. Wash saucepan before use, changing hot water several times until it is clean. Wooden spoon, sieve, strainer and skinner should also be kept separately, to be used for preserving only.

All equipments should be washed before and after use several times, in plenty of changes of water, until clean.

Pack fruits quickly into jars, to prevent staleness. Do not fill jars up to the top. This goes especially for bottled fruits and for cucumbers pickled in salted water with toasted bread, etc. If patent-bottles are not used, take care to seal up bottles tightly, by using cellophane, greaseproof paper, synthetic skin or ox-bladder. Use double rubber bands or thin, strong string, winding around several times, so as to keep the jars air-tight. Close jars, when packed, one by one, without delay. An exception may be made with jams, cooked thick, which should be left in a dry place for a day, until the surface skins over. Close jars only afterward. Wash the mouth of jars with a clean cloth steeped in hot water, then wipe with a clean cloth until dry.

When the water-bath method of sterilization is used, put bottles or jars into a metal saucepan of suitable size. Place a metal trivet into the saucepan and put the bottles or jars on it, side by side, not too close together. Put clean paper or cloth between jars, so as to prevent cracking, in case they should knock together during steaming. Pour as much water into the saucepan as to come up about two thirds of the bottles. The steaming time, given in recipes, must be counted from the time the water first comes to boil. Preserves may spoil quickly if they are insufficiently boiled, but if greens, vegetables and fruits are steamed too long, they may become much too soft. Cover steaming saucepan with a tightly fitting lid. Take out jars after steaming, wipe outer surface clean, and when cooled, put into the pantry.

If sterilized according to the dry steam method of sterilization, use a larger clothes-basket. Line bottom and sides of basket with pillows, place jars on top, side by side, not too closely. Jars should be filled previously with hot fruits, sealed quickly and wiped clean on the outside. Put pillows on top of the jars and cover everything with a suitable rug, so as to "insulate" jars well and keep out cold air. Leave preserves in dry steam between the pillows for 24 hrs., take them out the next day, wipe clean and put into the pantry.

Examine jars well after steaming, to make sure that the cellophane or other sealing material is still unbroken. If cracked, re-seal jar and only store afterwards.

Cook syrup, necessary for preservation, from lump or granulated sugar. Powdered sugar is not suitable for this purpose. While sugar boils, remove grey foam from the surface with a cleanly washed skimmer.

For pickles use French vinegar of good quality if possible. Great care must be taken to keep the saucepan, in which the water with the vinegar boils, scrupulously clean.

The success of good preservation depends on correct storing. The preserves may be kept for a long time without the danger of spoiling in a clean, cool, dry pantry or larder of even temperature, which can be aired easily. Strong sunshine, extreme changes of temperature, a high vapour percentage in the store-room, etc., may endanger the keeping of preserves.

We must check up, from time to time, that our preserves are not mouldy. If any traces of mould are found, the jar must be opened and the spoilt part taken out. Bring marmalade or jam to boil, boil well, and then pour back again into the freshly washed bottle, seal properly and put it away again. Cover fruits with fresh syrup and pickles with fresh vinegar and store away well closed.

PRESERVATION OF VEGETABLES

Leavened (Summer) Cucumbers

Wash uniform, medium sized cucumbers well, cut off both ends and score lengthwise in the middle, but do not cut in two. Put sprigs of fresh dill at the bottom of a wide-mouthed glass jar, arrange prepared cucumbers in jar, cover them with sprigs of dill again, and put in a few slices of bread as well. Pour in salt water, enough to cover cucumbers. Keep in the sun or in a warm place for 5—8 days to ripen. May be seasoned with a few cloves of garlic if preferred. Take 1 oz. of salt for 2 pt. of water.

Cucumbers Pickled in Salt Water (Dill Cucumbers)

Blanch neat, oblong, healthy cucumbers in an enamel or porcelain dish with a weak solution of alum. Drain off water a few minutes later, and place cucumbers on a clean, dry cloth. Pack into a glass jar, when dry. Arrange dill, horse-radish, morello cherry leaves and whole black pepper at the bottom and arrange cucumbers on top. Mix 2 oz. of salt into 2 pt. of water, bring to boil and pour boiling liquid slowly and gradually over cucumbers, taking care not to crack glass jar. Seal jar tightly with ox-bladder, soaked previously in water. Put jar in a well-aired place. Within two days the liquid will become cloudy; it will ferment first, and then clear gradually. Do not use parchment paper to seal dill cucumbers, but ox-bladder only. Fill jars up with cold salted water previously boiled, after 1—2 weeks, when the liquid diminishes.

Cucumbers Pickled in Vinegar

Wash small, freshly picked cucumbers (gherkins) well and blanch them. Place morello cherry leaves at the bottom of the jar and arrange cucumbers on top. Put slices of horse-radish, whole black pepper and bay leaves between cucumbers, cover with vine leaves and put some more whole pepper into it, then dilute with cooled salted water, mixed with vinegar, previously boiled and seal up tightly with ox-bladder. Different kinds of vinegars are of various concentration, the mixing proportion cannot be given therefore exactly, but water should be mixed according to taste with vinegar. The mixture ought to be sharp enough, however, because cucumbers may easily spoil otherwise. It is important to place a small wooden spatula across the neck of the jars, after filling them, and to press down cucumbers with it.

Cucumber Salad Preserve

Slice thinly healthy, young cucumbers, salt and leave in salt for 2 hrs., until quite saturated; then press well, squeezing out the juice with your hands. Repeat this procedure two or three times, until cucumbers are quite free of water. Afterwards, pack into a jar, first putting at the bottom an inch thickness of salt; arrange a layer of squeezed cucumbers on top, cover with salt again, arrange an other layer of cucumbers, repeating the procedure, until the jar is full. Press down cucumbers, then seal tightly with parchment paper and put to a well-aired place. (Take 1 oz. of salt for every $3\frac{1}{2}$ oz. of cucumbers.)

Green Paprikas Pickled in Vinegar

Wash uniform size green paprikas well and dry them, then pack into a jar. Place whole black pepper and horse-radish slices into the jar, on top of the green paprikas. Bring water to boil and when cooled, mix with vinegar. (For every 2 pt. of water take 1 pt. of vinegar and $\frac{3}{4}$ oz. of salt.) Mix well and pour over green paprikas. Place open jar into the pantry, and after about 5—6 days add the rest of the vinegar. Make sure, before sealing, that the paprikas on top are not soft.

Green Paprika Salad Pickled

Wash green paprikas well, remove cores and seeds, cut into even rings, blanch with salted water (take ¾ oz. of salt for every 2 pt. of water), mix well for 5—10 mins., then strain off and cool, in plenty of cold water. Pack drained paprikas in suitable jars, but not too closely. Take ¾ oz. of salt and 2 pt. of vinegar for every 2 pt. of water, and bring to boil. When cooled, pour over the green paprikas, to cover completely. A few grains of whole black pepper may be put into it as well. Sprinkle the top of paprikas with some salicyl and seal up jar with parchment paper.

Preserving of Mixed Pickles

Plane and salt cucumbers, together with onions and green tomatoes. Clean green paprikas, remove cores and cut them in rings. Squeeze cucumbers well and arrange the whole mixture in layers in the bottle, packing compactly and evenly, beginning with a layer of green paprikas, arranging a layer of onions on top, then a layer of cucumbers. Continue in this order, until the jar is full. Sprinkle each layer with finely ground black pepper. Pour vinegar, prepared previously (1¼ oz. of salt, for 2 pt. of water and 1 pt. of vinegar, brought to boil and cooled) on the mixed salad and seal tightly with ox-bladder.

Preserving of Green Paprikas for Stuffing

Remove the cores of green paprikas and cut off the ends, so as to fit one into another tightly, not allowing any vacuum when filling. Bring to boil plenty of water, put paprikas into it and stir round once, then drain straight away. Drain paprikas well on a sieve and put one into another, then arrange in a wide-mouthed jar, with pointed ends down. Pour thick tomato purée on paprikas packed in the jar, add some salicyl as well, seal tightly with parchment paper, and sterilize by the usual water-bath method (steaming).

Vegetable Marrow Preserved in Salt

Peel marrows, remove seeds, etc., plane and salt, then put away for 1—2 hrs. Squeeze well afterwards and place in a wide-mouthed jar, pressing down tightly, putting first salt at the bottom of the jar, placing a layer of marrows over it, and repeat this procedure, until the jar is full. Put salt on top, and seal up with ox-bladder, soaked well for 12 hrs. previously in cold water, changing water several times.

Vegetable Marrows Pickled in Vinegar

Salt planed marrows slightly, then after about half an hour squeeze well and rinse in cold water; then drain thoroughly. While draining, mix water with a little vinegar and bring to boil, then cool liquid. Place drained marrows on a clean dry cloth or serviette and dry with another cloth, then pack into a wide-mouthed jar, filling about three quarters of the jar only, and pour cold water with vinegar to reach up to the neck of the jar; seal tightly with parchment paper and steam.

French Beans Pickled in Salt

Peel the pods of freshly picked French beans the whole way round to remove the strings and then snip off ends; wash well and dry with a clean cloth. Cut cleaned beans about 2—3 inches long. Measure beans thus prepared and take $5\frac{1}{4}$ oz. of salt and $\frac{3}{4}$ oz. of sugar to each 2 lb. of beans. Mix salt and sugar together and pickle the chopped beans with this mixture. Put away for 24 hrs. and leave them. Beans will shrink somewhat in consequence of salting, and juice will come up. Pack salted beans into a jar, pour juice over them and seal up tightly with ox-bladder. Place into a well-aired pantry.

French Beans Pickled in Vinegar

Clean freshly picked, unblemished young French beans well, and wash. Bring some water to boil with a little vinegar, throw chopped beans into this water, when boiling and parboil them. Drain parboiled beans, and leave to cool. Bring water with vinegar to boil once more, and if the solution is very week, add some more vinegar to it, adding $\frac{1}{3}$ oz. of salt to every 2 pt. of water. Pack beans when cooled into a wide-mouthed jar, but do not fill it quite up when cooled; pour water with vinegar on top, and put a pinch of salicyl into each jar; seal up tightly with parchment paper and steam for about 15—20 mins. (Steaming time to be counted from the time the liquid begins to boil.) Take out jars from the steaming saucepan only when they have already cooled.

Preserving Tomatoes

Wash ripe tomatoes, remove stalks and placing into an enamel dish, squash them, then cook until soft. Pass cooked tomatoes through a sieve. Bring the tomato juice to boil and pour into the pre-heated bottles, while hot. Seal up bottles filled with tomato juice straight away with ox-bladder and place in hay-box. When cooled, take out bottles and store in a cool place.

Preserving Lecsó
(Stewed green paprikas and tomatoes with onions)

Ingredients: 12 lb. green paprikas, 6 lb. tomatoes.

Slice fleshy green paprikas neatly and cook in slightly salted water for 2 mins., then pour onto a sieve and drain well. Cook tomatoes and pass through a sieve, then boil, reducing, until quite thick. Pack jars with drained green paprikas, pour tomatoes on top, sprinkle with a pinch of salicyl and seal up well. Steam for 20—25 mins. and leave in the water to cool.

The other method of preserving lecsó is to cook green paprikas with the tomato juice (having passed tomatoes through the sieve previously), then mix into it a solution of natrium benzoicum and water, taking 1,5 g to every 2 lb. of lecsó. Pour into jars, and when cooled, seal up tightly. Lecsó thus preserved need not be steamed. Handle, before cooking, just as if fresh vegetables.

Fresh Dill Pickled in Salt

Clean and wash dill well, and dry thoroughly. Place salt at the bottom of a dry jar, arrange a layer of dill on top, and repeat this procedure until the jar is filled. Salt comes on top.

Pickling of Sauerkraut

For the purpose of pickling, we should choose stone-hard, full heads of winter cabbages. Remove all the outer, dead and bruised leaves, take out the centre stem with a suitable corer, plane cabbage or slice thinly, and pack in layers into a barrel, scrupulously scrubbed and rinsed previously. Salt and press down by treading well. When made at home, it is usual to season with whole black pepper, bay leaves, sliced quinces and whole, dried red paprikas.

Take care to tread out evenly. When barrel is filled, there should be already plenty of foamy water on top of the shredded cabbages. Cover cabbages with a clean cloth and place the covering boards of the barrel across the cloth on top, then put a wider board over it, press down thoroughly with stones and leave cabbage at a temperature of 65—80° Fahrenheit. Take care that the liquid should cover the cabbages during the whole time of fermentation. Put barrel into a cool place when fermented, to prevent destructive postfermentation. Should the liquid of cabbages diminish, either during or after fermentation, for any reason, make it up with slightly salted water, boiled and cooled previously.

The top layer of the sauerkraut should be cleaned from time to time, and the cabbages pressed down again well.

Pickling French Beans

Butter or Lima beans are most suitable for the purpose of pickling, while they are quite young and beans are hardly formed as yet in the tender pods. Remove fibres from around pods and cut off the ends, then cut to desired length, wash and blanch for 4—5 mins., then cool well and drain. Mix 2 pt. of water with 1 pt. of vinegar, adding ¾ oz. of natrium benzoicum, and bring to boil. Cool liquid, pack cleaned and cut French beans tightly into a jar (into patent-jars with rubber bands, if possible), pour water with vinegar over them, seal up and steam for 20 mins. at a temperature of 212° Fahrenheit.

Mixed Mushroom Salad Pickled in Vinegar

Grade medium sized, neat green cucumbers, wash them and plane roughly, with the skins on them or slice with a knife; then salt a little. Remove the seeds of white green paprikas, just turning pink in colour and cut into rings with a knife, then salt too.

Slice freshly picked hard truffles or chanterelle mushrooms, or take whole small fresh Champignon mushrooms, blend in water with a little lemon and cool. Remove the outer skins of spring onions (shallots) and blanch. Parboil the small middles in water with lemon for 2 mins. Squeeze cucumbers and paprikas slightly, when everything is prepared, and mix all ingredients together. Pack into jars and pour salted water with vinegar oven them. Take ¾ oz. of salt and about 1 pt. of vinegar to each 2 pt. of water, bring to boil, then cool.

Cover mixed salad packed into jars with this liquid, seal up, and keep in a cool place.

Keeping Green Paprikas for the Winter

Pick paprikas late in the season for this purpose; choose uncut and unblemished specimens, because they can be kept until spring only if perfectly sound and of good quality. Place paprikas in dried sand in layers, in a box, arranging them so that they should not touch, putting sand in between.

Store in a cool pantry or dry cellar.

Preserving Asparagus

Scrape off the shoots of asparagus, using a suitable knife, removing the white skin from the lower end, then cut the stalks into equal lengths, according to the size of the glass jar. Put in cold water when cleaned, so as to prevent discolouring. Place into a smaller colander or sieve, with tips upwards, and cook in boiling water in the following way: cook the lower, hard ends first, about half the length of the asparagus for 5 mins., then steep colander more into the water, and cook ¾ of asparagus stalks for 3 more mins., at last dip colander entirely into the water and cook tips as well for 2 more mins. Asparagus is ready when stalks may be bent, but do not break. Rinse with cold water, changing several times, until cool, then pack into patent-jars with rubber bands, dilute with boiled and cooled water and seal up carefully. Place in a water-bath, pouring enough water into the saucepan to cover jars, mix salt into water, thus raising the boiling point of water by 3—4 degrees. Cook for 90 mins. without lid. Repeat this procedure in 5—6 days time, in the same way and at the same temperature, but cook only for 15—20 mins. Use patent-jars only, with rubber bands previously washed in warm water, rinsed several times and drained well. It is advisable to steep rubber bands into hot water before use.

Preserving Green Peas

Sugar, express and perennial peas, even-sized ones, are most suitable for the purpose of preservation. Shell freshly picked peas, and shake through a suitably holed sieve, to sort out smaller peas, or grade peas when shelling. Cook graded peas for 3—5 mins., then cool well, and when cooled, pack into patent-jars with rubber bands, about 2 pt. in size. Salt and sugar water slightly, bring to boil, strain through a cloth, cool, then cover peas with this liquid, seal up and place in a water-bath straight away. Preserving process is then identical with that for the asparagus.

Preserving French Beans

Take tender and fleshy, young French or kidney beans for the purpose of preserving, in which the beans are not quite formed as yet. Remove the fibre from around the pods and cut off both ends; you may cut them into even pieces, if desired. Wash them and cook in boiling water for 3—4 mins., cool, and pack tightly into patent-jars, with rubber bands, then cover with boiled, cooled, slightly salted water and steam twice, after sealing jars, in the same way as for asparagus.

Preserving Mushrooms

It is best to blanch freshly picked, hard truffles or chanterelle mushrooms in water with lemon-juice. Should be preserved in the same way as French beans.

Attention!

10 thousandth part of salycil to boiling water may be used for the preserving of the greens and vegetables, described above; use 10 g of salicyl to 20 pt. of water.

KEEPING FRUITS AND PRESERVING FOR THE WINTER

Bottled Apricots

Peel slightly under-ripe apricots thinly, halve them and soak in cold water with alum (taking ¾ oz. of alum for 10 pt. of water). Bring water to boil, plunge apricots into boiling water, stir once, take them out with a wooden spoon and put into cold water, cool well, then drain and dry with a cloth. Pack into jars, pour cold syrup over them (taking 1 lb. 7 oz. of sugar to every 2 pt. of water) and steam well, after sealing tightly. Steam for 8—10 mins. counting the time from the beginning of boiling.

Bottled Cherries

Remove stalks of uncut, unblemished cherries, clean and wash them well, then dry with a cloth. Make syrup, taking 40 lumps of sugar for every 2 pt. of water. Pack washed and dried cherries into clean jars and pour sugar syrup over them, when cooled. Seal them up tightly and steam. The time of steaming for a jar of 1 pt. should take 9—10 mins., for 2 pt. jars 10—15 mins., counting the time from the beginning of boiling.

Bottled Greengages

Pick sound, unripe, green fruit for the purpose of preservation. Cut off half the stalks of greengages. Mix some vinegar into water, adding a pinch of bicarbonate of soda to it, and bring to boil. Prick greengages with a needle or fork and cook in the boiling water, till the skins of the fruits begin to crack. Take greengages out of the water and cool in cold water, drain well and pack into jars. Pour cold sugar syrup over them (taking 1 lb. of sugar to every 2 pt. of cold water, when making sugar syrup).

Bottled Pears

Use small sized pears whole, but cut big ones into quarters. Peel pears, then put into lemon-water. Cook in this water, until soft, then cool in cold water. Drain and pack into jars, pour cold syrup over them (12¾ oz. of sugar to every 2 pt. of water), seal tightly and steam for 15—20 mins.

Bottled Morello Cherries

Remove stalks of healthy, unblemished morello cherries, wash and pack them into jars, pour cold sugar syrup over them (1 lb. 7 oz. of sugar to every 2 pt. of water), seal up tightly with parchment paper and steam in the usual way for 15—20 mins.

Large Garden Strawberries Bottled

Take equal quantities of strawberries and sugar. Cook thick syrup from sugar, with the addition of a finely chopped lemon, vanilla and a little water. Blanch cleaned strawberries with boiling water, mixed with a small quantity of vinegar, drain straight away; add to syrup and bring to boil, together with the syrup. Take strawberries out of the syrup the next day, bring syrup once more to boil. Place strawberries back into the syrup again and boil together for 1 min. When completely cooled, pack into jars and seal up well.

Bottled Quinces

Peel quinces and slice them evenly. Remove cores, place quinces into lemon-water and cook in this water, until soft. When tender, cool in cold water, then drain on a sieve. Pack drained quinces into jars and pour cold sugar syrup over them (1 lb. 7 oz. of sugar to every 2 pt. of water). Seal up well, and steam in the usual way for 15—20 mins.

Bottled Golden Apples

Cut off the stalks of the apples, leaving about half an inch in length; clean fruits properly. Wash and dry thoroughly, then pack into jars, pour cold syrup over them and add a pinch of salicyl as well (take 2 lb. of sugar to 2 pt. of water; the so-called stock syrup). Seal and steam, but take care not to allow the apples to crack.

Quince Cheese

Wash yellow, ripe quinces, then slice and cook in an enamel saucepan until soft. Pass soft quinces through a sieve, having drained them well first. Then cook thick syrup, taking 2 lb. 7 oz. of sugar for every 2 lb. of fruit. Cook syrup separately, adding a small quantity of quince juice only and boiling until syrup candies when dipped into cold water with a wooden spoon. Mix quince purée into the syrup and cook together, constantly stirring, until the hard lumps of sugar completely disappear. Pour out into a wetted mould and when cooled, turn out and pack in greaseproof paper.

Cherry Jam

Wash cherries, remove stalks, stone them, and cook, without sugar, for about 25—30 mins. Take 1½ lb. of sugar for every 2 lb. of fruits. Cook thick syrup from sugar (it is ready when sugar breaks), add previously cooked cherries and continue cooking for about ½ hr. Add some salicyl before ready; pour into pre-heated jars and leave till the next day, until the surface skins over. Seal jars hermetically, and store in a dry, cool pantry.

Morello Cherry Jam

Wash ripe, fleshy morello cherries and stone them. Take 1 lb. 11 oz. of sugar for every 2 lb. of fruit. Cook morello cherries well in an enamel saucepan, then add sugar and cook well over strong flame, until thick enough. Pour into pre-heated jars and only seal the next day.

Apricot Jam

Wash and stone apricots, then measure and take 1 lb. 11 oz. of sugar to every 2 lb: of apricots. Place into an enamel saucepan and sprinkle with the sugar. Leave for the night in a cool place. Cook for 15—20 mins. over a strong fire the next day, until thick enough, and pour, while hot, into pre-heated jars. Seal hermetically the next day.

Plum Cheese without Sugar

Wash and stone ripe plums and cook in an enamel saucepan, constantly stirring, until quite thick. Pour into pre-heated jars, while hot, and seal up hermetically the next day.

FRUIT JAMS

Jams and jellies may be prepared from all fruits, but garden strawberries, wild strawberries, cherries, morello cherries, apricots, cranberries, redcurrants and cornel-cherries are favourites. All jams should be prepared in the same way, as described below.

Garden Strawberry Jam

Remove stalks from strawberries and place them onto a sieve or a large colander, and wash them in plenty of water, by dipping into water 2—3 times, then drain them well, and place into the saucepan straight away. (Copper saucepans are most suitable, do not use aluminium ones.) Take about 1 lb. 11 oz. of sugar to every 2 lb. of fruits, and besprinkle fruits with sugar. Leave for at least an hour, together with sugar, to draw juice, then cook on a strong fire, stirring constantly, until the jam drops in flakes from the wooden spoon.

Another test for gelling is to drop a little of the jam onto a dry plate, and if turns into shiny jelly and wrinkles, the jam is ready. Pour into jars straight away and seal up only when quite cooled.

Cherry and Apricot Jam

Use only 1 lb. or 1 lb. 3½ oz. of sugar to every 2 lb. of fruits for the making of these jams. The same method may be used as in the recipe above.

Red Currant Jam

Top and tail washed red currants, then measure weight. Take 1 lb. 12¾ oz. of sugar to every 2 lb. of fruits. Cook cleaned red currants in an enamel saucepan, then add sugar and cook until thick enough. Pour jam while hot into pre-heated jars when ready, and seal up the next day.

Red Currant Jelly

Ingredients: 3 lb. red currants, 1 lb. 11 oz. sugar. This will give a quantity of about 3 lb. 7½ oz. of jelly, when cooked.

Clean ripe red currants and squash them thoroughly in a dish, then boil together with 3—4 pt. of water, until the fruit is tender. Drain on a fine sieve or through a fine strainer or jelly-bag, then, adding about 1 lb. 11 oz. of sugar to every 2 lb. of juice, cook well, skimming frequently, and cooking until it gells, when dropped onto a plate. Pour into pre-heated, clean jars, while hot, and seal up the next day. Keep in a cool, dry place.

Raspberry Jelly

Ingredients: 2 lb. 11 oz. raspberries, 1 lb. 5½ oz. sugar.

Clean ripe raspberries and pass them raw through a hair sieve. Add sugar to raspberry purée, place into a saucepan, and cook well, stirring constantly. Skim frequently, take a sample after about 10 mins. time and if drops turn into jelly, pour into pre-heated, clean jars; seal them up the next day and keep in a cool, dry place.

Above quantity will give about 3 lb. of jelly, when cooked.

Rose-hip Jelly

Ingredients: 3 lb. hips, 1½ lb. sugar.

Remove stalks and tops of the ripe berries, and cook them in ⁴/₅ pt. of water, until soft, then pass through a fine hair sieve. (Take care not to squash seeds, because the fine, silky nut-gall inside them may make the jelly unfit to eat.) Measure purée-like substance and take 1½ lb. sugar to every 2 lb. of fruits, put on the fire to cook, and, constantly stirring, cook for about 25—30 mins., then pour into pre-heated clean jars. Seal up the next day and store in a cool, dark place.

The above quantity will yield about 3 lb. of jelly, when cooked.

Raspberry Syrup

Pick ripe raspberries for the making of raspberry syrup. Squash raspberries well and leave in an enamel or porcelain dish to ferment for 2—3 days, in a not too warm place. Frothing will stop on the third day and the juice will clear somewhat. Drain juice through a cloth and measure. Take 1½ lb. of sugar to every 2 lb. of juice. Take 1 pt. of water for every lb. sugar, and make a thick syrup, boiling for 10—15 mins., skimming frequently. Strain syrup through a cloth into an enamel saucepan, add raspberry juice and boil slowly and steadily for 20—25 mins., skimming again when necessary. Leave raspberry syrup to cool when cooked, then put into bottle, seal them, and keep in a dry, cool and dark place.

Garden Strawberries in Syrup

Wash fine specimens of ripe, firm strawberries and place on a sieve. Place in a dish after draining, arranging strawberries in layers, and alternately covering them up with castor sugar also in layers, put another layer of strawberries next, and put sugar on top. Continue this procedure until all strawberries are thus arranged.

Cover dish tightly with a cloth and leave in a warm place for about 5 hrs., until sugar melts. Pour off melted sugar syrup from strawberries and bring syrup to boil, then pour the boiling syrup over strawberries and put to cool. Repeat this procedure twice or three times, until the syrup is quite thick. Finally pour into jars, seal them up, and steam for a few minutes.

Green Walnuts Bottled

Prick quite tender green nuts with a needle or fork. Pour cold water over them and leave in water to soak for 10 days, changing the water daily. Make a sugar syrup after the 10 days are over, by taking 6 pt. of water for every 2 lb. of sugar. Cook for quarter of an hr.; scum must be skimmed off frequently; strain and cool. Throw nuts into the syrup and leave them in it. The next day take the nuts out of the syrup, bring syrup to boil, take off the fire after a few mins., put it aside, adding a few grains of cinnamon anc cloves in a linen-bag to this liquid. When cooled, place nuts into syrup again and leave till the next day. Repeat this procedure four or five times, until walnuts are completely free of water. At last bring syrup to boil, together with walnuts, and cook for a few mins., stirring all the time. When quite cooled, place into jars, together with cinnamon and store them, well sealed.

Musk-melon Bottled in Sugar

Skin not over-ripe melons (Canteloupe melons are best), then halve them and remove seeds, etc. If the flesh inside is soft, cut too soft parts out as well with a sharp spoon. Cut melons into slices, cutting slices in two if too long. Place into water slightly seasoned with lemon-juice, then drain. Arrange in one layer in an enamel saucepan, adding enough sugar syrup (taking 1 lb. of sugar to every 2 pt. of water), to cover the fruit, and bring to boil. Put saucepan away after boiling and leave till next day in a cool place. Place melon slices into a sieve the next day, and boil syrup in the meantime for 10—12 mins. When syrup is cooled, throw in melon slices and put it aside. Repeat this process the next day as for Green walnuts.

Preserving of Stoned Cherries or Morello Cherries for Rétes
(21 lb.)

Remove the stalks of cherries or morello cherries, wash and stone them. Place stoned cherries into an unchipped enamel saucepan.

Take 2 lb. of granulated sugar, 1 tbsp. of salicyl, $^1/_5$ pt. of rum, 2 cloves and a bit of cinnamon, mix well together with the cherries, cover, and keep in a cold place for 3 days. Stir well daily with a wooden spoon. Pour into jars after three days, packing tightly, and covering fruit with its juice, then put jars aside, sealed up. May be used when needed, the rest will not spoil.

Cherries and morello cherries can be bottled together.

Cherries, Morello Cherries or Plums in Rum

Take about 14 lb. of fruits, for a jar 10 pt. in size. Remove the stalks from sound, unblemished fruits and wash them well; then drain off on a sieve. Pack fruit together with 4 lb. of granulated sugar into jars in layers, pouring

$^3/_5$ pt. of rum (60% proof) and add a pinch of salicyl, sprinkling the top of fruits. Seal jars tightly and keep in the sun, until the liquid is cleared completely. Use ½ lb. more of sugar in case of morello cherries.

FRUITS PRESERVED IN WATER WITH SALICYL

Peaches

Blanch not over-ripe, freshly picked, medium sized, unblemished peaches in a large dish with hot water. Afterwards cool quickly and carefully, so as not to bruise them, pack them into larger jars. Previously bring water with salicyl to boil, cool and pour over peaches, seal them up and put away.

Take 20—25 g salicyl to every 20 pt. of water.

The same method may be applied in the case of apricots, morello cherries, greengages, plums and figs.

Preserving Grated Apples for Rétes

Apples which ripen at the end of August, are best for this purpose.

Take as many sound, unblemished, sour apples, as can be packed tightly in a 10 pt. jar, skin and grate them, and place into an enamel saucepan. Take $^1/_5$ pt. of rum and mix it with a tsp. of salicyl, then boil 4 lb. of sugar to a thick syrup with water. First pour rum with salicyl over the prepared apples, mix well, then add hot syrup, constantly stirring. Put into a 10 pt. jar pressing it down tightly and pour juice over it to cover (a little juice will be left over). Seal up jar with double parchment paper, place in a well-aired pantry and leave in one place for four weeks without moving. May be used afterwards at any time, the rest of the apples will not spoil. May be kept in smaller jars as well if preferred.

Bottled Figs

Pick ripe fruit, but take care to avoid over-ripe ones. Wash figs and prick them with a needle or fork and put into water seasoned with vinegar. Cook in this water until as tender as desired. Cool well afterwards and pack into patent-jars with rubber bands; then pour sugar solution over them (taking 1½ lb. of sugar to every 2 pt. of water), seal up, steam in a water-bath at a temperature of 212° Fahrenheit for 20 mins.

Fruits Preserved Prepared for Diabetic Patients

Fruits should be prepared by the same method, as described above, but sugar must be left out. Pack prepared fruits into jars (use exclusively patent-jars with rubber-bands, do not even try other sorts). Pour boiled, tepid water over fruits, seal up jars straight away and steam for 10—15 mins. at a temperature of 212° Fahrenheit.

Since sugar may not be used, use such fruits as will taste good even without sugar. Use saccharine when serving if necessary. But do not use it at the time of preservation.

DIET

We must not forget that for all patients and in all phases of an illness, the only diet to be recommended is the one prescribed by the doctor on the basis of an exact diagnosis. Only such food may be considered as real "dietary" cooking which completely corresponds with the doctor's orders. It is not only useless, but even dangerous to keep a diet, recommended by a layman or decided upon by ourselves. If the doctor prescribes the food to be consumed and the food to be avoided, it is the task of dietary cooking to execute the doctor's orders.

Diets should be prepared on the basis of the doctor's prescription and according to the patient's wishes, but we must try to introduce many variations into our menus and to compose appetizing meals.

The preparation of diets needs great care and attention, and in order to make the patient's meals as tasty as possible, we should not hesitate to do our best, by making our dishes palatable and serving them in an appetizing manner.

Light Menus, Diets

Disordered or delicate digestive organs are taken care of by a light diet. For cooking use butter or oil instead of lard or goose-fat, because the latter are not easily digestible. Season food carefully, using only as much black pepper, clove and even onions, as prescribed by the doctor. But such a restriction should not influence the flavour of the food. We must use other, milder seasonings, to substitute the appetizing flavour of stronger spices.

For light menus or diets, cook or steam food until tender, in order to soften fibres that would make digestion more difficult. Doctors are often not content with this, and prescribe puréed food as well.

As a rule the roux for thickening soups, fricassées and vegetable dishes, is not browned much in a light diet. Flour is mixed slowly into moderately heated butter or oil and fried, with constant stirring, until quite light brown in colour. Dishes prepared with such a light roux are usually cooked longer, in order to bring out the full flavour from the fibres, thus making up for the

334

lack of spices. Before cooking, dress meats properly, by removing films and sinews which are not digested easily. Take care not to fry them very "crisp" because the concentration of flavours on the surface of roast and fried meat increases their stimulating effect. When preparing cutlets, do not roll them in eggs and bread-crumbs, but rather in flour and beaten eggs. Fry them in hot fat, taking care to keep their colour light. Put them onto a sieve after frying, to drain off superfluous fat. Very rich and fat food is heavy for digestion. Use lemon-juice or citric acid for flavour, instead of vinegar, or use the juice of pickled cabbages (sauerkraut).

Skim clear meat soup or bouillon before serving. The quantity of each course and of all the meals should be carefully controlled, because delicate organisms cannot digest as much food as healthy ones. White and lean meats containing less stimulating substance are more suitable in a light diet, than red meats, the more so since they require less attention and are simpler to prepare. Red meats may also be included in a light diet, but we should boil them first, and thus extract most of their stimulating substance. Cream soups, especially barley and rice soups, are very suitable for a light diet. Cabbages and pulses, containing a high percentage of fibres, should not be included, at least not if prepared by the usual culinary methods. Leguminous vegetables may be introduced in a light diet only if rubbed through a sieve, but always in accordance with the patient's state of health. Since cabbage and pulses contain a high amount of roughage do not serve them in a light diet prepared in the usual way. Potatoes and rice, boiled or stewed, together with other vegetables, prepared in various ways, represent the basis of a light diet. It is important not to serve potato purée or tasteless boiled rice as a main course but to prepare the food in varied ways.

Fish, poultry or veal, free of fat, boiled until tender, or stewed, may be served in the form of hash or meat pudding as well. Do not include fattened duck, goose or pork, even if the fat has been removed before cooking, because the muscle fibres of such meats may also contain a lot of fat. If meat is separated from fat and grilled, and thus freed from most of the fat, they may be tried with care and in small portions only. Beef and game should be boiled first — putting stock aside for healthy people — and the meat may be used afterwards for the making of hash or meat pudding. Mild seasoning may also enliven light diet.

Most suitable of the farinaceous products are sweets made from sponge-rolls, soufflés, puddings and creams. Avoid pastries, prepared with yeast or fried in fat. Better leave out noodles and dumplings as well, and use pastas cut thinly into slices or squares. The fat-content and seasoning of pastries should also be properly controlled. Thin pasta, boiled in milk, especially if lightened with eggs, is quite suitable to vary the light diet, in the form of puddings, with different kinds of flavour (vanilla, chocolate, etc.).

Alcoholic liquors are generally not permitted, but beer and light wines, containing a low percentage of alcohol, may be included in the diet, in compliance with doctor's orders.

Diet for People Suffering from Heart and Kidney Diseases

For patients, suffering from heart and kidney diseases and high blood pressure, doctors prescribe the restriction of salt and liquids, and in graver cases, even fix a daily maximum. Since the use of strong spices is also forbidden in the case of these diseases, and also, for instance, the quantity of bouillons, the compilation of a diet is not an easy task. First of all, the quantity of liquids should be restricted; the limitation of salt and spices tends to serve the same purpose. It is well known that after consumption of food, free of salt and spices, thirst appears to be less, and the water-conserving capacity of the organism increases.

In the case of circulation disorders, foods causing flatulence directly influence the functions of the heart; therefore the consumption of pulses, cabbages and mushrooms, containing a high percentage of fibres, should be strongly restricted. Among vegetable dishes only vegetable marrows, carrots, spinach, green peas, French beans and asparagus may be given. These vegetable dishes should be prepared, of course, with very little salt and very small quantity of liquid only. The inclusion in the diet of potatoes, rice, barley, soufflés, fresh and stewed fruits, provide a varied diet, if prepared according to the recipes given below.

The consumption of alcoholic beverages should generally be avoided. Moderate consumption of black coffee may be permitted by the doctor. It is better to drink tea with milk instead of strong tea, and give patients a good variety of drinks, containing milk, or yoghurt.

Diet for People Suffering from Bilious Complaints

In the case of bilious and liver complaints, doctors strongly restrict the fat content of the meals. The use of lard and goose-fat is forbidden, and the consumption of butter and vegetable oil recommended instead, but their quantity should be also strictly limited, only as much as it is absolutely necessary being used. The use of strong spices (pepper, ginger, strong paprika, onions) should be avoided. It is not advisable to include foods (pulses, cabbages) which contain a high percentage of fibres, and cannot be digested easily; therefore in addition to potatoes, rice and barley, serve soups and vegetable dishes prepared from light vegetables only. It is permitted to use eggs in light puddings and sponges, but egg dishes (fried or scrambled) are generally not desirable. Leavened doughs should not be eaten when fresh, only in a dry or toasted condition. Pastries prepared with fat, as well as fattened meats, are not permitted, because of the restriction of fat consumption. Include lean, white meats in general, in the diet, cooked with little fat, together with light vegetables and stewed fruits.

336

Diet for People Suffering from Sluggishness of the Bowels and Diarrhoea

A diet may also be prescribed to decrease the excessive functioning of the bowels. In such cases, serve thick soups (rice, barley, oatmeal), boiled potatoes with very little fat, perhaps red wine and unsweetened tea. Give fresh fruits, greens and vegetables, only in small quantities or not at all, as long as the functioning of the bowels is not quite normal. Apples and quinces are exceptions; they may be served in stewed, boiled or raw, grated form, in order to restrict the excessive functioning of the bowels, and to cure this ailment. It is very important that patients, weakened by this illness, should be given salty soups, because the quantity of salt lost by diarrhoea should be recovered.

In case of sluggishness, the diet should tend to help the functioning of the bowels. For this purpose wholemeal bread, pulses, all sorts of cabbages and dried fruits are advisable, because they contain a high percentage of roughage. Vegetable dishes and sweets in abundance may also have a good effect. Fermented drinks (sour milk, yoghurt), and fermented pickles (sauerkraut, cucumber preserves) frequently help to regulate the functioning of sluggish bowels.

In case sluggishness and diarrhoea alternate each other, the doctor should first be consulted because it is no use to attempt a cure by diet alone.

Fattening and Slimming Diets

Very often it is necessary to increase or to decrease the weight of the body, by regulating food, that is, by arranging such menus which can help thin people to put on weight and fat ones to reduce.

In case of a reducing diet, make sure that the person who must lose weight should never be hungry. Give filling foods therefore, which nevertheless contain low calories, because fasting may decrease weight, but it is bad for general health at the same time. Besides, fasting is usually followed by abundant nourishment, and in consequence, weight is put on again. While in the case of light, curative diets, the varying of menus is to be recommended, in the case of a reducing diet, it may be neglected. On the contrary, a monotonous diet tends to lessen appetite, and thus successfully helps in loss of weight. Reducing should be gradual and should be undertaken only under the constant supervision of a doctor, because the patient may exaggerate reducing, and that may cause grave illnesses. First of all the diet should maintain the patient's usual weight, and only then, under the doctor's constant observation, should we attempt carefully to reduce the weight of the patient.

Do not include soups, vegetable dishes, pastries and meats containing a high percentage of fat in the diet. Serve soups with very few garnishes, prepare them without fat, and the quantity should not exceed a usual portion either. The correct regulation of liquid intake may help to decrease the weight of the body. Pastries or sweets should only be included in the menu on rare occasions and in small quantities, and the diet should mainly consist of boiled meats, greens, vegetables, salads and pickles. Green paprikas, radishes, cucumbers, different salads may be given several times a day, as well as sauerkraut and beetroots. As a rule, cherries, apples and sour fruits (gooseberry, red currant, etc.) may be served without restriction. The consumption of bread, pastries, potatoes, rice and barley should be strictly controlled. Use less sugar and lard in preparing meals, and saccharine may also be used sometimes instead of sugar. Milk, non-fatty cheeses, hard-boiled eggs may be given in abundance, but butter, cream, and fatty cheese should be avoided completely.

In order to increase weight, quite the contrary to the above diet should apply. Food should consist of frequent meals, containing high calories. The variety of food should be stressed, and the colour, state and temperature of the dishes is also very important. Give, first of all, the foods avoided in the reducing diet, i. e. bread, sweet pastries, fat meals, fruit containing much sugar, bottled fruits and jams, as well as sweets in all varieties. Serve meats with many garnishes, potatoes, rice or pastas, as desired. Fatty cheese and cream may also help considerably because the latter increases the nutritive value of the food, without making it less easy to digest. Of course fattening diets should not be undertaken without a doctor's supervision either, because the excessive consumption of fat food may overburden the digestive organs. Disorders of the digestive organs, in consequence, may cause an unfavourable utilization of nourishment, and the speedy losing of weight may follow.

Diabetic Diet

Special literature deals with the diet of diabetic patients. It is not possible to treat this question in detail without misleading by general advice or directions.

General Advice

It is evident that a "diet" need not necessarily mean caraway seed soup and potato purée. Light or special diets should not differ too much from ordinary fare, because the patient may find the doctor's remedies more irksome than his disease and he may deny the existence of his ailment, in order to escape the rigours of potato purée for lunch and oatmeal in milk for supper day after day.

A good cook therefore should keep in mind the patient's wishes and desires, preparing menus which tempt rather than repel the sluggish appetite. Unusual or new dishes must be tempting, tasty and neatly served to make the patient relish his food.

Healthy people, too, appreciate nicely served food; but this is even more important in the case of sick persons, because nourishment is much more important for them.

338

SOUPS

Caraway Seed Soup

Ingredients: 1½ oz. flour, ¼ tsp. salt, 2 oz. lard or butter, 1 roll, ½ oz. caraway seeds.

Make a roux with lard or butter and flour, brown well, throw caraway seeds into it, continue frying, then dilute with 3 pt. of cold water; salt, mix well until smooth and boil for 10—15 mins. Dice roll neatly in the meantime and fry in the rest of the lard or butter until golden. Pass soup through a fine sieve, whisk until smooth and serve hot. Skim off fat before serving. Serve fried dices of roll on a separate plate.

Thick Brown Soup

Ingredients and method of making are identical with those of the caraway seed soup, but leave out caraway seeds.

Fatfree Thick Brown Soup

Brown flour, without lard, in a saucepan on a steady, low fire, stirring frequently, until golden; then follow method for making caraway seed soup.

Clear Soup with Semolina

Ingredients: 2 pt. skimmed clear soup, 1½ oz. semolina.

Put semolina into the boiling clear soup, stirring constantly with a whisk; boil for 2—3 mins. and serve in cups.

Clear Soup with Tapioca

Prepare as for Clear soup with semolina.

Clear Soup with Mixed Vegetables (Julienne)

Ingredients: 2 pt. skimmed, slightly seasoned clear soup (see Clear Soup), 1½ oz. carrots, 1½ oz. turnips, 1½ oz. celery, 1½ oz. tender green peas.

Clean carrots, turnips and celery; wash well and chop into very fine slices (Julienne). Add shelled tender green peas and cook all vegetables in slightly salted water, until soft, but use only as much water as will reduce by the time vegetables are soft. Add clear soup afterwards, free from fat and only lightly seasoned, and serve, dividing vegetables proportionately, together with the soup. A few tender heads of asparagus may be cooked with other vegetables during the season.

Vegetable Bouillon

Ingredients: 5 oz. carrots, 5 oz. turnips, 2 oz. celery, 2 oz. mushrooms, 2 oz. kohlrabi, 2 oz. savoy cabbages, small bunch of parsley, half a tsp. salt, 1 tsp. tomato purée, $^1/_5$ pt. oil.

Clean vegetables and wash well. Grate carrots, celery, kohlrabi and mushrooms finely on a fine horse-radish grater and brown in oil, over a good fire, until golden. Drain off oil afterwards, add tomato purée, dilute with 3 pt. of water, mix well and bring to boil. Salt, add savoy cabbage, cut into fine slices and well washed parsley. Cook on a low, steady heat for 1—1½ hrs., until vegetables are all tender. Take off the fire, leave to settle, then strain through a fine cloth, as in the case of real bouillon; skim off fat completely and serve hot in pre-heated cups. The browned vegetables and tomatoes should give it a nice, golden colour.

Rice Cream Soup

Ingredients: 5 oz. rice, ½ tsp. salt, 1 egg-yolk, ½ pt. cream.

Wash rice several times, changing water, then cook in 3 pt. of salted water until soft (about 1—1½ hrs.). When soft, pass through a hair sieve, mix with a whisk until smooth and bring to boil once more. Serve hot, adding a mixture of the cream and egg-yolk, just before serving, and stirring well with a whisk. Rice cream soup should be thick, just like cream soups—because of the starch content of rice—without the addition of extra thickening substance. Leave out cream and egg-yolk, if the doctor does not allow their consumption.

Barley Cream Soup

Ingredients: 5 oz. barley groats, 1 egg-yolk, ½ tsp. salt, $^1/_5$ pt. cream.

Prepare as for Rice cream soup, but cook for 2—2½ hrs., because barley groats soften more slowly. Bring water to boil first, then pour off the water, and further cook barley groats in fresh water, until soft; then prepare just as for rice cream soup.

Chicken Purée Soup

Ingredients: 1 chicken about 1 lb. in weight, 7½ oz. mixed vegetables, 1 tsp. salt, 1½ oz. butter, 2 oz. flour, $^1/_5$ pt. cream, 1 egg-yolk, ½ lemon, small bunch of parsley.

Clean and dress chicken, wash, cut into pieces, and put into a saucepan in 2 pt. of water together with the cleaned, washed and sliced vegetables; cook, just as for meat soup, but, of course, without spices, adding salt only.

340

Cook until quite tender and the flesh comes off the bones easily. Remove meat from the bones, mince finely and brown slightly in butter, together with washed and finely chopped parsley. Sprinkle with flour, dilute with chicken broth, mix until smooth, season with salt again, and cook for 10—15 mins. Pass through a fine sieve, beat well with a whisk until smooth and mix egg-yolk and cream into it. Before serving, flavour with lemon-juice and serve hot. The soup should be thick, like a cream. Do not boil it any longer, after having added cream and yolk, because egg may curdle.

Veal Purée Soup

Prepare as for Chicken purée soup, but take 11 oz. of veal, not counting the weight of bones, instead of the chicken.

Potato Cream Soup

For ingredients and method see Soups.

Spinach Cream Soup

See Soups, but leave out ground black pepper and nutmeg from in-gredients.

Liver Purée Soup

Ingredients: 7½ oz. calf's or pig's liver, 1½ oz. butter, 2 oz. flour, ⅔ tsp. salt, 1 roll, 2 pt. bone stock (made with vegetables and without spices).

Prepare as for ordinary Liver purée soup, but without spices.

Apple Cream Soup

Ingredients: 1 lb. apples, 2 oz. flour, 1½ oz. butter, pinch of salt, ½ lemon, 1 egg-yolk, 2 oz. sugar, ⅕ pt. cream, 1 pt. milk.

Peel apples, remove cores and seeds, and slice. Cook, together with sugar, in about 1½ pt. of water. Make a light roux with butter and flour, dilute with milk, mix well, and add cooked apples, together with juice; salt, flavour with a little grated lemon peel and cook for 10 mins. Pass through a hair sieve, mix until smooth, add smooth mixture of cream and egg-yolk, stirring con-stantly with a whisk; flavour with lemon-juice and serve. Do not boil after having added cream and egg-yolk, because it may curdle.

Brains Purée Soup

Ingredients: 1 calf's brains, 1½ oz. butter, 2 oz. flour, ½ tsp. salt, small bunch of parsley, ½ lemon, ¹/₅ pt. cream, 1 egg-yolk, 2 pt. bone stock (made with vegetables and without spices).

Peel off thin membranes, wash brains well and cut finely with a knife. Clean parsley as well, wash well and chop finely. Fry brains together with parsley in butter; salt, add flour and brown together for a while; then dilute with bone stock and mix until smooth. Cook for 10—15 mins., then pass through a fine sieve. Beat well until smooth. Before serving mix cream well with egg-yolk, and add mixture to soup; then flavour with lemon-juice. Do not boil again after having added cream and egg-yolk.

Carrot Cream Soup

Ingredients: 11 oz. carrots, 1½ oz. butter, 2 oz. flour, ½ tsp. salt, 2 pt. calf's bone stock (cooked without spices), 1 oz. sugar, ¹/₅ pt. cream, 1 egg-yolk.

Clean carrots well, wash, and grate on a fine horse-radish grater; then partially cook in butter, sprinkle with flour and dilute with bone stock. Flavour with sugar, salt and cook until tender. Pass through a fine hair sieve and mix well again, until smooth. Mix egg-yolk and cream well together, and add this mixture to soup just before serving, stirring constantly with a whisk. Do not boil soup, after having added egg-yolk and cream, because it may curdle.

Vegetable Cream Soup

Ingredients: 7½ mixed vegetables, 1½ oz. butter, 2 oz. flour, ½ tsp. salt, 2 oz. celery, small bunch of parsley, small bunch of green celery tops, 2 pt. calf's bone stock (cooked without spices), ¹/₅ pt. cream, 1 egg-yolk.

Clean mixed vegetables and celery, wash and grate on a fine grater. Clean and wash parsley and green celery as well, and chop finely. Afterwards, brown celery in butter until golden together with grated vegetables; add chopped parsley and green celery top, sprinkle with flour, brown a little, salt and finally dilute with bone stock, and cook until vegetables are quite tender. Pass through a fine hair sieve when ready and beat with a whisk until smooth. Mix egg-yolk with cream well and add to hot soup, and re-season, if necessary, then serve. Do not boil after having added egg-yolk and cream.

Asparagus Cream Soup

Ingredients: 14 oz. asparagus, 1 oz. sugar, 1½ oz. butter, 2 oz. flour, ½ tsp. salt, 2 pt. calf's bone stock (cooked without spices), ¹/₅ pt. cream, 1 egg-yolk.

Clean and scrape asparagus carefully, cut into pieces, wash well. Cook asparagus in stock, seasoned slightly with sugar and salt, until tender. Prepare a light roux in the meantime with butter and flour, but do not brown, and thicken soup with it. Pass through a hair sieve, mix until smooth, flavour with sugar and salt, then serve. Flavour may be improved with cream and egg-yolk, added just before serving. Do not boil soup after the addition of cream and egg-yolk.

Celery Cream Soup

Ingredients: 14 oz. celery, 1½ oz. butter, 2 oz. flour, ½ tsp. salt, 2 pt. calf's bone stock (cooked without spices), ¹/₅ pt. cream, 1 egg-yolk.

Clean celery, slice, wash well and simmer in butter until half-cooked. Sprinkle with flour, brown a little longer, then dilute with bone stock; salt and cook until quite tender. Pass through a fine hair sieve when ready, mix well until smooth, then flavour. Mix cream and egg-yolk together, and add this to the soup, stirring constantly with a whisk, just before serving. Do not boil after the addition of cream and egg-yolk, because it may curdle.

ENTRÉES

Whipped Eggs

See warm egg dishes.

Calf's Brain Croquettes

See warm entrées for ingredients and method, but leave out onions and ground black pepper from ingredients, and prepare, dipping only in flour and eggs, before frying. Serve with potato purée or spinach cream.

Omelettes

For ingredients and method see warm entrées, but use butter for making, instead of lard.

Calf's Liver Soufflé

Ingredients: 14 oz. calf's liver, 3 oz. butter, 3½ oz. flour, ½ tsp. salt, 5 eggs, ³/₅ pt. milk, 5 portions of cheese sauce.

Slice calf's liver and fry lightly on both sides, then pass through a fine mincer or a strong wire sieve.

Make a light roux with 2½ oz. of flour, but do not brown it. Dilute with hot milk and stir quickly over the fire, until smooth and thick enough to serve as a milk sauce (béchamel sauce: see Hot Sauces). Add minced calf's liver, salt and mix well. Take off the fire afterwards and mix 5 egg-yolks into it gradually, one by one, stirring constantly. Whisk the whites until quite stiff; mix into the liver, folding it in carefully. Take 5 small pudding moulds, butter with the rest of the butter, sprinkle with the rest of the flour and put the soufflé in 5 equal portions into the buttered pudding moulds. Steam under cover in a saucepan, in very little water—to ensure plenty of hot steam—for about 15—20 mins. Soufflés will rise considerably. When they are cooked, turn them out by inverting moulds and serve with warm cheese sauce. (For cheese sauce: see Hot Sauces.) May be prepared from pig's or chicken-liver, if necessary.

Rolls Fried in Eggs and Flour

Ingredients: 5 rolls, $^3/_5$ pt. milk, $^1/_2$ tsp. salt, 3 oz. flour, 3 eggs, 7$^1/_2$ oz. oil or butter.

Slice rolls, soak in milk, then squeeze out moisture, salt, dip into beaten eggs, and flour and fry in hot oil, or butter, until golden-brown. Drain when ready on a clean serviette, and serve hot, together with spinach, potato purée or other dietetic light vegetable dish.

Eggs-en-cocotte

Ingredients: 10 eggs, 2 oz. butter, $^1/_2$ tsp. $^3/_{10}$ pt. cream.

Butter 5 fireproof cocottes or individual casseroles, put a little cream in each. Break 2 eggs into each, salt, and divide the rest of the cream equally, putting some on top of every cocotte. Place cocottes in a saucepan and pour a little water into the saucepan. Cover with a lid—to ensure the formation of steam—and heat for 4—5 mins. Then serve, straight away, while hot. The tops may be sprinkled with grated cheese.

Asparagus Fried with Cream and Eggs

Ingredients: 3 lb. asparagus, 1 oz. sugar, $^1/_2$ oz. salt, 2 oz. butter, $^3/_{10}$ pt. cream, 5 eggs.

Clean and scrape asparagus and cook in slightly salted and sugared water until tender; then drain and dry on a sieve. Whisk cream and eggs well together in the meantime and salt them a little. Take 5 fireproof dishes, butter, and divide into them all the asparagus, drained and dried previously. Finally pour cream and eggs on top. Bake in a hot oven for 7—8 mins. until they are a nice golden-brown, and rise like a soufflé. Bake just before serving, because they may collapse, when put aside. Melt the rest of butter and sprinkle asparagus with it before serving. The same dish may be prepared with tender French beans or cauliflower.

Risotto with Eggs

Ingredients: 6 hard-boiled eggs, 11 oz. rice, 11 oz. tinned green peas, 5 oz. butter, ½ tsp. salt, 3½ oz. grated cheese, small bunch of parsley, $1/_5$ pt. gravy (made with butter).

Steam rice in the usual way, together with 2 oz. of butter until soft. Shell hard-boiled eggs in the meantime and cut into even dices. Add butter and diced hard-boiled eggs to rice and lastly add green peas as well. Salt, add 2 oz. of grated cheese and finely chopped parsley; mix well together and put back into the oven for 5—10 mins. Steam under cover. Put into small pudding moulds afterwards, large enough for one person; turn out when set, sprinkle with the rest of the grated cheese, pour gravy around them and serve straight away.

FISH DISHES

Fish Mousse with Jelly

For ingredients and method see cold fish courses but omit Cayenne pepper and smoked salmon from the recipe.

Jack Salmon Fillets in Jelly with Asparagus

Ingredients: 2 lb. jack salmon fillets (boneless), 1 tsp. salt, 1 lemon, 1 lb. tinned asparagus, 2 hard-boiled eggs, 1 lb. 11 oz. aspic.

Season water lightly with salt and lemon-juice and cook jack salmon fillets in it, until tender; then take them out with a flat ladle and drain on a sieve. Drain tinned asparagus on a sieve as well, and slice hard-boiled eggs. Melt already prepared aspic, until tepid, and divide well drained fish into 5 fire-proof—or glass—dishes. Garnish tastefully with asparagus and sliced hard-boiled eggs, then pour melted aspic over them carefully, so as not to spoil decorations. (With jack salmon fillets in jelly, use aspic made, if possible, from fish bones, and for dietetic cooking, leave out onions, whole black pepper and bay leaf from the recipe, flavouring it with vegetables, salt and a little lemon-juice only.) Put on ice, until it sets, and serve, accompanied by carefully seasoned tartare sauce in a sauceboat.

Pike-perch Fillets with Lemon Sauce

Ingredients: 2 lb. pike-perch fillets (boneless), $3/_4$ oz. salt, 5 portions of boiled potatoes, 5 portions of lemon sauce.

Cook pike-perch fillets in lightly salted water and serve, accompanied by garnish of boiled potatoes and lemon sauce. (See Hot Sauces.)

345

Jack Salmon Fillets in Butter

For ingredients and method see warm fish courses. Serve, accompanied by buttered potatoes, with parsley and lemon slices.

Parisian Pike-perch or Jack Salmon Fillets

For ingredients and method see warm fish courses, but fry fillets in butter and oil, instead of lard. Serve with lightly seasoned tartare sauce, in a sauceboat.

Jack Salmon Strips Fried in Batter

Ingredients: 1½ lb. jack salmon fillets (boneless), ½ tsp. salt, 7½ oz. flour, 11 oz. oil or butter, 1 pt. milk, 3 eggs, 1 lemon.

Cut fillets into strips, ½ inch in thickness and salt. Make a thick pancake-like batter from 3½ oz. of flour, 3 egg-yolks and milk; add whites, whisked stiff, mix, folding whites in carefully and salt the mixture. Roll fish strips in flour, then dip in the batter, described above; and fry in hot oil or butter, until golden-brown. Drain on a clean serviette and serve hot. Garnish with lemon slices or dietetic tartare sauce, without seasoning.

Jack Salmon Fillets with Hollandaise Sauce

Ingredients: 2 lb. jack salmon fillets (boneless), ½ tsp. salt, ½ lemon, 5 portions of Hollandaise sauce.

Salt water lightly and flavour with lemon-juice. Cook jack salmon fillets in it; afterwards pour Hollandaise sauce over them (see Hot Sauces), and serve, accompanied by buttered potatoes with parsley.

Fish Soufflé

Ingredients: 1 lb. pike-perch or jack salmon (boneless), 4 oz. butter, 3½ oz. flour, ⁴/₅ pt. milk, ½ tsp. salt, 5 eggs, ½ lemon.

Salt water lightly and flavour with lemon-juice. Cook fish in it, until soft, then drain on a sieve and pass through a fine hair sieve while still hot. Make a light roux in the meantime with 2½ oz. butter and 2½ oz. flour; do not brown. Dilute roux with hot milk and mix quickly until smooth, thus preparing a good, stiff milk sauce (béchamel: see Hot Sauces). Dilute with some fish stock if sauce is too thick when taken off the fire. Afterwards add fish purée to it and mix 5 egg-yolks in as well; whisk whites until stiff, then fold into mixture carefully. Butter 5 small pudding moulds (each for one person), using 2 oz. of butter, then sprinkle with the rest of the flour and divide fish equally in five dishes. Put dishes into a saucepan and boil them under cover, for about 15—20 mins. in a little water—taking care not to moisten mixture with the steam. When soufflé rises, turn out onto a plate and serve hot. Serve, accompanied by cream, lemon or Hollandaise sauce (see Hot Sauces).

MEAT DISHES

Fricassée of Veal

For ingredients and method see Veal Stew (veal dishes), but make roux with butter and leave out onions and whole black pepper completely. Garnish, accompanied by boiled rice. May also be prepared with asparagus heads with lemon-juice or green peas.

Veal Pudding

For ingredients and method see Calf's Liver Soufflé (see under Entrées), but instead of calf's liver take the same quantity of veal and serve with potato purée, instead of cheese sauce. May be garnished with young, tender green peas or carrots, prepared in a white sauce.

Buttered Roast Veal

For ingredients and method see Roast Veal, but roast in butter instead of lard, and steam afterwards under cover, until quite tender. Leave tomato purée out from gravy. Serve, accompanied by light, dietetic vegetable dishes, potato purée, steamed rice.

Fillets of Veal in Butter

For ingredients and method see Escalopes of Veal (veal dishes), but use butter instead of lard, and steam after frying in the butter until quite tender, then serve with stewed carrots, asparagus and sugar peas.

Minced Veal Cutlets

For ingredients and method see veal dishes, but fry in butter instead of lard. Garnish with potato purée and spinach prepared with cream.

Mock Cutlets

Ingredients: 1 lb. veal, ½ tsp. salt, 4 oz. flour, ½ lb. oil or butter, 5 eggs, 2 oz. bread-crumbs, ³/₅ pt. milk.

Pass roast veal twice through mincer. Make a light roux in the meantime with 2 oz. oil or butter and 2 oz. flour; dilute with hot milk and mix well, stirring quickly, until smooth. Add minced veal, 2 eggs whole, bread-crumbs and salt and mix well into a thick stiff paste. Turn out onto a well floured wooden board, and leave to cool completely. When cooled, roll out and make slices from mixture, shaped like veal cutlets, roll in flour and dip into eggs, then fry in hot oil or butter until golden-brown. Drain on clean serviette, and serve hot, garnished with potato purée, or other dietetic vegetable dishes.

Parisian Veal Fillets

For ingredients and method see veal dishes, but fry in butter or oil, instead of lard. Serve, accompanied by dietetic vegetable dishes.

Minced Veal (Hash)

Ingredients: 1 lb. veal (boneless), 3½ oz. butter, ¹/₅ pt. cream, ½ tsp. salt, 5 oz. mixed vegetables, 2 oz. flour, 2 egg-yolks.

Cut veal into pieces, wash well. Clean, wash and slice mixed vegetables and put to cook, together with veal, in enough lightly salted water to cover, in a well covered saucepan. Take meat out of the stock and when cooled, pass twice through a meat mincer. Make a light roux in the meantime with 2 oz. butter and flour, dilute with veal stock and whisk until smooth, then boil for a few mins. Add minced veal to this sauce, taking care that sauce should not be too thin or too thick; mix in cream as well, salt and continue boiling on a low heat for a few more mins. Finally pass the whole mixture through a fine sieve, add egg-yolks and break in the rest of the butter gradually; whisk until smooth and serve. Flavour with a little lemon-juice. Serve, accompanied by steamed rice.

Sweetbreads in Butter

Ingredients: 1 lb. 11 oz. sweetbreads, 5 oz. butter, 2 oz. flour, ½ tsp. salt, ½ lemon.

Clean sweetbreads, by removing films and membranes, wash well and blanch, plunging into boiling water for 1—2 mins. Cool afterwards, drain and dry on cloth; slice, salt and, rolling in flour, fry on both sides in 3½ oz. of butter, taking care not to dry excessively. Putting in saucepan add 2 oz. butter gradually, and steam under cover on a low heat—adding a few drops of water, from time to time—until quite tender. Flavour with a little lemon-juice, before serving. Garnish with steamed rice, but it may also be served with young, tender vegetables.

Fricassée of Chicken with Lemon

For ingredients and method see poultry dishes, but leave out onions and whole black pepper from the recipe, and prepare roux with butter instead of lard. Serve with steamed rice.

Minced Chicken

For method see Minced veal, only take a young chicken, about 2 lb. 7½ oz. in weight, instead of veal.

Minced Chicken Breast in Butter

For ingredients and method see Minced breast of chicken (poultry dishes), but use butter instead of lard. Serve potato purée or dietetic vegetable dishes with it.

Young Chicken Stewed in Butter

For ingredients and method see Roast poulard, but leave out marjoram from the recipe and roast in butter instead of lard; then steam under cover—adding a little water from time to time—until quite tender. Do not put tomatoes in the gravy. Serve with steamed rice, buttered potatoes and various compotes.

Chicken Fillets Stewed in Butter

Ingredients: Breasts of 2½ chickens (about 4 lb.), ½ tsp. salt, 2 oz. flour, 5 oz. butter.

Remove meat from chicken breast, avoiding removal of wing bones, skin and beat with mallet into thin, neat slices. Salt, dredge in flour and fry in 3½ oz. of butter on both sides, until golden-brown. In the meantime cook a good, strong stock from the bones and reduce, boiling. Steam fillets in a saucepan under cover, adding stock from time to time, until quite tender. Add 2 oz. butter afterwards, mix well and serve, accompanied by steamed rice or tender, young green peas. Serve with lettuces, prepared with lemon, or with some kind of compote.

Poultry Croquettes

Ingredients: 2 lb. chicken or fowl, 12 oz. butter, 5 oz. flour, 1 tsp. salt, 2 egg-yolks, $^1/_5$ pt. milk, 2 oz. bread-crumbs, 3 eggs.

Cook meat in lightly salted water until quite tender (it is cooked when the meat comes off the bones easily); remove meat from bones and pass it twice through a fine meat mincer. Reduce stock in the meantime, until only about $^1/_5$ pt. is left. Make a light roux, with 2 oz. of butter and 2½ oz. flour, dilute with the reduced stock and milk, mix quickly until smooth; then add minced meat together with 2 egg-yolks, bread-crumbs and salt. Mix well together over the fire, until quite smooth and the mixture is thick enough. Turn out onto a floured wooden plate and leave to cool. Make small, neat croquettes from this mixture, roll in flour and beaten egg, and fry in hot butter until golden-brown. Drain on a clean serviette, and serve hot. Serve potato purée or young, tender dietetic vegetable dishes with it. May be fried in oil instead of butter.

Chicken with Green Peas

Ingredients: 2½ young chickens (about 3½ lb. in weight), 1 tsp. salt, 2 oz. flour, 4 oz. butter, 1 tsp. sugar, 14 oz. shelled young green peas, small bunch of parsley, $^1/_5$ pt. cream.

Clean chicken well, cut into pieces, wash and dry on a clean serviette; then salt, and, rolling in flour, fry lightly in butter. Add washed peas, and finely chopped parsley; season with salt and sugar and steam under cover, adding a little water from time to time, until both the chicken and peas are tender; at the same time reduce liquid gradually, until only thick, strong gravy is left. Add cream, bring to boil once more, re-season if necessary, and serve with steamed rice or buttered potatoes prepared with parsley. May be prepared without cream if necessary.

VEGETABLE DISHES

Carrots Prepared with White Sauce

For ingredients and method see vegetable dishes, but prepare with butter, instead of lard.

Carrot Purée

Pass carrots prepared with butter through a fine hair sieve and whisk until smooth. Put through sieve while still hot, because it is easier than when cold.

Potatoes Prepared with Sauce

Peel and slice potatoes finely, wash them well and cook in lightly salted water, until almost soft. Make a light roux in the meantime with butter and flour, and thicken potatoes with it. Add finely chopped parsley, washed previously, and sour cream; re-season, stir until smooth and bring once more to boil; then cook for a little longer, until potatoes are completely tender. Serve hot. May be prepared with cream as well, instead of sour cream.

Potato Purée

For ingredients and method see Garnishes.

Asparagus Prepared in White Sauce

Ingredients: 2½ lb. asparagus, ½ tsp. salt, 2 oz. butter, 1 oz. sugar, 2½ oz. flour, small bunch of parsley, $^3/_{10}$ pt. cream.

Clean asparagus, scrape stalks and cut into ½ inch long pieces; wash well and cook in water flavoured with sugar until quite soft. Make a light roux in the meantime, with butter and flour, and thicken asparagus with this. Mix until smooth, re-season with salt and sugar. Add finely chopped parsley, mix in cream, bring once more to boil and serve hot. Asparagus purée may be prepared in the same way, but the vegetable should be passed through a fine hair sieve when cooked, whisked until smooth and served hot. Roux should be somewhat thicker, if needed for purée.

Lettuces Prepared in White Sauce

Ingredients: 3 lb. lettuces, ½ tsp. salt, 2 oz. butter, 1 oz. sugar, small bunch of fresh dill, 1 lemon, $^1/_{10}$ pt. sour cream, 2½ oz. flour.

Clean lettuces and wash them in plenty of water, changing water several times, and cook them in boiling water. Drain and squeeze well, to get rid of moisture, then cut into moderate sized pieces. Put into a saucepan again with enough water to cover, and cook until almost soft. Make a light roux in the meantime, with flour and butter, and add to lettuces. Flavour with sugar, salt and lemon-juice; add washed and finely chopped dills, mix in sour cream and whisk well together. Bring to boil once more and serve hot. The gravy should be as thick as cream. Pass through a sieve, if you wish to make lettuce purée, but use a hair sieve for the purpose.

French Beans Prepared in White Sauce

Ingredients: 2 lb. French beans, ½ tsp. salt, 2 oz. butter, 1 lemon, 1 oz. sugar, 2½ oz. flour, small bunch of parsley, ³/₁₀ pt. sour cream.

Clean beans well, and cut them into about ½ inch long pieces; then wash several times in plenty of water and cook in lightly salted water until almost tender. Make a light roux in the meantime with butter and flour, and thicken French beans with this. Flavour with salt, sugar and lemon-juice, add sour cream and mix in finely chopped parsley, then bring to boil, and cook until beans are quite soft. Re-season and serve hot. Bean purée may be prepared in the same way, but pass through a fine hair sieve, when beans are tender, and mix well until smooth. Use cream instead of sour cream if necessary.

Vegetable Marrow Prepared in Cream with Dill

For ingredients and method see vegetable dishes, but leave out onions and paprika, and instead of sour cream use the same quantity of cream, and finally, flavour with lemon-juice instead of vinegar.

Vegetable Marrow Purée with Dill

Pass marrow prepared in cream with dill through a fine hair sieve; mix well with whisk until smooth and serve.

Spinach in White Sauce

Ingredients: 3 lb. spinach, pinch of bicarbonate of soda, ½ tsp. salt, ³/₁₀ pt. cream, 2 oz. butter, 1 tbsp. flour, 1 pt. milk.

Clean spinach, wash several times in plenty of water, then cook in boiling water with salt and bicarbonate of soda, until tender. Drain, rinse and, squeezing out moisture, pass through a fine hair sieve. Make a light roux in the meantime with butter and flour, dilute with milk and mix well until smooth with a whisk; add spinach purée and mix well again, until smooth, then bring to boil. Add cream and salt, mix thoroughly, bring to boil and serve hot. Thin with a little bouillon, if necessary. May be prepared without cream as well, in which case use a little more milk.

Fine Vegetables Prepared in White Sauce

For ingredients and method see Vegetables, but use asparagus heads instead of kohlrabi and prepare roux with butter instead of lard.

Fine Vegetable Purée

See Garnishes for ingredients and method, but leave out onions from the recipe. Pass through a fine sieve and mix well with a whisk, until smooth. Purée should be as thick as potato purée. Pass through the sieve, while hot.

Green Peas in White Sauce

For ingredients and method see Vegetables, but use butter instead of lard.

Green Pea Purée

Pass green peas, prepared with butter in white sauce, through a fine sieve and mix well with a whisk until smooth. Should be as thick as potato purée. Pass through the sieve while hot.

GARNISHES

Steamed Rice

See Garnishes for recipe, but leave out onions and use butter instead of lard.

Semolina Fried in Butter

Ingredients: 11 oz. semolina, 3½ oz. butter, ½ tsp. salt.

Fry semolina in butter, stirring constantly until golden-brown; then dilute with ²/₅ pt. of hot water, salt, stir quickly and take off the fire; then put aside to steam under cover, until it rises. Mix well with a fork and serve hot.

Carrots with Butter

Ingredients: 2 lb. carrots, ½ tsp. salt, 3½ oz. butter, 1 oz. sugar, small bunch of parsley.

Scrape carrots well, and cut into neat and even pieces, wash and cook in lightly salted water, until tender, then drain. Wash parsley and chop finely; put into heated butter, add cooked and drained carrots; mix well, re-season with sugar and salt, then serve hot. Young, tender carrots should be stewed in butter, under cover, adding a little water to them from time to time.

Buttered Potatoes with Parsley

Ingredients: 3 lb. potatoes, 3½ oz. butter, ½ tsp. salt, small bunch of parsley.

Peel potatoes, and cut into longish pieces, just as for potatoes with paprika; cook in salted water until tender, then drain. Wash parsley and chop finely, then put into heated butter. Add cooked and drained potatoes, mix well, re-season if necessary and serve hot. Cooked and drained potatoes may also be served in a serving dish, sprinkled with melted butter and with chopped parsley.

Buttered Green Peas Prepared with Parsley

Ingredients: 2 lb. young, tender green peas, ½ tsp. salt, 1 oz. sugar, small bunch of parsley, 3½ oz. butter.

Wash shelled peas and cook in plenty of boiling water. Flavour lightly with salt and sugar, boil until almost tender, then drain. Wash and chop parsley finely, and put into heated butter; then add drained green peas, re-seasoned with salt and sugar if necessary and allow to simmer, stirring frequently, until quite tender. Serve hot. Young, tender peas may be prepared in butter, under cover, by steaming them until soft, adding a little water from time to time.

Spring Garnishes

Ingredients: ½ lb. carrots, ½ lb. asparagus, ½ lb. cauliflower, ½ lb. green peas, ½ tsp. salt, 1½ oz. sugar, 1 bunch of parsley, 3½ oz. butter.

Clean carrots, asparagus and cauliflower well, wash and cut into suitable, neat pieces; then put to cook in separate saucepans in lightly salted water, together with a little sugar. Cook peas, shelled and washed previously, in a separate saucepan. Drain vegetables, when cooked and leave on a sieve, until free from most of the moisture. Wash parsley in the meantime, chop finely and put into melted butter; then add various vegetables, shake them well together, carefully, so as not to squash them. Re-season with salt and sugar and serve hot.

SWEETS

Sponges with Custard

For ingredients and method see sponge cakes and pastries. Prepare milk-custard in the same way as wine custard, but use milk instead of wine and leave out cinnamon and nutmeg, using vanilla and a little lemon peel instead. Beat milk-custard with a whisk, and serve in a sauceboat.

Rice Pudding

Ingredients: ½ lb. rice, $^3/_{10}$ pt. milk, 7½ oz. sugar.

Wash rice well and cook in milk on a low heat stirring frequently, until soft, and flavour with sugar. Serve with castor sugar, mixed with cinnamon or cocoa, but may be sprinkled with grated chocolate as well.

Semolina Pudding

Ingredients: ½ lb. semolina, ³⁄₁₀ pt. milk, 7½ oz. sugar.

Put semolina into boiling milk, cook for a few mins., stirring constantly with a whisk, and flavour with sugar. Serve with castor sugar, mixed with cinnamon or cocoa or grated chocolate.

Floating Islands

Ingredients: 2 pt. milk, 5 eggs, ¼ stick of vanilla, 7½ oz. sugar, 10 sponge cakes.

Put milk to boil, together with the vanilla and 3½ oz. sugar. Beat egg-whites in the meantime, until quite stiff; mix 2 oz. sugar into them and gradually add this mixture into the boiling milk with a spoon. Turn these noodles upside down in the milk so as to cook them on both sides. Take out with a ladle and drain. Mix egg-yolks with the rest of the sugar, then add hot milk —in which the noodles of egg-white were cooked—to yolks, stirring constantly; put on the fire again, and leave there, stirring all the time, until thickens. Do not boil, because yolks may curdle. When thick enough, cool, and serve in glass dishes or in goblets, dividing the so-called noodles evenly between these glasses. Serve with sponge cakes. May be sprinkled with finely chopped almonds, according to taste.

Omelette Confiture

Ingredients: 10 eggs, 5 oz. castor sugar, 7½ oz. flour, 11 oz. apricot jam, 1 oz. butter.

Mix yolks well with 3½ oz. of sugar, then add whipped, stiff whites and finally fold in flour, carefully and loosely, so as not to disturb the stiff froth. Butter a round baking tin, sprinkle with flour and place prepared sponge batter into it in the shape of a hemisphere. Bake in a moderate oven, then put onto a plate, spread with apricot jam—previously passed through a sieve—then fold up omelette, to give it the shape of a semi-circle; fill inside with jam and sprinkle top with the rest of the castor sugar, and serve hot. Heat apricot jam, before filling the omelette with it.

Omelette Soufflé

Ingredients: 10 egg whites, 3½ oz. castor sugar, ½ lb. apricot jam, 1 oz. butter.

Beat egg whites, until quite stiff, then add sugar and mix well, together with the previously sieved apricot jam. Pile this mixture onto a lightly buttered and floured fireproof dish and give it a neat shape; then bake in a hot oven for a few mins., until golden-brown. Sprinkle with sugar and serve straight away.

Semolina Soufflé

Ingredients: 1 pt. milk, 6 oz. semolina, 4 oz. sugar, 4 oz. butter, 6 eggs, a little lemon peel.

Put a little lemon peel and 3½ oz. of sugar into milk and boil. When it comes to boil, mix well with a whisk, stirring constantly and add semolina. Continue cooking, until quite soft and it has a thick, stiff, creamy consistency. Take off the fire, add 3 oz. of melted butter, stir and leave to cool. Mix egg-yolks very well and add to this mixture; beat whites afterwards, until quite stiff and fold carefully into semolina as well. Carefully butter 5 small pudding moulds with the rest of the butter (1½ oz.), covering the whole inner surface of the moulds; sprinkle with castor sugar and divide prepared pudding mixture equally between the moulds. Put a little water into a saucepan, place moulds into it; boil water and cook soufflés in hot steam under cover for 15—20 mins. When soufflés are nicely risen and cooked well, turn out onto plates, sprinkle with sugar and serve straight away. Serve raspberry juice or milk custard, prepared with vanilla, in separate sauceboat.

Vanilla Cream

Ingredients: 1 pt. milk, 5 egg-yolks, ¼ stick of vanilla, 5 sheets of gelatine, $^3/_5$ pt. cream.

Bring milk to boil, together with egg-yolks, sugar and vanilla, stirring constantly with a whisk. When it begins to thicken, take off and mix in gelatine, soaked previously and melted in some hot water. Leave to cool a little, then add $^2/_5$ pt. stiff cream, beaten well, and mix together. Divide in equal portions and pour into pudding moulds. Put on ice to set. Dip into hot water for a second, before serving, to separate cream from the mould. Turn out onto cold glass or porcelain plate, decorate with the rest of the cream ($^1/_5$ pt). beaten stiff, and serve with sponge cakes or waffles. May be served in goblets as well.

Apple Compote

For recipe see apple dishes (fruit preserves), but leave out cinnamon and nutmeg and flavour only with some lemon peel and juice. Cherry or pear compotes may be prepared in the same way.

Apple Purée

Should be prepared as for Apple compote, but pass fruit through a fine hair sieve when tender.

SPECIAL OCCASION MENUS

I

Mixed Savouries
Clear Soup in Cups
Fillets of Jack Salmon with White
      Wine Sauce
Tenderloin Steaks, Underdone
Parisian Garnishes
      (French Garnishes)
Hazelnut Pudding
Fruit Salad
Cheese
Black Coffee

II

Asparagus Cream Soup
Jellied Goose-liver Paste
Fattened Roast Chicken
Parisian Potatoes
Lettuces
Rosalinda Cake
Parfait
Fruit
Cheese
Black Coffee

III

Caviare, Served on Ice
Chicken Cream Soup
Vol-au-Vent with Mushroom Filling
Larded Pheasant
Apple Purée
Various Kinds of Rétes

Fruit
Cheese
Black Coffee

IV

Cold Fillets of Pike-perch with
      Rémoulade Sauce
Omelette with Chicken Liver
Fillets of Venison with Cumberland
      Sauce
Chocolate Soufflé
Fruit
Cheese
Black Coffee

V

Chicken Bouillon in Cups
Boiled Blue Trout
Larded Loin of Veal
Potato Doughnuts
Spring Garnishes
Sacher Cake
Peaches Melba
Cheese
Black Coffee

VI

Crayfish Soup
Chicken Galantine
Tenderloin Fillets with Béarnaise
      Sauce
Potato Crisps

Green Peas Stewed in Butter
Strawberry Cream Slices
Jardinette
Cheese
Black Coffee

VII

Cold Clear Soup
Fillets of Pike-perch
Roasted Young Goose or Duck
Roast Potatoes
Cucumber Salad
Alsatian Pear Cake
Fruit
Cheese
Black Coffee

VIII

Swedish Mixed Savouries
Asparagus Heads with Hollandaise
    Sauce
Young Chicken Fried in Bread-
    crumbs
Buttered Green Peas
Lettuces
Pancakes Filled with Walnuts, with
    Chocolate Icing
Wild Strawberry Parfait
Cheese
Black Coffee

INDEX

Ujházi's Chicken Broth 18

Vegetable Soup 18
Vegetarian Borshch 32

SAUCES

Anchovy Sauce 56
Apple Sauce 57
Asparagus Cream Sauce 51

Béarnaise Sauce 49
Béchamel Sauce 47
Beetroot Sauce 57
Bordelaise Sauce 46
Brown (Espagnole) Sauce 43
Brown Mushroom Sauce 45
Brown Tarragon Sauce 44
Burgundy Sauce 46

Caper Sauce 56
Celery Sauce 56
Chaudfroid Sauce (Brown) 42
Chaudfroid Sauce (White) 43
Cheese Sauce 48
Cherry Sauce 47
Chive Sauce 42
Choron Sauce 50
Crayfish Coral Butter 47
Crayfish Sauce 48
Cream Sauce 54
Cucumber Sauce 58
Cumberland Sauce 41

Demi-glace Sauce 44

Florentine Sauce 49
Fresh Dill Sauce 55

Garlic Sauce 55
Gooseberry Sauce 58
Green Sauce 42
Gribiche Sauce 41

Hollandaise Sauce 48
Horse-radish in Vinegar 42
Horse-radish Sauce 57
Horse-radish Sauce with Apples 40
Hot Brown Sauce (Fines–herbes Sauce) 46
Hunter Sauce 44

Italian Sauce 43

Lemon Sauce 52

Madeira Sauce 46
Mayonnaise 38
Mayonnaise Sauce 39
Mayonnaise Sauce with Caviare 41
Morello Sauce 57
Mornay Sauce or Sauce au Gratin 47

Moscow Sauce 50
Mushroom Sauce with Cream 54
Mushroom Sauce with Sour Cream 54
Mustard Sauce 40

Normandy Sauce 52

Onion Sauce 55

Paprika Sauce 55
Portuguese Sauce 50
Poulette Sauce 53
Provençal Sauce 45

Ravigote Sauce 40
Red Currant Sauce 58
Rémoulade Sauce 39
Robert Sauce 45
Russian Sauce 40

Sherry Sauce 45
Sorrel Sauce 56
Soubise Sauce 48
Supreme Sauce 52

Tarragon Sauce 40, 51
Tartare Sauce 39
Tomato Sauce 50
Tyrolean Sauce 41

Valenciennes Sauce 53
Vinaigrette Sauce 41

White (Velouté) Sauce 51
White Wine Sauce 53

COLD AND HOT ENTRÉES AND
SANDWICHES

Asparagus 83
Asparagus au Gratin 84
Asparagus with Buttered Bread-crumbs 84
Asparagus with Hollandaise Sauce 83
Aspic (Jelly) 60
Aubergines Fried in Bread-crumbs 84

Bolognese Macaroni or Spaghetti 80

Calf's Brains Croquette 75
Canapés Made from Brioches 71
Cheese Sandwiches 73
Chicken Croquettes 74
Chicken Galantine 64
Chicken Patties 65
Chicken Risotto 78
Chicken Salad 62
Crayfish Mayonnaise 62

Fish Croquette 74
Fish Galantine 68
Fish Mayonnaise 61
Fish Roe Salad 61

VEGETABLES AND GARNISHES

SALADS

Printed in Hungary 1977
Zrínyi Printing House Budapest
CO 1545 - h - 7779